ADOLESCENCE IN THE LIFE CYCLE
Psychological Change and Social Context

ADOLESCENCE IN THE LIFE CYCLE
Psychological Change and Social Context

Edited by

SIGMUND E. DRAGASTIN
*National Institute of Child Health
and Human Development*

and

GLEN H. ELDER, JR.
*Department of Sociology
University of North Carolina*

 **HEMISPHERE PUBLISHING
CORPORATION**

Washington, D.C.

A HALSTED PRESS BOOK

JOHN WILEY & SONS

New York   London   Sydney   Toronto

Hemisphere Publishing Corporation
1025 Vermont Ave., N.W., Washington, D.C. 20005

Distributed solely by Halsted Press, a Division of John Wiley & Sons, Inc.,
New York

Library of Congress Cataloging in Publication Data
Main entry under title:

Adolescence in the life cycle.

    Papers originally prepared for a research conference
sponsored by the Growth and Development Branch,
National Institute of Child Health and Human Development
and held Oct. 2-5, 1973, Hunt Valley, Md.
    Includes indexes.
    1. Adolescence—Addresses, essays, lectures.
2. Adolescent psychology—Addresses, essays, lectures.
3. Maturation (Psychology)—Addresses, essays, lectures.
I. Dragastin, Sigmund E., ed.   II. Elder, Glen H., ed.
III. United States. National Institute of Child
Health and Human Development. Growth and Development
Branch.   [DNLM: 1. Adolescence—Congresses.
2. Adolescent psychology—Congresses.   WS462 A233 1973]
HQ796.A3326   301.43'15   74–22002
ISBN 0–470–22155–0

Contents

Preface

This volume represents a group of papers prepared originally for a research conference on the psychology and sociology of adolescence sponsored by the Growth and Development Branch of the National Institute of Child Health and Human Development. The conference was held October 2–5, 1973, at Hunt Valley, Maryland. Dr. Sigmund Dragastin of the Growth and Development Branch, the National Institute of Child Health and Human Development, and Dr. Glen H. Elder, Jr., Department of Sociology, University of North Carolina, organized and co-chaired the conference.

The National Institute of Child Health and Human Development (NICHD) is one of ten mission-oriented Institutes of the National Institutes of Health (NIH), which make up the main medical research arm of the Public Health Service in the Department of Health, Education and Welfare.

Early in 1972, the National Advisory Council of the NICHD, representing scholars from both the biomedical and social sciences as well as representative laymen, recommended an expanded research effort in the area of adolescence. In response to this recommendation, staff members of the Growth and Development Branch, working with various consultants and experts on adolescence, identified five areas of research emphasis representing both the biological and behavioral interests of the NICHD. The five areas are:

1. The biological processes involved in the onset and completion of puberty—with emphasis on the hypothalamic-pituitary system, the extrahypothalamic central nervous system, and the mechanism of action of hormones, gonadotrophins, and releasing factors.
2. Nutrient needs—to determine nutrient needs and improved ways of expressing these needs, especially in the context of the adolescent growth spurt, rapidly changing metabolism, and adolescent pregnancy, as well as the relationship between nutritional requirements and endocrine function.
3. Intellectual development—emphasizing the qualitative changes in cognitive processes that take place during adolescence and the important interaction of cognitive processes with motives and attitudes.
4. Adolescent socialization—looking at the way social patterns and social structures help or hinder the adolescent to engage in appropriate role behavior during periods of rapid personal transitions.
5. The relationship between changing hormonal levels and psychosocial development and behavior.

In order to delineate some of these research areas, several conferences were held in 1972-73. The first conference concerned the biological processes involved in the onset of puberty and has been published under the title *The Control of the Onset of Puberty* (Wiley, 1974). The second conference concerned adolescent nutrient needs and was published under the title *Nutrient Requirements in Adolescence* (MIT Press, 1974). The third conference is represented by this volume and cuts across topics three and four in the above list of research priorities.

The conference on Adolescence in the Life Cycle was not designed to cover all the possibly important topics on the behavioral and social side of adolescent development. Rather, the organizers thought it important to take a broad look at adolescence as a developmental process and to see the process as it interacts with social factors in order to understand how process, social factors, and interactions facilitate or impede transitions to adult roles. For this reason, conference participants were drawn from the fields of psychology and sociology in almost equal numbers. In part, the goal was to assess what is currently known about adolescent development and in part to elucidate adolescence as a life cycle phenomenon. The conference organizers also thought it important that the papers be prepared by investigators deeply immersed in the research process.

Thanks are due to the conference participants who provided a great deal of challenging and stimulating discussion during the three-day meeting. It was impossible to include this interchange in the present volume and still have a manageable book. Some salient points of the discussion are, however, included, with appropriate credit, in the Epilogue. The organizers of the conference also wish to thank Drs. Joseph Adelson, John Janeway Conger, Robert Deisher,

Zahava Blum Doering, Dorothy Eichorn, Leon Eisenberg, Hans Furth, and Dale Garrell. These consultants to the Growth and Development Branch of NICHD contributed indirectly to the content of this conference.

Finally, I wish to thank Mrs. Jean DiSandro and Mrs. Christine Donnelly, who helped with the many tasks involved in organizing the conference. I also wish to thank Mrs. Marian Young, who was extremely helpful in managing the myriad details of getting this book to press.

Sigmund E. Dragastin

Bethesda, Maryland

Adolescence in the Life Cycle: An Introduction

GLEN H. ELDER, JR.
University of North Carolina

The concept of adolescence in the life cycle is rooted in three general premises. Adolescence (and the more inclusive category of youth) represents a socially defined stage in the life course; its study thus entails some understanding of adjacent periods, childhood and the adult years. Second, the social reality of adolescence, its boundaries, duration, and experience are variables in the process of social change, cyclical and evolutionary, and these also vary across ecological contexts at common points in historical time, such as between urban and rural farm settings. The latter point should serve to restrain broad generalizations regarding the nature of adolescence, even in contemporary urban America. Third, human development is a lifelong process; investigation of the biographical antecedents and consequences of development in adolescence necessitates a life span framework. Interest in the antecedent factors directs inquiries to childhood and social experience in the formative stage of personality development, whereas the appraisal of outcomes or consequences leads to the adult years.

In developing this anthology of papers, we sought to achieve variations on the common theme of adolescence in the life cycle, variations according to developmental foci and approach, both theoretical and methodological. The central theme is reflected in selective coverage of the life course of boys and girls

1

from childhood to the early adult years, of early antecedents and adult consequents of development and social experience in adolescence. The currently obvious notion that girls as well as boys make up the social world of adolescence and are interdependent participants in the process of socialization and human development was not so obvious some ten or more years ago. In fact, my review of the professional literature on adolescence in 1968 (*Adolescent Socialization and Personality Development*) might well have included a section entitled "Where Are the Girls?" The literature at that time was very largely a literature on male, white adolescents. Moreover, the available studies of adolescent girls were all too frequently informed by theoretical frameworks geared to the development and life course of boys. Since the mid-1960s research priorities and perceptions among analysts of human development have shifted slightly in the direction of correcting some of these deficiencies, owing partly to issues raised by the Women's Liberation movement.

We have organized the book around four sections, beginning with dimensions of human development and concluding with sociological aspects of the life course and youth involvement in social movements. Part I is concerned with two basic axes of human development: physical development and its social meaning from adolescence to adulthood (John Clausen); and cognitive aspects of development, with David Elkind's review of the literature on adolescent thinking and Joseph Adelson's research-based essay on the development of ideology through the adolescent years.

Analytic issues on adolescent development are the focal point of Part II. Dorothy Eichorn discusses some forms and consequences of asynchrony, a concept that refers to a lack of congruence between aspects or rates of development and between person and situation. Morris Rosenberg uses the concept "dissonant context" to refer to settings in which the adolescent finds himself at odds with other occupants (e.g., a black youth in a predominantly white school), and examines their effect on self-concepts. Situational dissonance and congruence identify consequential aspects of social transitions in the life course, and thus should prove useful in their conceptualization. Diana Baumrind's paper on the socialization antecedents in childhood of adolescent styles of competence concludes this section.

In Part III the focus shifts from dimensions of human development and the early phase of adolescence to social transitions in late adolescence, entry into adult roles (marriage, parenthood, etc), and status attainment through education and occupation. Each developmental dimension (physical, cognitive, self, competence) can be viewed as bearing on the adaptive potential and options of youth relative to entry into college (as analyzed by Norman Goodman and Kenneth Feldman), into occupational statuses (the research paper by Karl Alexander and Bruce Eckland), and into marriage and motherhood (as treated by Robert Lewis and Jessie Bernard). Part IV views adolescents within the social-historical process in "Youth and Social Movements," by Richard Braungart.

It should be clear from this overview that the volume covers selected aspects of adolescence in the life cycle. We chose not to include a presentation on sexual development, for example, since this was the subject of an earlier NICHD conference on adolescence, entitled "The Control of the Onset of Puberty" (Grumbach, Grave, & Mayer, 1974). Instead of a comprehensive treatment of adolescence, we sought thorough coverage of selected areas in the hope of generating fresh problem foci on adolescence within a life span framework. In order to encourage the exchange and cross-fertilization of ideas across disciplinary lines, authors were recruited from both psychology and sociology. This intellectual mix paid handsome dividends in the Adolescent Conference and accounts, in part, for the variety of problem areas and approaches represented in this book. As a field of inquiry, the life span is open to a wide array of problem foci, theoretical orientations, and preferences in method. Such diversity is reflected in this collection of papers.

In this introductory essay, I shall first review very briefly some developments that have given the life span framework new vitality during the past decade, with special emphasis on their relevance to adolescence. This is followed by a discussion of conceptual issues: the life cycle, its limitations, and the more inclusive concept of the life course; a set of social facts that bear on our view of adolescence; and a consideration of analytic approaches to adolescent socialization and development.

Before getting into these matters, some clarification is needed on the distinction between adolescence and youth as social stages in the life course. Recognition of adolescence as a social stage in the life span emerged in America around 1900, in large part through the writings of G. Stanley Hall (1904) and the growth of high school education. Despite a lack of consensus among social scientists on the social boundaries of contemporary adolescence, the clearest marker for entry into adolescence is the transition from primary to secondary school (from sixth to seventh grade). Entry into one or more adult roles (marriage, parenthood, full-time employment, financial independence) is commonly regarded as the upper boundary. In general usage, the stage of youth tends to represent a more inclusive part of the age structure than adolescence, since it includes young people in those ill-defined years between partial and complete independence relative to the family of origin, a time span that has increased over the past twenty years through the expansion of higher education (see Keniston's discussion of youth as a new "psychological stage of life," 1970). In this volume, adolescence and youth are employed interchangeably in reference to the years between the seventh grade and (relatively) complete independence from the family of origin.

THE LIFE SPAN APPROACH

Sensitivity to the reciprocal aspects of generational relations and socialization calls for a life span approach in research on human development. Thus the analyst would be aware of the interdependence of the middle-aged world of parents and the adolescent experience of their offspring. In practice, the career stage of parents (defined by particular demands, options, and resources) is seldom taken into account in studies of adolescent socialization. In fact, it would be difficult to find a study in the literature on child and adolescent socialization that has incorporated parental career stage in the analysis. As a result, we are poorly informed on a wide range of issues pertaining to the life course of parents and its consequence for the upbringing of their children. To what extent, for example, is the adolescent's role in orienting parents to the postparental years a factor in his own upbringing and relationships within the family? Neglect of the middle years (ages 40 to 60), "a major unexplored period in 'life span' research" (SSRC, 1973, p. 25), may well have some connection to such limitations in adolescent research. Here it is worth noting that the recent launching of a new program of support for research on adolescence at the National Institute of Child Health and Human Development coincides with the formation of an SSRC (Social Science Research Council) committee to foster research on work and personality in the middle years. Clearly neither adolescence nor the middle years stand alone in the course of human development.

In the past decade a number of developments have occurred in the application of life span concepts to human lives and the developmental process, to the family unit, and to cohorts (social aggregates defined by a common event, such as birth year, year of marriage, etc.). These include causal models of events and status relations in the life course, an approach that moves beyond relationships between variables measured at two points in time to the conceptualization and test of linkages, to explanatory analysis. Consider the well-established relationship between the socioeconomic status of father and son. Though much speculation has focused on status transmission, only recently have studies systematically explored this process and traced out the complex paths through which a father's status influences the status attainment of his son. Following this approach, Alexander and Eckland (selection 9 in this volume) focus on the mediating function of school experience and its complex chain of influences in the status attainment of young men and women. This study employs data from a large-scale follow-up of persons who were first surveyed as high school students in the late fifties.

Another noteworthy development is the remarkable surge of interest, both quantitative and qualitative, in the life history approach. While the history of this perspective can be traced at least as far back as the 1920s and 1930s in the work of W. I. Thomas, Ernest Burgess, and John Dollard, recent work has led to the development of methods that are well suited to the collection, retrieval, and quantification of detailed life history information (Ramsøy, 1972). Using sophisticated forms in the collection of retrospective information, the researcher links events and transitions in the life course (such as first full-time job, job changes, residential change, marriage, etc.) to both chronological age and historical time. Life history information is well suited to the measurement of temporal constructs, such as career lines and status fluctuations, and provides a degree of scope and depth that exceeds the traditional framework of causal models. (As one might expect, the quantitative analysis of such data presents a large number of stubborn problems; see Carr-Hill & MacDonald, 1973). The painstaking collection of relatively valid data from retrospective reports offers an alternative to prospective longitudinal studies in generating life records.

In developmental psychology, early emphasis on the life span is seen in the work of Charlotte Bühler, Else Frenkel-Brunswik, and various staff members of the longitudinal studies that were launched in the twenties and thirties. From the 1940s to the present, important theoretical contributions on the life span (such as Havighurst's concept of the developmental task) and valuable research findings have come from the Committee on Human Development at the University of Chicago. This early work influenced the formulation of a developmental theory of the family (Hill, 1964), a perspective distinguished by its temporal orientation and reliance on the life cycle concept. More will be said about this approach to the family in our subsequent discussion of the life cycle and life course concepts.

As a field of inquiry, life span developmental psychology gained coherence and visibility through a series of West Virginia Conferences from 1969 to 1972. Papers presented at these meetings have been published in three volumes under the major title of *Life-Span Developmental Psychology*: Volume I, *Research and Theory* (Goulet & Baltes, 1970); Volume II, *Methodological Issues* (Nesselroade & Reese, 1973); and Volume III, *Personality and Socialization* (Baltes & Schaie, 1973). As outlined in these volumes, the life span approach is defined by its concern with the description and explanation of age-related behavioral changes (ontogenetic) from birth to death. The explanatory thrust of this approach focuses on theory construction and on the specification of linkages in antecedent-consequent relationships within the life span, and thus directly confronts a major weakness in longitudinal studies of human development and socialization. In addition to theory building, research workers in this area have been especially productive in methodological innovation, as evidenced by the sequential-longitudinal design and the isolation of historical change from life course change in intellectual functioning.

An important development over the past decade bears directly on the developmental psychologist's sensitivity to the social-historical context of the life course and its influence: the comparative and internal analysis of cohorts, as proposed in the work of social demographers (see Ryder, 1965) and by the emerging sociological specialty of age stratification (Riley, Johnson, & Foner, 1972). The sociotemporal context of birth cohorts (of individuals born within the same time interval) varies according to the rapidity of social change. Furthermore, it is assumed that the consequences of such change for individuals vary according to their age or life stage, and are expressed in their subsequent course of development. "The cohort is distinctively marked by the career stage it occupies when prosperity or depression, and peace or war, impinge on it" (Ryder, 1965, p. 846).

Cohort differentiation has profound implications for adolescents to the extent that it shapes their socialization environment and options for entering adult roles. Some of these implications are evident in an ongoing comparative study of two birth cohorts (Elder, 1974b): members of the older cohort were born in 1920–21 and lived in Oakland, California; the younger cohort, born in 1928–29, grew up in the adjacent city of Berkeley. The Oakland children were beyond the critical early years of development during the Great Depression, but they were old enough to contribute to the household economy. They left high school during the early phase of war mobilization and consequently entered a labor market that offered opportunities that were a substantial improvement over the depressed thirties. Over 90 percent of the men in this cohort entered the military during World War II for an average of three years. By comparison, members of the Berkeley cohort were of preschool age during the most severe phase of the Great Depression, and thus are likely to have been more adversely influenced by family hardship than members of the Oakland cohort. The Berkeley children were too young to assume a major productive role in the household economy of their deprived families, and their world of adolescence was shaped by war and surging prosperity rather than by the depressed economy of the thirties. In sharp contrast to the Oakland men, only half of the young men from Berkeley ever served in the military and then primarily in the Korean War. Thus the experiences of depression and war, of scarcity and prosperity, differentiate these cohorts in complex ways. Richard Braungart relates some of these historical variations to the involvement of young people in social movements in his contribution to this volume.

From this brief overview, it is clear that the life span approach to adolescence is informed by a diverse intellectual history, a diversity that is well represented among the contributors to this volume. It is a perspective in ferment; in search of theoretical coherence and useful constructs that portray the process of human development and socialization. Since constructs inform and structure the research we undertake, the remainder of this introductory essay is devoted to matters of conceptualization: to limitations of the life cycle concept and a more promising life span formulation based on dimensions of the life course; to social facts that should inform our view of adolescence in society and life experience; and, last, to analytical frameworks in the study of human development in adolescence and the life span.

THE LIFE CYCLE AND LIFE COURSE

The life cycle and life course have often been used interchangeably in reference to the event-structured process of life. However, there are distinctions between these constructs worth noting, since they bear on our understanding of the life span and adolescence. By definition, the life cycle refers to cyclical aspects of the life course. A number of cyclical aspects come to mind as we survey the life span of an individual: the organismic sequence of birth, growth and maturation, aging, and death; the acquisition, performance, and gradual shedding of roles (occupational, marital, parental) in the later years of life through retirement, death of marital partner, the launching of children along adult paths; and the cycle of earning power, which reaches a high point in the middle years of life and generally declines in old age. Organismic change constitutes a principal source of structure in the life cycle of individuals and can be viewed as its developmental core.

There are facets of the temporal process of life experience that do not fit the cyclical format (worklife patterns, for example) and are best treated within the more inclusive framework of a multidimensional life course. This point is seen most clearly within the context of family studies, since the life cycle concept entered the sociological literature in application to the family, mainly through work in social demography (Glick, 1947; Glick & Parke, 1965), and has been developed subsequently by proponents of the developmental approach to families (Hill, 1964).

The family life cycle depicts changes that occur in the family unit "as a result of routinely expected variation in the size of families and in the roles of family members" (Burr, 1973, p. 218). These changes delineate stages of the family cycle, as seen in Reuben Hill's nine-stage formulation (1964).

1. Establishment—newly married, childless.
2. New parents—infant to 3 years old.
3. Preschool family—child 3 to 6 years old and possibly younger siblings.
4. School-age family—oldest child 6 to 12 years, possibly younger siblings.
5. Family with adolescent—oldest child 13 to 19 years, possibly younger siblings.
6. Family with young adult—oldest child 20 years and up, to when first child leaves home.
7. Family as launching center—from departure of first to last child.
8. Postparental family—the middle years, after children have left home until father retires.
9. Aging family—after retirement of father.

The core of this version of the family cycle is the reproductive process, both sexual and social; the typology barely touches base with father's worklife and refers not at all to mother's worklife. As structured by the birth of children, the typology is useless for childless couples, a segment of the population that is likely to increase in percentage in birth cohorts that reach marital age in the 1970s. Remarriages are also excluded. In short, the unmarried and variant family forms do not fit the typology outlined by Hill. Where marriage rates are low, as in Sweden, the excluded represent a very substantial component of the population (see Trost, 1973). These variant forms do not present a problem for the life course approach.

It is possible to avoid some of these limitations by broadening the array of types, by including spinster and childless categories, for instance, as seen in Peter

Uhlenberg's comparison (1974) of white and nonwhite birth cohorts of American females from 1890-94 through 1930-34. Five types were specified: (1) early death—female dies between the ages of 15 and 50; (2) spinster—female survives, does not marry before the age of 50; (3) childless—female survives and marries, but has no live births; (4) unstable marriage, with children—female survives, marries, bears at least one child, but first marriage is broken before the age of 50; and (5) preferred—female reaches age 50, living with first husband and having produced at least one child. Over the last fifty years, the data show a trend toward the preferred form of the family for both white and nonwhite females. This is a useful typology for the purpose at hand, to reveal demographic trends in family structure, but it yields only a skeletal picture of the life course of these women.

While the family cycle typology has proven its utility in descriptive research, despite its ill-defined and conglomerate structure, important analytic advantages can be gained by shifting to a multidimensional concept of the life course. This concept emerges in primitive form by simply decomposing the typological construction into its component dimensions: into histories of the marital relationship, household, childbearing, child rearing, worklife of husband and wife, mortality. By elaborating these dimensions and adding others (such as educational, residential, and consumption records), we end up with a multidimensional concept of the life course. From this vantage point, the family could be viewed, in Bernard Farber's phrase (1961) as "a set of mutually contingent careers." This strategy enables the analyst to work with the life course of each individual family member and of the family unit as a whole, to relate individual and group aspects of the life span. The sequential patterning and clustering of events are ascertained from empirical analysis, not from pre-judgments.

This version of the life course has direct relevance to the study of adolescents, their historical biography and prospective lines of action. In the age stratification system of complex, industrial societies, late adolescence in particular is characterized by a high degree of social differentiation along institutional sectors; social differentiation of the life course increases sharply as the young child becomes an adolescent and then enters the stages of youth and young adulthood. This is another way of saying that the late adolescent is in the process of entering lines of activity in adulthood—in worklife and economic role, in legal and political status, marriage and parenthood. At any point in time, a cross section of the youth population shows a high degree of variation in stage or position across dimensions of the life course. For example, a child may be born before marriage, economic independence, or the completion of education. For the individual, the social stage of youth frequently provides striking examples of asynchrony (see Cain, 1964, pp. 300-301). By relying on a multidimensional concept of the life course, we are able to capture this social reality.

The distinction between a concept of the "life course in general" and a multidimensional concept parallels the commonplace distinction between "development in general" and lines or dimensions of human development (on the latter distinction, see Keniston, 1971, p. 337). Development frequently consists of an uneven rate of change across developmental dimensions, and this is also true of situational change across dimensions of the life course. A differentiated view of the life course thus enables the analyst to achieve conceptual precision in studying social transitions that entail some degree of change in the relation between an individual and his proximal environment, to focus on age-related change in the parent-child relationship, points of continuity and discontinuity in the educational career of the young, the transition to full-time employment, marriage, parenthood. Transitions of this sort entail some measures of social separation and integration, of differentiation and consensual validation. Their psychosocial effects are contingent on the nature of the change and the adaptive potential of the individual, as defined by resources, social preparation, and support.

By dimensionalizing the life course and obtaining life records or histories on each dimension, we can obtain a differentiated and relatively complete characterization of lives in process. This approach is basic to the study of career lines and provides the ingredients for explanatory analyses of the life span through examination of the interdependencies and causal linkages between diverse events in the temporal process.

ADOLESCENCE IN SOCIETY AND LIFE EXPERIENCE

Our view of adolescence in society and its social history has been very strongly influenced by ideas regarding social growth and long-term social development. In theory, such development takes the form of a continuous transaction between "increasing differentiation and higher level integration of the social structure" (Smelser, 1968, p. 243). Within this framework, change in the family bears directly on the origin of adolescence in American society. Prolongation of dependency through the emergence of adolescence as a life stage in the twentieth century and the increased significance of the peer group in socialization are linked to conditions that diminished the family's role in upbringing and widened the gap between family experience and the requirements of adult life (see Eisenstadt, 1956; Parsons, 1964). These conditions include separation of the production function from the family unit and its transformation into a more specialized unit of socialization and consumption, the increased specialization of job skills resulting in higher educational requirements, and the growth of secondary education in response to these requirements and developmental concepts of the young person (see Demos & Demos, 1969; Kett, 1971). Technological developments that augmented the productivity of workers lessened the value of preadult labor and strengthened reform efforts to protect the young from exploitation by excluding them from the labor market.

Discontinuities between family experience and the requirements of adult life pose two interrelated problems for society and young people. Society's problem is to establish a bridge to adult roles through appropriate socialization and role allocation. For adolescents the problem consists of achieving independence, deciding on future alternatives, and establishing their identity. These conditions give rise to organized, adult-directed groups or agencies that prepare adolescents for and guide them toward the capacities and qualities desired in adults, and also create a propensity for adolescents to form peer groups. Decline of the family in preparing the young for adult roles is thus expressed in a more differentiated socialization environment, which is distinguished by the prominence of secondary school, adult-directed youth organizations, and peer groups.

Historically, the extension of schooling has made a substantial contribution to the segregation of young people from adult life and to restricted cross-age experience within the youth group. These social patterns have been singled out as more costly than beneficial to contemporary youth and society by the President's Panel on Youth (PSAC Report, 1973). Though not anticipated originally, the high school established a conducive setting for peer influence and mate selection beyond the constraints of parental control. A number of adult-directed youth organizations emerged between 1890 and 1920, including the Boy Scouts and youth groups in the YMCA. "The new youth organizations were pervaded by an incongruous tolerance of socialization by the peer group, by the idea that loyalty to age peers in youth could be sublimated into civic service in adulthood, a concept which conflicted with the rigid adult direction of youth organizations, but which was present all the same" (PSAC Report, 1973, p. 24).

Symptomatic of the presumed shift in relative contribution to socialization—from family to school and peers—is the conclusion that the concept of the generations (from parents to offspring) has outlived its usefulness as a framework for the study of social change. Societies undergoing rapid change "must generally break the grip of the family on the individual. In so doing [they] produce the kind of social milieu in which the cohort is the most appropriate unit of temporal analysis" (Ryder, 1965, p. 853). Most prominent in this milieu are the school, peer groups, and the latter's mediation of the mass culture, advertising, and so on.

The ascendance of the peer group in the social world of young people, as depicted in the long view of social development in American society, is reflected by three major appraisals of its social influence. Together they tend to underscore what might be regarded as the unapplauded consequences of peer association in an age-segregated society—David Riesman's *Lonely Crowd* (1950; see also Riesman, 1961), James Coleman's *Adolescent Society* (1961), and Urie Bronfenbrenner's *Two Worlds of Childhood* (1970). American and Soviet upbringing are the two worlds of childhood in Bronfenbrenner's study. It is important to distinguish between the empirical evidence marshaled by these authors and their interpretations. The interpretations have been effectively challenged by critics on a number of grounds, but the studies address well-documented developments in American society (such as age segregation) and pose important policy issues.

Riesman's provocative essay covers an exceedingly broad canvas on the relation between historical change and social character, but considerable attention is given to the emergence of other-directed peer groups in the upper middle class. It is the peer group, not the family, that dominates the lives of children in the other-directed society. Affluent parents continue to select appropriate environments for their children by their choice of neighborhood and school, but the social experience and destiny of the young are shaped largely by school and peers, social agencies that will help locate them in the social order. Lacking clear standards or measuring rods for child rearing, other-directed parents consult magazines, other parents, and their child's own peer group. The young learn how the parental role should be played from television and peers, and use this knowledge to achieve their ends. Peers represent the model and the group represents the measure for all endeavors. Group pressures enforce taste standardization and condition skills in consumership. Children may be "loved" toward maturity, but they are no longer "brought up" as were the children of inner-directed homes. In the land of the other-directed, parents have abdicated their responsibilities and authority in parenting to their children's peer group.

Riesman's analysis (which is much too complex to be presented in detail here) has been criticized on a number of points. As one critic has noted, Riesman "tends to 'reify' the peer group, as if it were the overwhelmingly predominant factor in socialization and constituted a kind of microcosm of the emerging adult 'other-directed' society" (Parsons, 1964, p. 221). Research studies have provided a more differentiated picture of the peer group's influence by specifying the conditions under which peers function as allies or adversaries of parents in adolescent socialization (Elder, 1968; Hirschi, 1969). Whatever the trend in family support, studies have shown that adolescents who fail to receive guidance, affection, and concern from parents—whether by parental inattention or absence—are likely to rely heavily on peers for emotional gratification, advice, and companionship, to anticipate a relatively unrewarding future, and to engage in antisocial activities (Bronfenbrenner, 1970, pp. 101-105; Hirschi, 1969).

Recently Riesman's depiction of peer-group dominance and parental abdication has been reemphasized by Urie Bronfenbrenner (1970) in the context of age segregation. One of the most significant trends toward age segregation over the past thirty years, according to Bronfenbrenner, consists of a decline in the amount of time parents and children spend together. He reinterprets the historical trend toward permissive child rearing as evidence of parental disengagement from the responsibilities of parenthood, a trend that is open to serious question in view of the available data. *"Children,"* he concludes, *"used to be brought up by their parents"* (p. 95), an assertion very much in keeping with Riesman's argument in *The Lonely Crowd*. Some recent studies by Bronfenbrenner (1970, pp. 98-99) and his associates suggest that contemporary American parents are less involved in child rearing than German and Soviet parents. In a survey of children in six nations, England was the only country in which parents ranked lower than American parents on companionship with children, involvement in child rearing, and affection (1970, p. 116). The relatively low position of American parents on parenting is explained in terms of "changed conditions"; yet some features of this change in parent-child relations—such precocious independence, loss of parental control—can be seen in the commentary of European visitors to Nineteenth-century America.

In the absence of substantial adult participation in child rearing and direction of peer relations, Bronfenbrenner sees little developmental value associated with heavy involvement in youth groups. The group is more likely to be a source of wayward conduct than a civilizing agent. Although the effects of peer involvement depend on the standards and activities of the group (see Kandel, 1973), Bronfenbrenner (1970) regards intense involvement in groups free of adult direction as a handicap to moral growth and development. "If children have contact only with their own age-mates, there is no possibility for learning culturally established patterns of cooperation and mutual concern" (p. 117).

The separation of adolescents from the adult community (in this case via the high school) also represents a major theme in Coleman's *Adolescent Society*, which reports a study of students in ten midwestern high schools. Two conclusions drawn from this study—the relatively stronger influence of peers, compared to that of parents, and the assumed cultural cleavage between the adolescent and adult communities—have been effectively questioned by critical reviews (see Jahoda & Warren, 1965). Coleman could not determine the extent and type of difference in norms and values between high school and the adult community, since he analyzed data only on students. Nevertheless, this research made an important contribution by highlighting the potential dysfunctions of age segregation (see PSAC Report, 1973), and by pointing to the conflicting incentives in youth groups and formal education.

Social integration of older and younger Americans has implications far beyond the unidirectional influence of adults on children and youth, which Bronfenbrenner stresses, for it is through such associations that the young convey their definitions of the situation, their aspirations, needs, and anxieties to the old. In cross-age relationships, older people are also socialized by the young in terms of the meanings and expectations they have acquired (Elder, 1967). Isolation of the young diminishes the accuracy of adults in taking the role of the young, in knowing how they feel, think, and perceive, and in applying this empathic knowledge to guide their own responses in socialization. Physical separation increases adult dependence on the mass-media stereotypes of the adolescent world, and these biased concepts may provide the sole basis for citizen response to the schools, student complaints, drugs, and so forth. Unlike Soviet youth, the problem for American young people is less that of having the right and opportunity to dissent or criticize than of being respected, listened to, and understood. The young's role as a mentor of adults has special significance in a rapidly changing society, for as Erikson (1962) observes, "No longer is it merely for the old to teach the young the meaning of life, whether individual or collective. It is the young who, by their responses and actions tell the old whether life as represented by the old and as presented to the young has meaning" (p. 24).

Up to this point, we have viewed adolescence from the perspective of societal development, a vantage point that neglects important social facts that bear on the position of young people. Since 1900, this position has been modified, at times drastically so, by swings in the economy, major wars, and correlated change in demographic processes, such as cohort fertility. The oft-stated assumption that prolonged dependency is a luxury of affluent societies generates a number of questions concerning the nature of adolescence during the Great Depression. Were adult responsibilities extended downward in the depressed thirties? What role did the young play in the labor-intensive economy of deprived families, and how does it differ from the household role of children in middle class families during the postwar era of prosperity (see Elder, 1974a)? In the absence of theoretical insight, knowledge of social history would at least sensitize us to the vulnerability of youth culture to economic conditions. "The collapse of the counter-culture of the 1920s in the face of economic depression suggests that one must eschew any linear theory of societal change. The cultural revolt of the present period presupposes economic stability and affluence, conditions which, given the cyclical behavior of capitalist economies, should not be taken for granted" (Mankoff & Flacks, 1972, pp. 56-57). This caution is underscored by transformations in social and cultural experience among youth since the late 1960s and by the awareness of growth limitations that has emerged from the energy crisis of the 1970s. Cyclical change in the economy differentiates birth cohorts, and thus the experience of adolescence and youth.

Economic cycles are correlated with demographic events that have profound consequences for the young, as dependents and in later life, and for society. Variations in cohort size, resulting from change in the birth rate, differentiate socialization experience and marital, occupational, and other life prospects. The drop in fertility during the Great Depression produced a cohort of relatively small size. In terms of jobs and job seekers, the supply–demand ratio favored the life chances of these young Americans as they entered the labor market of the fifties and early sixties. At the other extreme in cohort size are young people who entered the age group of 14- to 24-year-olds in the 1960s, most of whom were born in the postwar era of earlier marriage and rising fertility. This age category, which included 27 million young Americans in 1960, swelled to over 40 million by 1970, a gain (52 percent) that was absorbed mainly by the schools and military (PSAC, 1973, Ch. 3). Youth in the sixties thus became a larger component of the population relative to adults and rapidly overtaxed existing educational facilities and manpower.

The life situation of a small cohort may be likened to an "undermanned behavior setting" (to use Roger Barker's concept, 1968), which maximizes participation and responsibility opportunities for members, while the environment of a large cohort resembles that of an overmanned behavior setting in which challenging roles are limited to a smaller proportion of the occupants. In the latter case, the major challenge, that of absorption, is faced by the adult community. Noting that undermanned settings are becoming less prevalent in American society, Barker points out that its historically distinctive features are rooted in an idea that relates undermanned settings to a way of life—land of opportunity, people of plenty, and the free frontier. It is the idea that "there has been a superabundance of goals to be achieved and an excess of tasks to be done in relation to the nation's inhabitants, and that these have been important influences on the American society and people" (Barker, 1968, p. 189). Decline in the birth rate over the past decade and its continuation point to a smaller socialization task in the future as well as a potentially brighter future for the young worker.

As our last point regarding the social dimensions of adolescence, we take issue with assessments that are focused solely on adolescence and young people in society *as a whole*, that do not take ecological variations into account. As a matter of emphasis, our interest in societal development and economic growth over the past half century is apt to slight the uneven pace of change across sections of the country. This uneven pace has implications for the upbringing, duration of dependency, and social options of the young. On economic base and resources, age structure and population change (via natural increase and migration), low-income rural counties clearly represent very different socialization environments from those of affluent suburbs in metropolitan areas. A comparison of this urban world with that of rural farm youth in the open country of the Midwest brings to mind variation in the degree of discontinuity between family experience and adult life, a form of social discontinuity that is generally regarded as a major factor in prolonged dependency and in the life stages of adolescence and youth. From these contrasts we perceive the social existence and dimensions of adolescence as variables, not constants, in contemporary American society.

Morris Rosenberg takes contextual variations into account in his contribution to this volume and reminds us that young people do not live in the *total society*; they spend their life in specified contexts—in neighborhoods, schools, communities. These contexts serve as a frame of reference and evaluation for occupants. In this respect, Rosenberg's data show that the self-evaluations of black youth vary according to the racial composition of their school. Another example of contextual influence is seen in the distorted age-sex structure of some rural counties in the Deep South, a structure resulting from a large outmigration of black male adults in the early productive years and a high birth rate among black females. A relatively large number of children per adult in the productive years results in both economic and social deprivation. There are many children to be cared for, loved, and educated by a relatively small number of adult caretakers and teachers. Few competent young adults are around to serve as models for the children. Black boys see and interact with relatively few black males who are working, and most of these men have subsistence jobs. Aside from the poverty, one wonders how the impressions and attitudes of children who grow up in a setting populated mostly by children, women, and the elderly differ from those acquired by children who are reared in a setting with a more balanced age-sex ratio.

In this section, we have examined three categories of social facts that should inform our view of adolescence in life experience: (1) the general course of societal development through structural differentiation and higher-level integration, its relation to the emergence of prolonged dependency, as expressed in the social stages of adolescence and youth, and transformation of the relative contributions of adult agencies to socialization; (2) historical variations in the social dimensions of adolescence and youth in relation to swings in the economy, wars, and correlated demographic processes; and (3) ecological variations in these social dimensions within society at points in the historical process, variations that differentiate the proximal social contexts in which the young come to maturity. Societal development and historical variations differentiate the socialization environment and life chances of birth cohorts, and call for analytic sensitivity to historical change in human development. The social facts of ecological variation require specification of historical change within concrete social contexts. The course of human development to the adult years is shaped largely by the social matrix of these contexts.

MATTERS OF CONCEPT AND APPROACH

The familiar call for more theoretical development in a field of inquiry applies with particular force to human development in adolescence and the life course. What are the constructs that distinguish and comprise a life span framework? Since we are dealing with lives in process, first priority should be given to constructs that represent aspects of that process. Yet temporal formulations have not received the investment they warrant or require, especially on the subject of environmental change. Underlying this task is the more general need for greater emphasis on theory construction relative to extant theories that often have limited utility for the problem at hand. This need is most urgent in cross-level relations between social structure and personality (i.e., the psychological effects of class position as mediated by interactional contexts), since relations of this sort are typically neglected from a conceptual standpoint and generally require models that integrate elements of different theories.

In theory and research, the range of approach, analytic level, and focal point seems well beyond the reach of any coherent framework. What framework, for example, could be used to bring coherence to the developmental literatures in the physical, intellectual, achievement, competence, dependency, and moral domains? As common lines of inquiry in psychology, these developmental dimensions find much less favor among sociologists, who are more attuned to social sectors and roles, to adolescent socialization and status transitions relative to educational, occupational, marital, and political roles. As in the general literature, these two foci are expressed in the present volume; the initial chapters on developmental dimensions and issues are authored mainly by psychologists; the later chapters on social roles, by sociologists. Common ground can be found in a social-psychological approach to environmental influences and personality in the life course. Elements of this approach inform a number of papers in this book and represent a base from which to develop a general analytical perspective on adolescence in the life cycle. Group-level and individual-centered analyses provide a useful context in which to take up this cross-level perspective.

Group-level analyses include the comparative and historical study of adolescence as an age-grade in society, the comparative study of age cohorts, generations, and youth groups from large-scale social movements to the small circle of peers. Adolescents are studied as a social aggregate or collectivity; little or no attention is given to the individual in a social situation, to his socialization and personality development. Research problems posed by observed variations in the social position of youth as a social aggregate lead to investigations of causal factors in social change. What factors in the historical process were instrumental in the segregation of age groups, of boys and girls in educational institutions? Informed by sociological and anthropological theories, this mode of analysis is illustrated by perspectives in the preceding section of this essay (see also Musgrove, 1965) and by Braungart's essay, "Youth and Social Movements," in this volume.

A contrasting mode of inquiry centers on the study of organismic development with little emphasis on social processes or person-environment interactions. Examples may be found in the literature on physical and cognitive development. In selection 5 of the present volume, Eichorn illustrates this perspective in her examination of differential rates of development. Comparison of the focal points of group and individual brings out an important distinction between socialization and development (for a review of concepts of development, see Stevenson, 1966). Since socialization represents a process of induction into group ways, it is appropriately studied in terms of the matrix and requirements of group life. In this respect, the principles of socialization are not equivalent to the principles governing aspects of human development. In fact, group requirements and their social expression may at times run directly contrary to developmental interests, as in the case of the large, low-income family. Depending on social circumstances, socialization may entail costs as well as benefits for human growth and development.

Each mode of inquiry is distinguished by a specific class of research questions. Of special interest in this regard are the questions posed by the social-psychological approach, since it is concerned with the interplay of organism and environment in the developmental process. This perspective shifts attention from matters concerning the relative autonomy of data for presumably different levels of analysis to the question of relatedness. How are structural aspects of the environment related to psychological characteristics of the adolescent or young adult, his motives and concept of self? An understanding of the relationship entails explanatory analysis. Given the relationship between social class and the work values of adolescent boys, for example, we are led to investigate the process by which class exerts its influence (Elder, 1973). This approach provides an analytic focus for studies of the social environment in human development, a focus defined by research questions that orient investigation to linkages between aspects of social structure, personality, and behavior. Specification of linkages between constructs requires some measure of clarity in their definition, and thus may produce reformulations that offer greater conceptual coordination and precision.

This approach is most important for research on the relation between social structure and personality in the life span, since extant theories that are relevant to human development apply only to limited and highly diverse aspects of the conceptual domain (e.g., psychoanalytic, genetic-developmental, self-role, social learning, etc.). Frequently no single theory satisfies the explanatory requirements, as seen in Rosenberg's paper and in Alexander and Eckland's study of the complex causal chains in the status attainment process. A rudimentary outline of relations between key constructs is generally found in the statement of a research problem. By elaborating these constructs and their interrelations, the researcher formulates an analytic model, a conceptual map of the domain that specifies principal lines and boundaries for the research. Linkages identified in the model can thus be operationalized and put to an empirical test. To date, this procedure is the exception rather than the rule among studies of adolescents. In most cases research proceeds no further than the demonstration of a simple association between two variables that are assumed to be ordered in a causal sequence.

In relation to the adolescent, aspects of the social environment can be located on a proximal-distal continuum, from the interactional context of the family, for example, to the family's location in the class structure and the community's location within the regional economy. Proximal environments are thus potential linkages as we trace the psychological effects of larger social structures to the adolescent's life experience and personality development. It is commonly assumed that the behavioral effect of situations is mediated by the actor's interpretation, by his definition of the situation and attribution of causality. Social structures impinge on these concepts of reality and personality through the imperatives of social position (its social demands, constraints, task experience) and the proximal environment of interpersonal relationships and socialization. The relative importance of these two types of linkages depends in part on the age status of the individual. During the years of dependency, the interpersonal world of family, peers, and school assumes unusual significance as a link between the larger social structure and the individual. For the adult male, the more important mediator may well be the imperatives of social position, as Mel Kohn (1973) has argued from his studies of men in the labor force:

> A person's social class position affects his perceptions, values, and thinking processes
> primarily by shaping the everyday realities he must face, the demands he must try to
> meet, and not, to any very important degree, because it puts him into continuing

interaction with other members of his class, who share what some call a class culture. I do not deny the existence of class cultures, of shared values and beliefs. But I do argue that those beliefs stem directly from the realities faced by members of any given social class and will change when the realities change. Moreover, if the individual's own experiences are at variance with those of other members of his social class, his own experiences—not the beliefs and values of others—will come to shape his views (p. 3).

Given the usual limitations of resources and expertise, the scope of a single project must be restricted to only a segment of the network of relations that form a bridge between social structure and adolescent personality. But this does not mean that we can remain blind to the context in which this network is embedded. The risk in doing so is noted by Leo Bogart (1973) on the subject of birth order and personality. Family size is known to be related to social status, and yet clinical studies of birth order effects have not incorporated social status in the analysis.

Understandably, the students of this subject have concentrated on the nature of child rearing and on parent-child and sibling relationships in families with different structures, and their effects on personality. . . . Birth order appears to have an independent importance. But without the necessary controls on social class, how are we to interpret evidence of its influence on personality? This question typifies the problem of building generalizations from a succession of small studies. But it should also alert us to the difficulty of drawing intelligent generalizations from large studies in which psychological indicators are divorced from their social context (p. 997).

Another example of the price paid by ignoring contextual properties is found in the literature on the relative influence of parents and peers. Explanations of this influence include two prominent foci: adolescent subcultures that are rooted in the structure of communities and institutions; and family socialization that accounts for variation in adolescent vulnerability to peer influence. As a rule, work in the latter tradition excludes contextual variations from the analysis and even fails at times to consider the relevance of context for the problem at hand. Thus in two studies, which reported diametrically opposed findings on the nature of peer influence, contextual variations appear to be the principal explanation, and yet neither had much to say on this topic. Using a sample of adolescents and parents from the Lower East Side of New York City, Furstenberg (1971) found that the more the young participated in peer activities, as indicated by frequency and amount of interaction, the less they knew about or shared parental aspirations. This outcome begins to make sense when we note the sample composition (predominantly low-income, over half Puerto Rican and black) and the tradition of delinquent subcultures in the residential area (not discussed by Furstenberg). The other study of adolescents, their mothers, and close friends (Kandel & Lesser, 1969) is based on a sample that was drawn from students in three high schools in New England—one rural, another urban, and the third a consolidated school that recruited its student body from adjacent communities. Though no other evidence is presented on community setting, the New

England adolescents would most certainly rank higher on integration with adults than the New York City adolescents. In any case, close friends and parents of the New England youths generally shared the same educational goal, and association with peers did not lessen agreement with parents. The important point here is that the researchers failed to recognize the uniqueness of their respective contexts, and thus could not apply such information to their interpretations and generalizations. As a consequence, we are left without important clues to the conflicting results.

By viewing adolescence within a life span framework, lines of analysis include temporal distance in antecedent-consequent relations as well as the usual conceptual distance between social-structural and personality constructs that are measured at a point in time. In either case the analytic task of constructing linkages varies according to the distance involved. Consider, for example, an early study of Austrian and German adolescents. Paul Lazarsfeld found that "local variations in occupational choice tended to correspond with variations in the economic structure" (cited in Lipset & Bendix, 1959, p. 521). The larger the proportion of persons employed in a particular kind of occupation in a city, the larger the proportion of 14-year-old youths who desired to enter that occupation. The relevance of economic structure for the occupational choice of boys, an account of its chain of influence, is expressed in the hypothesized linkages that connect community structure to the life situations and subjective reality of the young. Variations in community structure bear on options in the local labor market and the likelihood of exposure to certain types of occupational models and networks (intergenerational and other) that orient the young to these options. In this regard, the proximal environments of family, school, and peer group are likely mediators of structural effects on the community level.

As we move into the adult years and identify outcomes of preadult life situations, linkages that connect these situations with social structure and individual behavior become building blocks in the construction of models that provide an account of the childhood-adult relation. Given the conceptual scope in problems of this sort, each interpretive model is likely to build on a number of received theories. A model of occupational choice and attainment might draw on structural theory for an account of a boy's differential access to occupational models and influences, on observational theory for an explanation of the psychosocial effects of such models, on allocation theory for the placement function of schools, and on a theory of structured commitments and options that sheds light on the relation between first and subsequent jobs in adult worklife. The explication of antecedent-consequent relations thus becomes an exceedingly complex process, as Alexander and Eckland demonstrate in this volume. Few problems are more critical to an understanding of adolescence in the life cycle than the process of status transmission across the generations, and yet we have only recently made efforts to conceptualize this process and subject these interpretations to empirical test.

In this introductory essay, I have emphasized selected theoretical issues in the study of adolescence in the life cycle: the identification and elaboration of constructs that capture the realities of the life course; concepts of adolescence and youth as stages in the life course, and their relation to social-historical conditions; and the conceptual implications of approaches to environmental influences in human development. If the state of theory and research on adolescence appears to resemble the fabled "Tower of Babel," there is common ground in an approach that focuses on the analytic task of linking social structure and personality in the developmental process. This volume will serve us well if it draws attention to this task and suggests fruitful directions for studies of adolescence in the life cycle.

REFERENCES

Baltes, P. B., & Schaie, K. W. (Eds.) *Life-span developmental psychology: Personality and socialization*. New York: Academic Press, 1973.

Barker, R. *Ecological psychology*. Stanford: Stanford University Press, 1968.

Bogart, L. Psychology on a large scale. *American Psychologist*, November 1973, 28, 994-999.

Bronfenbrenner, U. *Two worlds of childhood: U.S. and U.S.S.R.* New York: Russell Sage Foundation, 1970.

Burr, W. *Theory construction and the sociology of the family*. New York: Wiley-Interscience, 1973.

Cain, L. D., Jr. Life course and social structure. In R. E. L. Faris (Ed.), *Handbook of modern sociology*. Chicago: Rand McNally, 1964.

Carr-Hill, R. A., & MacDonald, K. I. Problems in the analysis of life histories. *Sociological Review Monographs*, July 1973, 19, 57-95.

Coleman, J. S. *The adolescent society*. New York: Free Press of Glencoe, 1961.

Demos, J., & Demos, V. Adolescence in historical perspective. *Journal of Marriage and the Family*, November 1969, 31, 632-638.

Elder, G. H., Jr. Age integration and socialization in an educational setting. *Harvard Educational Review*, Fall 1967, 37, 594-619.

Elder, G. H., Jr. *Adolescent socialization and personality development*. Chicago: Rand McNally, 1968.

Elder, G. H., Jr. On linking social structure and personality. *American Behavioral Scientist*, July-August 1973, 16, 785-800.

Elder, G. H., Jr. *Children of the great depression*. Chicago: University of Chicago Press, 1974. (a)

Elder, G. H., Jr. Social change in the family and life course. Unpublished outline of research program. Spring, 1974. (b)

Eisenstadt, S. N. *From generation to generation: Age groups and the social structure*. New York: Free Press of Glencoe, 1956.

Erikson, E. Youth: Fidelity and diversity. *Daedalus*, Winter 1962, 91, 5-27.

Farber, B. The family as a set of mutually contingent careers. In N. N. Foote (Ed.), *Household decision-making*. New York: New York University Press, 1961.

Furstenberg, F. F., Jr. The transmission of mobility orientation in the family. *Social Forces*, June 1971, 49, 595-603.

Glick, P. C. The family cycle. *American Sociological Review*, 1947, 12, 164-174.

Glick, P. C., & Parke, R., Jr. New approaches in studying the life cycle of the family. *Demography*, 1965, **2**, 187–202.

Goulet, L. R., & Baltes, P. B. (Eds.) *Life-span developmental psychology: Research and theory.* New York: Academic Press, 1970.

Grumbach, M. M., Grave, G. E., & Mayer, F. E. (Eds.) *The control of the onset of puberty.* New York: Wiley, 1974.

Hall, G. S. *Adolescence: Its psychology and its relations to physiology, anthropology, sociology, sex, crime, religion, and education.* New York: D. Appleton, 1904.

Hill, R. Methodological issues in family development research. *Family Process*, March 1964, **3**, 186–206.

Hirschi, T. *Causes of delinquency.* Berkeley: University of California Press, 1969.

Jahoda, M., & Warren, N. The myths of youth. *Sociology of Education*, Winter 1965, **38**, 138–149.

Kandel, D. Adolescent marihuana use: Role of parents and peers. *Science*, 14 September 1973, **181**, 1067–1070.

Kandel, D. B., & Lesser, G. S. Parental and peer influence on educational plans of adolescents. *American Sociological Review*, April 1969, **34**, 213–233.

Keniston, K. Youth, a (new) stage of life. *American Scholar*, Autumn 1970, **39**.

Keniston, K. Psychological development and historical change. *Journal of Interdisciplinary History*, Autum 1971, **11**(2), 329–345.

Kett, J. F. Adolescence and youth in nineteenth-century America. *Journal of Interdisciplinary History*, Autumn 1971, **11**(2), 283–298.

Kohn, M. L. Comments on Glen Elder's Linking social structure and personality. American Sociological Association Meetings, New York, August 1973.

Lipset, S. M., & Bendix, R. *Social mobility in industrial society.* Berkeley: University of California Press, 1959.

Mankoff, M., & Flacks, R. The changing base of the American student movement. In P. G. Altbach & R. S. Laufer (Eds.), *The new pilgrims: Youth protest in transition.* New York: McKay, 1972.

Musgrove, F. *Youth and the social order.* Bloomington, Ind.: Indiana University Press, 1965.

Nesselroade, J. R., & Reese, H. W. (Eds.) *Life-span developmental psychology: Methodological issues.* New York: Academic Press, 1973.

Parsons, T. *Social structure and personality.* New York: Free Press, 1964.

President's Science Advisory Commission, Panel on Youth. *Youth: Transition to adulthood.* Washington, D.C.: Office of Science and Technology, 1973.

Ramsøy, N. R. The Norwegian occupational life history study: Design, purpose, and a few preliminary results. Institute of Applied Social Research, Blindern, Oslo 3, 1972.

Riesman, D. (with N. Glazer & R. Denney) *The lonely crowd.* New Haven, Conn.: Yale University Press, 1950.

Riesman, D. (in collaboration with N. Glazer) The lonely crowd: A reconsideration in 1960. In S. M. Lipset & L. Lowenthal (Eds.), *Culture and social character.* New York: Free Press of Glencoe, 1961.

Riley, M. W., Johnson, M., & Foner, A. (Eds.) *A sociology of age stratification.* Vol. 3: *Aging and Society.* New York: Russell Sage Foundation, 1972.

Ryder, N. B. The cohort as a concept in the study of social change. *American Sociological Review*, December 1965, **30**, 843–861.

Smelser, N. Toward a general theory of social change. In N. Smelser, *Essays in sociological explanation.* Englewood Cliffs, N.J.: Prentice-Hall, 1968.

SSRC Committee on Work and Personality in the Middle Years. *Description of proposed activities.* New York: Social Science Research Council, June 1973.

Stevenson, H. W. Concept of development. *Monographs of the Society for Research in Child Development*, 1966, **31**, Whole No. 5, Serial No. 107.

Trost, J. The family life cycle: A problematic concept. Paper presented at the 13th International Seminar of the Committee on Family Research, of the International Sociological Association, Paris, September 24–28, 1973.

Uhlenberg, P. Cohort variations in family life cycle experiences of U.S. females. *Journal of Marriage and the Family*, May 1974, **36**, 284–292.

I

Aspects of Human Development

2

The Social Meaning
of Differential Physical
and Sexual Maturation

JOHN A. CLAUSEN
University of California, Berkeley

The interrelationships among physical development, cognitive development, temperament, and social behavior have been explored to only a very limited degree. A substantial segment of the research that has been done on the topic has come from the longitudinal studies at the Institute of Human Development at Berkeley. The present paper will draw primarily on publications of that research over the past three decades and on unpublished analyses that I have carried out in recent years. As a consequence, I must immediately offer a *caveat*: we shall be talking primarily about adolescents who matured a full generation ago. Insofar as there have been changes in valued attributes of physique or in activities for which particular aspects of physique put one at an advantage or

The data analyses on which this report is based were supported by grants MH-5300 and HD-4565 from the National Institute of Mental Health and the National Institute of Child Health and Human Development, respectively. The author is indebted to Caroline Kusch and Robert Dean for carrying out the computer analyses. He is also indebted to Norman Livson for an incisive discussion of the paper at the conference. A number of the points made by Dr. Livson have been incorporated into the paper and others have resulted in attempts to clarify the interpretation of the data. Needless to say, Dr. Livson is not responsible for the remaining inadequacies of this presentation.

disadvantage, there may well have been changes in the social meaning of differ-ential physical and sexual maturation. Available evidence does not, however, suggest that there have been marked shifts of this sort.

Before turning to consideration of the social meaning of maturation and physique, I want to make clear that I do not assume that there is nothing more to differences in physique than the social meanings attaching to such differences. On the contrary, I assume that there are genetic linkages as well. That is, certain genes may carry messages affecting physical *and* temperamental *and* mental ca-pacities or proclivities. In populations that contain a high mixture of genes, however—as in the ethnic mixtures that make up the general population in most areas of the United States—the confounding of influences on performance and personality make it all but impossible to establish what the genetic linkages may be, at least for the present. Therefore this discussion will focus on social mean-ings.

The course of development, from childhood through puberty to full maturity, and the kind of physique one develops, may themselves be considered messages. Recent research by Staffieri (1967) and by Lerner (1969) reveals that preference for an athletic build—muscular but neither fat nor thin—is already well established by age 7, and that stereotypic expectations attach to body build. Thus, asked to match personality attributes to silhouettes representing the dominant somatotypes formulated by Sheldon (1940), both preadolescents and adolescents attributed to mesomorphs—having muscular, stocky silhouettes—leadership ability, athletic prowess, many friends, aggressiveness, and relative immunity from nervous problems. Silhouettes of endomorphs—fat children—were negatively viewed, and those of ectomorphs—skinny children—were also somewhat devalued but to a lesser degree.

Just as there exist preferences for types of physique, it appears that there exist preferences for the timing at which various maturational stages are reached, though here the generalization rests less on direct data than on inference. In general, younger children try to emulate older ones, and especially as puberty is approached, children wish to be accorded more freedom from parental super-vision and to be treated more nearly like adults. There is a gradual shift from parents as primary affiliates to peer affiliations, occurring most often between the ages of 14 and 16 (perhaps a bit later for girls than for boys). Peers who appear to be older and more mature than their years are frequently the objects of admiration and envy. We would expect, therefore, that early maturing carries some of the same positive connotations as does an athletic build.

The following pages will briefly review the most salient findings, with refer-ence to effects on personality and social reputation of early versus late maturing and of particular aspects of body build. It appears that such effects come about in several different ways. First, and most obvious, relative maturity, size, and type of physique influence one's physical performance capacities. Thus, an early-maturing male will tend to be taller, heavier, and stronger than a late maturer in the middle of the pubertal age range. In athletics and in various other physical performances, the early maturer will for some years excel his later-maturing peers. Similarly, mesomorphic boys and girls are likely to excel their more ectomorphic peers in athletics. Second, maturity and physique influence one's social stimulus value (appearance, attributed personality traits) and the expectations that are held by one's peers and others. These expectations may be more or less constant over a considerable age range (e.g., those related to muscularity or linearity) or may shift with maturation (e.g., those related to early versus late maturing in boys). Moreover, capacities may not always agree with expectations. For example, the very tall boy who is not yet well coordinated may be at a disadvantage in sports, yet have more expected of him because of his size. Finally, it seems likely that one's self-image will be influenced both by one's capabilities and by the responses of others to one's appearance and capabilities.

My aim in this paper is to show how some of these linkages operate from the latency period through the adolescent years. Over the past few years, I have been examining interrelationships between various dimensions of physique and maturation and measured intelligence, parental responses to the child, personality ratings, and, where possible, peer relationships and ratings. The populations studied are those of the three longitudinal studies carried out at the Institute of Human Development at the University of California for more than four decades.

My analyses started with the data from the Oakland Growth Study, since I was responsible for this project for a number of years, and I was intrigued with the extent to which dimensions of physique (specifically, somatotypes) appeared to influence social reputation in the preadolescent and early adolescent period. Had I only confined my attention to this study, I could have published some years ago a rather coherent and convincing account of relationships between physique and personal development. When I turned to the other populations, however, I discovered that some relationships significant at the .01 level in the Oakland Growth sample were not necessarily replicated even in direction of relationship when I shifted to another sample. I hasten to add that some relationships have been found consistently, but this has certainly not been the rule.

PROBLEMS RELATING TO SAMPLING
AND POPULATION MIX

When one deals with the correlates of particular dimensions of physique, one inevitably must deal with a whole constellation of items that may be differently correlated in different samples. Any given subpopulation or sample thereof will contain a mixture of persons from varied ethnic backgrounds. Outside the southern states, for example, a white working-class sample is likely to contain more persons whose parents or grandparents immigrated to this country after 1900 and came from Mediterranean or Eastern European countries. They will tend to be shorter and stockier than the descendants of earlier immigrants who came from Northwestern Europe. More important for our purposes, the descendants of earlier immigrants are likely to have achieved higher social status and all the attributes that go with it, including cultural benefits and orientations toward education that result in higher scores on tests of intelligence, superior educational performance, and so forth. As intermarriage goes on between different ethnic stocks, such differences will tend to disappear, but they are still evident in the United States and probably will remain in evidence for some generations.

This means that the patterns of intercorrelation among various dimensions or measures of physique and between measures of physique and measures of performance (physical or intellectual) will vary from sample to sample and that generalizations will be more tenuous as a consequence. Differences from one sample to another will in part reflect unreliability of the measures employed and in part sampling error attributable to the relatively small samples drawn from heterogeneous populations. Beyond these sources of variation, however, there undoubtedly exist real differences in the mix of population from one community to another, and these may be far more significant in explaining research results than we generally assume. For example, differences in "mix" may be suggested when we compare the intercorrelations between dimensions of physique, strength, and intelligence by social class. As an illustration, let us look at intercorrelations of physical measures within the working-class and middle-class segments of the Oakland Growth Study (Table 2.1). In general, the pattern of correlations is fairly similar, but note some of the variations. Height and weight correlate similarly in the working and middle classes, but when we examine the correlates of strength by class, they differ rather markedly in this sample. In the working class, height at age 17-18 bears no relationship to strength (indexed by the sum of three separate measures of arm strength), whereas in the middle class the relationship is nearly .4 and is significant at the .01 level. In the working class strength is best predicted by mesomorphy (.61) and by masculinity of build (.60), while in the middle class it is best indexed by weight (.67) and by early maturing (− .42 with age of reaching 90 percent of mature height).

Since intelligence is a major influence on developmental pathways, I have shown IQ in the right-hand column on the table. We do not expect any substantial or significant relationships between dimensions of physique and intelligence, but, alas, in the working class we find a correlation of .39 between mean adolescent IQ and height at age 17-18. In the sample as a whole, the correlation between height and IQ is .14. Middle class boys averaged 117 in IQ while working-class boys averaged 112, but the classes differed very little in height, weight, or measured strength. Most of the differences in the levels of intercorrelation by class are probably chance differences, but some may reflect real differences in the populations sampled.

Turning to the comparable data for girls (Table 2.2), we again find a suggestion of class differences. In the case of strength, the correlate of weight is as

TABLE 2.1

Intercorrelations of Physical Measures, O.G.S.—Males, Age 17–18

Working class

	B	C	D	E	F	G	H	I	IQ
A. Height	.66**	-.00	.44*	.00	-.55**	.49*	-.12	.75**	.39*
B. Weight		.39*	-.29	.26	-.40*	.52**	.30	.12	.14
C. Strength			-.28	.60**	-.13	-.16	.61**	-.27	-.07
D. Ponderal index				-.22	-.32	-.27	-.42*	.80**	.17
E. Masculine build					.25	-.31	.83**	-.40*	-.09
F. Age 90% mature height						-.07	-.18	-.17	-.27
G. Endomorphic							-.24	.12	.27
H. Mesomorphic								-.61**	-.05
I. Ectomorphic									.14

Middle class

	B	C	D	E	F	G	H	I	IQ
A. Height	.60**	.39**	.48**	-.13	-.16	.18	-.23	.72**	.03
B. Weight		.67**	-.26	.25	-.42**	.39**	.44**	.04	-.04
C. Strength			-.21	.36*	-.42**	.10	.37*	.09	-.04
D. Ponderal index				-.28	.16	-.40**	-.56**	.75**	-.08
E. Masculine build					-.12	-.25	.71**	-.28*	-.12
F. Age 90% mature height						-.02	-.16	.15	-.05
G. Endomorphic							-.04	-.33*	.08
H. Mesomorphic								-.57**	-.13
I. Ectomorphic									.13

*p < .05.
**p < .01.

TABLE 2.2

Intercorrelations of Physical Measures, O.G.S.—Females, Age 17–18

Working class

	B	C	D	E	F	G	H	I	IQ
A. Height	.60**	.28	.28	.10	.24	−.22	−.30	.41*	.13
B. Weight		.41*	−.55**	.60**	−.23	.55**	.42**	−.44**	.05
C. Strength			−.27	.13	−.32	.23	.43**	−.20	.09
D. Ponderal index				−.57**	.48**	−.79**	−.68**	.77**	−.05
E. Feminine build					−.28	.69**	.40*	−.55**	.18
F. Age 90% mature height						.31	−.59**	.47**	.00
G. Endomorphy							.66**	−.87**	.07
H. Mesomorphy								−.82**	.01
I. Ectomorphy									−.05

Middle class

	B	C	D	E	F	G	H	I	IQ
A. Height	.39*	.28	.42*	−.12	.10	−.34	−.45**	.53**	.17
B. Weight		.39*	−.61**	.55**	−.29	.59**	.44**	−.48**	.30
C. Strength			−.09	−.12	.24	.17	.17	−.06	.01
D. Ponderal index				−.58**	.29	−.78**	−.80**	.90**	−.15
E. Feminine build					−.35	.81**	.39*	−.63**	−.15
F. Age 90% mature height						−.29	−.10	.38*	−.19
G. Endomorphy							.56**	−.78**	−.02
H. Mesomorphy								−.82**	.01
I. Ectomorphy									−.01

*$p < .05$.
**$p < .01$.

important in the working class as in the middle class, but again mesomorphy is more highly related to strength in the working class than in the middle class. Among the girls, early or late maturing is not significantly related to strength at age 17–18 in either class (but *would* be related to strength measured at age 14). There are no significant correlations between IQ and physique components, but the .30 coefficient between IQ and weight in the middle class could create some noise if we should seek personality correlates of weight.

The differing correlations between strength and certain other variables, by sex and social class, are summarized in Table 2.3. There are two points to be made here. One relates to the uncertainties that must be expected when one's analysis is based on small numbers of cases from population segments in which the variables of interest *may* be differently intercorrelated. About this, more in a moment. The second point relates to the substantially higher correlation between mesomorphy and measured strength in the working class as compared with the middle class. Strength is a more valued attribute of boys than of girls and is more highly valued in the working class than in the middle class. There is a suggestion in these data that a greater valuation of strength may lead to a higher development of the potential for strength that is inherent in the more heavily muscled mesomorph.

To return to the first point, I would like to stress that analyses carried out on relatively small samples almost inevitably preclude tracing the complex mediation of social contexts and relationships and sequences. The meaning of particular features of physique does not inhere in those individual features alone, but in the way in which they are combined with other features of the person that

TABLE 2.3

Correlations Between Strength at Age 17 and Selected Dimensions of Physique
and Maturing and Between Late Maturing and Mesomorphy
by Sex and Social Class, O.G.S.

	Males		Females	
	Working class	Middle class	Working class	Middle class
Dimensions of physique and maturing correlated with strength				
Height	.00	.39**	.28	.28
Weight	.39	.67**	.41**	.39*
Mesomorphy	.61**	.37*	.43**	.17
Age 90% of mature height	−.13	−.42**	−.32	.24
Age 90% of mature height vs. mesomorphy	.18	.16	−.59**	−.56**

*p < .05.
**p < .01.

influence performance in given contexts. Since rate of maturing, type of physique, and IQ are only minimally correlated, it is to be expected that certain constellations of values on these variables will work together to produce a greater effect than any one variable alone. Moreover, meanings will obviously differ from one cultural group to another and probably from one time to another. To the extent that energy level or activity level may be correlated with particular physiques, this will of course change the meaning of the given physique differentially in different settings. Finally, as already suggested above, the meaning of differential maturation or of particular dimensions of physique may be extremely significant for a short period of time and then fade away, or, either by virtue of persisting physique differences or because of the consequent channeling of interests and commitments at a critical period, the whole course of a life may be influenced.

GENERAL FORMULATIONS AND EARLIER RESEARCH

One's physique and appearance begin very early to influence the responses of others. The preschooler may have already received enough positive or negative commentary about his or her own appearance and that of other children to have incorporated some feeling about this aspect of self. In peer interaction in the play group, some children are rougher and more assertive, some are fearful and tend to withdraw. A number of studies (see Walker, 1962) are in agreement that stockier, mesomorphic children tend to be overrepresented among the more assertive and that taller, thinner ectomorphic children tend to be overrepresented among the timid and submissive. As noted earlier, even 7-year-olds are aware that this relationship exists, and they express a preference for a mesomorphic build.

In one of the earliest analyses of the relationships between physical maturing and behavior, Mary Jones and Nancy Bayley (1950) noted that early maturing boys were viewed as more attractive and more relaxed by adult observers. They appeared to have less need to strive for status. Mussen and Jones (1957), building on the earlier analysis, hypothesized that late-maturing boys would have feelings of inadequacy as a consequence of their disadvantageous competitive positions in many activities. Further, Mussen and Jones hypothesized that being treated as if they were still "little boys" at a time when early maturers were beginning to be treated as "men" might well lead the late maturers to have feelings of being dominated and rejected by adults. However, it is not clear that parents would be likely to treat late-maturing boys much differently from early maturers. Indeed, parents might be more responsive to the child's total range of behaviors and less responsive to physique and maturation than peers would be. On the other hand, late maturers might tend to have friendships with younger children and thereby be subject to somewhat lower expectations.

Although most of the early publications on the influence of maturation rate proceeded from the premise that early maturing was highly desirable for boys,

Harvey Peskin (1967) has proposed more recently that there may be drawbacks to early maturing if the criteria for evaluation go beyond conventional social success. Elaborating psychoanalytic formulations of the functions served by the latency period, Peskin notes that the early maturer has a shorter time in which to consolidate ego strength before having to cope with the hormonal and physiological changes of adolescence—changes that are bound to be stressful, even if socially valued. The early maturer may experience greater initial anxiety at the time of pubertal onset, being both chronologically and psychologically younger at this time than his later-maturing peers. Peskin suggests that the social recognition given to the early maturer may act as a source of anxiety reduction and thereby lead him to a long-term reliance on social participation and conformity to social expectations to maintain self-esteem. Along with this mode of coping, the early maturer is more likely to have a fearful conception of impulse release.

Peskin tested his formulation (with Guidance Study data) by comparison of behavior ratings and test scores for the early and late maturers equated not for chronological age but for years before or after the individual's pubertal onset. This mode of analysis permits one to see what differences existed prior to the onset of puberty and what changes occurred with puberty for early- and later-maturing boys. The later-maturing boys averaged roughly a year and a half older at the onset of secondary sexual characteristics. Certain of Peskin's findings for a series of behavior ratings are given in Figure 2.1, which has been reproduced from Peskin (1967).

In general, there were no significant differences in the prepubertal period between the early and late maturers in their scores on a wide range of motor, cognitive, social, and emotional dimensions. With the onset of puberty, however, early maturers became less active, less given to exploratory behavior, more submissive, less intellectually curious, more somber, temporarily more anxious, and so forth. Late maturers showed little or no consistent change in these ratings with the onset of puberty, though in some cases they show a change three to four years later. Significant differences tend, then, to be confined to the first few years after the onset of puberty, and they appear to bear out Peskin's expectation that the early maturer responds to pubertal onset with inhibition and rigidity.[1] The early maturer may be forced into a premature identity, having had too little time during the latency period to come to grips with his own feelings

---

[1] More recent analyses by Peskin (1973) suggest that the effects of early maturing on emotional and cognitive development may be mediated by the nature of the Oedipal situation in the family. Boys whose mothers were rated as giving their sons more love than they gave to their husbands (strong Oedipal) appeared to withdraw from internal stimuli and to constrict their intellectual interests if they were early maturers but not if they were late maturers. The opposite pattern was found for boys who were faced with a less strong Oedipal situation. That is, among boys whose mothers were rated as giving at least as much love to their husbands as to their sons, intellectual interests and insight tended to be associated with early rather than late maturing.

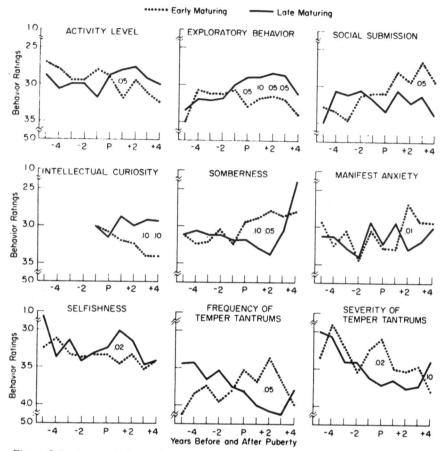

Figure 2.1 Average behavioral ratings by maturational age of early- and late-maturing boys. Significance levels are based on *t* tests, two-tailed. In all cases, a low rating indicates a higher degree of the titled trait. (From "Pubertal onset and ego functioning" by H. Peskin, *Journal of Abnormal Psychology*, 1967, 72, 1–15. Copyright 1967 by the American Psychological Association. Reprinted by permission.)

and the ambiguities of his world. The late maturer has a longer period to get ready for pubertal changes and may be able to handle them with more flexibility.

Most of the consistent research findings on the effects of early maturing refer to boys. We may note that the implications of early maturing differ greatly for boys and girls. The features of physique that lead to regarding a boy as attractive—masculinity of build and muscularity—are quite different from those that lead to regarding a girl as attractive. Early-maturing girls tend actually to be seen as less attractive than their later-maturing peers. Moreover, the implications of early physical development for a girl are quite different than they are for a boy. Among the boys, being larger and stronger than one's peers is definitely to be desired. One can compete athletically and one can move in older circles.

Early-maturing boys may be as physically mature as the average of girls in their age class. Early-maturing girls, however, will not only exceed most of their female age-mates in size but will be larger than many of the boys. Moreover, the physically mature girl, especially if she is well endowed with curves, is far more likely to be regarded as a sex object by older boys, and to be pressured into different kinds of peer relationships with the opposite sex. This is perhaps more likely to be true in the working class than in the middle class, since fewer working-class girls will anticipate going to college and deferring marriage.

SOURCES OF LASTING EFFECTS

Let us now consider more fully the ways in which differences in physique or maturation at a given point in time may have more lasting effects. To the extent that attributes or aspects of physical performance or of appearance are *valued* (i.e., regarded as desirable), we may hypothesize that persons who possess those attributes will be regarded more favorably than their peers who are less well endowed in these respects. Moreover, to the extent that a person is favored in any given respect—height, strength, energy level, beauty—we might expect that person to maximize his or her positive attributes and to have these become especially salient in his or her self-concept. Given two high school students with equal potential for intellectual development, but grossly different potential for athletic performance, for example, one low and the other very high, we might expect the person more favored in athletic physique to put greater effort into developing his athletic prowess, while his athletically inept peer would concentrate on academic performance.

Again, a handsome boy or beautiful girl will receive more positive feedback from peers explicitly referring to appearance, and is likely to reflect this in self concept and in aspirations. On the other hand, a child who comes to see himself or herself as homely must seek to cultivate other attributes to enhance self-esteem.

It is true that humans often seek to overcome their handicaps instead of simply compensating for them in other ways. The 97-pound weakling may work to build his strength by using Dr. Sampson's barbell and (possibly) become a Wee Geordie, Olympic hammer-throwing champion. However, this response does not appear to occur nearly as often as does the compensatory response of seeking a source of satisfaction and reward elsewhere than in physical prowess.

To carry the analysis further, let us examine the implications of a muscular build for personality development of an American male in the junior high and senior high school years. Assuming that Coleman's analysis (1961) of the social climate of American high schools in the 1950s still has considerable validity (and almost certainly had considerable validity as characterization of school climates several decades earlier), early-maturing boys and those with an athletic build should be more popular and more frequently involved in the leading cliques than boys who are unathletic in build. We are also assuming here that such a build has a significantly high relationship to athletic prowess (as it does to measured strength) so that those so possessed are considerably more likely to be athletes.

Among middle class boys, a high proportion will be oriented toward attending college and seeking careers that require substantial knowledge and are somewhat demanding intellectually. Far fewer working-class boys will hold such aspirations. Further, in the working class, physical prowess in males is more highly valued than it is in the middle class. Muscle is used more often in one's occupation. More generally, in the home, in recreational activities, and in the prevailing folklore, working-class men appear to be more directly "physical" in their behaviors than are middle class men. We would expect, then, that the working-class boy who is skinny and unathletic would be at a great disadvantage and would have less self-confidence and lower self-esteem than would either a more athletic working-class boy or a middle class boy of comparable physique.

We might expect that a more athletic, mesomorphic physique would lead to greater ease within and responsiveness to peer culture, while a less athletic, ectomorphic physique would lead to greater efforts to please adults by conforming to their wishes and values. To the extent that a late-maturing or an ectomorphic boy has high intellectual potential, we might expect greater effort to develop that potential.

Beyond the school years, occupational success and life satisfaction would seem to rest far less on appearance and far more on intellectual ability, ability to handle one's relationships with others, and technical knowledge based on education or training. Therefore we would expect some change in the correlates of physique, especially as regards self-esteem and self-assurance, as the individual demonstrates competence unrelated to physique.

THE COURSE AND CORRELATES
OF MATURATION

It may be helpful to briefly review the major features of maturation of boys and girls. In general, skeletal maturation, the appearance of secondary sexual characteristics, and the adolescent growth spurt are highly correlated, for both males and females. Neither linearity nor masculinity of build is appreciably related to the onset of puberty for males. Livson and McNeill (1962) concluded that ectomorphs and mesomorphs differ negligibly in mean age of reaching 90 percent of mature height, though ectomorphs seem to show less variability. Early-maturing boys begin to show change in secondary sex characteristics in the eleventh year, and maximum growth in the thirteenth, whereas their late-maturing peers may lag as much as two years behind them (Jones & Bayley, 1950). Early maturers will be taller, on the average, for a considerable number of years, and they will tend to be heavier and stronger as well. Differences in size and performance will be maximal at ages 14 to 16, toward the end of junior high school and in the early years of senior high school.

Maturation begins nearly two years earlier for girls than for boys, and the early maturers tend to be stocky, plumper girls (McNeill & Livson, 1963). The early maturers maintain a height advantage over their later-maturing peers until the latter are well along in their growth spurt, but the later matures ultimately become taller and tend to remain slimmer. Differences in size and weight between early and late maturers are greatest at ages 12 to 14, during the junior high school period.

SOME RECENT ANALYSES

In attempting to assess the social meaning of physique in developmental perspective, we shall note first some of the trends manifest in childhood. The Guidance Study, which followed a cross-sectional sample of children born in Berkeley in 1928–29, affords a good starting point. Behavior ratings, based on interviews with mother and child, were made annually from ages 5 to 16 and were composited for four three-year periods: ages 5 to 7, 8 to 10, 11 to 13, and 14 to 16. Correlation coefficients were computed between these behavior ratings, and a number of components of physique and physical development assessed at a single point in time (in general, near the end of adolescence). In the case of height and somatotype, the measures were those characterizing the individual after the attainment of maturity. In general, for height and for the mesomorphic and ectomorphic components, there was high stability of assessments made at various periods from childhood to adulthood, except that the correlations between mature height and height measured during the pubertal period dropped somewhat, height at this time being partially dependent on whether one was an early or late maturer. Endomorphy, on the other hand, proved to have only moderate stability, so that its social meaning cannot be adequately assessed by using a measure at any single point in time.

Figure 2.2 illustrates trends in the relationships between mature height and three of the behavior ratings that show significant patterns. Although many of the correlations are modest, it is reasonably clear that taller boys were consistently rated low on show-off behaviors and on demand for attention and that they tended, except at the very earliest period, to be seen as reserved. From the earliest period the taller boys were seen as being significantly more submissive than their shorter peers, but in each succeeding period the correlation drops off, until in adolescence height is not seen as being at all related to submissiveness. Tall boys were also consistently seen as somewhat shyer and somewhat more somber than their peers. We might note that the tendencies toward reserve and avoiding show-off behaviors were strongest in the age range 11–13, when the earlier maturers were just beginning their growth spurts. Thus one may surmise that being tall had a quite different meaning for a preadolescent or pubescent boy than it would come to have in later years.

Table 2.4 presents data on a single rating, running from "underactivity" to "overactivity," correlated with age of reaching 90 percent of mature height,

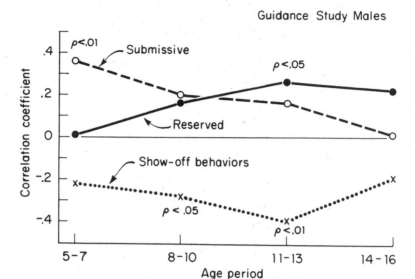

Figure 2.2 Correlations between mature height and selected behavior ratings at four age periods.

somatotype, and lowest ponderal index (the last providing an excellent objective measure of linearity or ectomorphy). Note that boys high in endomorphy as of late adolescence went from being rated significantly *over*active to being significantly *under*active over the twelve-year period under consideration. Mesomorphs tended to be seen as slightly overactive, but significantly so only in the final period, when most of them had reached puberty. Ectomorphs, on the other hand, went from being significantly underactive (at the .01 level) to being

TABLE 2.4

Changing Correlations Between "Over vs. Underactivity" Rating at Four Age Levels and Physique Components, Guidance Study Males

Age period	Late maturing	Endomorphy	Mesomorphy	Ectomorphy	Lowest ponderal index
5–7	− .04	.26*	.14	− .30**	− .31**
8–10	− .05	.04	.10	− .16	− .16
11–13	.16	− .14	.02	.08	.15
14–16	− .02	− .31*	.31*	− .02	.17

Note: Sample size decreases with increasing age.
*$p < .05$.
**$p < .01$.

rated just about average on activity level. Interestingly enough, whether or not a child was an early or late maturer showed no relationship to rated activity level for any of the four periods for Guidance Study males.

For both boys and girls, the endomorphic component was associated with demands for attention and show-off behaviors, but for girls this was true only in the periods prior to puberty. It will be recalled that the endomorphic girls tended to mature early. Among girls, mature height turned out to be the best predictor of a number of nonproblematic behaviors, with those who ultimately became tallest rating significantly lower on excessive modesty, lying, frequency of temper tantrums, and competitiveness in most periods. At ages 11 to 13, these girls (who tended to be late maturers) were rated significantly higher on submissiveness, but at ages 14 to 16 they were average for both competitiveness and submissiveness.

In the Guidance Study, IQ proved to be a stronger correlate of the age-composite behavior ratings than any of the physical measures. Thus, of thirty-five measures examined over four periods, giving 140 ratings, IQ was related at the .05 level or better with 27 ratings for girls and 17 for boys. In general, where there is a significant relationship at one age level, the correlations for the other age groups are consistent and do not vary greatly from one age level to another. However, those behaviors that are indicative of self-assurance (high self-reliance, low dependency, low submissiveness, low rating on shyness) tend to be somewhat more highly associated with IQ at the last two age levels. Mature height was the next most significant correlate of behavior ratings, among the dimensions of physique examined, with somatotype components a bit further back and early versus late maturing only minimally associated with the behavior ratings.

Both the mesomorphic and ectomorphic components of physique show a number of relationships with ratings of personality in childhood. Indeed, data from the Berkeley Growth Study suggest that males who were rated strongly ectomorphic at maturity had as infants been seen as significantly shyer, *not* active, *not* happy, and *not* positive in their behaviors, whereas the reverse had been true of those rated high on the mesomorphic component.[2] The most

[2] The subjects of the Berkeley Growth Study were observed from the early months of life. The study population was small, and the number of subjects for whom both early observational data and mature somatotypes are available was even smaller. Nevertheless a number of correlations between components of somatotype assessed in late adolescence and ratings of behavior for the first two years of life showed high consistency from quarter to quarter. Thus boys rated highly ectomorphic at maturity were seen in the first two years as shy, not calm, not happy, and as manifesting negative behaviors. Several of the correlation coefficients at successive periods were significant at $p < .05$. It must be reported, however, that the girls of the Berkeley Growth Study show almost a complete reversal of rated attributes. Until data on subjects in other longitudinal studies can be brought to bear, the findings for infant males who were later to be rated highly ectomorphic should be regarded as merely suggestive, but note that they are in agreement with the Guidance Study data for the youngest age group (5–7).

substantial correlates of these physique components, however, are found in peer evaluations.

Let me give an example from the Oakland Growth Study. The subjects attended the same junior high school, and each year all the students present completed a "reputation test," designating which of their classmates best fitted certain descriptions, twenty pairs of polar opposites that can be summarized by such terms as restless-quiet, leader-follower, daring-afraid, grown-up–childish, etc. Although for any given year the distributions of scores are far from normal, by compositing scores over the junior high school years and standardizing them, it is feasible to use these scores for correlational analysis. We can then examine which measures of maturation and physique are most highly related to social reputation. For the male junior high students, age of sexual maturing was significantly related to only one of these peer ratings, "assured." On the other hand, height was significantly related to four ratings, masculinity of build was related to six, measured strength to ten, and mesomorphy to fourteen of the twenty. Incidentally, IQ was significantly related to only two of these ratings, brighter boys being seen as somewhat less restless and less talkative.

As already noted, stereotypic expectations for the mesomorphic physique are developed very early. And we have already commented on the greater valuation of strength and physical prowess in the working class. Table 2.5 shows the correlations between the fourteen peer ratings with which components of physique were significantly correlated and two of the components, mesomorphy and ectomorphy, by social class.

It is immediately apparent that there are more significant relationships in the working class than in the middle class. In both classes the boy who was seen as highly active, a leader, a fighter, etc., was highly mesomorphic in build, but more so in the working class. This is true of all the items that connote aggressiveness but not of items that relate to friendliness or appearance.[3] Perhaps even more striking, the working-class ectomorph, the skinny, relatively weak boy, was seen very negatively. He was the follower, afraid rather than daring, avoiding fights, etc. Note that the middle class ectomorph was *not* significantly devalued by his peers.[4]

The previously cited studies of Lerner (1969) and Staffieri (1967) found that endomorphic physiques were most devalued by preadolescents. Rather surprisingly, in view of the negative stereotype of fat boys and girls, we found only

---

[3] If we confine attention to those items that load on the first factor (defined by elements of daring and aggressiveness) emerging from a factor analysis of the reputation test items, six out of six show a higher correlation with mesomorphy in the working class than in the middle class. On the other hand, those items that load on the second factor (defined by friendliness and appearance) are apparently not related differentially to mesomorphy by social class. If anything, the relationship may be stronger in the middle class.

[4] Note that correlation coefficients are significant only in the working class, despite the smaller sample of working-class boys. Again a simple comparison of the number of instances in which the working-class correlation coefficient exceeds that for the middle class suggests a significant pattern.

TABLE 2.5

Correlations Between Somatotype Components and Peer
Ratings in Junior High School, by Social Class,
O.G.S. Males

	Mesomorphy		Ectomorphy	
	Working class	Middle class	Working class	Middle class
Talkative	.45*	.06	− .26	− .21
Active	.57**	.56**	− .35	− .18
Humor (jokes)	.47*	.28	− .02	− .18
Friendly	.27	.31*	− .19	− .23
Leader	.59**	.45**	− .55*	− .13
Fights	.78**	.49**	− .42*	− .14
Assured in class	.13	− .02	− .46*	.00
Daring	.63**	.54**	− .42*	− .11
Has older friends	.20	.33*	− .06	− .08
Popular	.46*	.25	− .33	− .15
Happy	.51**	.20	− .38	− .24
Enthusiastic	.22	.34*	− .29	− .04
Bossy	.49*	.45**	− .13	− .09
Good-looking	.12	.34*	− .30	− .07

*$p < .05$.
**$p < .01$.

weak relationships between endomorphy and peer ratings in junior high school. In general, in both social classes, endomorphic boys were less likely to be viewed by their peers as active, popular, daring, and friendly, but the correlation coefficients seldom exceed .3. Endomorphs seemed to have been perceived more negatively in the middle class than in the working class.

When other correlates of peer evaluations are examined by social class, measured strength emerges as the most potent correlate of the aggressive-daring-masculine component of the peer ratings in the working class, exceeding even mesomorphy. On the other hand, the second component found in factor analyzing the peer ratings (friendly, assured) is most significantly related to mesomorphy in the working class but is even more highly *negatively* related to height in the middle class. In other words, the boys regarded by their peers as least friendly and least assured tended to be the tallest. This is in accordance with the Guidance Study data reported previously, suggesting tendencies to submissiveness and reserve among tall boys.

With some slight variation, the same general pattern of findings relating to somatotype and peer ratings in junior high school occurs for girls as for boys, but the correlations between physical components and peer ratings are consistently lower for girls. Among working-class girls, positive evaluation by peers tended to go with higher scores not only on the mesomorphic but also on the endomorphic components of physique (on eleven out of twelve comparisons where significant correlations are found, they are higher in the working class than in the middle class). In the middle class, endomorphy showed no consistent pattern of relationships with peer ratings, and even mesomorphy was only modestly related to peer evaluations. Again, the ectomorphic girls were perceived more negatively in the working class than in the middle class (in seven out of seven comparisons).

Preadolescents are obviously highly influenced in their interpersonal perceptions of their peers by the physiques of those peers. Ratings by staff members of the same Oakland Growth Study boys show less great but still significant correlations of physique with various social and psychological measures. Boys high on the mesomorphic component were rated by staff psychologists as more overtly aggressive, more popular, less introspective, less egotistical, and more socially mature than were boys who were low on the mesomorphic component. In every instance of a significant correlation overall between a rating of manifest traits and the mesomorphic component, the correlation coefficient was somewhat higher in the working class than in the middle class.

Next we turn to evidence that the perceptions of peers and adult observers has an impact on the self-perceptions of the boys themselves. A self-report inventory used in both junior and senior high school reveals that working-class boys high in mesomorphy were significantly more likely to see themselves as social leaders and as athletes than were those low in mesomorphy. The same general trend was found in the middle class, but it was not significant. More striking are findings relating to an index of psychoneurotic tendencies (emotional upset, dysphoria, psychosomatic complaints). Working-class boys high in ectomorphy were significantly more likely to report a number of symptoms and complaints than were those high in mesomorphy ($r = .41, p < .05$). In the middle class, on the other hand, there was no relationship between psychoneurotic tendencies and ectomorphy.

EARLY VERSUS LATE MATURING

Although the behavior ratings reported earlier for the Guidance Study subjects suggest relatively little influence of early maturing, Q sorts of interpersonal tendencies suggest somewhat greater influence, in line with differences earlier reported by Jones and Bayley (1950) and by Mussen and Jones (1957). In their analyses of subjects of the Oakland Growth Study, they found early-maturing boys to be significantly more poised, relaxed, good natured, and unaffected. Late-maturing boys were found to be expressive, dynamic, and buoyant but were also rated as tenser and more affected in their high school years.

A comparison of findings for Oakland Growth Study males and Guidance Study males reveals both certain consistent findings and the kind of variant

TABLE 2.6

Correlations Between Late Sexual Maturity and Selected Interpersonal
Q-Sort Items, Junior and Senior High School, O.G.S. and G.S. Males

Q-sort item	Oakland Growth Study			Guidance Study	
	Junior high	Senior high		Junior high	Senior high
	Total	Working class	Middle class		
Perceives parents as restraining his activities	− .12	.47*	− .21	.24	.44*
Feels parents accept his steps toward maturity	.03	.18	.05	.09	− .44*
Acts younger than age	.23	.34	.56**	.39	.48*
Has social poise with peers	.06	− .51*	.03	− .17	− .43*
Achieves leadership with peers	− .09	− .60**	− .13	− .31	− .33
Expresses hostile feelings directly to peers	.04	.45*	.16	.37	.09
Is butt of group—tends to be the "fall guy"	.12	.40	.34	.19	.24
Arouses liking in peers	− .27	− .54*	− .15	− .16	− .21

*p < .05.
**p < .01.

results that have been so puzzling in this research. The data are presented in
Table 2.6.

The most striking finding that emerges from an examination of Guidance
Study data is the marked change in assessment of the boy's relationship with his
parents between the junior high and senior high school years. Late maturers were
already seen as acting somewhat younger than their ages on the basis of all the
data available for the junior high school years, and this tendency becomes more
pronounced during the senior high school years. In junior high school, early and
late maturers did not appear to differ significantly in their perceptions of their
parents or their relationships with them, but in the senior high school years late
maturers perceive their parents as more restrictive, less egalitarian, as old-
fashioned, as not accepting their growth and steps toward maturity, and as
singling out the late maturer for special evaluation and treatment. Thus the
prediction of Mussen and Jones (1957) is borne out more strongly by Guidance
Study data than by the Oakland Growth Study data they employed.

Findings with reference to changing peer relationships were not significant in
the Guidance Study sample, except for a marked change in the assessment of
social poise and presence with peers. In the Oakland Growth Study, on the other
hand, we find fewer significant relationships between early and late maturing and

the adolescent boy's perceptions of his parents, though the working-class correlations show the same general trends for the senior high years as do Guidance Study data. What comes through to a greater degree in the Oakland Growth Study data is the importance of early maturing for the boy's status with his peers during the senior high years. In junior high school, leadership is, by far, best predicted by mesomorphic build, especially in the working class. In the senior high years, it is best predicted by early maturing. Again, however, the relationship is much stronger in the working class than it is in the middle class. The correlation between age at achieving 90 percent of mature height (that is, late maturing) and the Q-sort item "achieves leadership in roles with peers" is $-.60$ in the working class and $-.13$ in the middle class. Early-maturing males are seen as significantly more poised, freer in expressing hostile feelings directly to peers, and at the same time more likely to arouse liking in peers than are their later-maturing counterparts. All of these relationships are stronger in the working class than in the middle class; indeed none achieve statistical significance in the middle class.

Quite clearly, then, early maturing exerts significant influences especially during the years of senior high school, influences that extend both to peer relationships and to relationships in the family. The effects of early maturing do not, however, mean that other components of physique are no longer important. Mesomorphs continue to be seen as more poised, more assertive, and oriented more to their peers than to adults. Ectomorphs continue to be seen as somewhat submissive, especially in the working class, but the very negative connotations of ectomorphy for social poise and assertiveness are considerably diminished in the senior high school years. It is now the late maturer rather than the ectomorph who is most deficient in performing according to the values of working-class males.

In both the Guidance Study and the Oakland Growth Study, boys with a strong endomorphic rating had the most problematic peer relationships, especially in the junior high years. They were seen as not being knowledgeable in the peer culture, as most often being the butt of the group, as not selective in choosing friends, and, in general, as seeking peer acceptance in any way they could get it.[5]

The Block personality Q sort was used to assess personality attributes in the junior and senior high school years and in adulthood. In both studies, only a few items show a relationship to early versus late maturing, and these are primarily items dealing with satisfaction with one's own appearance, physical

---

[5] It is puzzling to find stronger relationships between endomorphy and peer relationships as assessed by the interpersonal Q sort than between endomorphy and direct peer assessments among Oakland Growth Study boys, but there are many more significant correlations in the former set of data. Since the judges using the Q sort had pictures of the subjects as well as data on physique (along with the great bulk of data for each time period), the possibility exists that the judges reacted more to their own stereotypes than to the data on observed or reported behavior, attitudes, and feelings.

attractiveness, and satisfaction with self. Generally, but not universally, these items show significant relationships only in the senior high years. No Q-sort item assessed from interviews at age 30 correlates significantly with maturation rate of Guidance Study males, and for Oakland Growth Study males only two items out of the hundred in the deck retain at age 38 a significant relationship with early maturing: priding self on being objective and being seen as conventional.

Jones (1965), using Oakland Growth Study subjects, and Peskin (1967), using Guidance Study subjects, have reported substantial lasting effects of early versus late maturing on the careers and personalities of these individuals. Jones found especially strong relationships with a number of California Psychological Inventory (CPI) scales, assessed at age 30. Early maturers were significantly and most substantially higher on scales for dominance, socialization (which has a strong element of conformity), and good impression, while late maturers were higher on the psychoneurotic scale. When I examined the data by social class, the correlations were a bit higher in the working-class segment of the Oakland Growth Study (that is, subjects who originally came from working-class families) but not to such a degree that one would conclude that class differences are significant.

I examined the same CPI scales, assessed in adulthood, for the Guidance Study males, but found not a single significant relationship and indeed very few correlations over .2. Here is a real puzzle and one that I have been quite unable to unravel. The group means and standard deviations look reasonable, and I can find no basis for the vast differences in two cohorts drawn from roughly comparable settings only seven or eight years apart.

Before concluding, I do want to mention a few of the Q-sort items that quite consistently (in junior high school, senior high school and at ages 30 to 40) relate to components of physique and especially to the muscular-linear polarity, if one can stress the respect in which those high on the mesomorphic component differ from those high on the ectomorphic component. The thinner, less muscular boys (and men) are consistently seen as more emotionally controlled, *not* self-indulgent, as having high aspiration levels, and as aesthetically reactive. In many respects, the profile of the mesomorphic type is the obverse, with assertiveness and conventionality of thought thrown in. Somatotypes come just behind IQ in the number of significant associations with adult personality, though the associations are not necessarily those predicted by Sheldon.

I have presented very little of the data on girls, partly because of the limits of space but primarily because of divergent findings. To give one example, it appears that early-maturing of girls in our Oakland Growth Study sample was positively related to self-confidence and to several other CPI scales for middle class girls and strongly negatively related for working-class girls. Peskin (1973) finds substantial changes between adolescence and the adult years in the correlates of early maturing for Guidance Study females, with early maturing having far more positive valence when one views the adult subjects.

As Norman Livson commented at the Adolescent Conference, this paper makes even more complicated an already very complicated situation. The consequences of one's physique and biological maturation do not merely inhere in organic processes but emerge from the interaction of biological givens with the developmental tasks of childhood and adolescence and with the expectations of close associates. Long before puberty, the child becomes aware of his or her body by virtue of internal stimuli, comparisons of self to others, and body-based interpretations made by others. With puberty, new self-definitions must be achieved; they are shaped in part by prior preparation and by criteria of social desirability. To some extent every person must come to grips with the problem of incorporating his body image, his physical capacities, and his developmental history into an identity. It seems reasonably clear that both internal clocks and social responses lead to patterned outcomes. Yet it is also clear that the meaning attached to one's physique and whether one matures early or late will in part depend on the kinds of intellectual interests and personal commitments one forms early in life.

The data presented here do not permit us to trace adequately the ways in which the person's choices at various life stages are responsive to his physical development. Indeed, small sample size precludes examining the effects of combinations of physical attributes. It would be desirable, for example, to test the notion that the combination of extreme ectomorphy and late maturing in a boy (especially in a working-class boy) leads to greater deficits in social poise and peer-group status than does either ectomorphy or late maturing alone. Our sample of subjects was too small to trace out career contingencies for such a group, but there is one bit of suggestive evidence. A comparison of median age at marriage for subjects characterized as dominantly mesomorphic or ectomorphic, cross-classified by early or late maturing, reveals the lowest marital age for mesomorphs who were early maturers (22.0) and the highest for ectomorphs who were late maturers (25.5), with the other two groups intermediate. Substantially larger samples will be needed to assess the long-term personality correlates of such combinations of attributes and to view them in the social contexts that help endow them with meaning.

Whatever their long-term consequences, however, there can be little doubt that during the years of childhood and early adolescence, physique and sexual maturation vie with and interact with cognitive skills and emotional expressiveness in contributing to the social identity of the adolescent.

REFERENCES

Coleman, J. S. *The adolescent society.* New York: Free Press, 1961.
Jones, M. C. Psychological correlates of somatic development. *Child Development*, 1965, 36, 899–911.
Jones, M. C., & Bayley, N. Physical maturing among boys as related to behavior. *Journal of Educational Psychology*, 1950, 41, 129–148.
Jones, M. C., & Mussen, P. H. Self-conceptions, motivations, and interpersonal attitudes of early- and late-maturing girls. *Child Development*, 1958, 29, 491–501.

Lerner, R. M. The development of stereotyped expectancies of body build–behavior relations. *Child Development*, 1969, **40**, 137–141.

Livson, N., & McNeill, D. Physique and maturation rate in male adolescents. *Child Development*, 1962, **33**, 145–152.

McNeill, D., & Livson, N. Maturation rate and body build in women. *Child Development*, 1963, **34**, 25–32.

Mussen, P. H., & Jones, M. C. Self-conceptions, motivations, and interpersonal attitudes of late- and early-maturing boys. *Child Development*, 1957, **28**, 243–256.

Peskin, H. Pubertal onset and ego functioning. *Journal of Abnormal Psychology*, 1967, **72**, 1–15.

Peskin, H. Influence of the developmental schedule of puberty on learning and ego development. *Journal of Youth and Adolescence*, 1973, **2**, 273–290.

Sheldon, W. H. *The varieties of human physique.* New York: Harper & Brothers, 1940.

Staffieri, J. R. A study of social stereotype of body image in children. *Journal of Personality and Social Psychology*, 1967, **7**, 101–104.

Walker, R. N. Body build and behavior in young children: I. Body build and nursery school teachers' ratings. *Monographs of the Society for Research in Child Development*, 1962, **27**(3, Whole No. 84).

3

Recent Research on Cognitive Development in Adolescence

DAVID ELKIND
University of Rochester

Studies of cognitive development in adolescence have generally comprised only a small fraction of the total number of studies of mental growth. G. Stanley Hall (1904) complained of this situation almost three-quarters of a century ago, and he would be equally chagrined if he looked at the research literature today. The reasons for the relative dearth of studies on adolescent thinking are multiple and intricate. One of the most important of these is the diversity and the complexity of adolescent thinking, which requires equally complex and diverse methods of investigation. We have only just begun to develop methods for exploring the manner in which adolescents think. Another reason for the paucity of studies in this area is that adolescents are, generally, less accessible and are likely to be less cooperative than children.

Despite these and other difficulties in investigating adolescent thought, research continues to be done in this area, but it is centered around only a few problems. One of these problems has to do with moral judgment and behavior, another with the generality of formal operations in adolescence, still another deals with the self-concept in adolescence, and a fourth is concerned with conceptual orientation shifts, the ease with which children and adolescents shift from one level of cognitive functioning to another. A final problem, not limited to adolescent cognition, has to do with ethnic differences in cognitive ability. No effort will be made in this paper to survey every study done on each of these issues. Rather, some representative recent studies will be reviewed to illustrate the problems, the methods of investigation, and some characteristic findings.

MORAL JUDGMENT

Most of the recent work in moral judgment in adolescents derives from Kohlberg's elaboration (1963) of the Piagetian work on the moral judgment of the child. As is well known, Piaget found two stages of moral development. Among young children, moral judgments are made on an objective basis, on an estimate of the amount of damage done. A child who has broken twelve cups is judged more culpable than one who has broken one cup, regardless of the circumstances. Among older children (usually middle childhood, ages 8 to 12), moral judgments are usually made on a subjective basis, on an estimate of the child's intention rather than on the objective amount of damage done.

Kohlberg (1963) has elaborated this scheme to six different stages, which he describes as ordered at three levels of moral orientation.

I. Premoral level—control of conduct is external.
   Stage 1. Obedience and punishment orientation, deference to superior power and prestige.
   Stage 2. Naive, hedonistic, and instrumental orientation; acts that satisfy the self and sometimes others are defined as right.
II. Morality of conventional role conformity—morality is defined in terms of performing good acts and maintaining the conventional social order.
   Stage 3. Morality of maintaining good relations; orientation to approval and to pleasing and helping others.
   Stage 4. Orientation to authority, law, duty, to maintaining a fixed order, whether social or religious, which is assumed as a primary value.
III. Morality of self-accepted moral principles—morality is defined in terms of conformity to shared or sharable standards, rights, or duties.
   Stage 5. Morality of contract, individual rights, and democratically accepted law.
   Stage 6. Morality of individual principles of conscience; orientation not only to existing rules and standards, but also to conscience as a directing agent.

One of the adolescent research issues that derive from this formulation has to do with the rigidity or educability of moral judgments, while the other concerns the relation of moral judgments to actual behavior. As to the shifting, Rest, Turiel, and Kohlberg (1969) report that when children are given a choice, they prefer moral judgments at a more advanced level than the judgments they make on their own. Turiel and Rothman (1972) found that exposing children at different levels to moral reasoning led to a shift upward for stage 4 subjects, but not for subjects below that level.

In a related study, Birnbaum (1972) tested for the effects of anxiety on moral judgment. She found no support for the hypothesis that castration anxiety will lead to greater rigidity in moral judgments. Other types of anxiety, particularly anxiety over the loss of parental love, may, however, produce some rigidity of moral position. In Birnbaum's study, peer acceptance appeared to be the most important factor in the development of a flexible independence from adult rules. There was clearly a reciprocal effect inasmuch as adolescent flexibility also played a role in gaining peer acceptance.

A couple of recent investigations have dealt with the relations of level of moral judgment to behavior. In one study (Fodor, 1973) 30 psychopathic and 30 nonpsychopathic delinquents were compared with one another on level of moral development as assessed by the Kohlberg interview. The psychopathic delinquents displayed a lower level of moral development than the nonpsychopathic delinquents. In retrospect, psychopathic delinquents saw their fathers as less nurturant than did nonpsychopathic delinquents. Mothers of the psychopathic patients were less demanding of achievement than the mothers of nonpsychopathic delinquents.

In another study (Saltzstein, Diamond, & Belenky, 1971) the moral judgment level of 63 seventh-grade boys and girls was assessed in individual interviews following the Kohlberg procedure. Each subject was also observed in a modified Asch-type group influence situation under independent and dependent goal conditions. These investigators found a curvilinear relationship between conforming behavior and moral judgment level. Stage 3 (approval-seeking) children were more likely to conform under the influence of group pressure than children at stages 2, 4, or 5. Children at stages 4 and 5 were particularly resistant to group-imposed conformity.

The implication of these studies is that the stages of moral development defined by Kohlberg may eventually have relevance for the prediction of overt behavior. Many questions, of course, remain unanswered despite these suggestive findings. Scoring of the Kohlberg interviews still leaves considerable room for error, and the validity and reliability of the assessments of stages of moral development are still far from being well established. Even so, the Kohlberg description of moral development has stimulated a great deal of discussion and research that is likely to be beneficial regardless of the eventual verdict on the Kohlbert stages themselves.

GENERALITY OF FORMAL OPERATIONS
IN ADOLESCENCE

Some years ago, as part of a series of replication studies of Piaget's research, I came across a surprising finding. While my results (Elkind, 1961a) supported those of Piaget with respect to the ages at which mass and weight were conserved, they did not support Piaget's finding that the conservation of volume is attained by 75 percent of 11- to 12-year-old children. In my study, only 27 percent of the 11- to 12-year-old youngsters gave evidence of an abstract conception of volume. This failure to confirm Piaget's age for the attainment of the volume conception in elementary school children led to a second replication (Elkind, 1961b) using junior and senior high school students, ages 12 to 18. Results showed that of the 469 students tested, 87 percent had demonstrated conservation of mass and weight, but only 47 percent demonstrated conservation of volume. In a third replication (Elkind, 1962), with 240 college students, comparable results were obtained. While 92 percent of the college students demonstrated the conservation of mass and weight, only 58 percent gave evidence of volume conservation. It was also found that among the junior and senior high school students, as well as among the college students, significantly more men than women gave evidence of volume conservation.

My reading of these findings at that time was that while all adolescents of average intellectual ability probably attain formal operations, they do not apply them equally to all aspects of reality. In adolescence, girls for social role reasons, are more likely to apply their formal operational thinking to interpersonal matters than to matters of science. The absence of volume conservation in some adolescents and particularly among women was seen as a matter of differential application of mental abilities and not as evidence for the absence of formal operational thinking. Piaget (1972) has made the same argument in his recent discussion of intellectual evolution from adolescence to adulthood.

Other investigators, however, doubt that most individuals attain formal operations in the sense described by Inhelder and Piaget (1958). Bynum, Thomas, and Weitz (1972) for example, question the Inhelder and Piaget assumption that formal operational thinkers use all sixteen binary operations of truth-functional logic in solving problems. In their investigation, they found evidence for only eight of the sixteen operations described by Inhelder and Piaget. In addition, they believe the Inhelder-Piaget logical analysis of the multiple variable, tasks, and of adolescents' responses to them, to be faulty in its demonstration that subjects used all sixteen binary operations.

Other studies report findings comparable to those that I obtained in the Piaget replication studies. Hobbs (1973) tested 906 young people in grades 7 through 12 with weight and volume tasks at several difficulty levels. Ninety-six percent of the subjects conserved weight when the task involved recognizing that a ball of clay remained the same in weight when rolled into a sausage. While 40 to 50 percent of the boys demonstrated volume conservation, only 20 to 30 percent of the young women did so. For both men and women and for both mass and volume, conservation was more difficult when the transformation involved a change of state (e.g., solid to liquid) than when it involved only a change in form.

Similar findings were reported by Tomlinson-Keasey (1972), who tested three groups of females, whose ages were 11, 19, and 54 years, respectively. She examined them on Piaget's pendulum balance and flexibility problems. Thirty-two percent of the 11-year-olds, 67 percent of the 19-year-olds, and 57 percent of the 54-year-olds were at the formal level of thinking. Attainment of the highest level of formal operational thinking was rare at all age levels.

Working with minimally educated adults, Graves (1972) used the group testing procedures I had employed in my studies. The subjects in her study were 120 adults (black and white) who were enrolled in night school basic education classes. Graves observed that 78 percent of her subjects attained the conservation of mass, and 67 percent conserved weight, but only 24 percent conserved volume. These figures are lower than those I obtained with college students and may reflect cultural and IQ differences. It would be wrong, however, to infer from these findings that the subjects who failed the volume conservation task were deficient in formal operations. What needs to be done is to test such subjects in tasks that require formal operations, but that are in their particular domain of expertise.

A somewhat different approach to the problem of the universality of formal operations was taken by Siegler, Liebert, and Liebert (1973), who trained preadolescents to solve the Piagetian pendulum problem. The training involved presenting young people with a conceptual framework for approaching the problem and with analogous problems. The unaided 10- and 11-year-old children did not solve the pendulum problem, but they were able to solve it after training. As in all training studies, this one raises as many questions as it answers. The crucial question is: Does training affect competence, or does it merely alter performance? Unfortunately, this training study, like so many others, provides no information on whether the effects demonstrate improved performance or enhanced ability.

In general the work on the universality of formal operations remains an open question. Piaget's suggestion (1972) that people be tested in formal operations in their area of specialization seems reasonable in principle but difficult to achieve in practice. How does a salesman, a shoe clerk or a carpenter use formal operations? To be sure some areas of specialization may require formal operational thinking, but not all occupations do. Devising tests of formal operations for specific fields is a difficult task but one that has to be attempted if the question of the generality or universality of formal operations is to be answered.

ADOLESCENT SELF-CONCEPT

The domain of cognitive psychology is ill defined at best and particularly so where the self-concept is concerned. To the extent that the self-concept is considered a concept, it clearly falls within the domain of cognitive psychology. As soon as the self-concept is considered an affective schema whose measurement reveals facets of personality, the boundaries between the affective and the cognitive domains become more blurred. Many of the studies of self-concept reside in the never-never land between the cognitive and the affective domains.

At the risk of stepping on another contributor's prerogatives, a few studies of adolescent self-concept will be described here.

Some of the most extensive work on adolescent self-concept has been done in Europe and is reported in two recent books. In *Le Moi et l'Autre dans la Conscience de l'Adolescent*, Rodriguez Tomé (1972) presents a theoretically oriented questionnaire study of adolescents' conceptions of themselves and others. Tomé distinguished three dimensions of adolescent self-conceptions: egotism (e.g., the tendency to feel superior); self-control (e.g., the ability to solve problems without help); and sociability (e.g., confidence). Tomé found that these three factors were statistically almost completely independent of one another.

Tomé distinguished between the individual's self-image proper and his social self-image. Subjects were asked to describe themselves as they saw themselves (self-image proper) and as they thought other people saw them (social self-image). The same three factors of personality appeared in both descriptions and were as uncorrelated for descriptions of the self-image proper as they were for the social self-image. There was almost no change with age for boys (from 12 to 18 years) and girls (from 12 to 21 years) in the relative weights that were given to egotism, self-control, and sociability. At all age levels, adolescents ranked themselves highest on sociability and lowest on egotism.

Tomé also compared the adolescent's self-image with the images his parents held of him. He found that parents generally regarded their offspring as more egotistical and less self-controlled than did the adolescent himself. Parents and their offspring did agree on the adolescent's sociability. Mothers and fathers were in good agreement as to their appraisal of their adolescent children. Tomé also had each adolescent judge himself as he thought his parents would judge him and had the parents judge the adolescent as they thought the adolescent would judge himself. The adolescents were closer to the mark than were the parents. It appeared that the adolescents had a better picture of what the parents thought of them than the parents had of what the adolescents thought of themselves.

In another comprehensive study, Gérard Lutte (1971) looked at the evolution of the ego ideal in children between the ages of 10-11 and 16-17 in several different countries. It is not possible to summarize all the findings, but some of the most striking results can be reported. First, the ego ideal does not develop in the same manner in different cultures. In America, the ego ideal is first the parent, but this changes in adolescence. In Germany and Portugal, however, parents remain an important ego ideal from age 10 through age 17. Likewise, the model for the ego ideal is different for boys than it is for girls between the ages of 10 and 13. For the girl, the model is often a friend, whereas for the boy it is more likely to be a celebrity. Lutte argues that it is hard to defend the position that the ego ideal evolves in regular stages because it is affected by so many different variables.

Among the factors that affect the adolescent's self-concept is his social class. Lutte found that adolescents from both the middle class and the working class aspired to better occupational and financial positions in life. But the adolescents of low socioeconomic status aspired too high and placed between their dreams and reality obstacles difficult to surmount given their station and the society in which they lived. Middle class adolescents were more realistic about their limitations and gave more weight to such factors as intelligence and willpower in attaining success. This finding among European young people replicates comparable findings among American adolescents.

Several other recent studies of adolescent self-concept will illustrate the nature of work in this area. In a factor analytic study of developmental trends in self-concept, Monge (1973) found that semantic differential factors remained constant among young people in grades 6 through 12. This consistency of self-evaluation was greater for boys than it was for girls. There were some exceptions. Boys, but not girls, showed an increase in both achievement and leadership. For both sexes, congeniality and sociability increased after grade 10. Both boys and girls scored lower on adjustment with increasing age, and this was particularly true for girls. Both boys and girls scored higher on scales of masculinity with increasing age.

In a somewhat different type of study, Sinha (1972) looked at the readiness of adolescents to reveal themselves on a "self-disclosure inventory." Her subjects were 250 adolescent girls living in an urban area of India. Sinha found that the readiness of adolescents to reveal themselves declined with increasing age. Social environment also affects self-esteem in systematic ways. A study of adolescents raised on a kibbutz suggested that such young people were more social and had higher self-esteem (at least among boys) than did children who were raised on moshavim (Long, Henderson, & Platt, 1973).

While the studies of adolescent self-concept are of interest from a descriptive point of view, they lack theoretical direction and coherence. The one exception is the study by Tomé (1972), but the theory employed in that study was more sociological then developmental. In particular, the role of cognitive development in the elaboration of the self-concept during adolescence needs to be articulated and explored systematically. The formal operations described by Piaget make it possible for the young person to see himself from the perspective of others, and this must have a significant impact upon the self. Moreover, the ability to think about thinking allows the adolescent to discover the privateness of his thoughts and the social isolation of his reflective self. How the adolescent handles these new discoveries and the changes in his body and in his social relations has yet to be explored in a systematic way.

CONCEPTUAL ORIENTATION SHIFTS IN
CHILDREN AND ADOLESCENTS

One of the problems of adolescent thinking that our research group has been exploring deals with what we have called conceptual orientation shifts. We assumed that there are particular conceptual orientations that relate to the child's level of cognitive ability. Preschool children, who are at the preoperational stage of development, tend to conceptualize on a perceptual basis. School-age children, who are at the concrete operational period, tend to conceptualize at a functional level, and adolescents, who are at the formal operational stage, tend to conceptualize at the abstract or categorical level. That young people at different age levels do tend to conceptualize in these different ways was demonstrated by Reichard, Schneider, and Rapaport (1944).

While young people at different levels of cognitive development may well have preferred orientations toward conceptualization, these orientations will always interact with the nature of the stimuli to be conceptualized. That is, some forms of stimuli are more likely to elicit perceptual types of conceptualization, others are more likely to elicit functional modes of conceptualization, and still others are likely to elicit categorical modes. The stimulus dimensions are both qualitative and quantitative. Pictures, for example, are more likely to elicit perceptual modes of conceptualization than are words. And pictures of a class of objects are more likely to elicit an abstract categorization than would a picture of a single object.

Our studies had a twofold aim: (1) to explore the relations between mode of conceptualization elicited by the stimuli and the preferred mode of conceptualization of the subjects, and (2) to look at the ease with children and adolescents shift from their preferred mode of conceptualization to another mode. Our hypothesis was that adolescents would shift more readily than would children because formal operations provide for greater flexibility of thought than do concrete operations.

In the first study (Elkind, 1966) children and adolescents (ages 9 and 14, respectively) were presented with two concept formation tasks. At each grade level, one half of the subjects had to attain a functional concept of vehicles, and the other half had to attain a functional concept of tools. Then the subjects who had first learned a vehicle concept had to attain a concept of unwheeled *tools*, the subjects who had first learned a tool concept had to attain a concept of unwheeled *vehicles*. In effect, both the children and the adolescents had to shift from a functional concept to a perceptual concept. The results were clear-cut. There was no difference between the children and the adolescents in the ease of attaining the functional concepts, but adolescents attained the perceptual concept much more easily than did the children.

One difficulty with this study was that the perceptual concept might also be regarded as a disjunctive concept, and thus it might be argued that it was too difficult for the children. In order to test this question, we presented the same children and adolescents with a simple discrimination learning task. A deck of cards was divided into two piles in such a way that if the top card of each pile were turned over, one of the two upturned cards would always be of a red suit and the other would always be of a black suit. The right-left positions of the red and black cards were randomized. The subjects were told that one of the cards in the two piles was right and the other wrong, and that they would have to guess which one of the two was right. Each time the experimenter would tell them if their choice was correct. They were to learn the rule that would allow them to tell which card was right every time. The rule was that all of the black or red cards were right. Adolescents learned the rule very quickly, but children had to go through the deck several times, and many did not arrive at the solution even then.

To test this finding in still another way, we (Elkind, Barocas, & Johnson, 1969) employed pictures of three concrete objects and their verbal labels in a concept production task. Children and adolescents were asked to produce as many ideas to these stimuli as they could. We found that there was no difference between the children and the adolescents (again ages 9 and 14, respectively) in the number of concepts they produced to pictures but that there was a significant difference in favor of the adolescents regarding concept production to words. This suggested that adolescents had no trouble shifting down to the functional and perceptual modes of conceptualization but that children had trouble shifting up to the categorical mode suggested by the words.

These preliminary studies still left many questions unanswered, particularly as to the level of concept produced by the children and adolescents as well as the number of concepts produced. In a more elaborate study (Elkind, Medvene, & Rockway, 1969) we tried to answer some of these questions. We used three series of paired stimuli, with ten pairs in each series. One of the series was entirely pictorial, another was entirely verbal, and another was a combination of pictorial and verbal stimuli. Our aims were (1) to demonstrate that the number of concepts produced by the children, but not by the adolescents, would be directly related to the level of representation of the stimuli, and (2) the percentage of perceptual responses given by the adolescents, but not by the children, would be directly related to the level of representation within a particular series.

The results of the study (there were 120 subjects) were straightforward. The total number of concepts produced by the adolescents was greater than the total produced by the children. There was also a significant interaction between series and age. For the adolescents there was no significant difference between the absolute number of responses they produced to the three series. For the children, however, the number of concepts produced was directly related to the amount of pictorial material in the series. In addition, the number of perceptual responses produced by the adolescents, but not the number produced by the children, varied directly with the level of representation of the stimuli. Again the hypothesis that adolescents make conceptual orientation shifts more readily than children was upheld.

In our most recent study in this domain (Gesten, Elkind, & Cassell, 1971) we looked at the quantitative dimension of stimuli. The materials were pictures and words depicting single objects and pictures and words depicting classes to which the single objects belonged. For example, there were pictures of a penny and the word "penny" and pictures of a group of coins and the word "coins." Groups of children and adolescents were asked to produce concepts to these different stimuli. In general, pictures and words of single objects elicited more concepts than pictures and words of classes of objects. There were no differences between children and adolescents in their concept production to pictures of single objects, but there were differences in favor of the adolescents in concept production for words of single objects and for pictures of classes of objects. The one surprising finding was that adolescents had almost as much trouble as children in producing concepts to words of classes.

There is obviously much more work to be done on the problem of conceptual orientation shifts, particularly on the conditions that facilitate and hinder such shifting. The problem is related to other problems, such as functional fixedness in problem solving. Our tentative results suggest that the functional fixedness of children may be more a matter of intellectual immaturity than one of rigidity. In any case, the study of conceptual orientation shifts has many possible educational implications, as well as theoretical significance.

ETHNIC DIFFERENCES IN COGNITIVE DEVELOPMENT

One of the issues that has received considerable public as well as professional airing in recent years concerns ethnic differences in IQ. Much of the discussion was generated by Jensen's article (1969) in which he suggested that compensatory education failed because the children it served were not really capable of profiting from the extra educational push. On the basis of a vast marshaling of research studies, Jensen concluded that blacks differed significantly from whites in IQ and were better at associative learning while whites were better at abstract thinking.

Jensen's work has been criticized from many points of view (Moore, 1969). Anthropologists and biologists have pointed out that racial differences are hard to establish. Because of intermarriage, the gene pools of black and whites in America are, at most, only several generations apart. Developmental psychologists point out that the difference in associative versus abstract thinking is developmental rather than genetic. Black children may simply attain abstract thinking at a later age than the relatively young black and white children studied by Jensen. And, finally, statisticians point out that, in any case, the ethnic differences are only relative. Even if one accepts the overall statistical difference as valid, intelligence is still distributed according to a bell-shaped curve for both blacks and whites. Accordingly, 50 percent of the blacks are still brighter than 33 percent of the whites.

One of the questions raised by Jensen's paper and the subsequent discussion concerning it relates to the intellectual ability of black adolescents. To what extent, one might ask, are such adolescents deficient in abstract thinking, and to what extent, if any, can this deficiency be attributed to genetic factors? It was to this issue that a recent paper (Elkind, 1973) was addressed. It built upon my more than ten years of work with delinquent adolescents. The aim of the paper was to demonstrate that intelligence test scores of low-income adolescents are meaningless when they are interpreted independently of the sociocultural context in which they are obtained.

Basically, in clinical practice, one can observe two types of low-income adolescents who score low on intelligence tests but who give other indications of average intellectual development. These types of adolescents are not limited to delinquents and are to be found among low-income blacks (and whites) who never come to the attention of the authorities. In the absence of a clinical evaluation of their test performances, however, their obtained test scores are apt to be grossly misleading.

One type of low-income adolescent who scores low in IQ tests might be called "prematurely structured." Such young people have, from an early age, had to cope with some rather harsh realities. They have had to care for themselves and their siblings (and sometimes for their parents) and to forage for food and clothing. They had little time for play, and their cognitive skills were developed in the service of survival. To adults they seem crafty, shrewd, and worldly wise beyond their years. But this premature structuring of their practical intelligence is purchased at the price of the development of abstract intelligence. There is nothing genetic about the intellectual limitations of these young people; rather, the limitations are quite adaptive given the circumstances of their existence.

Another type of low-income adolescent develops his abstract intelligence but in directions not measured by standard intelligence tests. Such adolescents often model their behavior after successful adults in their society. By the age of 13 or 14 they may have several girls working for them, may be pushing dope, and may also be involved in robbery and extortion. They know how to stay out of trouble with the law, how to con the "Johns" and other "dudes," and how to dominate women and other men. They have a rich vocabulary of words and phrases that one would never find in Webster's dictionary and an array of interpersonal skills and talents that would be the pride of any used-car salesman. These young people have shown an *alternative elaboration* of their intellectual abilities that is never assessed by standard intelligence tests.

These clinical observations, or so it seems to me, point up still another danger of using intelligence test data to make inferences about genetics and heredity. Mental tests assume that mental development follows a path common to all individuals. But that is simply not the case, and there are exceptional patterns of development that are occasioned by sociocultural factors. The work of Cole, Gay, Glick, and Sharp (1971) gives further evidence of the influence of these sociocultural factors on intellectual development and test performances. Such a vast conceptual gulf exists between the level of gene complexes and the level of psychological test performance that any inferences made from one to the other must be regarded as highly conjectural.

REFERENCES

Birnbaum, M. P. Anxiety and moral judgment in early adolescence. *Journal of Genetic Psychology*, 1972, **120**, 13–26.

Bynum, T. W., Thomas, J. A., & Weitz, L. J. Truth functional logic in formal operational thinking: Inhelder & Piaget's evidence. *Developmental Psychology*, 1972, 7, 129–132.

Cole, M., Gay, J., Glick, J. A., & Sharp, D. W. *The cultural context of learning and thinking.* New York: Basic Books, 1971.

Elkind, D. Children's discovery of the conservation of mass, weight and volume. *Journal of Genetic Psychology*, 1961, 98, 219–227. (a)

Elkind, D. Quantity conceptions in junior and senior high school students. *Child Development*, 1961, **32**, 551–560. (b)

Elkind, D. Quantity conceptions in college students. *Journal of Social Psychology*, 1962, 57, 459–465.

Elkind, D. Conceptual orientation shifts in children and adolescents. *Child Development*, 1966, **37**, 493–498.

Elkind, D. Borderline retardation in low and middle income adolescents. In R. M. Allen, A. D. Artazzo, & R. P. Toister (Eds.), *Theories of cognitive development.* Coral Gables, Florida: University of Miami Press, 1973.

Elkind, D., Barocas, R., & Johnson, P. Concept production in children and adolescents. *Human Development*, 1969, **12**, 10–21.

Elkind, D., Medvene, L., & Rockway, A. S. Representational level and concept production in children and adolescents. *Developmental Psychology*, 1969, 2(1), 85–89.

Fodor, E. M. Moral development and parent behavior antecedents in adolescent psychopaths. *Journal of Genetic Psychology*, 1973, **122**, 37–43.

Gesten, E., Elkind, D., & Cassell, S. Concept production to individual and class stimuli. Unpublished paper, University of Rochester, 1971.

Graves, A. J. Attainment of mass, weight and volume in minimally educated adults. *Developmental Psychology*, 1972, 7, 223.

Hall, G. S. *Adolescence: Its psychology and its relations to physiology, anthropology, sociology, sex, crime, religion and education.* Vol. 1. New York: Appleton, 1904.

Hobbs, E. D. Adolescents' concepts of physical quantity. *Developmental Psychology*, 1973, 9, 431.

Inhelder, B., & Piaget, J. *The growth of logical thinking from childhood to adolescence.* New York: Basic Books, 1958.

Jensen, A. R. How much can we boost IQ and scholastic achievement? *Harvard Educational Review*, 1969, **39**, 1–123.

Kohlberg, L. The development of children's orientation toward a moral order: Sequence in the development of moral thought. *Vita Humana*, 1963, **6**, 11–33.

Long, B. H., Henderson, E. H., & Platt, L. Self-other orientations of Israeli adolescents reared in kibbutzim and moshavim. *Developmental Psychology*, 1973, **3**, 300–308.

Lutte, G. *Le moi idéal de l'adolescent.* Brussels: Dessart, 1971.

Monge, R. H. Developmental trends in factors of adolescent self-concept. *Developmental Psychology*, 1973, 8, 382–393.

Moore, D. R. (Ed.) How much can we boost IQ and scholastic achievement? A Discussion. *Harvard Educational Review*, 1969, **39**, 273–356.

Piaget, J. Intellectual evolution from adolescence to adulthood. *Human Development*, 1972, **15**, 1–12.

Reichard, S., Schneider, M., & Rapaport, D. The development of concept formation in children. *American Journal of Orthopsychiatry*, 1944, **14**, 156–162.

Rest, J., Turiel, E., & Kohlberg, L. Relations between level of moral judgment and preference and comprehension of the moral judgment of others. *Journal of Personality*, 1969, **37**, 225–252.

Saltzstein, H. D., Diamond, R. M., & Belenky, M. Moral judgment level and conformity behavior. *Developmental Psychology*, 1971, 7, 327–336.

Siegler, R. S., Liebert, D. E., & Liebert, R. M. Inhelder and Piaget's pendulum problem: Teaching preadolescents to act as scientists. *Developmental Psychology*, 1973, 9, 97–101.

Sinha, V. Age differences in self-disclosure. *Developmental Psychology*, 1972, 7, 257–258.

Tomé, H. R. *Le moi et l'autre dans la conscience de l'adolescent.* Paris: Delachaux & Niestle, 1972.

Tomlinson-Keasey, C. Formal operations in females from eleven to fifty-four years of age. *Developmental Psychology*, 1972, 6, 364.

Turiel, E., & Rothman, G. R. The influence of reasoning on behavioral choices at different stages of moral development. *Child Development*, 1972, 43, 741–756.

4

The Development of Ideology in Adolescence

JOSEPH ADELSON
University of Michigan

One is tempted to say that we know next to nothing about the development of ideology in adolescence; that may be too stark, but certainly we know very little. Although ideology has been much written about, often brilliantly, it has not yet received much systematic study. There seems to be little agreement about how we ought to define ideology; nor do we know very much about its structure, its functions in the lives of individuals, its origins, or its development and change through the life cycle. So it should come as no surprise that we know little about the particular vicissitudes of ideology in adolescence. Nevertheless, the mere fact that this paper is being written should provide some small occasion for optimism, since as recently as ten or fifteen years ago the topic did not, for all intents and purposes, exist. No textbook, no survey of adolescence would have thought to treat it. One might have come across some wistful remarks about adolescent idealism (on which, more later), or some ominous broodings about the apparent political ignorance of the typical teen-ager, but one would not have seen any serious attempt to consider the role of ideology in the adolescent experience. We now seem to be prepared to make a beginning.

Let me say a few words on how this paper will construe "ideology," for there are few terms in social science used so variously. For example, in intellectual (as against scholarly) discourse, the word is now commonly pejorative—to be ideological is to be intensely dogmatic or to be so captured and choked by abstractions as to lose all sense of the world's actualities. In the scholarly context itself, the term may be focused narrowly or broadly. A narrow tuning takes ideology to be more or less synonymous with the direction of sentiment; thus political ideology can be viewed as the central tendency of opinion—liberal or conservative or radical or what have you. The broadest focus, as we find it in most Marxist writing, or in the sociology of knowledge, takes ideology to encompass not merely opinion and belief, but almost all of the nonmaterialist domains of culture—ethics, theology, social and economic theory, and beyond that, even literature, science, and the arts. By and large, sociologists and historians of ideas have tended to employ broader, and psychologists narrower, definitions of ideology.

This essay locates its interest somewhere between these extremes. Our studies of adolescent political thought (Adelson & Beall, 1970; Adelson, Green, & O'Neil, 1969; Adelson & O'Neil, 1966; Beall, 1967; Bush, 1970; Gallatin, 1972; Gallatin & Adelson, 1970; Gallatin & Adelson, 1971) have given little attention to the partisan inclinations of our respondents or to their views on current issues; rather, we have concentrated on a wider (but by no means the widest) domain of ideology—how they conceive of and judge the fundamental workings of society, politics, and government. Thus, given a topic such as crime, we were interested less in whether our subjects favored, say, the death penalty, or (to be fanciful) the *Miranda* opinion, and far more interested in their conceptions of such issues as the root sources of crime, or the inevitability of crime, or the power of government to prevent crime and to reform offenders.

What follows is a synthesis of several studies of adolescent political ideology that we have carried out during the last decade. Our first extensive research compared (largely) middle class youngsters in the United States, Great Britain, and West Germany; the most recent research, just completed, involved (largely) working-class black and white adolescents in an American metropolis. We have now interviewed about a thousand adolescents, ages 11 to 18. The interviews, though varying somewhat in content over the years, have had the same general format: The interviewee is asked to imagine that a thousand people leave their country to form a new society, and once settled, confront the myriad problems involved in establishing and maintaining a social and political order. The format permits us to pose a wide array of semiprojective questions on a large number of topics—on the structure and functions of government, on crime and justice, on the citizen's rights and obligations, on the interactions of state and citizens, on the utopian possibilities of government, and so on.

This paper will center on our developmental findings, since these are without question the most substantial and significant we have. The earliest lesson we learned in our work, and the one we have relearned since, is that neither sex, nor race, nor level of intelligence, nor social class, nor national origin is as potent a factor in determining the course of political thought in adolescence as is the youngster's sheer maturation. From the end of grade school to the end of high school, we witness some truly extraordinary changes in how the child organizes his thinking about society and government, and this paper will attempt to report these changes.

Previously I suggested that we distinguish between opinion alone and the larger frameworks of political thought. It is a distinction particularly apposite to the study of adolescence, for we may be easily misled by the child's readiness and capacity to state attitudes. Let us imagine a 12-year-old, a bright and opinionated one, and let us imagine further that we are discussing political parties with him—what he thinks of them, what his allegiances are, and so on. He might well tell us the following: that there are Democrats and Republicans, that his father and mother are Democrats and he is too, that the Democrats are nice people and stand for the best things, that they are against pollution and war, and are in favor of being fair to everybody. Since the child has opinions, strong ones, and since these, though rudimentary and naive, make sense in a rough and ready way, we are prepared to impute to him some general grasp of the role parties play in the political process.

But we could not be more mistaken. The ordinary child at the age of 12, at the threshold of adolescence, cannot tell you, that is, cannot put into coherent language, what a political party is, or what it does, or what part it plays in democratic politics. Now, I mean this literally; depending on the question you ask and how you ask it, anywhere between 50 and 90 percent of 12-year-olds either draw a blank, or lapse into confusion, or are deeply in error about the nature and function of the political party (Bush, 1970). Some of them think that a party is just that—a party, where you meet people and have fun; some confuse parties with the governmental process in general, and think that parties pass or enforce laws; some understand that parties are somehow connected with voting, but cannot say how or why. Even that minority who give passable answers do not give good ones—they may understand that parties represent differing stances on issues, but are unable to say much beyond that. Of the 160 or so 11- and 12-year-olds we have interviewed, we have yet to discover one, however otherwise precocious, who could offer an intelligent account of the function of the political party.

By an "intelligent account" I do not mean textbook-clever; I mean little more than an ordinary man-in-the-street response. Here, as an example, is an 18-year-old American high school girl, of average intelligence, telling us what she believes to be the advantages of political parties: "Well, if you have a whole bunch of people with different ideas about how the government is to be run, you are not going to get much accomplished, but if you put them together in a group, and then they pool their assets and ideas, then they have enough power to do something about what they want, than everybody just talking about what they want." I think you will agree that there is nothing intellectually powerful about this statement, yet its common-sense accents frame ideas that are totally beyond the grasp of nearly all children just six years younger. Her answer shows that she understands that parties are a medium for the expression of political views; only about 10 percent of young adolescents can recognize this. More important, she stresses the efficiency and potency of unified political belief; that is, she links ideas with unity with power, in recognizing that a collective body can fuse separate voices and so amplify its claims for political attention. To an adult this notion is nothing if not commonplace, and because it is, because it is so much a part of our repertoire of tacit assumptions, we may fail to sense that it represents a significant intellectual acquisition. The idea is so rare as to be exotic in the spontaneous discourse of 12-year-olds. They are unable to cognize organized, collective action and thus do not understand that politics involves the collision of collectivities devoted to separate interests. Hence they cannot truly grasp the idea of "party"; for the same reason they are confused, or indifferent, or ignorant about such collectivities as the trade union, the lobby, the pressure group, the voluntary association, the voting bloc. It is not merely that some of these phenomena are recondite and require sophisticated information; even if the child had that information, he could do little with it, since he lacks the conceptual context that would allow him to make sense of it. For example, when we ask a young adolescent what a minority economic group, farmers, might do to protect its interests against a majority of nonfarmers—the question is of course phrased more tactfully—he will likely offer answers that are either amusing or baroque or both, but he is almost never able to answer realistically, in adult terms, since he cannot cognize concerted action by a formally organized collectivity, or by its representatives. His political world is occupied by single actors behaving against or for other single actors, or at best, by individuals who are only hazily connected with each other, a world that is lonely and stark, though at times dramatic.

Let me continue in this illustrative vein and move now to the domain of crime and justice. Children are not really interested in politics; but they are quite interested in wickedness and its retribution, and they bring to it all that passion and heat and apocalyptic sentiment that some of them will later bring to the question of politics. The child's moral sense is activated far more by crime than by politics, and this being the case, we may perhaps grasp the connections between morality and cognitive competence as these emerge during the adolescent years.

At the outset of adolescence, the child's mind is all fierce, retributory moralism on the one hand, and deficient competence on the other. How does one treat the thief? Clap him in jail, and if he will not learn his lesson, double or triple his sentence, or put him in solitary confinement, or torture him. How would you keep people from breaking a law against cigarette smoking? Spies and informers and secret surveillance. It is a mind we have lately become familiar with, the mind of G. Gordon Liddy. The imagination is so captured by glorious ends as to overwhelm any feeling for prudent means. It is an imagination so bemused by the sheer energy of the will as to be deeply defective in its apprehension of outcomes. It lacks skepticism. It lacks common sense. Anything goes.

Later in adolescence, the child pondering crime and justice speaks altogether differently. He tells us that we must try to understand the sources of crime and that these are likely to be found in the criminal's motives and these in turn are rooted in past and present milieus, in family and companions. He argues that we ought to think beyond punishment to rehabilitation and that jailing someone merely puts him in bad company and reinforces bad habits. A few, the most *au courant*, may feel that the roots of crime run so deep as to require psychotherapy. If you believe in original sin, you may find these ideas shallow, and, to be sure, one sometimes senses that the child confessing these sentiments is merely showing off his acquisition of liberal clichés. Nevertheless, these ideas, even if superficial, or superficially felt, reflect a remarkable advance over what went before.

It is an advance in sensibility. The preadolescent's mind is held by the act itself and cannot see past the act to origins, or ahead of the act to outcomes. It is frozen into the present, into the actness of the act. The criminal is seen to intend wicked purposes without apparent motivation, aside from the execution of these purposes. Nothing symbolic, nothing gestural is seen to reside in the act. To the criminal's act the state responds with an act of its own, and since the child's sensibility contains no fine sense of sources and outcomes, no notion of symbol and gesture, no enlarged view of meaning and motive, and no clear comprehension of human mutability, he would have the state react reflexively, without imagining itself into the situations that produced the act, or into those potential situations that might amend the character of the actor. This sensibility, concrete and narrow, is swept away as the child advances through his adolescence. He is ever more able to transcend the sheer particularity of the act, to place behavior within a web of circumstance. He does so by expanding and commanding time, linking past to present and present to future; the act has a history and its effects extend forward into time. He is increasingly able to see man as a social creature; thus the given act arises as a response to a range of social forces, and the consequences of the act are felt communally. He acquires a vocabulary of motives; the act has meanings and intentions, though these may be obscure, complex; thus the state's response to the act need not be merely condign, but may address itself, at least in part, to the motives that activated the act. Finally, he gives up the absolutism that earlier possessed him. All things change and all things are relative to other things. Men are mutable, as are laws, as is government and society itself, and since human character can be amended, men can be redeemed, and that then ought to be the aim of state action to the criminal.

Let me pause here, and pass from a discursive to a didactic mode, reviewing what our studies have suggested to us about the cognitive transitions that take place in the adolescent years.

1. *Abstractness.* What dominates our illustrations, and indeed what dominates the political discourse of the young adolescent—those between the ages of

11 and 13—is a difficulty in managing abstract concepts. We have seen that the child has his troubles in talking and thinking about collectivities—about parties, unions, and associations. This difficulty is evident whenever adequate discourse involves the intangible and the general. The young adolescent can imagine a church but not the church, the teacher and the school but not education, the policeman and the judge and the jail but not the law, the public official but not the government. And he is, as you might imagine, totally at sea when adequate discourse depends on the mastery of highly abstract words and ideas—equality, authority, justice, and so on. The child enters adolescence almost totally unable to manage abstract ideas, and he leaves it with that capacity well developed. Table 4.1, from Lynnette Beall's research (1967), shows us the swiftness and implacability of that advance.

2. *Time.* The celebrated lines which open T. S. Eliot's *Four Quartets* state that times present and past are present in time future, and time future contained in the past. It is precisely the sense, the intended meaning, of these lines that is beyond the grasp of the young adolescent. As we have seen, he is locked into presentness. He has no strong sense of history, of time past and its bearing on time present; nor does he discern well the larger impact of time present on time future. His view of the future is constricted; he may grasp the effect of today on tomorrow, but not on the day after tomorrow. He does not perceive the later reverberations of acts undertaken in the present. His feeling for historical causality is at best dim; and his judgments on public policy tend to be naive, since these should involve some apprehension of the remote consequences of action. There is a distinct improvement as the child matures; though here I should mention my impression that the gains achieved through adolescence are modest. Older adolescents rarely show an adequate sense of history, nor will they often peer boldly into the remote future.

3. *Change.* As the foregoing suggests, the political universe of the young adolescent is strangely static. It is, as we have seen, fixed in the present. There is little sense of the dynamic of history, nor is there much feeling for the

TABLE 4.1

Capacity to Deal with Abstract Ideas

	Concrete	Low-level abstraction	High-level abstraction
Fifth grade	57	28	0
Seventh grade	24	64	7
Ninth grade	7	51	42
Twelfth grade	0	16	71

Note: Full documentation of all tabular material in this article will be found in the publications cited.

mutability of men and of human institutions. We see this most vividly in the attitudes toward laws, which are held to be permanent and unalterable. To be sure, the child may, if you first suggest it, acquiesce to the abolition of a law; but he is not likely to propose abolition, and will almost never spontaneously imagine the amendment of a law. As he advances further into adolescence, he increasingly recognizes and accepts the tractability of all things human, of human disposition, of the laws men make, and the social forms they create. Politics and government become, increasingly, exercises in experiment.

4. *Costs and benefits.* The preadolescent's mind, as it ponders politics, is enviably innocent in that it has little sense of the costs to some that follow from the benefits to others. The older adolescent is wiser, or at least more skeptical, in that he recognizes that politics involves competing interests, their inevitable collision, and their necessary compromise. If we ask a young adolescent to choose between two difficult options, he may choose one rather grandly, and then defend his choice arbitrarily, or he may be overcome by moral paralysis. The older adolescent will more often—though by no means always—come to his decision by cost-benefit reasoning, examining the gains and losses of party A and party B, projecting these into the future, and then trying to find some formula, some moral equation that will produce some degree of equity for each party. As the child grows older, he is much more likely to understand that one of the parties in question is society, or the common good; one of the most striking findings we have is that preadolescent youngsters rarely grasp the needs and interests of the total community, presumably because the idea of collectivity is as yet beyond their grasp. And as the child grows older, he increasingly makes these decisions by reference to some general formula, that is, by seeking out a principle that is germane to the problem.

5. *Principles.* If you ask the young adolescent why a citizen or a state should or should not do a certain thing, and if he does not know, he will usually tell you so. But sometimes, either to please you or to please himself, he may venture an answer. If you then pursue the matter further, asking him to offer some reason for his answer, you may find him doing one of several things: he may justify his answers on the grounds of custom ("that is what they do"); or he may attempt an intuitive response in terms of some latent standard of fairness; or he may offer some rhetorical incantations, bringing in such words as "democracy," "freedom," and so on. In each case the child is straining after the appropriate principle; and in almost all instances he cannot achieve it. He may not know the guiding principle, but even if he "knows" it, that is, if he has been taught the words or the phrase, he will not understand the precise terms of its application to real events. (For example, many preadolescents know that "the majority rules," but few of them know what a majority is, and some even think it means a unanimity.) As the child matures, his grasp of principles grows steadily. For one thing, his knowledge of political principles advances; but more to the point, he is cognitively readier to judge particularities in terms of universals. He understands that the concrete event can and should be subsumed under a more binding

general rubric. These rubrics, or contexts, or frameworks, or what you will, must themselves relate to others in some sort of hierarchy or at least harmony. Human action is seen to be governed by conventions, many of these moral in nature, and these form a larger and more or less coherent network of principles. The functional (as against nominal) acquisition of principle is of course vital to the development of a consistent and articulate framework of political belief—that is, to forensic ideology. It is my impression—I emphasize that it is only an impression—that the acquisition of a sense of principle takes place far later than the other changes I have described; it is only at the end of the high school years that we see youngsters, and even then only a minority of them, adverting to principle as they discuss their political ideas. And even in these cases, one often does not have much sense that principles are applied consistently and co-herently.

The account I have offered may seem to celebrate the virtues of abstractness, and so it does. We have seen that the child's mind moves from the simple to the complex, from the particular to the general, from the local to the cosmopolitan, from the personal to the impersonal, from concrete to formal operations; and in doing so, it apprehends social and political reality ever more fully, powerfully, subtly. The limits of the concrete mind are clear enough, so clear that we are less likely to recognize the corruptibility of the abstract mode itself. In her recent novel, *The Black Prince*, Iris Murdoch has one of her characters say to another, at a critical moment between them: "Please don't use that abstract sort of language, it's a way of lying." In politics, perhaps more than elsewhere, the abstract mode can be employed to deceive and to self-deceive, to posture and obfuscate, to preserve one's blessed innocence and excuse one's bloody hands. The guiding test for these matters is George Orwell's great essay, "Politics and the English Language," which remains the classic statement on the uses of high-minded cant to conceal low and even squalid purposes in the realm of politics. Abstractness may be necessary for political intelligence, but by itself it does not suffice.

In line with this, I would caution us to resist the impulse to use develop-mental findings to construct a system of ideological virtue. That impulse has not been resisted in the study of moral ideology in Kohlberg's work, which argues (on the basis of very slim evidence) for a ladder of moral merit based on the putative cognitive superiority of a few. I do not want to dwell here on the philosophical and empirical problems of Kohlberg's position, since they are brilliantly examined in a forthcoming paper by Elizabeth Simpson (in press), and in the writings of Hogan (1973). But let me recognize that our findings might lend themselves to that impulse. We find, for example, that there is a sharp decline in authoritarianism in all nations and groups we have studied, as the child moves through adolescence. The preadolescent is arbitrary and even brutal in his view of miscreants; he is, relatively speaking, attracted to the idea of one-man rule; he is all in favor of coercive and indeed totalitarian modes of government. By late adolescence, the child has become liberal, humane, and democratic. Since all of us will find this movement of mind agreeable, we are tempted to take the next step, which is to posit a connection, perhaps a universal one, between democratic values and cognitive maturity. But now let us imagine a new Grand Inquisitor arguing, with the utmost intellectual power and subtlety, that the spiritual health of the polity would be elevated less by acts of mercy and more by the disciplines of retribution; or that men thrive on the conditions of order and rigor, and that the turmoil we see all about us stems from the confusions generated by democratic politics; or, with Aristotle, that some men are by nature noble and others by nature slaves. I would not myself recommend these sentiments, but I remind you that some of the great minds of political theory—Plato, Aristotle, Hobbes, Dostoevski, and many more—minds greater than our own, minds of the widest scope and deepest complication, have held views like these, views that are, by our light, authoritarian. All of which is to make a point that should be obvious, but does not seem to be so today: that we must distinguish sharply between the realm of belief itself and the processes—cognitive, emotional, or cultural—that generate or accompany belief.

The pursuit of adolescent idealism has proven to be like other celebrated quests—such as the searches for the Abominable Snowman and the Loch Ness Monster, for example. Rumors are heard that it exists, sightings are made, footsteps are found. Finally a scientific expedition equipped with the latest technology is sent out, and it returns to report that no reliable evidence can be found. Still, the rumors persist, as do reports of sightings, findings, and deathbed testimony. There are some things we want to believe and therefore do believe, and no evidence to the contrary will persuade us otherwise. I have suggested on another occasion that the adolescent serves as a projective figure in the American mind; one of the qualities we impute to that figure is a heightened idealism, the view that he is not yet corrupted by circumstance, but tingles with a fresh sense of the possibilities for mankind (Adelson, 1964).

As we commonly use the term, we imply one or both of the following in our understanding of idealism: First, ingenuousness, by which we mean having insufficient awareness of the gravity and complication of the given; we counterpose ingenuousness to realism, or perhaps to cynicism. Second, we may mean optimism, the belief that matters will, over time, tend for the better, and in a political context, a belief in the perfectibility of society toward the ultimate perfection of man. It is in both these senses—innocence and optimism—that Americans are, or were, held to be idealistic; and so too, presumably, with adolescents. If we accept this definition, our findings are quite clear; the adolescent years see a marked decline in idealism.

In our most recent work we repeated and extended previous findings to this effect. This project, under the direction of Judith Gallatin (1972), involved an interview study of 463 black and white adolescents, ages 12 to 18, living in the inner city of Detroit and in a racially mixed suburb. Many of our questions had

TABLE 4.2

Pessimistic Responses, by Age, to the
Question "Would It Ever Be
Possible to Eliminate . . . ?"

Age	Crime	Poverty	Racial prejudice
12	48	9	45
14	66	40	80
16	72	54	85
18	75	53	76

to do with crime, poverty, racial prejudice, and other aspects of urban malaise. For each of these topics, we asked whether it would ever be possible to eliminate the phenomenon in question, that is, to get rid of crime, poverty, or racial bias. In Table 4.2 we have a coding of the percentage of openly pessimistic answers, by age, to each of these questions. Note that the degree of pessimism varies with the topic, that our youngsters are not merely giving stock responses, for they deem poverty more tractable than crime or prejudice. Note too that there is a slight lessening of pessimism between the ages of 16 and 18 on the issue of prejudice. But the trend is unmistakable. As the child matures, he is ever less sanguine that social problems can be decisively eliminated. Findings by other investigators on other topics suggest the same. Tolley (1973), for example, finds that from latency to adolescence, children increasingly see wars as inevitable.

As to ingenuousness, the case is even stronger. As youngsters leave childhood behind, they show a decided increase in political realism. The confusion, the simplistic moralism, the intellectual coarctation that I have previously documented give way to and are replaced by an enhanced sense of how things work in the domain of politics. One could adduce literally hundreds of tables and charts to document this shift in political perceptiveness. Indeed, our most commonly used coding category is "confusion, simplistic," to denote answers that are essentially uncodable because the child is unable to manage the cognitive level that an adequate response requires, or has an inadequate understanding of elementary political processes. Between 25 and 60 percent of all responses given by 12-year-olds are so coded, depending on the item. Most of the time there is a sharp drop between the ages of 12 and 14, and some of the time the drop is between ages 14 and 16. By age 16, sometimes earlier, almost all children are giving answers that suggest a fundamental degree of competence in political judgment. As we have seen, the loss of innocence may show itself in an apparent pessimism, or fatalism, about chiliastic expectations for the human condition. In some instances it shows itself as well in a heightened cynicism. For example, in the course of a series of questions dealing with the citizen's influence on the

TABLE 4.3

Affirmative Responses, by Age, to
the Question "Are Only the
Important People Listened
to in Our Society?"

Age	Cynicism
12	0
14	6
16	22
18	25

legislative process, we asked if "only the important people are listened to in our society." Table 4.3 shows the increase in overtly cynical (or, if you will, realistic) answers as adolescence advances.

Given such findings, it is tempting to turn the notion of adolescent idealism squarely on its head and argue instead that what we see in this period is the growth of *Weltschmerz* and alienation—that is, the loss of confidence and morale. One might even be fashionably apocalyptic and say that an oppressive social system erodes the child's natural buoyancy. To my mind, however, neither view of adolescence—as idealistic or as alienated—is entirely adequate. Consider the following findings. We asked what might be done if a city council were proving itself unresponsive to the concerns of the average person. Table 4.4 shows the distribution of the major types of response: the simplistic-moralistic category expresses either indignation or in a primitive sense of process ("That's not fair," or "Talk to them real nice"); the pessimistic responses express sheer despair ("There is nothing you can do"); the pragmatic category suggests elective action or the deputation of spokesmen.

These findings and many more like them suggest that the dominating tendency is neither pessimism nor optimism, neither alienation nor enthusiasm, but

TABLE 4.4

Responses to What Might Be Done About an
Unresponsive City Council, by Age

Age	Simplistic, moralistic	Pessimistic, alienated	Pragmatic
12	62	17	17
14	40	15	38
16	16	22	10
18	10	35	50

rather the replacement of ingenuousness and naive moralism by more complex attitudes founded on an augmented realism. Both the pragmatic outlook and the pessimistic or cynical one are essentially modes of realism. One emphasizes action, the other despairs of it. One is attuned to tactics and process, the other to passive-aggressive mastery of destiny. Neither attitude is necessarily correct or incorrect; either may involve an objectively mistaken apprehension of reality. But both involve some effort to apprehend reality. The pragmatic adolescent's "realism" speaks for itself; it may be less apparent that the young cynic is simply showing a curdled version of realism, a sort of inside dopesterism.

I am not suggesting that we close the book on adolescent idealism, only that we recognize how complicated a matter it is likely to be. I have not dealt, for example, with one possibly important aspect of the "idealistic" syndrome, and that is sincerity. It may be that what we take to be idealism is a certain affective posture, that intense expression of seemingly genuine feeling we call sincerity. But sincerity is hard to appraise, much less measure reliably. For what it is worth, I offer the impression that the many adolescents I have conversed with on politics did not seem notably sincere as a group, nor for that matter notably insincere. Those who did seem sincere or intense were the indignants, the moralists, the dogmatists, and the incipiently fanatic. They make up a small proportion of the total. They are outnumbered by the indifferent, who regard politics as part of a world they never made; and by the cool rationalists who see it as a puzzle the world offers for solution. And I do not wish to foreclose other possibilities. It may well be that idealism is a late-adolescent or postadolescent event, that it matures after the child has achieved some degree of cognitive mastery. At that point perhaps—only perhaps—moral impulses are joined to an overweening cognitive self-confidence, and this connection produces a tendency toward idealistic and even utopian constructions of political possiblity.

A few words about utopian thinking among adolescents: We made a number of efforts, as in the questions on the inevitability of crime and poverty and racial injustice, to get our adolescents to talk about deep political and social change, and, as we have seen, the prevailing mood is pessimistic. Only about 5 to 10 percent of our responses are optimistic, and even these tend to be diffident, hedged about with qualifications. The last question in the interview directly asks the youngster to imagine an ideal society, to construct one mentally. Of the thousand or so adolescents we have talked to over the years, at the most four or five venture beyond commonplace reformist ideas. Let me illustrate by performing a little demonstration; for as I write this, I note that I have a stack of interview transcripts on my desk. I will now choose at random the protocols of three 18-year-olds and transcribe here their answers.

1. "A society that everyone gets along and knows each other's problems and try to sit down and figure out each other's problem and get along like that."

2. "I think right now that the only society I would have would be the exact same one as we have now, although it does have its faults, I think we do have a good government now."
3. "Well, I would set up a society of helping out people like when there would be crime, like I said before, I would put these criminals in there for life because when they get out they would want to do it again and all that."

As chance would have it, statement 1 is hazier, 2 more complacent, and 3 more bloody-minded than most, and the three taken together are rather thinner conceptually than is ordinarily the case among high school seniors. Yet they are on the whole more characteristic than not. Note the low intellectual energy of these responses. None seems to reflect any general sense of the social order; the suggestions made are either diffuse ("everyone getting along") or concrete ("jailing criminals for life"). We have often wondered why utopian statements are invariably so lackluster and can only guess why. It is likely that most adolescents (like most adults) are essentially conservative, in that they take the world as it is, except on those matters that abrade them directly. It is also likely that for most adolescents, general political questions are not of great importance. All the data we have on the level of political information argues for the low salience and low cathexis of the political. (Only 2 percent of 13-year-olds and 14 percent of 17-year-olds in 1969 knew the name of the Secretary of State; only 31 percent of 18-year-olds knew that a United States senator serves for a term of six years; and so on.) It is my impression, too, that even those adolescents whose sentiments are potentially utopian are not yet ready to deploy their recently achieved cognitive skills except in relation to rather focal political questions. They may be willing to propose ideas on the remediation of crime and poverty, but they will be hesitant to try their minds out on the formidably complex problems of the total society. Utopian thought is, after all, extraordinarily difficult. It involves not only a willingness to resist the world as it is, but requires as well the very highest level of political intelligence. Even the most politicized college students and adults are rarely utopian in thought, though they may be so in sentiment; their ideas generally reflect already packaged doctrines. All in all, it is not surprising that adolescents are not utopian. What may be surprising is that we find this surprising, that we are somehow affronted by the recognition. We hunger to believe otherwise.

And this brings me to my final topic, which is the connection between moral and political ideology. Work along these lines has already begun, and it is not altogether reassuring. We seek and have begun to find rough parallels between the modes of thought involved in moral and political reasoning, not too surprisingly. We would expect, for example, that a hard-line authoritarianism exposed in the analysis of moral dilemmas would also be displayed when the task is a political one. Yet in drawing attention to these parallels, we have drawn attention away from important differences; more particularly, we simplify what is involved in political reasoning.

As an illustration, let me contrast a moral dilemma with a roughly equivalent political one, to show how the analytic tasks differ in the two instances. Consider a moral problem that the Kohlberg method proposes, the well-known story about the man whose wife is mortally ill, and the greedy druggist who demands an exorbitant sum for the drug that would save her life. What should the man do? Is he entitled to steal the drug? Note that the analytic task is fairly simple, in that there is little ambiguity about goals, and that means and ends are closely tied. The issue is the legitimacy of means, and the values involved in determining that legitimacy. Now, let me translate that story into a political context; as it happens, startling similar dilemmas are beginning to appear in real life with the advent of elaborate and expensive medical technology. We now have a 62-year-old man whose 60-year-old wife is mortally ill and whose life might be saved through an experimental heart operation. The operation will cost $25,000, but cost is not the primary factor, since the man has medical insurance, and in any case, much of the expense will be borne by federal subsidies to the hospital. Arrayed against our man is not a greedy druggist, but another man who might profit from the operation, a 45-year-old mechanic with four teen-age children. The decision is not being made in the marketplace, but by a well-meaning and harassed panel of physicians, who are weighing the following elements: The housewife is older and her children are grown. On the other hand, she is a better risk to survive the operation. On still another hand, from a purely research standpoint, more would be learned from the mechanic's operation. Looking over the shoulder of the local panel is another panel of harassed medical bureaucrats who are asking themselves these questions and others besides: Should we invest $25,000 per patient? Will the costs come down once the method is perfected, and if not, ought one to put funds elsewhere? Assuming there are ten thousand patients per year whose lives will be saved, that would amount to a quarter of a billion dollars, and most of the patients would be at the end of the life span. Ought one to fund basic cardiovascular research instead? Or research on diseases affecting younger age groups? And behind that panel is someone from the Bureau of the Budget, or on the staff of the House Appropriations Committee, pondering just how much money ought to go into medicine, as against education or welfare or defense or foreign aid, or what have you.

Note how far we have come from the dying wife and the mercenary druggist. We have gone from a one-on-one collision of values to far more complicated issues: the relation of variable means to variable ends; the relation of uncertain means to uncertain ends; the relation between short- and long-term ends; the relation between individualistic and collective goods; the distinction between particularistic and universalistic orientations; the collision between values, and also the collision between interests, and between interests and values. We are in the realm of politics, which is cognitively more difficult than the realm of morals, which must subsume morals and venture beyond, neither ignoring morals nor being dominated by them.

What we have been seeing in recent research on the politics of the young is the tendency to emphasize the moral component and, ultimately, to reduce politics to morality. It is a tendency that runs deep in the American grain; and the feverish politics of the 1960s reinforced it. From John Winthrop and the Bay Colony to the dolorous present, American politics has been haunted by the illusion of politics-as-ethics, the belief that mere good conscience will generate an adequate politics. It will not, as the magisterial work of Reinhold Niebuhr (1960) should have taught us; that we believe it will is a form, a peculiarly American form, of the sin of pride.

If we believe it will as social scientists, we will assimilate politics to morality, and thus the more complex domain to the simpler one. We will in fact be doing what adolescents sometimes do when they are under cognitive stress, when they cannot quite grasp the dimensions of a question we pose to them—they retreat to a moralistic posture, suggesting that we be nice to people or put them in jail or teach them the Ten Commandments, as though a display of righteousness will overcome the dilemmas involved in political judgment. Such adjurations to piety have been evidenced in American political forensics, from the lowest to the highest, and now they seem to be quickly infecting our understanding of adolescent politics.

What I am getting to is that the study of political ideology, in depth, will require the simultaneous study of ethics and pragmatics, and of the interactions between them. Neither will suffice alone. To follow Niebuhr (1960), the ethical (or "idealistic") standpoint does not take adequate account of the human propensity for power and self-interest and "is inclined to take . . . moral pretensions . . . at face value," whereas the pragmatic ("realistic") outlook is insensitive both to "new possibilities" and to the "moral and social imperatives" generated by history. The task of an adequate political philosophy is to fuse both perspectives.

And it is likewise the task of an adequate social science. Adolescence offers us one opportunity to achieve this, for it is where serious politics begins and where, in many cases, it ends. The essence of adolescent politics is the concurrent nascence of morals and strategy, both brought to bear on the problem of the social order. What ought we do? What can we do? And how do oughtness and capacity, the ideal and the practical, modify and dominate and temper each other? The dialectic between the two is at the very nexus of adolescent ideology, and the dispassionate study of adolescence will allow us to see serious politics in the making, to watch ethics and pragmatics in their earliest opposition and reconciliation. But we will do so, I think, only if we give up sentimentalizing the political adolescent, stop seeing him only as an idealist, or a utopian, or as an agent of the higher morality, and begin to appreciate that larger side of him that is a struggling intelligence.

REFERENCES

Adelson, J. The mystique of adolescence. *Psychiatry,* 1964, 27, 1–6.

Adelson, J., & Beall, L. Adolescent perspectives on law and government. *Law and Society Review*, 1970, 495–504.

Adelson, J., Green, B., & O'Neil, R. The growth of the idea of law in adolescence. *Developmental Psychology*, 1969, 1, 327–332.

Adelson, J., & O'Neil, R. The development of political thought in adolescence. *Journal of Personality and Social Psychology*, 1966, 4, 295–306.

Beall, L. *Political thinking in adolescence.* Doctoral dissertation, University of Michigan, 1967.

Bush, M. *A developmental study of adolescent political thinking.* Doctoral dissertation, University of Michigan, 1970.

Gallatin, J. *The development of political thinking in urban adolescents.* Final report to the Office of Education, 1972.

Gallatin, J., & Adelson, J. Individual rights and the public good. *Comparative Political Studies*, 1970, 226–242.

Gallatin, J., & Adelson, J. Legal guarantees of individual freedom. *Journal of Social Issues*, 1971, 27.

Hogan, R. Moral conduct and moral character. *Psychological Bulletin*, 1973, 79, 217–232.

Niebuhr, R. In H. Davis & R. Good (Eds.), *Reinhold Niebuhr on politics.* New York: Scribner's, 1960.

Simpson, E. Moral development research: An examination of cultural bias. *Human Development*, in press.

Tolley, H. *Children and war.* New York: Teachers College Press, 1973.

II

Some Issues Concerning the Developmental Process

5

Asynchronizations in Adolescent Development

DOROTHY H. EICHORN
University of California, Berkeley

INTRODUCTION

Don't send a beginning student or a mindless computer to search the literature on asynchronies in development. He, she, or it is unlikely to find much under that descriptor. A review of some forty widely adopted texts on adolescent psychology or physical development and more than three times that number of journal articles and chapters in handbooks revealed only a few (e.g., Stolz & Stolz, 1951; Stone & Church, 1968) in which the term asynchrony was even used, much less appeared in the index. Yet the literature reviewed included the most recent texts on adolescence (e.g., Conger, 1973) and physical growth (e.g., Baer, 1973) and the most authoritative compendium on developmental psychology, *Carmichael's Manual of Child Psychology* (Mussen, 1970). At least some aspect of asynchronous development during adolescence was, nevertheless, discussed in most works.

How, then, is the thing called? Ausubel (1954) speaks of "discrepancies or unevenness in rates of growth" and Cole and Hall (1970) of "proportional growth." Conger (1973), Horrocks (1962), Jersild (1963), Maresh (1964) and McCandless (1970) avoid labels. Tanner, who has probably written more extensively on the topic than anyone else, uses different terms in each of several works—disorganization (1961), disunity (1969), and heterochrony and disharmonic (1970)—and none in his classic *Growth at Adolescence* (1962).

VARIETIES OF ASYNCHRONY

We must also expand on Roger Brown (1958) and ask: What thing or things are called by such names? Webster's Collegiate Dictionary defines asynchrony simply as "not concurrent in time." Thus, in principle, the term may be applied to differential growth rates of the various parts or functions of an individual (intraindividual asynchronies) or to interindividual differences in rates of growth in one or more characteristics among members of a group who, by virtue of some communality, such as chronological age or familial relationship, might be expected to have similar developmental patterns.

Clausen's paper (selection 2 in this volume) dealt with interindividual differences in rate of maturing, and the organizers of the Adolescent Conference asked me to emphasize intraindividual asynchronies, such as contrasts between physical and social or cognitive and emotional development. As will become evident, however, the two forms of asynchrony are often linked and difficult to separate.

In context all of the terms cited in the alphabetic sampling of authors referred to intraindividual variations in developmental rates. Despite this fact, asynchronies of this sort receive less attention in the literature than do interindividual differences. Whereas most of the textbooks reviewed only mention intraindividual variations, all have sections on deviations from normative developmental patterns. Where both types of asynchrony are included, they are treated in combination or juxtaposition, with typically much more extensive discussion of interindividual differences, but few authors distinguish sharply between the two types.

Some textbooks stress the normality of both intraindividual and interindividual differences in rates of growth and the fact that these occur throughout the life span. Others use precocious puberty, an abnormal extreme, to illustrate asynchrony. This disorder exemplifies both intraindividual and interindividual discrepancies in rates of growth, for persons with puberty praecox have not been found to show cognitive advancement, nor does their psychosocial development keep pace with their endocrinological and primary and secondary sexual development. The favorite textbook examples of normal intraindividual asynchronizations during adolescence are differences in the timing of the growth spurts of the feet, legs, arms, nose, and chin.

Use of illustrations from physical development in behavioral textbooks is understandable. Much more research is available on physical development than on psychological characteristics, although studies of interindividual and intergroup differences predominate in the biological as well as behavioral literatures.

The most thorough analyses of asynchronies in physical development during adolescence are those of Stolz and Stolz (1951) for boys and of Shuttleworth

(1939) for both sexes. Tanner (1962, 1970) summarizes these and other data showing that the most common pattern is for the foot to reach its final size earlier than other dimensions except probably those of the head. Peak growth in leg length precedes that in trunk length by about a year, with the peak for total height between the two and about six months before the weight peak. Acceleration in leg length also precedes that for hip width and chest breadth. Peak growth in shoulder breadth comes next, followed by trunk length and chest depth. Like the legs, the arms accelerate early and show a peripheral to proximal gradient, that is, calf before thigh and forearm before upper arm. The apex of the spurt in muscle growth seems to be about three months after the height growth apex, but peak gains in dynamometric strength do not come until eleven months after the muscle peak. This list does not, of course, exhaust the varieties of dimensional asynchronies. Shuttleworth (1939), for example, showed that each of twenty-two dimensions assessed in the children of the Harvard Growth Study had a characteristic growth pattern that, although similar for children of both sexes and of both Northern European and Italian ancestry, was in most instances distinct from that of each other dimension.

That sequences of physical development are less variable than is the timing of the events of the adolescent cycle is widely cited. Rarely noted is the fact that interindividual differences in the various developmental sequences do, nevertheless, occur frequently. Another way of stating this observation is that intra-individual asynchronies are not similar in all persons. Even the ossification sequence, which forms the basis for the most commonly used ratings of skeletal age, is far from invariant. For example, Garn (1966) found fifteen different "sequence polymorphisms" among only six of the carpal centers of the hand in 154 boys and girls. Among a number of types of sequential variations reported by Stolz and Stolz (1951) are fifty-one different arrangements in the timing of the adolescent growth apices of five dimensions (height, leg length, stem length, bi-iliac, and biacromial) among 67 boys.

Tanner, who has often stressed the point that "though there is much individual variation in the age at which puberty takes place, as a rule all the events of puberty occur together in a definite and not very variable sequence" (1969, p. 38), has also recently published graphs of pubertal events in girls (1969, 1970) showing that "the individual variability is considerable. Some children seem to have looser linkages between the events than others. At one extreme one may find a girl who has not yet menstruated, though she has reached adult breast and pubic hair ratings and is already two years past her peak height velocity; and at the other a girl who has passed all stages of puberty within the space of two years" (1969, p. 39).

Variations in the intervals between adolescent events and in the duration of the adolescent cycle are also evident in the analyses of Stolz and Stolz (1951) and Reynolds and Wines (1951). Even disorders that result in decidedly deviant ages at puberty are not necessarily characterized by deviance in all events of the adolescent cycle. An example from the pediatric literature is a boy with precocious puberty who, as is typical of this syndrome, achieved his final height very early (age 11 in this case), did not have temporary enlargement of the breasts until 12 years, the typical age for many normal males (Tanner, 1969, p. 40–citing Keizer, 1956).

It is worth mentioning that Tanner's graphs (1969, 1970) illustrating inter-individual differences in intraindividual asynchrony are plotted in terms of years of deviation from age at peak height velocity. Considerable use has been made of this technique in research on adolescent physical and physiological development. Whether the zero point from which years before and after are plotted is age at peak height velocity, age at menarche, age at reaching 90 percent of mature height, or some other developmental point, this technique markedly reduces the extent of the interindividual variation in various functions, such as metabolic rate, heart rate, and height, at the various developmental ages (e.g., -2 or $+1$ years from menarche) as compared with plots against chronological age. It is interesting that this method also clearly reveals variations in the nature of intraindividual asynchronizations.

Another way of examining the extent of association or dissociation between growth curves or developmental events is to compute the correlations between indices of developmental status or level in different domains or subsystems. This approach has usually been used in the context of assessing the "generality" of growth trends, for example, the adolescent spurt. Viewed conversely, the inter-correlations indicate the likelihood of varying degrees of asynchrony, because marked discrepancies in growth rate are most likely when two aspects of development are not closely associated and least likely when they are highly correlated.

Paralleling what can be seen in individual graphs such as Tanner's, tables of intercorrelations show that the development of secondary sexual characteristics, such as pubic hair and breasts, is less closely linked in either sex to skeletal and reproductive development than are the latter with each other (Nicholson & Hanley, 1953). Although chronological age at menarche, at peak height velocity, and at reaching certain skeletal ages and certain percentages of mature height have intercorrelations as high as .9, even correlations of this magnitude allow for considerable individual variation. Stating that a correlation of .9 leaves 19 percent of the variance unaccounted is less revealing in this connection than noting that this level of correlation reduces the standard deviation by about one-half. Thus, given a correlation of .9 between age at menarche and age at peak height velocity and a normal range of about five years in age at menarche, the range of age at menarche in relation to peak height velocity is still about two and a half years.

Tables of intercorrelations also reveal that the associations between skeletal maturity and percentage of mature size in height and other dimensions are moderately high even early in life (Bayley, 1943; Nicholson & Hanley, 1953; Simmons & Greulich, 1943). They increase steadily, reaching a peak around puberty. Some diminution is observed thereafter (as it is in correlations with secondary sexual characteristics), although in general the correlations remain high throughout adolescence. Why asynchronies are of particular interest during adolescence even though the "unity of growth" is greater than during childhood will be discussed later (pp. 88, 89).

When dimensional measures are maturity measures (i.e., percentages of mature size), correlations among them or between them and skeletal maturity are higher than when "size ages" (e.g., height age) are used. Studies of dwarfs and excessively tall children also show greater deviations from normal patterns in height age than in bone age (Van der Werff Ten Bosch & Enthoven, 1966; Van Gelderen, 1966). Measures such as "height age" are, of course, derived from the size of the average boy or girl at successive chronological ages. Because a child may be large or small at any age because he or she is maturing more or less rapidly than the average child or because he or she is an average-maturing child of genetically large or small size, "size ages" confound these factors. Some confounding may also arise from environmental circumstances, such as nutritional state or illness. However, such factors also tend to affect maturational rate, although the relative effect on maturation and size may not be equivalent. Skeletal age is a true maturity score, since all normal persons eventually achieve the same skeletal maturity. Although adult height and other dimensions differ, percentage of adult size is, nevertheless, also a maturity measure and, hence, reflects relative acceleration or retardation in maturational rate rather than size per se. (Reference to this important distinction is made on p. 86 in considering the assessment of behavioral development and asynchronies.)

As is often remarked in critiques of the concept of "organismic age" (a single maturational age derived by averaging a variety of developmental ages), dental development and cognitive development (measured as mental age) have only low positive correlations with other aspects of development. Indeed, development of the deciduous and permanent teeth is quite independent. The low order of association between mental age and other maturational ages may in part be a function of the sort of measurement problem described previously for ages based on physical dimensions. Additional measurement problems plague attempts to study cognitive and other behavioral asynchronies, however, as will be discussed later.

Even at pathological extremes of small stature or mental deficiency, the two forms of retardation are associated to varying degrees. That is, in some disorders one form of retardation is present without the other, in some both statural and mental retardation are profound, and in some one form of retardation is marked and the other only moderate (Drash, Greenberg, & Money, 1968; Money, 1968; Van Gelderen, 1966). Variations in personality have also been observed among different forms of dwarfism (Drash, Greenberg, & Money, 1968). Research on interindividual asynchronies within the normal range has, of course, demonstrated some fairly consistent associations between rate of physical maturation and some aspects of social and emotional development. Most of these data are, however, in the form of contrasts between means for groups of early-, average-, and late-maturing adolescents rather than correlations.

Studies on asynchronies within or across behavioral domains are few compared to the number on physical development. Several of the textbooks reviewed do summarize group data on differential rates of growth among mental abilities, drawing on longitudinal and cross-sectional data derived from standardized IQ tests, such as the Stanford-Binet, and on Thurstone's studies (1955) of primary mental abilities. Data taken from IQ tests show, for example, an earlier asympote for relatively simple tasks, such as digit span, than for more difficult tasks, such as reasoning and comprehension. As noted later in the section on methodology, however, one cannot be sure that these differences are not artifacts of measurement, for there is no reason to believe that the various scales have equal intervals, ceilings, and the like. Thurstone's curves showing different forms for the development of such abilities as perceptual speed, reasoning, and verbal comprehension are at least plotted in terms of proportion of adult status, although there is no guarantee that the scales are similar in the adequacy with which they sample the different functions at any or all ages.

A number of textbooks also include sections on mental retardation or acceleration ("giftedness") and on academic underachievement or overachievement, with emphasis in either case on the lower end of the distribution, that is, retardation and underachievement. Rarely, however, are such topics dealt with in the framework of either intraindividual or interindividual asynchrony despite the fact that in most instances both are involved. Indeed, only a few writers even speculate about the existence and nature of psychological asynchronies. Stone and Church (1968) comment, "We are not sure what the psychological equivalents of asynchronous growth and discontinuity of growth may be, but it is certain that children do have periods of greater receptivity to certain kinds of learning and thinking" (p. 202).

Thus far only asynchronies within or between domains (physical, cognitive, social, etc.) in an individual's growth or between individuals in an age peer cohort have been mentioned. Lack of developmental complementarity between generations can also be conceptualized as a form of asynchrony or as a source of it. This type of asynchrony is peculiar to adolescence because the adolescent sometimes develops in relation to two generations. On the one hand, his developmental course is affected by that of his parents and other adults. If, for example, parents are unable to provide the proper degree of autonomy or emotional support at an optimal time relative to the adolescent's needs, asynchronies in personality-social, cognitive, or even motor development may result. On the other hand, some adolescents become parents. This role may not only either promote or retard some aspects of their development but may produce asynchronies in their offspring if, say, the adolescent parents are too immature to engage in the kind of emotional giving and self-denial that parenting sometimes requires.

SOURCES OF ASYNCHRONIZATIONS

Many types of differential growth rates are, of course, programmed into all living organisms. Such species-specific genetic programming determines physical differences between pumpkins and squashes, horses and donkeys, men and monkeys, and developmental differences in proportions such as those between the large-headed, short-legged human infant and the long-legged adolescent. Among members of the same species, interindividual and intraindividual variations in growth rates and sequences of physical development can have both genetic and environmental bases. To cite but one example, atypical sequences of skeletal development have been noted in nutritional deficiencies (Dreizen, Snodgrasse, Webb-Peploe, & Spies, 1958). Yet Garn (1966) has demonstrated sex-specific and genetically controlled sequence deviations in a normal and adequately nourished sample. With respect to individual differences in the "tightness" or "looseness" of linkage between various aspects of physical development during adolescence, Tanner (1970) has hypothesized that the basis lies in variations in the degree to which hypothalamic and pituitary processes are integrated, since different groups of hormones control the adolescent height spurt, pubic hair development, and breast development.

Tanner (1961) has also speculated about the sources of psychological asynchronies:

> Disharmonized development in the psychological sphere could signify simply a disharmonious development of brain structure leading to an abnormality of personality, such as the mental defect often occurring in persons with chromosomal abnormalities. Perhaps a similar, though not detrimental, disharmony of development may lead to the extreme development of a gift for music or mathematics or drawing. . . . Different psychological functions develop in an individual in a distinct order, and . . . we can say that they too may develop disharmoniously, perhaps because of interaction between the child and his parents or teachers. Thus if the interaction necessary for the development of one psychological activity is too little, then the next activity to develop may fail to appear, or may appear late or in a distorted form. Perhaps, even, restraint applied to prevent one activity from being manifested may, by a sort of back-pressure, prevent or distort the appearance of subsequent activities (pp. 60–61).

In a later paper (1970) he adds:

> Variation in the speed of development of different structures and functions (heterochronisms) underlie many individual differences in bodily structure. . . . It is an open question to what extent similar heterochronisms may explain differences in personality structure. Some psychological abnormalities or culturally excessive deviations from the average (analogous with an inconvenient degree or nearsightedness) may arise from insufficient harmonization of the speeds at which different structures and functions develop. This could occur either for genetical reasons, the child carrying, by chance, a relatively dysharmonic set of genes, or for environmental reasons, the development of one area of the personality having been speeded up by external forces, perhaps early in childhood, while another was relatively retarded (pp. 130–131).

Whereas these quotations emphasize abnormalities, Ausubel (1954), who has given more attention to this topic than any other psychologist dealing with adolescence, treats asynchronies as normal and inevitable, particularly during periods of transition:

> In nature, the characteristics of any growth process are uniquely determined by the special conditions relevant to its development. Hence, it is extremely unlikely that the particular constellation of genetic and environmental factors regulating the development of any given trait or capacity would completely overlap the set of regulatory factors involved in the development of any other trait. . . . As the tempo of development (or decline) accelerates and as discontinuities in the growth patterns of particular functions occur, greater opportunities prevail for wider disparities to develop between the relative levels of maturity attained by these different functions. . . . at least initially, glaring discrepancies in rate of growth constitute a characteristic and invariable feature of transitional phases of development. . . . When growth in one area is a necessary precondition for or stimulant of growth in another area, a certain amount of lag is inevitable. Thus, muscle strength lags behind the increase in muscle mass, but it precedes the gain in neuromuscular coordination. The growth spurts in social and emotional development necessarily begin *after* the physiological and physical growth spurts. . . . In some cases, unevenness in the total growth pattern is caused by the lack of a growth spurt in certain areas. An illustration of this is intellectual development, which is singularly unresponsive to the stimulus of physiological maturation, but may be adversely affected by emotional instability and the sudden influx of competing interests powered by emerging new drives. . . . In personality development, differences in social attitudes and expectations, in the availability of certain types of status-giving activities, and in the relative flexibility of various social institutions result in marked differences in maturity levels characterizing the several indices of adult personality status (pp. 62–64).

Speculation about the role of social institutions and cultural customs in engendering behavioral disharmonies among adolescents and youth is one exception to the general tendency to stress asynchronies in physical growth and overlook possible psychological analogs. During the past decade attention has been called increasingly to the possibly detrimental effects of progressively prolonged economic dependence in generations displaying the secular trend toward accelerated physical, social, and academic development. Both clinical experience (Otterstadt, 1960; Seidmann, 1963) and some research data (Engelmann, 1962; Heath, 1968) have been interpreted as indicating that this sort of discrepancy has resulted in retardation in emotional and moral development and in an increase in adolescent and intergenerational conflicts. Although the evidence for advancement in physical, social, and educational development is considerable, that for emotional and moral retardation is not, and, as Muuss (1970) notes, generalizations about the latter go beyond the data. Nevertheless, the possibility that lack of opportunity for independent responsibility commensurate with physical, cognitive, and social skills is having deleterious psychological and social consequences has been considered serious enough to warrant examination at the level of public policy (Coleman, Bremner, Clark, Davis, Eichorn, Griliches, Kett, Ryder, Blum, & Mays, 1973).

Very recently Gutmann (1973) has suggested that the philosophies of some current subcultures may be having an opposite effect; that is, they may be promoting premature senescence in personality development. He points to studies showing that older men, as compared with younger ones, are milder and less competitive, "more interested in receiving than in producing," in "communion than in agency," and that food, religion, and the assurance of love are their sources of pleasure and security. Because the counterculture stresses these values, Gutmann argues that it promotes premature psychological senility. According to his thesis, affluence and consumerism have generated a number of "mythologies," especially a psychic collectivism, and these in turn have had an "aging" effect on ego development during adolescence and postadolescence.

Familial economic and social circumstances and parental values and practices can also produce asynchronies, whether or not these factors reflect societal or subcultural patterns. Such influences have been documented in research on mental acceleration and retardation and on underachievement and overachievement (see, for example, summaries in Conger, 1973; and McCandless, 1970), and at least the clinical literature suggests parallels in personality development. Reference to asynchronies resulting from lack of generational complementarity, both between adolescent and parent and between the adolescent parent and offspring, was made at the end of the section on varieties of asynchronizations.

SIGNIFICANCE OF ASYNCHRONIZATIONS

Presumably asynchronies in physical growth rates are of interest to educators and behavioral and social scientists primarily because of their bearing on, or interactions with, behavior and psychological adjustment. It is, therefore, worthwhile to examine what authorities on behavioral development consider to be the significance of such asynchronizations during adolescence. Although more dramatically stated than most, the following quotations are representative of textbook illustrations and interpretations:

> Since most of his increased height is due to growth in the legs, many a boy finds himself equipped wih pedal extremities that get him across a room rather faster than he expected, causing him to overrun his objective; they also tend to get tangled in the furniture. His arms, having grown 4 or 5 inches in length, also contribute to his miscalculations of distance and lead him into a long series of minor tragedies, from knocking over his waterglass because his hand reached it too soon to throwing a forward pass 6 feet over the receiver's head, because his elongated arm automatically produced far greater leverage than he has been accustomed to (Cole & Hall, 1970, p. 22).

> Asynchrony . . . is especially evident during pubescence, when arms, legs, nose, and chin may seem suddenly to sprout individually, with no regard for overall proportions or harmony. . . . One of the characteristics of adolescence is a feeling of being out of step, and asynchrony may enhance that feeling. Moreover, any deviation from the group average is likely to make the child feel out of step (Stone & Church, 1968, p. 477).

Also widely cited are the data of Schonfeld (1950) and Stolz and Stolz (1944) on the incidence of adjustment problems associated with adolescent physical development and the physical characteristics reported as sources of distress. Actually, most if not all of these characteristics involve deviations from the norm or ideal rather than simply intraindividual asynchronies. Other than occasional case histories, data on psychological disturbance stemming directly from asynchronous physical growth are lacking, although most psychologists seem to assume that the phenomenon is widespread.

In general, interpretations of the psychological significance of intraindividual asynchronies in physical development parallel those for interindividual differences. That is, they stress the adolescent's preoccupation with himself and his body, the effect on self-concept of deviations from peers or cultural ideals and of discontinuity from previous status, and the abruptness of onset and intensity of the adolescent spurt. These factors are also offered as reasons that physical asynchronizations seem to be more disturbing during adolescence than during other periods of the life span despite the fact that they are no greater, and, indeed, are usually less, than during infancy and childhood.

Among textbook writers, only Ausubel (1954) considers in depth the implications of biobehavioral and psychosocial asynchronies for personality development:

> Just as maturation in one area may precipitate or facilitate maturation in another area, the converse holds equally true: relative retardation in a slowly growing function inevitably limits the full expression and complete development of a more rapidly growing function. ... Thus, whenever growth in a given function greatly outstrips development in related, supporting functions, only two possibilities of expression exist: The relatively precocious function will (1) be utilized immediately, before the supporting areas are adequately developed, and therefore prematurely; or (2) its utilization will be deferred until related maturational tasks are completed. But regardless of the alternative, the results will prove unsatisfactory. Premature utilization can never be wholly effective or satisfying and often leads to serious dysfunction. ... On the other hand, postponement of functional expression until related maturational readiness would lead to emotional tension because of the frustration of current needs, and to developmental retardation resulting from disuse and insufficient role-playing experience (pp. 64–65).

That retardation in one ability may have far-reaching consequences is documented in research on school dropouts, whose educational failure is accompanied by personality problems and difficulties in social relationships. Although academic retardation often accompanies mental retardation, growth in mental age of many dropouts is average or even accelerated. Among such youngsters greater retardation in reading than in other skills is found regularly. The further one goes in school, the more success in most subjects depends on reading ability.

Research on educational arrangements for children and adolescents at both extremes of the IQ distribution shows not only how frequently asynchronies between mental and educational development occur, but also how difficult it is to avoid increasing the likelihood of one type of asynchrony while trying to remedy another. As McCandless's review (1970) of the literature makes evident, the educational achievement ages of both mentally gifted and handicapped youngsters tend to be lower than their mental ages. The handicapped do better academically in regular classes but are happier in segregated ones. High IQ youngsters make greater educational progress in segregated classes, but currently such arrangements are rarely used because of concern about possible deleterious effects on their personal-social development. Parenthetically, it should be noted that the rather voluminous literature on the mentally handicapped contains relatively little on the special problems of the adolescent and youth. A retarded child somehow fits better in the world of children than does the older adolescent in a cohort preparing for or undertaking the responsibilities of self-support, marriage, and parenthood.

If even some forms of asynchrony are the source of developmental difficulties, then asynchronies are significant simply in terms of the statistical probabilities of the magnitude of the problem. Suppose one defines normality as being within the middle 50 percent of an age distribution. The likelihood of being synchronous in this sense in two uncorrelated characteristics is only .25 (.5 × .5). Given hundreds of physical and psychological characteristics, the probability of being synchronous in all is virtually zero, or, conversely, the probability that any individual will have developmental asynchronies between and within some domains is essentially 1. In this regard Bloom (1969) has pointed out that using only the seven tests in Thurstone's battery of Primary Mental Abilities (1955), about half the population should score in the top 10 percent on at least one test. Were more factors added—Guilford (1967) posits 120 combinations of mental abilities—everyone could expect to be at the top as well as the bottom in at least one.

For an individual, a deviation from the age mean much smaller than that necessary to place him in the upper or lower 25 percent may be meaningful. It may well be, for example, that a boy assesses his height not against the middle 50 percent but the upper 50 percent, or that a person compares his intellectual capacities not with the general population but with his close friends or family, who may be at either end of the distribution. Analogously, an intraindividual asynchrony of relatively small magnitude between two aspects of development may have more repercussions than a larger variation between two others.

Clearly, intraindividual variations are a source of error variance that can make it difficult to detect group differences on one variable or associations between variables in one or more groups. In his introduction to a monograph on human variation, Keys (1966) gives several illustrations from biosocial research, as well as putting the problem well: "Unexplained variability is exasperating, but the collection of data in such a way that variability is unrecognized can be disastrous. But variability is not merely a confounding nuisance; it is a challenge for explanation; careful attention to it can provide unexpected and valuable clues.

Unexplained variability means that one or more influential variables is being overlooked" (p. 506).

A case in point is the observation by Livson and Bronson (1961) that maximum growth age (MGA) and menarcheal age, although strongly and positively correlated, had sizable and *opposite* correlations with degree of over-control in a longitudinal sample of girls. Scatterplots revealed that those whose growth spurts were relatively early and whose menarche was later than average tended toward "extreme overcontrol of impulses." Further, mean scores on overcontrol and impulsivity differed depending on whether the interval between MGA and menarche was two or more years, one to two years, or less than a year. One recalls here the data of Tanner (1969, 1970) and of Stolz and Stolz (1951), cited earlier, showing marked individual differences in the duration and timing of adolescent events. Livson and Bronson (1961) comment that "despite the existence of a strong general factor coordinating the various processes of maturation during adolescence, there may be useful information in the temporal patterning of these processes. If this is so, then—to take one example—investigations of personality correlates of maturational rate may be made more powerful by a consideration of the possible impact of asynchronies among the various components of development in adolescence" (p. 87).

RESEARCH ISSUES, PROBLEMS, AND STRATEGIES

Had the topic of intraindividual asynchronies been well explored, data on the following would be available for a variety of combinations of behavioral and physical traits:

1. Differences between the pairs of growth curves across the life span in rate of increment or decline, duration of periods of growth or decline, age at onset, peak, and offset of each phase, and the directions of the asynchronies, that is, in which member of the pair of curves development occurs earlier or more rapidly.
2. The incidence (range of occurrence) and prevalence (frequency of instances for a given period of the life span or subject population) of each asynchrony, or, more generally, whether a particular asynchrony is typical or atypical of a developmental phase or subject population.
3. The "side effects" of each asynchrony, that is, whether it disturbs or enhances other aspects of development, and whether the "side effects" vary with the direction and/or degree of the asynchrony.
4. The source(s) of the asynchrony, that is, whether it is inherent in the developmental process of the species or a result of environmental circumstances or some combination of these factors.
5. Methods of preventing or remedying disturbing asynchronies or their effects or of promoting beneficial asynchronies.

Contrasting this list with the literature reviewed in preceding sections makes it apparent that these points represent primarily a statement of research issues for investigation rather than a summary of the current state of knowledge.

Also missing from the discussions of authors who posit the existence of intraindividual asynchronies and concomitant behavioral disturbances is consideration of the methodological pitfalls facing investigators who attempt to improve the state of the art. One major source of difficulty is the inadequacies of the instruments available for measuring most developmental characteristics. In order to derive a valid growth curve, one must have a single instrument with equal intervals and a known zero point that measures the same factor or factors across the life span. Once one moves beyond physical dimensions assessed with yardsticks, tape measures, calipers, or balance scales, even the best instruments are "rubber yardsticks." The intervals are not necessarily equal (e.g., is each primary or secondary tooth or each mental test item equivalent?), the zero point is usually unknown (e.g., when does memory begin?), and the upper limit is often restricted (e.g., how can one advance beyond skeletal maturity?). A scale bearing a single label, for example, "intelligence" or "responsibility," may not be sampling the same factor or factors at different developmental points. Development in some psychological, social, and physical characteristics is known or hypothesized to be qualitative, that is, discontinuous, in nature. Illustrations of such characteristics are stages of secondary sexual development, Erikson's stages of ego development, Piaget's stages of cognitive development, and Kohlberg's stages of moral development. At most, growth in these areas can be assessed with a single metric scale only in very restricted segments of the life span. Although many discontinuous developmental sequences can be ordered in a hierarchy, not all are susceptible to even ordinal scaling. Would one, for example, regard being divorced, widowed, or remarried as being a more advanced developmental status than an existing first marriage?

Even when metric instruments are available for assessing a behavioral characteristic, we have no assurance that they yield a valid measure of the growth process. Indeed, one may have as many different growth curves for a function as one has scales, a point well illustrated in the history of intelligence testing. Despite the fact that more attention has been given to the measurement of intelligence than any other behavioral trait, we do not know that any test yet devised accurately reflects the "true" developmental curve. Mental age scales are deliberately designed to produce mean scores for the standardization population that are a straight-line function of chronological age. However, this procedure is successful only until an individual is about 16 years old, although there is considerable evidence that intellectual development continues beyond this age in many, if not most, persons. "Absolute scaling" of intelligence tests based on point scores rather than on mental age yields a sigmoid growth curve that is steeply accelerated during the early years of life and gradually decelerates (Guilford, 1967). Attempts to scale except by gross stages or within very limited growth periods are contradicted by theories that cognitive development is discontinuous.

In principle the problems posed by the inadequacies of measures for deriving growth curves are not different from those to which any behavioral scientist who works with developmental processes and comparisons between ages or stages is accustomed; they are simply compounded by dealing with two variables simultaneously. Thus even greater caution in drawing inferences about the "state of nature" and greater care in the selection of appropriate instruments and scoring techniques are necessary. For example, if asynchrony between mental age and grade placement is the subject of study, mental age rather than "absolute" scale scores would be the measure of choice because both mental age and grade placement are, on the average, straight-line functions of chronological age. However, "absolute" scale scores would be more appropriate if intellectual development and growth in height were the variables concerned, for here both growth curves are sigmoid.

A problem in research design peculiar to studies of asynchrony is that of differentiating the effects of intraindividual and interindividual asynchrony. This problem arises because an individual who has an asynchrony between two characteristics in excess of the normal range may well be deviant from the peer group in at least one of those characteristics. Conversely, a person who is markedly deviant from the peer group in a given trait is also likely to have an atypical asynchrony between that characteristic and one or more others. Whether the object of the research is the effects of intraindividual or interindividual asynchrony, the results will be confounded.

In many instances this pitfall in design can be circumvented by selecting subjects who are within the normal range on both variables but fairly discrepant in the two "ages" under study. For example, during adolescence the standard deviation for both mental age (MA) and skeletal age (SA) is about one year. Thus an individual with a chronological age of 14, an MA of 15, and an SA of 13 would be within the middle 67 percent of the age group in the two variables of interest but would have a discrepancy of two years between MA and SA. By comparing groups deviating in this way in each direction, that is, MA greater than SA and SA greater than MA, with groups congruent in MA and SA but advanced, average, or retarded in both on a third measure, say, popularity, any differential effects of intraindividual and interindividual asynchrony in either direction could be detected. Adaptation and application of this strategy to other developmental phases could make it possible to draw inferences about the relative effects of asynchronies at different stages. Such a desirable result would contribute further to the aim of this conference—understanding the role of adolescence in the life cycle.

REFERENCES

Ausubel, D. P. *Theory and problems of adolescent development.* New York: Grune & Stratton, 1954.

Baer, M. J. *Growth and maturation.* Cambridge, Mass.: Doyle, 1973.

Bayley, N. Skeletal maturing in adolescence as a basis for determining percentage of completed growth. *Child Development*, 1943, **14**, 1–46.

Bloom, B. S. Replies to Dr. Jensen's article. *ERIC Clearinghouse on Early Childhood Education*, May 1, 1969, 3(4).

Brown, R. How shall a thing be called? *Psychological Review*, 1958, **65**, 14–21.

Cole, L., & Hall, I. M. *Psychology of adolescence.* (7th ed.) New York: Holt, Rinehart & Winston, 1970.

Coleman, J., Bremner, R., Clark, B., Davis, J., Eichorn, D., Griliches, Z., Kett, J., Ryder, N., Blum, Z., & Mays, J. *Youth: transition to adulthood.* Report of the Panel on Youth of the President's Science Advisory Committee. Chicago: University of Chicago Press, 1973.

Conger, J. J. *Adolescence and youth.* New York: Harper & Row, 1973.

Drash, P. W., Greenberg, N. E., & Money, J. Intelligence and personality in four syndromes of dwarfism. In D. B. Cheek (Ed.), *Human growth.* Philadelphia: Lea & Febiger, 1968.

Dreizen, S., Snodgrasse, R. M., Webb-Peploe, H., & Spies, T. D. The retarding effect of protracted undernutrition on the appearance of the postnatal ossification centers in the hand and wrist. *Human biology*, 1958, **19**, 365–372.

Engelmann, W. Reifungsentwicklung und Reifungsveranderungen im gefuhlsbetonten Werungsbereich unserer Jugend. *Psychologische Rundschau*, 1962, **13**, 131–140.

Garn, S. N. The evolutionary and genetic control of variability in man. *Annals of the New York Academy of Sciences*, 1966, **134**, 602–615.

Guilford, J. P. *The nature of human intelligence.* New York: McGraw-Hill, 1967.

Gutmann, D. The new mythologies and premature aging in the youth culture. *Journal of Youth and Adolescence*, 1973, **2**, 139–155.

Heath, D. H. *Growing up in college.* San Francisco: Jossey-Bass, 1968.

Horrocks, J. A. *Psychology of adolescence.* Boston: Houghton Mifflin, 1962.

Jersild, A. T. *The psychology of adolescence.* (2nd ed.) New York: Macmillan, 1963.

Keys, A. Introductory statement. *Annals of the New York Academy of Sciences*, 1966, **134**, 505–506.

Livson, N., & Bronson, W. C. Explorations of patterns of impulse control in early adolescence. *Child Development*, 1961, **32**, 75–88.

Maresh, M. M. Variations in patterns of linear growth and skeletal maturation. *Physical Therapy*, 1964, **44**, 881–890.

McCandless, B. R. *Adolescents: behavior and development.* Hinsdale, Ill.: Dryden, 1970.

Money, J. Intellect, brain, and biologic age: Introduction. In D. B. Cheek (Ed.), *Human growth.* Philadelphia: Lea & Febiger, 1968.

Mussen, P. H. (Ed.) *Carmichael's manual of child psychology.* New York: Wiley, 1970.

Muuss, R. E. Adolescent development and the secular trend. *Adolescence*, 1970, **5**, 267–284.

Nicholson, A. B., & Hanley, C. Indices of physiological maturity: Derivation and interrelationships. *Child Development*, 1953, **24**, 3–38.

Otterstadt, H. Akzeleration und Stoffplan. *Psychologische Rundschau*, 1960, **11**, 45–51.

Reynolds, E. L., & Wines, J. V. Physical changes associated with adolescence in boys. *American Journal of the Diseases of Children*, 1951, **82**, 529–547.

Schonfeld, W. A. Inadequate masculine physique as a factor in personality development of adolescent boys. *Psychosomatic Medicine*, 1950, **12**, 49–54.

Seidmann, P. *Moderne Jugend.* Zurich & Stuttgart: Rascher Verlag, 1963.

Shuttleworth, F. K. The physical and mental growth of boys and girls aged six through nineteen in relation to age of maximum growth. *Monographs of the Society for Research in Child Development*, 1939, 4(3).

Simmons, K., & Greulich, W. W. Menarcheal age and the height, weight and skeletal age of girls age 7 to 17 years. *Journal of Pediatrics*, 1943, **22**, 518–548.

Stolz, H. R., & Stolz, L. M. Adolescent problems related to somatic variation. *Yearbook of the National Society for the Study of Education*, 1944, 43, Part 1, 81–99.

Stolz, H. R., & Stolz, L. M. *Somatic development of adolescent boys.* New York: Macmillan, 1951.

Stone, L. J., & Church, J. *Childhood and adolescence.* (2nd ed.) New York: Random House, 1968.

Tanner, J. M. *Education and physical growth.* London: University of London Press, 1961.

Tanner, J. M. *Growth at adolescence.* Oxford: Blackwell, 1962.

Tanner, J. M. Growth and endocrinology of the adolescent. In L. Gardner (Ed.), *Endocrine and genetic diseases of childhood.* Philadelphia: Saunders, 1969.

Tanner, J. M. Physical growth. In P. H. Mussen (Ed.), *Carmichael's manual of child psychology.* New York: Wiley, 1970.

Thurstone, L. L. *The differential growth of mental abilities.* Chapel Hill, N.C.: University of North Carolina, Psychometric Laboratory, 1955.

Van der Werff Ten Bosch, J. J., & Enthoven, R. The tall child. In J. J. Van der Werff Ten Bosch & A. Haak (Eds.), *Somatic growth of the child.* Springfield, Ill.: Charles C Thomas, 1966.

Van Gelderen, H. H. Dwarfism and mental deficiency. In J. J. Van der Werff Ten Bosch & A. Haak (Eds.), *Somatic growth of the child*, Springfield, Ill.: Charles C Thomas, 1966.

6

The Dissonant Context and the Adolescent Self-Concept

MORRIS ROSENBERG
State University of New York at Buffalo

Although the idea of "group atmosphere" (Lippitt & White, 1947), ward atmosphere (Caudill, 1958; Stanton & Schwartz, 1954), "climate of opinion" (Bryce, 1916; Coleman, 1961b), *Zeitgeist*, and other contextual terms have had a long tradition in sociology, systematic sociological research on contexts is of relatively recent origin.[1] A respectable literature (e.g., Campbell & Alexander, 1965; Meyer, 1970; Michael, 1961, 1966; Sewell, 1966; Turner, 1964; Wilson, 1959) has by now appeared dealing with different aspects of the social context.[2]

---

[1] Most of these studies date from the explication of the contextual analysis approach in Lazarsfeld and Rosenberg (1955).

[2] There are several different types of contextual analyses, each suitable for examining somewhat different contextual effects. The most common type treats the context as simply one additional independent variable. The investigator, for example, might ask if people in metropolitan areas are more cultured or more impersonal than those in rural areas; if people in crowded areas are more neurotic than people in less crowded areas; if adolescents in predominantly middle class schools are more likely to want to go to college; etc. In other words, people located in different contexts are compared in terms of attitudes, personality, or behavior and the differences attributed to the context.

A second type of contextual analysis focuses on the context as a "condition" or "test factor" category. We know that the strength and even the sign of relationships between

This paper focuses on a relatively neglected aspect of the social context—its consonance or dissonance—and considers its possible impact on the self-concept of adolescents.

The special nature of contextual dissonance or consonance can be highlighted by comparing it with two related approaches in sociology and social psychology. The first might be called the individual characteristic approach, the second the collective characteristic approach.

Undoubtedly the dominant procedure in sociological research is the individual characteristic approach. In sociology, socially relevant characteristics of the individual—groups, statuses, or social categories—are usually treated as independent variables. Thus, a sociologist will ask such questions as: What is the relation of social class to political ideology? of rural-urban residence to mental hospitalization? of race to self-esteem? of age to alienation? In each case, some socially defined quality of the individual is assumed to influence his experience in such a way as to bear on his particular attitudes or behavior.

The collective characteristic approach, on the other hand, is aimed at understanding the bearing of some general property of the group on the thoughts, acts, or norms of its constituent members. Thus, much valuable information has been obtained by asking such questions as: What effect does immersion in a client-oriented group have on the attitudes of the individual social worker (Blau, 1960)? Are professors in large, prestigious universities more or less apprehensive than their colleagues in small, lesser-known colleges (Lazarsfeld & Thielens, 1958)? In general, these have been labeled "structural effects."

In turning to the issue of dissonance, we are primarily concerned with the *relationship* or *interaction* between the individual characteristic and the collective characteristic. Neither is primary; it is the agreement of the two that is decisive. The explanation of attitudes or behavior is thus seen to rest in the immersion of a particular individual characteristic in a group-determined field. In this view, the environment is not seen as dissonant or consonant in itself; it is only dissonant or consonant for a given individual.[3]

Despite its general neglect, contextual dissonance or consonance is a quintessentially sociological phenomenon, directly concerning the relation of the individual to his environment. This paper calls attention to the diversity of contexts to which the individual may be exposed and notes some of the

---

variables may differ under varying conditions—the so-called conditional relations. Thus, the relationship between family structure and self-esteem is found to vary with the racial composition of the secondary school (Rosenberg & Simmons, 1972); the relationship between occupational position and party vote is stronger in metropolitan than in rural areas (Ennis, 1962).

Contextual dissonance, the focus of this paper, constitutes a third type of contextual analysis.

[3] This view, originally presented in Rosenberg (1962a), differs from that of Hessler, New, Kubish, Ellison, & Taylor (1971), who believe that the collective unit itself should be treated as dissonant or consonant.

self-concept consequences of their dissonance or consonance. Three aspects of the self-concept will be considered: self-esteem, stability of the self-concept, and group identification.

SELF-ESTEEM

That the dissonance or consonance of the individual's environment bears upon his global feeling of self-worth seems evident. The person in a dissonant context is, through circumstances usually beyond his control, sociologically deviant in his environment; this situation might have negative effects on his self-esteem.

But there are different kinds of dissonant contexts: identity contexts, competence contexts, values contexts, and others. The bearing of these types of contexts on self-esteem will therefore be considered separately.

Identity Contexts

An individual's social identity consists of the groups, statuses, collectives, or social categories by which he is socially recognized and classified in the society. [4] These include such components as race, religion, sex, national origin, age, class, and occupation. Many of these categories of social identity, being immutable and outside the realm of voluntary control, represent the firmest aspects of the self-concept. But their significance for the individual will often depend on their immersion in a particular context. For example, what is the self-image impact of membership in the lower class? This impact may be very different if the lower class individual is surrounded by higher class people or by lower class people. Similarly, one must not ask simply if the individual is Mexican American, but also if he lives in a Mexican American neighborhood. We will consider the following social identity contexts: religion, race, and class.

Data. Unless otherwise noted, the data presented in this report are drawn from one of two studies: (1) a study of 5,024 high school juniors and seniors in ten New York State high schools in 1960; (2) a study of 1,988 children in grades 3 to 12 in twenty-six Baltimore City schools in 1968. (Details on these samples are presented in Rosenberg, 1965; and Rosenberg & Simmons, 1972.)

Religion. The New York State (NYS) study presented a good opportunity to examine the religious context. In the course of completing questionnaires dealing with the values, goals, and self-conceptions of youth, these high school students were asked about the religious composition of the neighborhoods in which they had lived. Knowing the adolescent's own religious background, it was possible to determine whether he was reared in a predominantly dissonant, mixed, or predominantly consonant religious environment. Table 6.1 shows that

---

[4] According to Gordon (1968, p. 118), "the individual's major role and social type categorizations are here conceptualized as his social identity." These include the individual's ascribed characteristics as well as the various roles and memberships largely under the individual's control. Kuhn and McPartland (1954) used the term "consensual categories" for the chief elements of social identity.

TABLE 6.1

Religious Dissonance and Self-Esteem, NYS

Self-esteem	Catholics		Protestants		Jews	
	In non-Catholic neighbor-hoods	In Catholic or mixed neighbor-hoods	In non-Protestant neighbor-hoods	In Protestant or mixed neighbor-hoods	In non-Jewish neighbor-hoods	In Jewish or mixed neighbor-hoods
Low	41%	29%	31%	25%	29%	18%
Medium	30	25	27	30	10	23
High	30	46	42	45	61	60
$N = 100\%$	37	458	164	241	41	80

Source: "The Dissonant Religious Context and Emotional Disturbance" by M. Rosenberg, *American Journal of Sociology*, 1962, **68**, 1–10. Copyright 1962 by the University of Chicago Press. Reprinted by permission.

*p < .05, for adjacent groups.

**p < .01, for adjacent groups.

those adolescents raised in dissonant religious environments were more likely to have low self-esteem than were those raised in mixed or consonant religious environments. For example, Catholics raised in non-Catholic neighborhoods had lower self-esteem than Catholics raised in Catholic or mixed neighborhoods; Jews raised in non-Jewish neighborhoods had lower self-esteem than Jews raised in Jewish or mixed neighborhoods; and Protestants raised in non-Protestant neighborhoods had lower self-esteem than Protestants raised in Protestant or mixed neighborhoods. The differences, while not extremely large, were nevertheless consistent.

Race. One situation of dissonance or consonance, usually not recognized as such, is racial integration or segregation. The confusion is probably due to the connotations of the terms involved. We tend to think of dissonance as bad but integration as good, of consonance as good but segregation as bad. Yet technically—and, as we shall see, psychologically—the one is an exact expression of the other.

In Baltimore, when black adolescents attending segregated and desegregated schools were compared, the results showed that the dissonant context appeared to have deleterious effects on self-esteem (Rosenberg & Simmons, 1972, p. 25). At the junior high level, black children attending white schools had lower self-esteem than blacks attending predominantly black schools, and this difference was greater at the senior high level.[5]

[5] There is no difference among elementary school children, but the number of black elementary school children in predominantly white schools was so small that no conclusions seemed warranted. And, as one might anticipate, there were almost no white children in predominantly black schools.

The small amount of other research in this area supports this finding. Powell and Fuller (1970) studied the self-esteem of 614 white and black students in grades 7 to 9 in segregated and desegregated schools in a city in the Central South. Using the Fitts Tennessee Self-Concept Scale (Total Net Positive Score), they found that black students in segregated schools had higher self-esteem than black students in integrated schools. Their results were quite strong; blacks in the consonant contexts averaged in the sixtieth percentile on self-esteem while blacks in the dissonant context were in the fortieth percentile. Bachman's nationwide study (1970) of 10th-grade boys yielded similar results. Using a ten-item self-esteem measure, Bachman also found that blacks in segregated schools had higher self-esteem scores than blacks in integrated schools. (These results are actually strengthened when family socioeconomic background is controlled and are strengthened further when intelligence is also controlled.) Finally, Coleman's study (1966), dealing with "academic self-concept," noted that "for each group as the proportion white in the school increases, the child's . . . self-concept decreases." In sum, the desegregated school may have certain advantages for the child, but self-esteem does not appear to be one of them.

Social class. When we speak of higher, middle, or lower classes, we are of course using relative terms; these terms achieve their meaning only by reference to certain anchorage points, as symbolized in the story of the unfortunate Hollywood film writer in the fifties whose peers looked down on him because he earned "only" $50,000 a year. To some extent, certainly, one *feels* rich or poor by comparing oneself to those in the same environment. What effect, then, does socioeconomic consonance or dissonance have on self-esteem?

The evidence available is sparse and at best suggestive. Nevertheless, consider the white children attending predominantly white schools in the Baltimore sample. These *pupils* have been classified according to the Hollingshead social class scale. Since Baltimore is primarily a working-class city, respondents are divided into three class groups: class 1-3 (middle), class 4 (working), and class 5 (lower). The schools these respondents attend have also been classified according to their average socioeconomic levels. These schools have been divided into the "high" (mean socioeconomic status of 1.0-3.4) and the "low" (mean socioeconomic status of 3.5-5.0).

Table 6.2 shows that middle or upper middle class children attending lower class schools had significantly lower self-esteem than middle or upper middle class children attending higher class schools; that, in the working class, no difference appears; and that lower class children in higher class schools have lower self-esteem than lower class children in lower class schools. For both upper and lower class children, then, dissonant socioeconomic environments appear hostile to self-esteem.[6]

[6] It is not possible to test this effect among black children in predominantly black schools because no black school had a mean SES level that was high (i.e., 1.0-3.4). Some black children do attend higher SES schools, but these are either racially mixed or predominantly white schools.

TABLE 6.2

Dissonant Socioeconomic Contexts and Self-Esteem Among Whites in Predominantly White Schools, Baltimore

Self-esteem	Pupil's socioeconomic level					
	Middle or upper middle class		Working class		Lower class	
	School socioeconomic level					
	High (1-3.4)	Low (3.5-5)	High (1-3.4)	Low (3.5-5)	High (1-3.4)	Low (3.5-5)
Low	25% **	59%	36%	36%	53%	40%
Medium	36	28	30	30	18	30
High	39	13	34	34	29	30
$N = 100\%$	163	46	91	184	17	80

$*p < .05$, for adjacent groups.
$**p < .01$, for adjacent groups.

In considering such aspects of social identity as religion, race, and class, we are obviously dealing with social categories evaluated as higher or lower, better or worse, in the society. While the data at hand are less than fully persuasive, they suggest that if groups are differentially evaluated in the society, then contextual dissonance will tend to have deleterious effects on the self-esteem of the lower-status group member and *may* have deleterious effects on the higher-status group member. Whether similar effects would appear with regard to social categories that are *not* socially ranked, or in environments in which the minority group members satisfy some special need or fulfill some special function, is unknown.

Competence Contexts

In addition to the groups, statuses, or social categories that constitute the individual's social identity, he is endowed with a multiplicity of traits. Insofar as these traits represent socially evaluated characteristics, their sociological relevance for self-esteem is obvious.

This is particularly likely to be true in areas of competence. Is the individual smart or dull, attractive or unattractive, fast or slow? To make a judgment, the individual requires some point of reference, and this will usually be his comparison reference group. This point can be illustrated by considering experience and abilities contexts.

Experience contexts. In "The American Soldier" studies (Stouffer et al., 1949a, b), the Research Branch considered the following contexts: green troops in green outfits; equally inexperienced replacements in divisions otherwise composed of combat veterans; and the veterans themselves in these divisions. Among numerous questions put to these soldiers was the individual's confidence in his ability to take charge of a group in combat. As one might expect, the veterans were more likely than the green troops to express confidence in their ability to take charge of a group of men. The interesting comparison, however, was between the green troops in green outfits and the green troops in veteran outfits. It turns out that the inexperienced soldier in a dissonant context—that is, a veteran outfit—was less confident that he could take charge of a group of men than was the green soldier in a green outfit. In other words, relative to the veterans, the replacements were aware of their inexperience and felt less capable of leadership than did equally inexperienced soldiers in inexperienced outfits; the competence was the same, but the contexts were different.

Abilities context. It seems obvious that the individual's assessment of his abilities and perhaps of his general worth will depend in part on the abilities of those around him. As Festinger (1954) noted: "There exists, in the human organism, a drive to evaluate his opinions and his abilities. . . . To the extent that objective, non-social means are not available, people evaluate their opinions and abilities by comparison respectively with the opinions and abilities of others." For young people, at least, these "others" are likely to be those in their immediate environments. For example, in making career decisions, Davis (1966) shows that college men are more strongly affected by their grade-point averages than by the general intellectual caliber of the student bodies of their schools. Graduate and professional schools, of course, do take account of the general level of the school as well as the average performance of the student. Students, on the other hand, apparently compare themselves with those within their schools and not with those in other schools with whom they are also competing.

It is difficult to examine the importance of the abilities context in our Baltimore data because so few students have A averages and because the bulk of the students—those with B or C averages—are little different from the school average. We are thus obliged to confine our attention to the poor students—those with borderline or failing averages (D or F); furthermore, because of insufficient white cases, we must confine our analysis to blacks in predominantly black schools. Is the self-esteem of such pupils affected by whether the average marks in their school are high or low? Table 6.3 suggests that it is. Borderline or failing pupils attending schools in which the average marks are relatively high have lower self-esteem than do similar students in schools in which the average level of work is closer to their own.

Since our data enable us to examine the abilities context for only one small subgroup of the sample, they are little better than suggestive. The general principle, however, does appear to be a matter of common observation. For example, well-functioning retardates in retardate classes are reported to suffer disturbance when transferred to classes of normal children. Indeed, even high achievers may suffer rude blows to their self-esteem when finding themselves in

TABLE 6.3

Self-Esteem of Poorly Performing Black Pupils
in Predominantly Black Schools with
Varying Average Marks, Baltimore

Self-esteem	Black D or F pupils attending black schools in which average marks are relatively . . .		
	High	Medium	Low
Low	33%	28%	27%
Medium	54	39	25
High	13	33	48
$N = 100\%$	24	36	48

Note: $\chi^2 = 9.88, df = 4, p < .05.$

the company of still higher achievers. This is an experience frequently reported by students who, having been outstanding high school seniors, suddenly find themselves to be mediocre as freshmen at a highly select college.

It would thus appear that, especially for the conspicuously inferior per-former, the dissonant abilities context is likely to be damaging to self-esteem. This is probably one of the reasons why performance, as measured by some general yardstick, often correlates only moderately with global self-esteem; the psychological impact of a given performance level depends on the general performance or achievement level in the immediate environment.

The Values Context

Thus far we have treated the notion of dissonance or consonance as a reflection of the relationship between a characteristic of the individual and the prevalence of that characteristic in his immediate environment. When we turn to the values context, the concept of dissonance is broadened to include not only the literal identity of the individual and collective characteristics but what might also be called their "congeniality." Here consonance or dissonance would be reflected in the relationship between a particular characteristic of an individual and the value attached to that characteristic in his environment.

An interesting example appears in Coleman's study (1961a) of adolescents. Using ten high schools, Coleman first classified the schools into those in which athletic ability was highly valued and those in which it was not. Having sociometric data for the school population, he was also able to select out the boys chosen as the best athletes in their schools. He considered a crude indicator of negative self-evaluation to be the proportion of students who said they would "want to be somewhat different." Considering only the boys named as best athletes, Coleman found that, in the schools in which athletic achievement was highly valued, only 9 percent of the boys wanted to be somewhat different; in the schools in which athletic achievement was less highly valued, however, 15 percent wanted to be somewhat different. It is thus not only the actual achievement of the individual—the boys in both groups were named as best athletes—but also the value attached to that particular ability in the context that influenced the feeling of self-satisfaction or self-dissatisfaction.

What is true of the value attached to traits is equally true of the value attached to statuses. Consider family structure. The most desirable family structure in American society is the intact nuclear family, the least desirable is the unmarried or abandoned mother and child. The normal expectation would be that children from the latter family structure would have lower self-esteem. Often overlooked, however, is the valuation or disvaluation of given statuses in different contexts.

In the Baltimore study, 30 percent of the black children came from separated or never-married families, compared to only 6 percent of the whites. We do not know what proportion of these families represent illegitimacy, what proportion abandonment, and what proportion legal separation. However, in light of the fact that 31 percent of nonwhite children were illegitimate in 1968—and this percentage was higher in the northern urban ghettos (Farley & Hermalin, 1971, p. 8)—it seems reasonable to infer that a very substantial proportion of these black children are illegitimate or abandoned by a legal father. The probable consequences for the self-esteem of these children appear obvious.

But these consequences, it turns out, depend on the context in which this family structure is embedded. In this case it is the racial context. Comparing black children from separated or never-married families with black children from other family structures, we find that, in predominantly black schools, there is no difference in self-esteem levels. But if black children from separated or never-married families attending mixed or predominantly white schools are compared with other black children in these racially dissonant schools, then they are much more likely to have low self-esteem. Specifically, 42 percent of them have low self-esteem compared with only 19 percent of the other black children in the mixed or white schools (Table 6.4). Thus the impact of family structure on the black adolescent's self-esteem depends on whether he is in a black or white school context. A socially undesirable family background may do little damage to self-esteem except in environments in which that background is reprehended. It may further be noted that white children from separated or never-married families, almost all of whom attend white schools, also have significantly lower self-esteem than do white children from intact families.

Various contexts then—identity contexts, competence contexts, values contexts—may all bear on the child's and adolescent's global self-esteem. From a psychological viewpoint, this finding is far from trivial, for self-esteem is surely one of the fundamental human attitudes; indeed, McDougall (1932) went so far

TABLE 6.4

Self-Esteem and Family Structure of Black Children Within Different
Racial Contexts, Baltimore

Self-esteem	Predominantly black schools		Mixed or predominantly white schools	
	Family structure			
	Separated or never-married	Other	Separated or never-married	Other
Low	19%	18%	42%**	19%
Medium	32	36	33	37
High	49	46	25	44
N = 100%	290	601	36	162

Source: "Black and White Self-Esteem" by M. Rosenberg and R. G. Simmons, *Rose Monograph*, 1971, 78. Copyright 1971 by the American Sociological Association. Reprinted by permission.

  *$p < .05$, for adjacent groups.
  **$p < .01$, for adjacent groups.

as to characterize it as the "master sentiment." But other aspects of the self-concept are also important. For example, Schwartz and Stryker (1970) assert that "persons seek to create and maintain stable coherent identities [and that] persons prefer to evaluate their identities positively." In other words, people want not only positive self-attitudes but stable ones as well. How contextual dissonance or consonance bears on the stability of the self-concept will be considered next.

STABILITY OF THE SELF-CONCEPT

The individual's strong motivation to maintain stable attitudes is evidenced by his strong resistance to changing these attitudes. Gordon Allport (1954) offered a persuasive explanation for this motive:

> Without guiding attitudes the individual is confused and baffled. Some kind of preparation is essential before he can make a satisfactory observation, pass suitable judgment, or make any but the most primitive reflex type of response. Attitudes determine for each individual what he will see and hear, what he will think and what he will do. To borrow a phrase from William James, they "engender meaning upon the world"; they are our methods for finding our way about in an ambiguous universe (p. 44).

The general need to maintain stable attitudes is amplified enormously when we turn to self-attitudes. Without some picture of what he is like—his traits, statuses, interests—the individual is virtually immobilized. Insofar as he is an actor in any situation, he must operate on at least some implicit assumption of what kind of person he is and how others see him.

Many writers, using different terminology, have expressed essentially the same view. It is a major aspect of what Erikson (1959) terms "identity diffusion" or "identity confusion" (although Erikson includes not only the current self-picture but also the individual's commitment to a future self). Perhaps the importance of stability and clarity has been expressed most vividly by Lecky (1945): "The self is the basic axiom of [the individual's] life theory."

It is thus not surprising to find that among adolescents the stability of the self-concept is strongly related to certain psychophysiological indicators of anxiety (Rosenberg, 1965, p. 143). Unfortunately, we are aware of no other research dealing with the social conditions likely to generate instability. Here we shall deal with one of these conditions, namely, the dissonant context.

Race

The Baltimore study utilized a seven-item Guttman scale of "stability of self-concept" with a Reproducibility Coefficient of 89 percent and a Scalability Coefficient of 65 percent.[7] Since self-esteem is related to both stability of self and contextual dissonance, Table 6.5 presents the relationship of contextual dissonance to stability, controlling on self-esteem by test factor standardization (Rosenberg, 1962b). At each school level, black children in dissonant racial contexts are conspicuously more likely to have unstable self-concepts than are black children in consonant contexts. The latter are not more likely to show high stability but to show medium stability.

Religion

The New York State study lacked sufficient information on race, but data were available on the religious contexts of the neighborhoods in which the adolescents were raised (Table 6.6). Once again, it is necessary to present the data controlling on self-esteem. While the data do not show any association between contextual dissonance and instability[8] of self-concept among Jews (actually, there is an association, but it is entirely due to self-esteem), there is some

---

[7] The items in this scale were: 1. How sure are you that you know what kind of person you really are? 2. How often do you feel mixed up about yourself, about what you are really like? 3. Do you feel like this: "I know just what I'm like. I'm really sure about it." 4. A kid told me: "Some days I like the way I am. Some days I do not like the way I am." Do your feelings *change* like this? 5. A kid told me: "Some days I am happy with the kind of person I am, other days I am not happy with the kind of person I am." Do your feelings *change* like this? 6. Do you know for sure how nice a person you are, or do your ideas about how nice you are change a lot? 7. A kid told me: "Some days I think I am one kind of a person, other days a different kind of person." Do your feelings *change* like this? These items, of course, were scattered throughout the interview.

[8] A five-item Guttman scale of stability of self-concept was employed. The scale items appear in Rosenberg (1965, Appendix D-2, pp. 308–309).

TABLE 6.5

Stability of Self-Concept of Black Children Attending Racially Desegregated
or Segregated Schools, by School Level (Self-Esteem
Standardized), Baltimore

	Elementary		Junior high		Senior high	
	School context is predominantly . . .					
	Black	White	Black	White	Black	White
Unstable	23% *	43%	26% *	43%	29% *	43%
Medium	57	36	54	33	53	40
Stable	20	21	20	24	18	17
$N = 100\%$	603	25	145	43	181	65

*$p < .05$, for adjacent groups.
**$p < .01$, for adjacent groups.

association between these variables among Protestants, and a definite association
among Catholics, even with self-esteem controlled. Religious dissonance thus
appears to exercise some effect on self-concept stability independent of
self-esteem.

Our data do not permit us to pin down precisely what it is about the
dissonant context that is responsible for generating self-image instability, but the

TABLE 6.6

Religious Context and Stability of Self-Concept
(Self-Esteem Standardized), NYS

	Catholics		Protestants		Jews	
	In non-Catholic neighbor-hoods	In Catholic or mixed neighbor-hoods	In non-Protestant neighbor-hoods	In Protestant or mixed neighbor-hoods	In non-Jewish neighbor-hoods	In Jewish or mixed neighbor-hoods
Stable	29%	41%	37%	43%	47%	49%
Intermediate	30	30	30	29	26	26
Unstable	46	29	34	28	27	25
$N = 100\%$	34	420	161	227	40	76

*$p < .05$, for adjacent groups.
**$p < .01$, for adjacent groups.

point is of sufficient interest to warrant speculation. In part it may be due to the fact that group identification becomes more equivocal for the child in the dissonant context. We would, however, suggest an additional possibility: that the dissonant context *may fail to provide interpersonal confirmation for the individual's self-hypothesis.*

Attitudes, including self-attitudes, tend to have a quality of inertia and are likely to persist indefinitely unless confronted by some stimulus challenging them. At the same time, many self-attitudes (except in certain schizophrenics) require confirmation. Among the various types of evidence confirming or disconfirming a self-hypothesis, probably the most important is interpersonal; the individual requires confirmation of his self-hypothesis in the action of others toward him.[9] For example, if a person considers himself likable, then others must act as if they like him; if he sees himself as intelligent, others must show some respect for his intelligence; and so on. In general, others must behave toward the individual in a fashion consistent with his picture of what he is like if he is to maintain a stable self-concept.

Thus, with regard to the racial context, the greater self-image instability of black children in dissonant settings may be due to the fact that the white children and teachers in these settings do not provide sufficient confirmation for the black child's self-concept. While he may see himself as physically attractive, mild in disposition, and honest, at least some proportion of the prejudiced white children may not appreciate his good looks and may act as though he is threatening, aggressive, or dishonest. Such behavior would challenge the black child's picture of himself. But any kind of prejudice—prejudgment—*including the excessively positive*, may have this effect. The "liberal" white teacher who publicly asserts how smart and cute and otherwise wonderful the black child is, whether or not the child actually is like this at all, may generate equal uncertainty and insecurity in the child and produce an unstable self-concept.

All this, of course, is speculative, and outstrips our data. The results do suggest, however, that dissonant racial and religious contexts are associated with somewhat greater instability of the self-concept. Further data would be needed to determine whether these speculations are sound.

GROUP IDENTIFICATION

The various elements of social identity considered earlier constitute bases of social definition and of self-definition. Although the individual is virtually obliged to define himself in terms of these socially recognized categories, this

---

[9] Needless to say, the individual's interpretation of the evidence is not necessarily objective or accurate. Discussions of selective interpretation appear in Rosenberg (1967, 1973).

says nothing about whether he identifies or disidentifies with them. Much of the discussion of group pride, group self-hatred (Lewin, 1948; Kardiner & Ovesey, 1951), or "identity conflict" (Proshansky & Newton, 1968) essentially deals with this issue. Speaking of race, Silberman (1964, pp. 112–114) describes such disidentification as "the flight from blackness, the hatred of self, the yearning to be white." Other discussions of "self-hatred among Jews" (Lewin, 1948) or "black self-hatred" (Kardiner & Ovesey, 1951) are also concerned with whether the individual identifies with the categories to which he is socially recognized as belonging and that constitute elements of his self-concept.

What effect does the dissonant context have on such group identification? The answer is far from self-evident. On the one hand, one might expect the minority group member in a given context to become more aware of his group membership by contrast with the dominant majority and to identify more strongly with his group (Durkheim, 1951). On the other hand, it might equally be contended that the minority group member, eager to achieve acceptance by the higher-status majority group, will be ashamed of his group membership and will disidentify with it (Lewin, 1948).

The Baltimore study contained six items[10] that, in one way or another, appeared to reflect group identification. These items were combined to form a score of racial identification, and the pupils in consonant or dissonant racial contexts were compared.

The results (Table 6.7) show that in junior high schools the context appears to have no effect on racial identification, but in the elementary and senior high schools contextual dissonance is associated with somewhat weaker identification.[11] It should be stressed that only in the rarest of instances do we find the kind of strong racial disidentification implied by Kardiner, Erikson, Lewin, and others; there is little evidence of real black self-hatred. The effect of the dissonant context, rather, appears to be to make racial identification slightly more equivocal or uncertain than would otherwise be the case, but not to produce strong group rejection or shame of oneself as a black.

Actually, the data in Table 6.7 may conceal as much as they reveal. It is possible that integration may strengthen racial identification among some and weaken it among others, producing a large total effect but little net effect. For

[10] Although some of the items are more questionable than others, all generally appear to reflect the dimension under consideration. The items, scattered in different sections of the questionnaire, are as follows: 1. If you could be anything in the world when you grow up, would you want to be Negro, white, or something else? 2. If you could be born again, would you like to be born of a different race, not Negro or colored? 3. Do you think you would be happier if you were not Negro? 4. If someone said something bad about the NEGRO or COLORED RACE, would you feel almost as if they had said something bad about you? 5. Is being Negro or colored very important to you, pretty important, or not important to you? 6. Do you feel very proud of being Negro, pretty proud, not very proud, or not at all proud of being Negro?

[11] At the elementary school level, the number of black children in integrated schools is so small that these data are no more than suggestive.

TABLE 6.7

Racial Identification of Black Children in Desegregated or Segregated
Schools, by School Level, Baltimore

Racial identification	Elementary		Junior high		Senior high	
	School context is predominantly ...					
	Black	White	Black	White	Black	White
Strong	29% **	7%	26%	23%	35% **	12%
Medium	13	34	13	16	11	15
Weak	58	59	61	61	54	73
$N = 100\%$	696	29	156	51	194	68

*$p < .05$, for adjacent groups.
**$p < .01$, for adjacent groups.

example, Armor (1972) reports that integration is associated with increased black militancy, including increased separatist ideology, ideological solidarity, and behavior withdrawal.[12] At the same time, other data (Rosenberg & Simmons, 1972) report more interracial friendships in these settings, and Crain and Weissman (1972) show that black adults who had attended racially integrated schools were more likely to want to live in racially integrated neighborhoods and to have more favorable attitudes toward whites.

In addition, it is necessary to take account of the fact that in the dissonant context the individual is more likely to be exposed to prejudice. Does exposure to prejudice enhance or weaken identification? Yinger (1961) notes that where prejudice is strong, there are "pressures to escape the group, tendencies toward self-hatred, and intragroup conflict." At the same time, prejudice may drive people together, enhancing their group identification and pride (Lewin, 1948; Durkheim, 1951). These various counteracting influences may all contribute in some complex fashion to the observed association between contextual dissonance and group identification.

Many questions remain. Militancy and identification are probably related but certainly are not identical; while militants no doubt identify with their groups, one can also identify without being militant. Furthermore, we have no idea why dissonance is associated with enhanced disidentification in the elementary and senior high school but not in junior high school. Hence, while our data are suggestive, additional research is needed if we are to obtain a satisfactory understanding of the impact of dissonance on identification.

[12] Pettigrew, Useem, Normand, and Smith (1973) have demonstrated that in view of the flaws of the study these results should not be taken very seriously.

SUMMARY AND DISCUSSION

That the social environment is an important factor in personality development and social behavior is both a matter of immediate experience and an established dictum of social psychology. Yet the same social environment will affect different people differently. One reason is that this environment may be consonant for some, dissonant for others.

This paper has focused on the possible impact of contextual dissonance on three aspects of the self-concept: self-esteem, stability of the self-concept, and group identification. Different types of contextual dissonance have been distinguished: social identity contexts—religion, race, and social class; competence contexts, such as experience or ability; and values contexts, relating the trait or status of the individual to the valuation or disvaluation of that trait or status in his environment. Each of these may have an effect on self-esteem. Stability of the self-concept and group identification may also be affected by social identity contexts, according to our data.

The enhancement and protection of the self are widely recognized as two of the fundamental motivations of the individual (Lecky, 1945; Murphy, 1947; Schwartz & Stryker, 1970); that is why our attention in this paper has centered on self-esteem and stability of the self-concept. Different contexts have different effects on subjects who are otherwise the same. On the whole, however, the data suggest that contextual dissonance tends to have a deleterious effect on the individual's self-concept if that trait or status is disvalued in the broader society or in the immediate group. Furthermore, in some cases at least, the higher status group member may also experience an assault on self-esteem in the dissonant context, although this may not be universally true. Occupying a minority status in an environment in which that status is especially functional for group needs or is otherwise valued might be conducive to high self-esteem.

Aside from its contribution to understanding the social determination of the self-concept, the perspective of contextual dissonance sheds light on a number of issues that, in the absence of this perspective, would be puzzling or contradictory.

For one thing, the perspective of contextual dissonance casts new light on the traditional concept of minority groups. What is generally overlooked in the massive literature in this field is that "minority group" is a *contextual* concept, and its consequences cannot be understood outside that framework. For example, about one out of nine Americans is black, clearly indicating that blacks are a minority relative to the majority whites. Jews represent perhaps 3 percent of the population and are thus a clear minority relative to Christians. When inferences about the effects of minority status are made, however, the total society is usually taken as the context. *The point is that this perspective does not represent the actual experience of the individual.* No individual lives in the total society; he spends his life in specified contexts. Thus, if 95 percent of the residents of a neighborhood or pupils of a school are black and 5 percent white, are blacks the minority group? As a matter of fact, in a school that is 90 percent Jewish and 10 percent Protestant, who is more likely to show prejudice toward whom? The dissonant context thus refers to minority group membership within a specified contextual unit; the same group may be alternately a minority and a majority group.

Contextual dissonance analysis has been particularly valuable in understanding the relationship between social structure and the self-concept, for it helps to account for a number of findings on race and self-esteem that in the absence of this perspective appear to be anomalous. Consider some of these:

1. In 1954 the Supreme Court ruled that school segregation was inherently demeaning, branding the black child by virtue of his race as inferior. This ruling was widely interpreted as signifying that black children in segregated schools would have lower self-esteem. While the evidence is not entirely firm, what evidence there is points to the opposite conclusion. How to explain?

2. If social experience bears on the development of the self-concept, as Mead (1934) and Sullivan (1953) teach us, then certain conditions of living would be expected to reduce feelings of self-worth: low racial status, low socioeconomic status, membership in a stigmatized family structure, poor school marks. In each of these respects, black children and adolescents fare much more poorly than whites. Yet blacks do not have lower self-esteem. How to explain?

3. Given the theory of reflected appraisals (Mead, 1934; Cooley, 1912), the individual's level of self-acceptance should depend in part on the social prestige or disesteem in which his group or social category is held. People from lower-status nationality groups, religious groups, racial groups, or social classes should have lower self-esteem than others. Although the evidence is mixed and uncertain, to date we believe it points to the conclusion that among children these effects are either weak or absent. Such a result runs squarely counter to fundamental social psychological theory. How to explain?

These are only a few of the anomalies that appear in the literature. Yet if one views these findings from the perspective of contextual dissonance, many are no longer puzzling. One reason black children in desegregated schools appear to have lower self-esteem, contrary to expectations, is that the desegregated school is a dissonant context. One reason black children, despite their greater poverty, membership in stigmatized families, and poorer school performance, do not have lower self-esteem than whites is that their comparison reference groups are chiefly in consonant contexts; comparing themselves with others of equal poverty, similar family structure, and equivalent school performance, their average self-esteem is not damaged. One reason that, among children, socioeconomic status or racial, religious, or nationality prestige is so weakly related to self-esteem is that the structure of society minimizes the amount of social identity dissonance that actually exists; it tends to segregate, or at least separate, groups. There is no way to say precisely how much separation actually exists, but there is little question that it is massive. Economic separation is well nigh universal. People in different social classes tend to live in different neighborhoods, join different clubs, eat at different restaurants, etc., and their children attend different schools. Racial segregation is perhaps equally widespread (U.S. Department of Labor, 1971, pp. 14-15) and nowhere is this more evident than in the schools. The physical separation of Mexican Americans, Puerto Ricans, Jews, and other ethnic and religious groups varies from extreme to moderate. Our society is so structured that, with reference to some of the major axes of social identity, there is far less dissonance than one might anticipate.

Since contextual dissonance research is in its infancy, the generalizations enunciated in this paper will not necessarily apply to *all* conditions that can appropriately be characterized as dissonance or consonance. These conditions may depend on general attitudes toward the group (if prejudice against a group declines, the impact of dissonance on self-concept may be reduced); on the social desirability or functional necessity of a group member (the effects of being a minority female in a majority male college are not likely to be negative, nor are the effects of being bright in a dull group, expert in an amateur group, etc.); on the salience of the trait or social category (regional dissonance may be less salient and less important than educational dissonance); and so on. The conditions under which contextual dissonance will have noxious self-concept effects still remain to be specified.

Although the focus of this paper has been on the self-concept, contextual dissonance obviously may have many other effects. Advocates or opponents of group separation often leave the impression that the effects of the dissonant context will have the same direction of desirability. There is a tendency for people to think that all good things go together. Thus, many advocates of desegregation have argued that it is not only morally just, but that it is also conducive to mental health (raises self-esteem), improves black school performance, increases intergroup friendship and harmony, eliminates identity diffusion, and so forth. What is often overlooked is that the same influence—the dissonant context—may have some effects that are positive and others that are negative. As we read the current data, the dissonant racial context appears to have somewhat negative effects on self-esteem, somewhat positive effects on learning (Pettigrew et al., 1973); it results in increased friendship between the races but also more conflict; it appears to be associated with better social adjustment and fewer social problems later in life (Crain & Weissman, 1972); and so on. The point is that the effects of contextual dissonance are diverse, some desirable, others not. What is moral is not necessarily mentally healthy, and what is effective is not necessarily associated with either of the others. Future research must spell out and document these diverse effects for various groups in various contexts.

Contextual dissonance is an essentially sociological concept. Greater attention to this neglected area should provide a deeper understanding of how social experience, governed by broader social forces, affects various aspects of the individual's self-concept, as well as cast light on many other aspects of human personality and behavior.

REFERENCES

Allport, G. W. The historical background of modern social psychology. In G. Lindzey (Ed.), *Handbook of social psychology*. Vol. 1. Cambridge, Mass.: Addison-Wesley, 1954.

Armor, D. J. The evidence on busing. *The Public Interest*, 1972, 28, 90–126.

Bachman, J. G. *The impact of family background and intelligence on tenth-grade boys. Vol. 2. Youth in transition*. Ann Arbor, Mich.: Survey Research Center, Institute for Social Research, 1970.

Blau, P. M. Structural effects. *American Sociological Review*, 1960, 25, 178–193.

Bryce, J. *The American commonwealth*. New York: Macmillan, 1916.

Campbell, E. Q., & Alexander, N. C. Structural effects and interpersonal relationships. *American Journal of Sociology*, 1965, 71, 284–289.

Caudill, W. *The psychiatric hospital as a small society*. Cambridge, Mass.: Harvard University Press, 1958.

Coleman, J. S. *The adolescent society: The social life of the teenager and its impact on education*. New York: Free Press, Macmillan, 1961. (a)

Coleman, J. S. Comment on three "climate of opinion" studies. *Public Opinion Quarterly*, 1961, 25(4), 607–610. (b)

Coleman, J. S. *Equality of educational opportunity*. Washington, D.C.: Office of Education, U.S. Department of Health, Education and Welfare, 1966.

Cooley, C. H. *Human nature and the social order*. New York: Scribner's, 1912.

Crain, R. L., & Weissman, C. S. *Discrimination, personality, and achievement*. New York: Seminar Press, 1972.

Davis, J. A. The campus as a frog pond. *American Journal of Sociology*, 1966, 72, 17–31.

Durkheim, E. *Suicide*. Glencoe, Ill.: Free Press, 1951.

Ennis, P. H. The contextual dimension in voting. In W. McPhee & W. A. Glaser (Eds.), *Public opinion and congressional elections*. New York: Free Press, 1962.

Erikson, E. H. The problem of ego identity. *Psychological Issues: Identity and the Life Cycle*, 1959, 1(1), 50–100.

Farley, R., & Hermalin, A. I. Family stability: A comparison of trends between blacks and whites. *American Sociological Review*, 1971, 36, 1–17.

Festinger, L. A theory of social comparison processes. *Human Relations*, 1954, 7, 117–140.

Gordon, C. Self-conceptions: Configurations of content. In C. Gordon & K. Gergen (Eds.), *The self in social interaction*. New York: Wiley, 1968.

Hessler, R. M., New, P. K., Kubish, P., Ellison, D. L., & Taylor, F. H. Demographic context, social interaction, and perceived health status: Excedrin headache #1. *Journal of Health and Social Behavior*, 1971, 12, 191–199.

Kardiner, A., & Ovesey, L. *The mark of oppression*. New York: Norton, 1951.

Kuhn, M. H., & McPartland, T. An empirical investigation of self-attitudes. *American Sociological Review*, 1954, 19, 68–76.

Lazarsfeld, P. F., & Rosenberg, M. (Eds.) *The language of social research*. Glencoe, Ill.: Free Press, 1955.

Lazarsfeld, P. F., & Thielens, W. *The academic mind*. New York: Free Press, Macmillan, 1958.

Lecky, P. Self-consistency: A theory of personality. New York: Island Press, 1945.

Lewin, K. *Resolving social conflicts*. New York: Harper, 1948.

Lippitt, R., & White, R. K. An experimental study of leadership and group life. In T. M. Newcomb & E. L. Hartley (Eds.), *Readings in social psychology*. New York: Holt, Rinehart, 1947.

McDougall, W. *The energies of men*. London: Methuen, 1932.

Mead, G. H. *Mind, self and society*. Chicago: University of Chicago Press, 1934.

Meyer, J. W. High school effects on college intentions. *American Journal of Sociology*, 1970, **76**, 59–70.

Michael, J. A. High school climates and plans for entering college. *Public Opinion Quarterly*, 1961, **25**, 585–595.

Michael, J. A. On neighborhood context and college plans (II). *American Sociological Review*, 1966, **31**, 702–706.

Murphy, G. *Personality*. New York: Harper, 1947.

Pettigrew, T. F., Useem, E. L., Normand, C., & Smith, M. S. Busing: A review of "the evidence." *The Public Interest*, 1973, **30**, 88–118.

Powell, G. J., & Fuller, M. School desegregation and self-concept. Paper presented at 47th Annual Meeting of the American Orthopsychiatric Association in San Francisco, California, March 23–26, 1970.

Proshansky, H., & Newton, P. The nature and meaning of Negro self-identity. In M. Deutsch, I. Katz, & A. R. Jensen (Eds.), *Social class, race, and psychological development*. New York: Holt, Rinehart and Winston, 1968.

Rosenberg, M. The dissonant religious context and emotional disturbance. *American Journal of Sociology*, 1962, **68**, 1–10. (a)

Rosenberg, M. Test factor standardization as a method of interpretation. *Social Forces*, 1962, **41**, 53–61. (b)

Rosenberg, M. *Society and the adolescent self-image*. Princeton: Princeton University Press, 1965.

Rosenberg, M. Psychological selectivity in self-esteem formation. In C. Sherif & M. Sherif (Eds.), *Attitudes, ego-involvement and change*. New York: Wiley, 1967.

Rosenberg, M. Which significant others? *American Behavioral Scientist*, 1973, **16**, 829–860.

Rosenberg, M., & Simmons, R. G. Black and white self-esteem: The urban school child. ASA Rose Monograph Series Publication, Washington, D.C.: American Sociological Association, 1972.

Schwartz, M., & Stryker, S. Deviance, selves and others. ASA Rose Monograph Series Publication, Washington, D.C.: American Sociological Association, 1970.

Sewell, W. H., & Armer, M. Neighborhood context and college plans. *American Sociological Review*, 1966, **31**, 159–168.

Silberman, C. E. *Crisis in black and white*. New York: Knopf, 1964.

Stanton, A. H., & Schwartz, M. S. *The mental hospital*. New York: Basic Books, 1954.

Stouffer, S. A., Lumsdaine, A. A., Lumsdaine, M. H., Williams, R. M., Smith, M. B., Janis, I. L., Star, S. A., & Cottrell, L. S. *The American soldier: Combat and its aftermath*. Princeton: Princeton University Press, 1949.

Stouffer, S. A., Suchman, E. A., DeVinney, L. C., Star, S. A., & Williams, R. M. *The American soldier: Adjustment during army life*. Princeton: Princeton University Press, 1949.

Sullivan, H. S. *The interpersonal theory of psychiatry*. New York: Norton, 1953.

Turner, R. H. *The social context of ambition*. San Francisco: Chandler, 1964.

U.S. Department of Labor. Black Americans, a chartbook. Bulletin 1699. Washington, D.C.: U.S. Government Printing Office, 1971.

Wilson, A. B. Residential segregation of social classes and aspirations of high school boys. *American Sociological Review*, 1959, **24**, 836–845.

Yinger, J. M. Social forces involved in group identification or withdrawal. *Daedalus*, 1961, **48**, 247–262.

7

Early Socialization and Adolescent Competence

DIANA BAUMRIND
University of California, Berkeley

INTRODUCTION

Psychosocial Adolescence

Competence in adolescence may be achieved by circumventing the adolescent crisis or by emerging from that crisis with a viable life style and an individuated thesis regarded by the individual as worthy of personal commitment. The boundaries of adolescence can be defined conveniently as the onset and termination of accelerated physical change. The concept of psychosocial adolescence implies, in addition, identity formation as the outcome of adolescent crisis. Identity formation according to Erikson (1959) is the outcome of adolescent experimentation with different life styles, resolution of bisexual conflicts, and emancipation from childhood dependency, eventuating in crucial decisions concerning school, love, and work. Psychosocial adolescence is a luxury afforded the

The program of research discussed in this paper was supported by the National Institute of Child Health and Human Development under Research Grant HD-02228 with supplementary support from the Grant Foundation, Inc. I am indebted to Glen Elder (1968) and Robert Grinder (1973) for their excellent reviews of the literature concerned with family antecedents of adolescent behavior and identity formation.

highly civilized and the affluent, since crises of survival preclude crises of meaning. When the onset of accelerated physical change also signals entry into the world of adult responsibilities, the "storm and stress" of the adolescent crisis is largely circumvented. Adolescence in the psychosocial sense was not recognized as a separate developmental stage until the advent of the twentieth century and the monumental classic on the subject by G. Stanley Hall (1904).

The adolescent, as contrasted with the postpubertal youth, even today does not exist as a reality in most of the world. In Mexico, boys frequently share responsibility for family support by age 13, and in Thailand or on the Jordanian desert, adult duties may be assumed even earlier. In Indochina, teen-age boys fight and die alongside their fathers. In societies characterized by monolithic ideology, adolescents may willingly accept the opportunity to participate meaningfully in a culture with shared values, and thus with little internal stress achieve a socially defined identity. During periods of national crisis a similar renunciation of personal identity occurs, compensated for by a shared sense of fellowship and community. Psychosocial adolescence, then, is not a universal experience even among affluent members of postmodern society. Personal autonomy and individuation are not universally accepted defining characteristics of the mature person, a fact American behavioral scientists are prone to overlook. Particularly today, species survival may require fusion of agentic and communal elements rather than the overemphasis on agentic values characteristic of Western cultures (Bakan, 1966).

The adolescent, who has negotiated the transition between concrete and formal operational thought can now distinguish between the real and the possible. He is in limbo between the literal, safe reality of childhood and the intransigent, indeterminate reality of adult commitment. Liberated from the literal reality to which he was confined as a child but not yet constrained by the realities of adult commitment to work and love relations, the adolescent is omnipotent in imagination yet relatively impotent in action. As Kramer (1972, p. 31) points out, the social matrix for the adolescent is "only a hypothetical matrix from which he is withheld and from which he withholds himself in non-commitment." But "morality is the quality of *real* encounters." While the adult must pursue "his moral structuring of situations in a concrete behavior arena," the adolescent may engage in the "busy work of hypothecating first principles and performing mental operations upon them." The adolescent newly awakened to the imperfection and hypocrisy of the adult world rejects and criticizes this world with freedom born of nonengagement and noncommitment.

The adolescent is literally "taken over" by inner acceleration in development, empowered further by sexual imagery. He experiences, even without drugs, rapid alterations of consciousness and mood which he cannot monitor. As the trustees of society lose control over the social structure in a period of rapid social change, so does the individual undergoing accelerated inner change lose control over imagery and action. Adolescents may transfer control to demagogues, gurus, and drugs in an effort to relieve inner pressure. Easy access to drugs may pacify many adolescents who will then avoid either entering the adult world or undertaking the construction of a viable personal identity.

The struggle for control between the generations becomes intensified at adolescence. Power relations within the family shift sharply. Adolescents may reject the legitimacy of parental authority and parents as models, going so far as to assume a negative identity (Erikson, 1959, p. 174), "i.e., an identity perversely based on all those identifications and roles which, as critical stages of development, had been presented to the individual as most undesirable or dangerous." Parents then may refuse to support an adolescent whose life style threatens theirs. The implicit contract between parent and child becomes inoperative and a common ground for negotiating a new one must now be found.

In late adolescence, if not earlier, the young person makes a preliminary attempt to define his essence, a process of negotiation between what a person is and what he could be, which should continue through life. Affluent society grants the adolescent a "psychosocial moratorium" (Erikson, 1968), so that he may have time with security to discover the unique niche in society through which he can best contribute. However, the psychosocial moratorium, rather than providing the bridge to adult commitment, may, in a society which has lost its thrust, lead instead to prolonged wallowing in nihilism and escapism.

Socialization Processes and Their General Effects

Socialization is the process by which a young person, through education, training, and imitation, acquires his culture as well as the habits and values congruent with adaptation to that culture. The processes by which one person may influence the development of another include at least five mechanisms. The first three, identified by the major theories of learning as reinforcement, identification, and cognitive insight, need no further review. The last two, less frequently mentioned, acknowledge that the family is a complex system and that the effects of the transactions which occur are often incidental to those which were intended. Adolescent identity in particular may be affected by these two mechanisms—reciprocal role assumption and psychological reactance. By *reciprocal role assumption* is meant the effects which prior role assumptions by other family members have on the roles the individual may assume. For example, if both parents are exceptionally competent managers, the children may not develop managerial skills since, while readily available for modeling, these skills are not needed within the family setting. Similarly, if the mother assumes a childlike dependent role, her eldest daughter may fill the void by assuming the role of mother. *Psychological reactance*, a term coined by Brehm (1972), refers to the fact that an individual threatened by abridgment of a freedom becomes motivationally aroused to regain that freedom. This may motivate the development of a negative identity status. An individual seeing peers with a freedom he does not possess may react in the same manner as an individual threatened by a loss of freedom. An adolescent may be reactively stimulated to greater self-reliance by real or imagined curtailments of his freedom to act.

Early socialization experiences may set limits on the kind of person the adolescent will become by depriving him of experiences he needs to advance developmentally. A child deprived of early love experiences may find it difficult to trust another person in later life. An understimulated or malnourished child may never develop his full cognitive capacities. A child who has not experienced firm, contingent discipline may be crippled in his ability to cope with the tension and anxiety of the adolescent crisis. A child brought up in a chaotic environment may regard natural or social laws as nonexistent or unknowable. A child who has been overprotected and shielded from danger may not learn how to cope with ambiguity and danger. Conversely, parents may develop in the child vigorous physical health, instrumental skills, and cognitive and moral maturity, thus providing a base for formation of a strong identity in adolescence.

EARLY CHILDHOOD SOCIALIZATION ASSOCIATED WITH PROTOTYPIC ADOLESCENT LIFE STYLES

Developmental and secular factors may interact in important ways with the effect on the child of a particular socialization practice. About that we have little systematic knowledge. The fact that differences in magnitude of correlations are found at different time periods does not necessarily signal the discovery of a delayed association between parental behavior at one time period and child behavior at another time period (e.g., the "sleeper effect" of Moss & Kagan, 1964). Differences in magnitude of correlations at different time periods may well be the result of measurement error. Therefore, in the discussion which follows, patterns of parent-child relationships will not be considered separately for each developmental stage and secular period. As a way of organizing hypotheses and available data on the effects of early socialization, I have constructed eight adolescent prototypes, corresponding to the eight possible combinations of high and low scores on the three dimensions of social behavior identified most commonly by students of individual differences. The three dimensions are:

1. *Social Responsibility (high versus low).* Social responsibility refers to behavior which is friendly rather than hostile to peers, facilitative rather than disruptive of others' work, and cooperative rather than resistive of adult-led activities. In the preschool and school-age child, qualities of obedience, conformity, and achievement orientation should feature prominently. In adolescence, qualities of objectivity and self-control should surface.
2. *Active-Passive.* Traits included in this dimension are reserved-expressive, reactive-phlegmatic, explosive-calm, and vital-sluggish—all qualities of temperament which show a high degree of stability from early childhood to adolescence (Yarrow, 1964; Bronson, 1966).
3. *Individualistic-Suggestible.* This dimension refers to behavior which is ascendant rather than submissive, purposive rather than aimless, and

individualistic rather than conforming. Its importance as a source of variance increases as the child approaches adolescence.

The first two dimensions coincide with the two orthogonal factor axes which emerged in two of my previous studies (Baumrind, 1967, 1971a); in a study by Schaefer (1961), working with the Berkeley Growth Study data; and in a study by Becker and Krug (1964), reworking Becker's data for 5-year-olds. The third dimension, which emerged as a very weak factor in earlier studies of preschool children (Baumrind & Black, 1967), should become most prominent in early adolescence, coinciding with the emergence of formal thought.

The eight prototypes formed by all combinations of these three dimensions are summarized in Table 7.1.

These eight prototypes, or patterns, were then combined into four sets of complementary patterns. Each pattern does in fact correspond to a recognizable life style, and its complement to an opposite life style. For each of the four sets of patterns thus constructed, several propositions relating childhood experience to their development could then be formulated. Each of the interlocking propositions which I will advocate has received support at more than one developmental stage, and in studies at different secular periods. Nonetheless, with possibly two exceptions, one that traditional upbringing deters alienation and the second that arbitrary, punitive, and inconsistent upbringing is closely associated with delinquency, the propositions which follow are in reality hypotheses which while consistent with the studies cited require further systematic study. Where theory or common sense suggests important developmental or secular effects, a brief section containing the appropriate qualifications follows the discussion of the proposition.

The patterns in the first set to be discussed are designated Social Agent and its complement, Social Victim.

TABLE 7.1

Adolescent Prototypes

	Dimensions of social behavior		
Prototype	Socially responsible	Active	Individualistic
A. Social Agent	High	High	High
B. Social Victim	Low	Low	Low
C. Traditionalist	High	High	Low
D. Alienated	Low	Low	High
E. Socialized	High	Low	Low
F. Delinquent	Low	High	High
G. Humanist	High	Low	High
H. Antihumanist	Low	High	Low

Social Agent versus Social Victim

	Social Responsibility	Active	Individualistic
A. Social Agent	High	High	High
B. Social Victim	Low	Low	Low

The central issue for this polarity concerns potence versus impotence; the Social Agent experiencing himself as potent, the Social Victim as impotent. The Social Agent expresses strong commitment to occupational and ideological choices. His self-concept is based on an internal, as opposed to an external, frame of reference (Marcia, 1967). The Social Agent, high in social responsibility, activity, and individuality, corresponds to the Competent children in Baumrind's 1967 study, to the children of Authoritative parents in Baumrind's 1971(a) study, to the youths of parents with symmetrical power structures in Elder's study (1961), and to some of the youths Peck and Havighurst (1960) designated as Rational-Altruistic. In addition to the above, published studies I will refer throughout this discussion to an unpublished pilot study that I conducted in 1968 (Baumrind, 1971c). In that study 103 tenth-grade students from the local public high school were interviewed concerning their attitudes toward authority, use of drugs, sexual experience, and relations with their parents. Sixty-six variables with a response of 95 percent or better were intercorrelated, so that clusters of defining variables could be formed. A number of adolescent profiles emerged, for black and white students separately, which will be included as data here.

A profile emerged from that study called Principled Humanists (fifteen white and nine black youths divided equally between boys and girls). These tenth graders were achieving, self-aware, highly intelligent, and accomplished in school; they had experimented with but did not now use psychedelic drugs. They felt positively about the authority arrangements in their family, describing their parents as firm yet democratic.

The Social Agent may be either a conserver of the culture or a political activist engaged in *constructive* dissent. Activism is after all a traditional American value. Whether conservative or dissenting, Social Agents are principled, self-disciplined, and committed. The findings from most studies of student social protest (Flacks, 1967; Keniston, 1968, 1969; Smith, Haan, & Block, 1970) show that there is in fact a sizable subgroup of politically active liberal-to-radical students who do not reject their parents' values, and that the characteristics of those who do not reject their parents' values are similar to those we call Social Agents.

The Social Victim, low on all three dimensions, corresponds to the Immature children in Baumrind's 1967 study and to the Expedient youths in the Peck and Havighurst study (1960). The Social Victim as defined here is apolitical and too passive to be chronically delinquent, although he may act out violently in response to prolonged frustration.

Proposition A. High social status and self-esteem should characterize the parents of Social Agents but not the parents of Social Victims.

The above proposition is similar to the status-envy hypothesis of Burton and Whiting (1961), which holds that the child is motivated to identify with the characteristics of a model whose privileges and status he envies, especially if he is required to conform to parental demands in order to obtain the privileges which parental status can confer. This hypothesis is supported by the work of Gold (1963), Smelser (1963), and Douvan (1963). Gold found that the influence of the father on his offspring was directly related to the prestige rank of his profession. Smelser found that sons born in 1928 with high-status and upwardly mobile parents were most likely to perceive their fathers as strong and competent and themselves to be independent and masterful persons. Douvan showed that the adolescent daughters of middle class women who were happily employed were themselves more ambitious and more admiring of their mothers. If parents achieve status in the eyes of youth through delinquent activities, they should also act as effective models, this time however of delinquent rather than of socially responsible behavior.

Social Victims should be most likely to come from homes where parents have few resources and/or arbitrarily withhold and dispense rewards. Inconsistent reinforcement signifies to the child that he is powerless to produce an outcome, and that those in power are not self-governed by rules or principles and therefore are not worthy of trust or respect.

Developmental and secular factors. The status-envy hypothesis is relevant only when the child or adolescent regards instrumental competence and vocational success as status-conferring, values the privileges which social status confers, and lacks the power and prestige which he attributes to his parents—all factors less characteristic of this generation than of previous generations.

Proposition B. Contingent criticism of the child's achievement behavior should be associated with achievement and independence, salient characteristics present in Social Agents and absent in Social Victims, provided that the parents' aspirations for the child are realistic.

Unconditional approval and overprotective parental practices were in fact associated with dependence and relatively low achievement in all of my studies of preschool children. Parents whose children were independent were rated low on measures of passive-acceptance and high on measures of maturity demands (Baumrind, 1967, 1971a). These findings concerning the negative effects of a high degree of passive-acceptance on children (girls in particular) are supported by observations of other investigators.

Thus Rosen and D'Andrade (1959) found that high achievement motivation was facilitated by high maternal hostility and rejection when the child was displeasing to the parent as well as by high maternal warmth when the child pleased the parent. Hoffman, Rosen, and Lippitt (1960) found that mothers of achieving boys were more coercive than were mothers of boys who performed poorly. Kagan and Moss (1962) reported that, in their early childhood, achieving adult women had mothers who were unaffectionate, "pushy," and not over-protective. Probably the parent, by being self-assertive and self-confident, pro-vides a model of similar behavior for the child. Thus Norman (1966) found that the same-sex parents of gifted achieving children had significantly lower con-formity and higher independence scores than did the same-sex parents of gifted children who were not achieving. Kagan and Moss (1962) reported that maternal acceleration at ages 3 through 6 was most conducive to the expression of leadership at adolescence, while McClelland (1961) reported that the critical age for achievement training was between 6 and 8.

However, when parents have unrealistically high aspirations for the child, the child may develop high aspirations which he cannot fulfill and thus ulti-mately become withdrawn and discouraged. Thus Cramer, Bowerman, and Campbell (1966) found that parental practices and goals relevant to achieve-ment training were relatively unrelated to the educational goals of black ado-lescents, while they were related for white youth. Another study with adolescents (Baumrind, 1971c) revealed the same discrepancy. A subgroup emerged for black, but not for white, students, in which subjects were docile and highly achievement-oriented, reporting that their parents had high aspira-tions for them. The members of this subgroup unfortunately had the lowest intelligence and achievement scores in the sample. Similarly, Stinchcombe (1964) identified a syndrome common to low-ability boys, in which the boys internalized parental standards that they would go to college despite their repeated failure to achieve in school.

Proposition C. Social Agency in adolescence should be facilitated by use of reason and high levels of communication throughout childhood.

To the extent that the parent uses verbal cues judiciously, he or she increases the child's ability to discriminate, differentiate, and generalize. According to Luria (1960) and Vygotsky (1962), the child's ability to "order" his own behavior is based on verbal instruction from the adult, which, when heeded and obeyed, permits eventual *cognitive* control by the child of his own behavior. Thus, when the adult legitimizes power, labels actions clearly as praiseworthy or changeworthy, explains rules and encourages vigorous verbal give and take, obedience is not likely to be achieved with the undesired side effect of passive dependence. In pursuing a policy of open and vigorous verbal interaction, the parent contributes to the development in the child of socially constructive power skills. The child, and later the adolescent, receives important training in constructive dissent and thus some confidence in his ability to effect change through self-assertive but nonviolent means. A young child who experiences ex-planatory feedback from one upon whom he is dependent should be expected to develop his ability at role-taking at an earlier age than one whose parent's re-sponses are generally expressive or punitive but not explanatory (Kerchoff, 1969).

The use of rational control rather than repressive control is associated with prosocial aggression (Baumrind & Black, 1967) but not with antisocial aggression (Glueck & Glueck, 1950; McCord & McCord, 1958) or discord with parents (Bowerman & Elder, 1962; Baumrind, 1967, 1971a). When parents use reason to legitimate authority, they provide the child with an experience of consistency in transition from the not always rational control appropriate to childhood to the rational control required in adolescents.

Developmental factors. Power per se legitimates authority in childhood. By virtue of his greater size, experience, and control of resources a parent can impose restraints and restrict autonomy. The child accepts as legitimate even very strict control because he is not yet capable of principled objections. By being presented with an orderly series of experiences, the child learns to express his individuality within limits acceptable to his parents and thus to distinguish between conforming and deviant behavior. However, when in adolescence the youth becomes capable of reflection and abstraction, he can formulate principles by which to judge his own activities and evaluate those of others. Because the adolescent can imagine viable alternatives to parental directives, the parent must be ready to defend his or her directives on rational grounds. The legitimacy of demands and control may be recognized when both parent and adolescent vigorously defend their positions until consensus is reached. Adolescents whose memories of early childhood include explanation of rules are more likely to model themselves after their parents. The acceptance and expression of legitimate authority is an essential characteristic of the Social Agent, in contrast to the Social Victim who is more likely to punctuate complete withdrawal with occasional violent episodes of antisocial aggression.

In summary, high social status, contingent, consistent reinforcement, and rational methods of control should characterize the upbringing of the Social Agent, and their absence or opposite the upbringing of the Social Victim.

Traditionalists versus Alienated

		Social Responsibility	Active	Individualistic
C.	Traditionalist	High	High	Low
D.	Alienated	Low	Low	High

The central issue separating the Traditionalist from the Alienated is that of meaning versus anomia. The Traditionalist accepts a commitment to an occupation and ideology which is in accord with parental standards and values, thus experiencing a sense of continuity and order as long as he remains embedded in the type of situation in which his identity was formed. Traditionalists have not experienced an identity crisis. Traditionalist identification characterized the foreclosure individual in Marcia's study (1967), and Block, Haan, and Smith's *continuous conservative* students, who were affiliative with *both* their society and their families. They were either conventionalists who were active only in nonpolitical social groups or constructivists who were active in social service but not in protest activities (Block, Haan, & Smith, 1969). By contrast, the Alienated adolescent lacks internalized norms, guiding fictions, or a sense of the world as orderly and supportive of realistic aspirations. The Alienated syndrome is defined by Keniston (1960) as "an explicit rejection of what are seen as the dominant values of the surrounding society" (p. 174). The Alienated differs from the Victim in that his protest is more individualized. However, like the Victim, the Alienated has not found meaning in achievement through creative effort, in the experience of love, or in the suffering he feels forced to undergo. Among the thirteen outlooks described by Keniston as characterizing the Alienated are: pessimism, distrust, egocentricity, social and cultural alienation, vacillation, and the feeling of being an outsider. Keniston's analysis is based on a very small sample of Harvard students interviewed in the late fifties and early sixties, consisting of only 11 alienated students, 10 traditional students, and 12 controls. However, the personality type he describes would fit the heavy drug user or "head" of today with two important exceptions: heads generally drop out of demanding universities such as Harvard, and the drug intensifies the passive, despairing, isolating aspects of the alienation syndrome.

Proposition A. The upbringing of the Traditionalist will emphasize firm discipline accompanied by strong affectional family ties and sanctioning of adult authority by appeal to religious and patriotic values.

Coherent, consistent upbringing, including that achieved by apparently authoritarian upbringing, may sustain meaning and hope during adolescence and thus prevent the rejection of life which characterizes the alienated individual. This proposition is very strongly supported by the data. The traditional family in America is generally labeled authoritarian (e.g., Marcia, 1967), although such a pejorative appellation would not be applied in Europe where the traditional family is still regarded as normative. In the traditional family very firm control is exerted in early childhood but may be relaxed considerably by mid-adolescence. Kandel and Lesser (1969) in a survey of several thousand American and Danish adolescents showed that Danish parents exercised greater control during childhood but imposed far fewer rules on adolescents. Because of this exercise of control in early childhood, Danish adolescents were able to behave in an approved fashion without external constraints. Similar results were found by Karr and Wesley (1966) in their comparison of German and American childrearing practices from infancy through adolescence. In an interesting study of social norms and authoritarianism, Kagitcibasi (1970) showed that her subjects in the United States who scored high on content areas of authoritarianism (i.e., respect for authority and high value placed on obedience) were more likely to suffer from the authoritarian personality syndrome (i.e., dogmatic and intolerant attitudes, motivated by repressed anger, emotional coldness, and a sense of impotence) than their Turkish counterparts. As the author notes, obedience to justified authority is a basic code of decency and morality in Turkey and part of a historical tradition still valued. Obedience coming from social norms carries different overtones than the unquestioned obedience and submission, mixed with repressed hostility, that is associated with the authoritarian personality.

In a series of cross-national studies, Bronfenbrenner (1970a, b) found that American parents, particularly by comparison with German or Russian parents, pay less attention to their children. German parents play a greater role in the lives of their adolescents, and the peer group a lesser one, because the family spends more of its leisure time together. In the Soviet Union, the peer group is controlled by adult society. Using matched groups of Soviet children attending day and boarding schools, Bronfenbrenner (1970a) found that children brought up in the boarding schools subscribed more strongly to culturally approved values and conformed more completely to social pressure in their immediate environment. In one recent study (Baumrind, 1972a), black daughters of Authoritarian parents, when compared with white girls, were significantly more Independent and Dominant. These differences are striking because there were no significant black-white differences in child behavior in the total sample. The socialization practices which characterized these black families, while authoritarian by white standards, reflect traditional values within the black culture which appear to be beneficial in that culture.

Within American society, families who maintain a strong belief system and a traditional family structure seem best able to shield their youth from drug use and anomie. Thus youth from homes in which both parents are religious and abstainers from alcohol are more likely to internalize an abstinence norm and refrain from drinking after making the transition from home to college environment (Campbell, 1964). Similarly, Clausen (1966) found in an analysis of Oakland Growth Study data that youth who demonstrated compliant dependence on their parents and whose parents did not smoke internalized the smoking prohibitions of their parents. Similar results were found by Blum (1972) for families in which drug abuse was prevalent by comparison with those in which it was not. Blum found that adolescent drug use was least prevalent among traditional families who both disciplined their children and spent much time with them, and for whom religion played an ongoing part in family and community life. In another study (Baumrind, 1968), adolescents who claimed to never have used illicit drugs were rater higher than others on clusters designated Concordance with Parents, Achievement-Oriented, Obeys Rules Willingly, and seeks Social Acceptability. This group submitted markedly more applications to better colleges and universities although, consistent with their somewhat lower SES, they were somewhat less intelligent than other students interviewed. Middle class youth who remain encapsulated within a traditional family structure in a traditional community may circumvent the adolescent crisis altogether as may lower class youth whose lives are given meaning by the struggle to survive. Whether this is regarded as a good or a bad effect may be a matter of the investigator's own cultural values.

The assumption that mature reasoning and moral judgment require that the individual embrace an ethic of personal conscience as opposed to an ethic of social responsibility (see Hogan, 1970) underlies the work of Piaget and Kohlberg and of most American behavioral scientists. On the other hand, a Mexican psychologist (Diaz-Guerrero, 1965) and a Chicano psychologist (Ramirez 1971–1972) point out in separate articles that although most American behavioral scientists, if asked whether obedience helps the development of an adolescent, would answer no, Mexicans and Chicanos would answer yes. American social scientists would conclude that Mexican American culture interferes with the intellectual and social development of Chicano children, whereas the Mexican American psychologist would disagree. For example, as Ramirez points out, research with the Rod and Frame Test shows that Chicano children are, in general, more field dependent than Anglo children. Most American researchers assume the advantages of field independence and the disadvantages of field dependence and conclude that Chicano children are disadvantaged in this respect. Ramirez argues that Mexican American families, unlike Anglo middle class families, reward children consistently for obedient and cooperative behavior and actually value field dependent behavior.

Proposition B. Parents who are themselves afflicted with existential despair would be least helpful as resources for adolescents facing the same problems.

The unifying theme of the life style of the Alienated is unbelief and rejection of trusting, optimistic, socially responsible, other-oriented values; a rejection of concern for others' and one's own future welfare. Whatever keeps the adolescent from committing himself in action should increase alienation, since every *choice* of action establishes value preferences defining for the adolescent the person he will become, i.e., his identity.

The parents of Keniston's eleven alienated Harvard youths were afflicted with existential despair (1965). These young men described their mothers as talented, intense, sensuous, and charismatic women who renounced vocational interests, channeling their efforts instead through their husbands and sons. Fathers were described as frustrated and disillusioned men who, like their wives, were unable to fulfill their youthful dreams. Alienated sons expressed deep sympathy for the plight of both their parents, whose predicament they most certainly did not wish to share. While Keniston stresses the repudiation by alienated sons of parental values, I am struck by the extent to which the parents' despair and anomie are shared by their sons.

Alienated youth may come either from restrictive families whose views they reject or from liberal families where the persons but not the views of the parents are rejected. Thus, adolescents (Baumrind, 1971c) who claimed heavy drug use came equally from permissive and restrictive homes. Whether permissive or restrictive, the parents were described as insufficient to the challenge of rearing children and as indecisive, depressed people whom their children did not wish to emulate. The way in which parents handle the crises adolescents precipitate in their own lives may in turn affect their function as models. As Scherz (1967) observed, the turbulent middle years for an adolescent frequently coincide with the middle years of his parents, who are struggling with changes in career status, family relations, and sex life.

The negative attitude of many adults toward themselves and their generation, exemplified in the wave of *mea culpa* literature which has appeared on the market (e.g., Osborne's *How to Deal with Parents and Other Problems*, 1962; Friedenberg's *Anti-American Generation*, 1971; and Reich's *Greening of America*, 1970), does nothing to fill the existential vacuum which afflicts many adolescents who are groping for meaning. The search for meaning is certainly a central, if not a universal, motive of man. Parents enveloped in an existential vacuum become part of the problem their efforts should be designed to cure.

Block's analysis (1972) of the causes of societal rejection among a subject pool drawn from the San Francisco Bay area suggests that parents of alienated students are overinvolved with their children and disappointed with their own lives. The child-rearing orientation of parents whose children rejected both their families and society lacked coherence; mothers tended to be permissive and overly involved in some areas, yet demanded submission and compliance in others. Fathers described their relationships with their children as ambivalent and conflicted.

In summary, parents of traditional adolescents will themselves strongly and unambivalently adhere to traditional values, behaving warmly and strictly toward their children. Parents of alienated middle class children will be ambivalent, despairing, and estranged—looking for meaning from their children's lives and not finding it there either.

Socialized versus Delinquent

		Social Responsibility	Active	Individualistic
E.	Socialized	High	Low	Low
F.	Delinquent	Low	High	High

The central issue for this polarity concerns naive trust versus basic distrust. The socialized individual trusts that authorities will treat him fairly, whereas the delinquent individual expects to be treated unjustly. The Socialized adolescent is a friendly, docile individual and a conforming citizen who avoids breaking the rules so that he will not suffer the disapproval of church, community, or peers. Unlike the Social Agent or Traditionalist, the highly Socialized adolescent is a rule follower and not a rule maker or active maintainer. The Socialized prototype corresponds to Peck and Havighurst's Conforming Type (1960), to the Overconformist in my adolescent study (1971c), and to the political Inactives in the Block study (1972).

The Delinquent expects to be treated unjustly. He is an active violator of the laws and mores of his society. He is the victimizer as well as the victim of that society. He is either amoral or a moral realist. Neither the Socialized nor the Delinquent life styles can be considered optimum. Each is characterized by an extreme of social conformity, the Socialized by overconformity and the

Delinquent by antisocial aggression. The following propositions will consider the antecedents of antisocial versus prosocial aggression and of overconformity versus responsible conformity.

Proposition A. Authoritative parental control will be associated with conformity rather than overconformity, and with prosocial rather than antisocial aggression, whereas restrictive parental control will be associated with both oversocialized and undersocialized adolescent behavior.

Authoritative control includes the following attitudes and practices: the child is directed firmly, consistently and rationally; issues rather than personalities are focused on; the parent both explains reasons behind demands and encourages verbal give and take; the parent uses power when necessary; the parent values both obedience to adult requirements and independence in the child; the parent sets standards and enforces them firmly but does not regard self as infallible; the parent listens to the child but does not base decisions solely on the child's desires.

Findings from two separate studies investigating patterns of parental control showed that authoritative parental control, as compared to either authoritarian or permissive control, was associated with responsible, assertive, and self-reliant behavior in preschool children (Baumrind, 1967, 1971a). In a separate correlational study (Baumrind & Black, 1967) parents' willingness to offer justification for their directives and to listen to the child when directing him was associated with indices of independence and social responsibility in both boys and girls. Parental restrictiveness and refusal to grant sufficient independence were by contrast associated (in boys) with dependent and passive behavior.

It is important to distinguish between the effects on the child of firm control and of restrictive control (in which extensive proscriptions and prescriptions cover many areas of the child's life and need systems, and arbitrary limits are placed on his autonomous strivings to try out new skills and make decisions for himself). In general, as Becker (1964) indicates, restrictive discipline does appear to lead to "fearful, dependent and submissive behaviors, a dulling of intellectual strivings and inhibited hostility." Whether the child perceives the ways in which parental authority is expressed to be arbitrary and overprotective or instead justified in terms of his own welfare may determine how well that authority is accepted and whether behavioral compliance is accompanied by immaturity and rebellion, or by independence in the child.

The contrasting effects of authority viewed as justified versus authority viewed as illegitimate should become particularly apparent at adolescence. Thus Pikas (1961), in his survey of 656 Swedish adolescents, showed that significant differences occurred in their acceptance of parental authority, depending on the reason for the directive. Authority that was based on rational concern for the child's welfare was accepted well by the child, while authority based on the adult's desire to dominate or exploit the child was rejected. The former, which Pikas calls rational authority, is similar to what we have designated authoritative or firm control, and the latter, which he calls inhibiting authority, is similar to what we have designated authoritarian or restrictive control. His results are supported by Middleton and Putney (1963) who found that parental discipline regarded by the child as either very strict or very permissive was associated with lack of closeness between parent and child and with rebellion against the parent's political viewpoints. Similarly, Elder (1963) found that junior and senior high school students were more likely to model themselves after their parents and to associate with parent-approved peers if their parents used reason to explain decisions and demands. Longstreth and Rice (1964) found that aggressive high school boys, as compared with well-adjusted boys, described their parents as unloving, whereas boys who described their parents as both loving and controlling identified with their parents in both these characteristics. Peck and Havighurst (1960) found that lack of consistency was most common in families of Amoral children. If values are inconsistently enforced, the child questions their validity. The typical (and more effective) Conformers in the Peck and Havighurst study had parents who were consistent and well organized but autocratic and rather severe. His Conformers accepted their parents' code and felt positively toward their parents. They were willing to do just as they were told so long as the authorities directing them were seen as good and respectable people like their parents.

Developmental and secular factors. With age, the optimum magnitude of control should decrease, and of independence-granting increase. With psychosocial adolescence reached at earlier ages, it may be particularly important for parents to be sensitive to the changing developmental needs of their children for less control. Too firm control, particularly as the child approaches adolescence, should be experienced as restrictive and affect the child adversely in the ways discussed earlier.

Proposition B. The development of independence in girls rather than over-conformity is associated with high parental demands and an absence of overprotection.

Resistiveness to adult authority is not related to low achievement in girls, although it may be so related for boys. It was found (Baumrind & Black, 1967) that resistiveness toward adults, although highly correlated negatively with achievement-oriented behavior for boys, was not at all correlated for girls. Moreover, for girls, as compared to boys, domineering behavior toward peers was related to dominant and purposive behavior and less related to hostile behavior. Dominance and stridency in girls, relative to other girls, may signify that they are resisting sex-role pressure to undercompete and underachieve. Thus it may be important in socializing girls to stimulate reactive aggression in order to assure independence and achievement (Baumrind, 1972b).

It is of interest in this regard that in a number of studies (e.g., Baumrind & Black, 1967) parental punitiveness was associated positively with indices of independence in girls. Crandall made a similar observation about the effects of maternal criticality and stress. In a recent progress report (1972) to the National Institute of Mental Health she noted:

> Perhaps internality at later developmental stages is best predicted by some degree of maternal "coolness," criticality, and stress, so that offspring were not allowed to rely on overly indulgent affective relationships with parents but were forced to learn objective cause-effect contingencies, adjust to them, and recognize their own instrumentality in causing those outcomes. . . . The data further suggested that internals' mothers . . . participated more frequently with their children in achievement activities, but were less protective, had lower intensity and frequency of contact with them, and rejected their dependency overtures. In fact, it is possible that this cluster of behaviors, together with the criticality and lack of affection cited above may have served to thrust the child "out of the nest" and into more active contact with his physical and social world (pp. 38–39).

The positive association shown in these studies between independent behavior for girls and absence of uncritical acceptance supports Bronfenbrenner's observation (1961) that among educationally advantaged subgroups too much warmth and support seem to have a "debilitating" effect on girls. Disciplinary techniques which foster self-reliance, whether by placing demands for high-level performance or by encouraging independent action, seem to facilitate assertive, independent behavior in girls. In attempting to understand the "debilitating" effects on girls of passive acceptance by parents, the hypothesis (advanced by Wolpe, 1958, among others) that avoidance and self-assertion are reciprocally inhibiting responses to threatening or frustrating experiences deserves consideration. The aspect of the fundamental fight-flight reaction to such experiences that will predominate for a given individual will be a function largely of prior experience. Vigorous, abrasive interaction in which assertive responses are stimulated and either not punished or rewarded should increase the likelihood that the individual so stimulated will react assertively rather than with avoidance to threatening or frustrating stimuli.

The passive-acceptant and overprotective attitudes of many parents of girls, as compared to boys, may explain in part why girls and women are found to be more affiliative, field dependent, suggestible, and obedient than men (Witkin, Dyk, Faterson, Goodenough, & Karp, 1954; Janis & Field, 1959; Walker & Heyns, 1962). In summarizing some of Douvan and Adelson's findings (1966) on the adolescent experience, Bardwick and Douvan (1971) observed that the overwhelming majority of adolescent girls remain dependent on others for feelings of affirmation. They speculated that unless the girl exhibited in early life the aggression or sexuality usually displayed by boys, and thereby experienced significant parental prohibitions, that there would be little likelihood that she would develop independent inner-oriented sources of self-esteem. That is, it is important for a child to discover that he or she can stand up to parental disapproval, pursuing a course of action not supported by significant others, in order to be willing to gamble with the threat of loss of love.

Douvan (1963) notes that daughters of working mothers are more likely to be independent and aggressive. In particular, daughters of working mothers who enjoy their vocation are less conforming and passive (Douvan, 1963; Hartley, 1970; Rossi, 1971). Douvan stresses the modeling theory as the causal link between mother's employment status and the child's instrumental competence.

Secular effects. Liberation from sex-role stereotypes means that independence and achievement will be valued increasingly in girls. Conversely, timidity and passivity in girls will become less acceptable. It may be particularly important at this time, then, that parents expose girls to maturity demands and vigorous, abrasive interaction and reward them for acts of independence and achievement.

Proposition C. Harsh, exploitative, arbitrary treatment by parents is strongly associated with antisocial rather than prosocial aggression in children and adolescents.

This proposition (together with proposition A in the last section, which asserted that traditionalist parents most effectively circumvent the alienating effects of the society) has received the most extensive support in the research literature. These findings hold equally for delinquent adolescent males (Bandura & Walters, 1959; Glueck & Glueck, 1950; Hetherington, Stouwie, & Ridberg, 1971; McCord, McCord, & Zola, 1959; Wittman & Huffman, 1945), for delinquent adolescent females (Hetherington et al., 1971; Wittman & Huffman, 1945), and for all ages studied (Becker, Peterson, Hellmer, Shoemaker, & Quay, 1959; Martin & Hetherington, 1971; McCord, McCord, & Howard, 1961; Winder & Rau, 1962). They hold for both middle and lower class families. Harsh parental treatment may convince the adolescent that morality is inevitably arbitrary and self-serving, thus providing a rationale in experience for amorality or moral realism. Punitive approaches to discipline, including verbal and physical abuse and unreasonable deprivations of privilege, are associated with low expressions of guilt and an external orientation to transgression. These crude displays of parental power characterize parents of delinquent youth. Frequently, parents of delinquent youth engage in illegal displays of power as well, thus modeling antisocial aggression both inside and outside the home setting. Not infrequently, aggressive boys are found to come from homes in which discipline is lax and inconsistent and one parent is highly punitive and the other is not (McCord et al., 1961). Inconsistent reinforcement for aggressive behavior serves to perpetuate that behavior on two counts: the child escalates his aggressive behavior, knowing that eventually it will be rewarded, and the legitimization of parental authority is undermined by intraparental and interparental inconsistency.

Proposition D. Middle class delinquency should be associated with a disregard or habitual violation of the principle of reciprocity by adult authorities.

As Elkind points out (1967), there is an implicit contract between middle class parents and their children at all ages. Parents agree to provide for the physical and emotional well-being of their children, who, in return, agree to obey the norms of middle class society which their parents support. According to Elkind, a major cause of middle class delinquency is that the parent breaks the terms of the implicit contract by chronically exploiting his child. The parent may exploit the child's accomplishments to enhance his own status, or use the adolescent to gain entry into the youth culture. Such a parent may be capricious, sadistic, and childishly egocentric while at the same time demanding that the child conform to his subjective standards.

Reciprocity is the core of principled morality. Contracts and due process are fundamental to the justice conception which develops in adolescence, particularly among educated middle class youth. The social contract presupposes that those governed consent to their status, expecting the authority to act for them, not against them. Since the making of contracts presupposes the liberty of the contractees, an adolescent who does not experience himself as a morally free agent will not feel required to abide by the explicit or implicit contracts he has with his parents or with society. Unless adult authorities are respected as moral agents, adolescents will not feel obliged ethically to abide by their rules.

During childhood, power is asymmetrical in the family unit. As Dubin and Dubin (1963) point out, by the imposition of parental authority in the early years the child learns to express his social individuality within the confines of what the culture will accept. However, power cannot be used by parents to legitimate or enforce their authority once the young person acquires formal operational thought. The asymmetry of power, which characterizes childhood, does not exist in adolescence. While head-on confrontation may serve to strengthen parental authority in the authority inception period, it should undermine parental authority in adolescence. Negotiation and intellectual exchange are more effective than confrontation in arriving at agreement as to what is just.

Humanist versus Antihumanist

	Social Responsibility	Active	Individualistic
G. Humanist	High	Low	High
H. Antihumanist	Low	High	Low

The central issue for this polarity concerns benevolence versus malevolence. The Humanist is empathic and acts accordingly; the Antihumanist sees himself as an outcast having little in common with others and therefore no reason to refrain from harming them where it serves his self-interest.

The Humanist adolescent, like the Social Agent, is both socially responsible and individualistic. Unlike the Social Agent, the Humanist is not interested in using power as a means of social control. Like the Socialized adolescent the Humanist is socially responsible and desirous of avoiding conflict. Unlike the Socialized type, he or she is highly individualized and autonomous. The Humanist corresponds to the Harmonious pattern in my study (1971b) and to a subgroup of adolescents of the Rational Altruistic type in the Peck and

Havighurst (1960) study. In my adolescent study, Harmonious subjects obeyed their parents' rules willingly, since these rules were in accord with their own values; they valued equanimity and harmony in daily life; they did not yet wish to become involved in drug or sexual experiences. These Harmonious adolescents claimed to not value achievement or status, although their grade-point averages were high and they received more honors than others. Proportionately fewer of them applied to colleges, but those who did applied to the "better" colleges and universities. These adolescents, while extremely competent intellectually, were predominantly interested in pursuing creative vocations, unlike their wealthy and successful professional parents. They felt, however, that their parents approved of their life styles and future vocational interests.

The Antihumanist type, unlike the Delinquent with whom he shares a rejection of the ethics of social responsibility and an interest in gaining social power, lacks individuality. Unlike the Social Victim, with whom he shares a lack of social responsibility and individuality, he is willing to become active in power games. Likely candidates for the Lumpenproletariat or revisionist movements, such individuals seek to relieve their sense of estrangement, alienation, and social inferiority by identifying with their aggressors, turning against others oppressed like themselves.

Proposition A. The pattern of upbringing most conducive to the development of the Humanist life style should be one in which conformity is achieved through reason and love more than through reinforcement or strict control, where parental standards are modeled more than extolled, and where gentleness and rationality are highly valued.

In my study of preschool children (Baumrind, 1971a), a subgroup of families were identified and called Harmonious (1971b). Although in the study proper (1971a), pattern membership was determined by multiple criteria, the eight families of preschool children placed in the Harmonious pattern had one common identifying characteristic—the observer assigned to study the family would not rate the family for the construct designated Firm Enforcement. In each case, the observer stated that any rating on these items would be misleading since the parents almost never *exercised control*, but seemed to *have control* in the sense that the child generally took pains to intuit what the parent wanted him to do and did it. The atmosphere in these families was characterized by harmony, equanimity, and rationality. Harmonious parents were equalitarian in that they recognized differences based on knowledge and personality, and tried to create an environment in which all family members could operate from the same vantage point, one in which the recognized differences in power did not put the child at a disadvantage. In their hierarchy of values honesty, harmony, love, and rationality in human relations took precedence over power, achievement, control, and order, although they also saw the practical importance of the latter values. Parents were generally drawn from the highest educational levels and were either very well to do, or, as was true of two families, had "dropped out" of that class.

The effects of Harmonious child-rearing patterns on children appeared to be sex-related. The six daughters of Harmonious parents were extraordinarily competent and very similar in their scores on the child behavior measures. Their average Stanford-Binet IQ was 136 (that of the entire sample was also high, 128). On clusters derived from scores on the Preschool Behavior Q Sort, when compared with the girls in all other categories combined, these girls were achievement oriented (.05), friendly (.05), and independent (n.s.). These characteristics were not apparent for the two boys whose parents were classified as Harmonious (Baumrind, 1971b). Peck and Havighurst (1960) identified an earlier expression of the harmonious lifestyle in a sub-group of the Rational-Altruistic type, described as a continuously maturing person whose capacities were effectively at work to improve his own well-being consonant with the promotion of the interests of his community, friends, and family, possessing an inner harmony and a conscience fully integrated with the rest of his ego structure. The Rational-Altruistic youth resembled most closely the individual who has reached the postconventional level of morality within the Kohlberg system, particularly stage 6. The families were democratic in that they encouraged the child to explore his world and make his own decisions. Although lenient, they were highly consistent in their discipline. They were approving of the child and his activities, and, in the words of Peck and Havighurst (1960), were "the most harmonious" of all families studied.

Secular factors. Some Humanists come close to Lifton's description (1971) of what he thinks is a newly emerging character type, which he calls Protean Man. Protean Man is characterized by an initiation of an ongoing series of experiments in identity formation, each of which is readily abandoned for the next. Protean Man has a permanently diffuse identity. He adapts with ease to the requirements of a changing social structure but may be incapable of firm commitment or prolonged personal attachments. He is a principled relativist.

Proposition B. By contrast, the pattern of upbringing most conducive to the development of the Antihumanist life style should be arbitrary discipline, emotional lability, brusqueness, and chaotic home management.

In the Peck and Havighurst study (1960) the least mature adolescents were designated Amoral, corresponding closely to the Antihumanist prototype. These youths showed hostile, immature emotionality. They had a very inaccurate perception of social situations, other people, and themselves. They had poor control over impulses and were unwilling to accept self-restraints or societal control because they felt active generalized hostility toward the world around them. The most striking feature of Antihumanist families was marked lability and swings between opposite polarities of emotion and action. While some families were autocratic and others lenient, in no case was consistent discipline or love expressed. In all cases parents were distrustful of how their children used whatever freedom they were offered.

There is some evidence that a similar pattern of child rearing may characterize families of students drawn to the more violent and revolutionary forms of radicalism. In the Block study (1972), child-rearing orientations of parents of students who rejected their families and society were comparatively incoherent and inconsistent and their disciplinary measures were insensitive, suppressive, and punitive. Such students resembled those in Fishkin, Keniston, and MacKinnon's even more recent study (1973). In that study a disproportionate number of subjects showing preconventional, fear-oriented, morally egoistic justifications favored violent radical ideology.

Summary of Proposed Parent-Child Relationships

The adolescent life styles just discussed may be grouped into two sets on the basis of their placement on the dimension of social responsibility. There are important similarities in the pattern of upbringing of the adolescents low on the dimension of social responsibility, designated Victims, Alienated, Delinquent, or Antihumanist. The parents of youths characterized as low in social responsibility generally lack consistency or adherence to a principled moral code. Families of Victims appear to be characterized, in addition to inconsistency, by a lack of social status and personal resources; families of Alienated by indecisiveness and an existential vacuum; families of Delinquents by selfishness, acquisitiveness, and exploitiveness; and families of Antihumanists by irrationality and emotional lability. While differing in many respects, the patterns of upbringing for the second set of adolescents, all high in social responsibility, are characterized by consistent adherence to a code of ethics or conventions and benevolent regard for their children and other persons. Adolescents in the second set, described as Social Agents, Traditionalists, Socialized, and Humanists, appear to differ more sharply from each other than adolescents in the first set. Social Agents are characterized by unusual self-confidence matched by instrumental competence; their parents possess high status and are potent and competent. Traditionalists, like their parents, are politically conservative and insulated from social change, so that they continue to identify with and actively uphold traditional values, taking pride in their status as contributing members of their country and community. Socialized adolescents are conforming and docile; the special quality of their upbringing is the high value which their parents put on "fitting in" and not making waves, and the relative absence of pressure in the home for achievement. Humanists are motivated to lead a harmonious and balanced life in which concern for others plays a prominent part, rather than to use their outstanding abilities and plentiful resources to predict and control natural or social events through knowledge or interpersonal power; their parents, in possession of material comfort and high social status, value neither status nor comfort as much as they value living in peace and harmony with other human beings and species.

SECULAR FACTORS AND ADOLESCENT IDENTITY FORMATION: SOME PREDICTIONS

An important factor eroding adult authority has been the steady decline of American prestige. The image of America as a progressive and moral force was sullied in 1945 with the atomic bombing of Hiroshima and Nagasaki. Our current foreign policy in Indochina established America as a major war criminal in the minds of many principled citizens of all ages. The Watergate revelations further exposed the hypocrisy of official American political morality, instrumental relativism masquerading as principled relativism. Prior to 1945, most adults believed in the American tradition and socialized their children to uphold that tradition. Now many parents, appalled by institutionalized illegality and deceit, regard conformity with institutionalized mores as immoral. Social responsibility includes both conformity with legitimate authority and resistance against illegitimate authority. Neither is possible where all governmental authority appears corrupt and unresponsive, as has been increasingly the case for the last thirty years.

A most striking change in the same period has been the increased recognition accorded youth and the abridgment of adult authority over adolescents in all spheres of life. It would appear today that many parents envy the status of their offspring rather than the reverse. The technical expertise of youth and the unprecedented acceleration of secular change account in part for the dramatic decline in adult authority. As was true of immigrants in previous eras, even well-educated parents today find themselves outdistanced by their offspring in the acquisition of technological skills. Many parents disaffected with federal authority and the structure of their own lives embrace a counterculture ethic and life style, at least in imagination. Adult advocates of Esalen fun and games and Consciousness III seek resolution of existential dilemmas through counterculture mythology and forms, rather than merely using these new forms to add hedonic and spiritual depth to their ordinary lives.

While adolescents have always played a large role in the ongoing development of their parents, acting as interpreters of the emergent values and life style, parents have been able in the past to bring perspective and experience to the generational dialogue. Adolescents have need of adults with whom they can dispute and from whom they can learn. They do not need adult worshipers, followers, and indulgent providers. Without mature rational guidance, adolescents easily fall prey to one of the host of phony gurus or demigods quite willing to take over where parents leave off. Today the inner chaos of the adolescent is matched by the outer chaos of the society. It is doubtful that there are many young persons who can function effectively with the diffuse identity characteristic of Lifton's Protean Man. Youth of the next generation are more likely to turn to conservative, even totalitarian, sources for structure and counsel than to embrace by choice a permanently diffuse identity. The Puritan ethic may disappear, a casualty of the population explosion and the apparent irrelevance of the nuclear family; the Protestant work ethic, still needed, should survive in modified form.

Use of consciousness-altering drugs remains an important cause as well as symptom of identity diffusion and existential void among adolescents. Habits and values established in early childhood may be suppressed or lost as a result of prolonged ingestion of psychedelic agents. Communication between drug-using adolescents and non-drug-using parents appears to break down. Unless a parent has experimented with drugs himself, he has no way of sharing his child's experience, and even then the experience is affected dramatically by stage of development. The sought-after effect of drugs is a qualitative alteration in consciousness. That effect may not be reversible. Reality, after prolonged drug use, may seem relative, shifting, and impermanent. Everything becomes possible and nothing is attainable. Everything matters equally and so nothing matters very much. To what extent does such a perception of reality interfere with the formation of a stable sense of self in adolescence? The effects of prior socialization experiences on the drug-using adolescent are almost entirely unknown and deserve serious investigation.

This is the first generation which must seriously question the value of progress. Modern technology, whose purpose was to increase human comfort and freedom, is now viewed with anxiety as the source of man's destruction. Generativity through work and procreation are no longer of certain positive value. The roles of provider and child bearer are both downgraded. An adolescent must now achieve an identity as a *person* rather than a man or a woman, lacking models of what a person is apart from sex role. Without a normatively sanctioned way to progress, many adolescents may regress, forming an identity based on rejection of adult roles. Alienated adolescents may seek a charismatic leader or a national movement to provide meaning to their lives. The Hitler-Jugend provided such meaning in Nazi society. As a member of Hitler Youth an adolescent had well-defined rights and obligations and could fall into predictable behavior patterns serving the power elite of the nation. We may face a similar threat to democratic values today. Witness the rapidly burgeoning Jesus Freak movement and its equally autocratic opponents.

The family as an institution is undergoing rapid change. It is not likely that women will be content to live vicariously through their husbands and children. The special status which accompanied the role of martyred mother is gone, I think, forever. Millett (1969) and Jones (1970) derogate and disparage the maternal role. Shirley Radl (1973) tells it like it is in a new book aptly titled *Mother's Day Is Over*. Both parents may now acknowledge more openly the anticipated benefits to themselves of having and rearing children and the limits of their tolerance for deviation from their central values.

Until the present decade parents were compensated for the very real discomforts and sacrifice of self entailed in rearing children, by material and symbolic rewards. In passing on their culture and values to their adolescent children, parents could achieve symbolic immortality. Child rearing is no longer a reliable source of personal meaning. In this postmodern era, adolescent children may damage rather than enhance their parents' self-esteem by repudiating their central values. Further erosion of parental authority, if it should occur, is likely to be accompanied by an increase in rejection by parents of adolescents; adults may well abandon their parental role earlier in the life cycle. The reduction of legal adult status to age 18 may be a first important step designed to liberate parents from their children. The investigation of these and other secular trends will be of major concern to the student of socialization effects in the future.

Since the family may be the social unit most responsive to rational influence, its importance as the unit of socialization should be underlined. There are many positive life styles and more than one route by which each can be reached. However, there are routes parents take that reliably lead in a direction opposite to the one that was intended. Even parents who value social conformity may reject unquestioning obedience in favor of principled conformity. Similarly, most parents who value highly, personal autonomy do not welcome the consequences of "unmitigated agency." A significant contribution of the behavioral scientist, then, is to assist parents to understand the unintended consequences of their intended acts within the family setting.

REFERENCES

Bakan, D. *The duality of human existence.* Chicago: Rand McNally, 1966.

Bandura, A., & Walters, R. H. *Adolescent aggression: A study of the influences of child-training practices and family interrelations.* New York: Ronald Press, 1959.

Bardwick, J. M., & Douvan, E. Ambivalence: The socialization of women. In V. Gornick & B. K. Moran (Eds.), *Women in sexist society.* New York: Basic Books, 1971.

Baumrind, D. Child care practices anteceding three patterns of preschool behavior. *Genetic Psychology Monographs*, 1967, 75, 43–88.

Baumrind, D. Authoritarian versus authoritative parental control. *Adolescence*, 1968, 3, 255–272.

Baumrind, D. Current patterns of parental authority. *Developmental Psychology Monograph*, 1971, 4(Whole No. 1). (a)

Baumrind, D. Harmonious parents and their preschool children. *Developmental Psychology*, 1971, 4, 99–102. (b)

Baumrind, D. Types of adolescent life-styles. Unpublished manuscript, Berkeley, Calif., 1971. (c)

Baumrind, D. An exploratory study of socialization effects on black children: Some black-white comparisons. *Child Development*, 1972, 43, 261–267. (a)

Baumrind, D. From each according to her ability. *School Review*, 1972, 80(2), 161–197. (b)

Baumrind, D., & Black, A. E. Socialization practices associated with dimensions of competence in preschool boys and girls. *Child Development*, 1967, 38(2), 291–327.

Becker, W. C. Consequences of different kinds of parental discipline. In M. L. Hoffman & L. W. Hoffman (Eds.), *Review of child development research.* Vol. 1. New York: Russell Sage Foundation, 1964.

Becker, W. C., & Krug, R. S. A circumplex model for social behavior in children. *Child Development*, 1964, 35, 371–396.

Becker, W. C., Peterson, D. R., Hellmer, L. A., Shoemaker, D. J., & Quay, H. C. Factors in parental behavior and personality as related to problem behavior in children. *Journal of Consulting Psychology*, 1959, 23, 107–118.

Block, J. H. Generational continuity and discontinuity in the understanding of societal rejection. *Journal of Personality and Social Psychology*, 1972, **22**(3), 333–345.

Block, J. H., Haan, N., & Smith, M. B. Socialization correlates of student activism. *Journal of Social Issues*, 1969, **25**(4), 143–177.

Blum, R. H., and associates. *Horatio Alger's children*. San Francisco: Jossey-Bass, 1972.

Bowerman, C. E., & Elder, G. H., Jr. The adolescent and his family. Unpublished manuscript, 1962.

Brehm, J. W. *Responses to loss of freedom: A theory of psychological reactance*. Morristown, N.J.: General Learning Press, 1972.

Bronfenbrenner, U. Some familial antecedents of responsibility and leadership in adolescents. In L. Petrullo & B. Bass (Eds.), *Leadership and interpersonal behavior*. New York: Holt, Rinehart and Winston, 1961.

Bronfenbrenner, U. Reaction to social pressure from adults versus peers among Soviet day school and boarding pupils in the perspective of an American sample. *Journal of Personality and Social Psychology*, 1970, **5**, 179–189. (a)

Bronfenbrenner, U. *Two worlds of childhood*. New York: Russell Sage Foundation, 1970. (b)

Bronson, W. C. Central orientations: A study of behavior organization from childhood to adolescence. *Child Development*, 1966, **37**, 125–155.

Burton, R. V., & Whiting, J. W. M. The absent father and cross-sex identity. *Merrill-Palmer Quarterly of Behavior and Development*, 1961, **7**, 85–95.

Campbell, E. Q. The internalization of moral norms. *Sociometry*, 1964, **27**, 391–412.

Clausen, J. A. Family structure, socialization, and personality. In L. W. Hoffman & M. L. Hoffman (Eds.), *Review of child development research*. Vol. 2. New York: Russell Sage Foundation, 1966.

Cramer, M. R., Bowerman, C. E., & Campbell, E. Q. *Social factors in educational achievement and aspirations among Negro adolescents*. Chapel Hill, N.C.: Institute for Social Research in Social Science, 1966, mimeo.

Crandall, V. Progress report to the National Institute of Mental Health, 1972, Grant No. MH-02238.

Diaz-Guerrero, R. Sociocultural and psychodynamic processes in adolescent transition and mental health. In M. Sherif and C. W. Sherif (Eds.), *Problems of youth: Transition to adulthood in a changing world*. Chicago: Aldine, 1965.

Douvan, E. Employment and the adolescent. In F. I. Nye & L. W. Hoffman (Eds.), *The employed mother in America*. Chicago: Rand McNally, 1963.

Douvan, E., & Adelson, J. *The adolescent experience*. New York: Wiley, 1966.

Dubin, E. R., & Dubin, R. The authority inception period in socialization. *Child Development*, 1963, **34**, 885–898.

Elder, G. H., Jr. Family structure and the transmission of values and norms in the process of child rearing. Unpublished doctoral dissertation, University of North Carolina, 1961.

Elder, G. H., Jr. Parental power legitimation and its effect on the adolescent. *Sociometry*, 1963, **26**, 50–65.

Elder, G. H., Jr. *Adolescent socialization and personality development*. Chicago: Rand McNally, 1968.

Elkind, D. Middle-class delinquency. *Mental Health*, 1967, **5**(1), 80–84.

Erikson, E. H. Identity and the life cycle. *Psychological Issues*, 1959, **1**(Whole No. 1).

Erikson, E. H. *Identity: Youth and crisis*. New York: Norton, 1968.

Fishkin, J., Keniston, K., & MacKinnon, C. Moral reasoning and political ideology. *Journal of Personality and Social Psychology*, 1973, **27**(1), 109–119.

Flacks, R. The liberated generation: An exploration of the roots of student protest. *Journal of Social Issues*, 1967, **23**(3), 52–75.

Friedenberg, E. Z. (Ed.), *The anti-American generation*. New Brunswick, N.J.: Transaction, 1971.

Glueck, S., & Glueck, E. *Unraveling juvenile delinquency.* New York: Commonwealth Fund, 1950.

Gold, M. *Status forces in delinquent boys.* Ann Arbor, Mich.: Institute for Social Research, University of Michigan, 1963.

Grinder, R. E. *Adolescence.* New York: Wiley, 1973.

Hall, G. S. *Adolescence.* New York: Appleton, 1904.

Hartley, R. E. American core culture: Change and continuities. In G. H. Seward & R. C. Williamson (Eds.), *Sex roles in changing society.* New York: Random House, 1970.

Hetherington, E. M., Stouwie, R. J., & Ridberg, E. H. Patterns of family interaction and child-rearing attitudes related to three dimensions of juvenile delinquency. *Journal of Abnormal Psychology,* 1971, **78**, 160–176.

Hoffman, L., Rosen, S., & Lippitt, R. Parental coerciveness, child autonomy, and child's role at school. *Sociometry,* 1960, **23**, 15–22.

Hogan, R. A Dimension of Moral Judgment. *Journal of Consulting and Clinical Psychology,* 1970, **35**, 205–212.

Janis, I. L., & Field, P. B. Sex differences and personality factors related to persuasibility. In I. L. Janis & C. I. Hovland (Eds.), *Personality and persuasibility.* New Haven, Conn.: Yale University Press, 1959.

Jones, B. The dynamics of marriage and motherhood. In R. Morgan (Eds.), *Sisterhood is powerful.* New York: Vintage, 1970.

Kagan, J., & Moss, H. A. *Birth to maturity: A study in psychological development.* New York: Wiley, 1962.

Kagitcibasi, C. Social norms and authoritarianism: A Turkish-American comparison. *Journal of Personality and Social Psychology,* 1970, **16**, 444–451.

Kandel, D., & Lesser, G. S. Parent-adolescent relationships and adolescent independence in the United States and Denmark. *Journal of Marriage and the Family,* 1969, **31**, 348–358.

Karr, C., & Wesley, F. Comparison of German and United States childrearing practices. *Child Development,* 1966, **37**, 715–723.

Keniston, K. *Youth and dissent: The rise of a new opposition.* New York: Harcourt Brace Jovanovich, 1960.

Keniston, K. *The uncommitted: Alienated youth in America.* New York: Dell, 1965.

Keniston, K. *Young radicals: Notes on committed youth.* New York: Harcourt, Brace & World, 1968.

Keniston, K. Notes on young radicals. *Change,* 1969, **1**, 25–33.

Kerchoff, A. C. Early antecedents of role-taking and role-playing ability. *Merrill-Palmer Quarterly of Behavior and Development,* 1969, **15**, 229–247.

Kramer, R. B. On the development of moral maturity. Unpublished manuscript, 1972.

Lifton, R. J. *Boundaries: Psychological man in revolution.* New York: Random House, 1970.

Lifton, R. J. *History and human survival.* New York: Random House, 1971.

Longstreth, L. E., & Rice, R. E. Perceptions of parental behavior and identification with parents by three groups of boys differing in school adjustment. *Journal of Educational Psychology,* 1964, **55**, 144–151.

Luria, A. R. Experimental analysis of the development of voluntary action in children. In *The central nervous system and behavior.* Bethesda, Md.: National Institutes of Health, 1960.

Marcia, J. E. Ego identity status: Relationship to change in self-esteem, "general maladjustment," and authoritarianism. *Journal of Personality,* 1967, **35**, 118–133.

Martin, B., & Hetherington, E. M. Family interaction and aggression, withdrawal, and nondeviancy in children. Progress Report, University of Wisconsin, Project No. MH 12474, National Institute of Mental Health, 1971.

McClelland, D. C. *The achieving society.* Princeton, N.J.: Van Nostrand, 1961.

McCord, J., & McCord, W. The effects of parental role models on criminality. *Journal of Social Issues*, 1958, **14**(3), 66–75.

McCord, W., McCord, J., & Howard, A. Familial correlates of aggression in nondelinquent male children. *Journal of Abnormal and Social Psychology*, 1961, **62**, 79–93.

McCord, W., McCord, J., & Zola, I. K. *Origins of crime*. New York: Columbia University Press, 1959.

Middleton, R., & Putney, S. Political expression of adolescent rebellion, *American Journal of Sociology*, 1963, **68**, 527–535.

Millett, K. *Sexual politics*. New York: Doubleday, 1969.

Moss, H. A., & Kagan, J. Report on personality consistency and change from the Fels Longitudinal Study. *Vita Humana*, 1964, **7**, 127–138.

Norman, R. D. Interpersonal values of parents of achieving and nonachieving gifted children. *Journal of Psychology*, 1966, **64**, 49–57.

Osborne, E. G. *How to deal with parents and other problems*. New York: Grosset & Dunlap, 1962.

Peck, R. F., & Havighurst, R. J. *The psychology of character development*. New York: Wiley, 1960.

Pikas, A. Children's attitudes toward rational versus inhibiting parental authority. *Journal of Abnormal Social Psychology*, 1961, **62**, 315–321.

Radl, S. *Mother's Day is over*. New York: McKay, 1973.

Ramirez, M. Social responsibilities and failure in psychology: The case of the Mexican-American. *Journal of Clinical Child Psychology*, 1971–72, **1**(1), 5–7.

Reich, C. *The greening of America*. New York: Random House, 1970.

Rosen, B. C., & D'Andrade, R. The psychological origins of achievement motivation. *Sociometry*, 1959, **22**, 185–218.

Rossi, A. S. Changing sex roles and family development. Unpublished manuscript, Goucher College, 1971.

Schaefer, E. S. Converging conceptual models for maternal behavior and for child behavior. In J. C. Glidewell (Ed.), *Parental attitudes and child behavior*. Springfield, Ill.: Charles C Thomas, 1961.

Scherz, F. The crisis of adolescence in family life. *Social Casework*, 1967, **48**, 209–215.

Smelser, W. T. Adolescent and adult occupational choice as a function of family in socio-economic history. *Sociometry*, 1963, **26**, 393–409.

Smith, M. B., Haan, N., & Block, J. H. Social-psychological aspects of student activism. *Youth & Society*, 1970, **1**, 261–288.

Stinchcombe, A. L. *Rebellion in a high school*. Chicago: Quadrangle Books, 1964.

Vygotsky, L. S. *Thought and language*. Cambridge, Mass.: MIT Press, 1962.

Walker, E. L., & Heyns, R. *An anatomy for conformity*. Englewood Cliffs, N.J.: Prentice-Hall, 1962.

Winder, C. L., & Rau, L. Parental attitudes associated with social deviance in preadolescent boys. *Journal of Abnormal and Social Psychology*, 1962, **64**, 418–424.

Witkin, H. A., Dyk, R. B., Faterson, H. F., Goodenough, D. R., & Karp, S. A. *Personality through perception*. New York: Harper, 1954.

Wittman, M. P., & Huffman, A. V. A comparative study of developmental adjustment, and personality characteristics of psychotics, psychoneurotics, delinquent, and normally adjusted teen-aged youths. *Journal of Genetic Psychology*, 1945, **66**, 167–182.

Wolpe, J. *Psychotherapy by reciprocal inhibition*. Stanford, Calif.: Stanford University Press, 1958.

Yarrow, L. J. (Ed.) Symposium on personality consistency and change: Perspectives from a longitudinal research. *Vita Humana*, 1964, **7**(Whole No. 2).

III

Events and Processes in the Life Course

Expectations, Ideals, and Reality: Youth Enters College

NORMAN GOODMAN
and
KENNETH A. FELDMAN
State University of New York at Stony Brook

The period of life commonly called "adolescence" may well be a societal "invention" of the last hundred years or so, as Bennett Berger (1965) has put it. Being such, of course, makes it no less real and no less problematic for those who must somehow work their way through it. What at one time seems to have been a difficult but relatively short transitional stage is becoming an increasingly prolonged period in a person's life (cf. Berger, 1965, 1971, pp. 87–98). A major feature of this increasingly long transitional period from one status (child) to another (adult) is the interplay of hopes, desires, and expectations, on the one hand, and reality on the other. The confrontation between the two, traumatic for some, is generally a slow, continuous process; their adequate blending may be considered a sign of maturity, as most adults know it. But in some areas of the adolescents' experiences (and for some adolescents), this confrontation is likely to be more abrupt and unsettling. One such area for many adolescents involves the transition from high school to college, particularly when a

The study reported in this paper was initially designed, and the relevant data were collected, by Norman Goodman with the collaboration of Jerome E. Singer. We gratefully acknowledge the assistance of Andris Grunde, through the cooperation of James Bess and Joseph Katz, with the computer analysis.

residential college is involved. It is this more specific transition point in adolescence, and the issue of expectations and reality surrounding it, that forms the major concern of this paper and supplies the basis for the research that will be discussed (and for the more general analysis that follows).

It would seem at first glance that to study the process of transition from high school to college is to work in a very crowded area of research. For six years running, Stanley Cramer and Richard Stevic (1967, 1968-69, 1969, 1970-71, 1971, 1972) have reviewed articles in selected journals that seemed to them to be relevant to this particular field of study. Even with a modal number of only nineteen journals per year, the items of their bibliography total to some 423 entries over the six years. The topics of these articles include factors affecting college choice, patterns of financial aid, special admission programs, intellective and nonintellective predictors of academic success in college, measurement of college characteristics and environment, personality, attitudinal and value change during college, college student attrition and migration, types of college students, and types of subcultures in college, to name only a few of the areas.

From this partial listing alone, it should be clear that the studies reviewed by Cramer and Stevic vary widely in the degree to which they directly and systematically research the transition from high school to college. For example, studies of subcultures within college generally have had only a very indirect bearing. It is true that both the subcultures picked by students and the types of influence that these subenvironments have on them are presumably affected by what students are like before they enter college and by the exact nature of the transition to college they experience. These are not the matters, however, on which the college subcultural literature has generally focused. Research on the personal and social determinants of college aspirations and selection, on the other hand, clearly has a more direct bearing on the school-to-college transition, although many of the existing studies in this area stop at the point where the individual and the college have picked one another. Studies that actually begin with students in one or more high schools *and* then trace these students into (if not through) a college setting have been done. Though such studies are increasing in number, they are still relatively infrequent (for some of these studies, in addition to one reported herein, see Trent & Medsker, 1968; Herr, 1971; Taube & Vreeland, 1972; Offer & Offer, 1969; Offer, Marcus, & Offer, 1970; Remaly, 1969; Folger, Astin, & Bayer, 1970; McMahon & Wagner, 1973; Flanagan & Cooley, 1966; Sewell & Hauser, 1972, 1974).

Before presenting the specifics of the present research, we might note that the present study is at once similar and dissimilar in general design to other studies also focusing on the correspondence between prefreshmen's views of college and the actuality they perceive once there. During the late fifties and approximately the first half of the sixties, research on the fit between prefreshmen's expectations and the actuality of college was usually cross-sectional in design. In such studies, the reports of college recruits regarding their expectations of the colleges they were entering are compared with statements made by students (and sometimes faculty) already there (for a review of these earlier studies, see Feldman & Newcomb, 1969, pp. 71-82). In recent years, research has shifted to a longitudinal design, whereby prefreshmen are compared with themselves at one or more points in time after they are in the college setting; the study reported here follows this design (for others, see Bagley, 1969; Berdie, 1968; Buckley, 1971a; Caple, 1971; Chapman and Sedlacek, 1969; Herr, 1971; Pate, 1970; Quay and Dole, 1972; Schoemer and McConnell, 1968; Sockloff and Uhl, 1969; Stanfiel and Watts, 1970; and Walsh and McKinnon, 1969).

In both the cross-sectional and longitudinal research, initial measurement has almost always been at the time of entrance (usually during the freshman orientation period) rather than at some earlier period when students are still in high school. Since it is quite possible that persons become more knowledgeable about the college environment during their first few days there (see Feldman & Newcomb, 1969, pp. 73), the design of the present research—in which high school students completed an initial questionnaire well before their arrival on a college campus—probably gives a somewhat "purer" picture of precollege expectations. Finally, to the best of our knowledge, the design of the present study is distinctive, if not unique, in allowing comparisons between students who declined the acceptance of a given college in order to matriculate elsewhere with those students who were accepted by the particular college and actually attended it.

THE RESEARCH

Research Design

Two samples of college students were studied at two different points in time. One group consisted of a sample of students who were accepted for admission to a large public university (State) *and* who came to study there. This sample is labeled AA, indicating that they were *a*dmitted to State and *a*ccepted the offer. The second set of adolescents consist of those who applied and were accepted by State but decided to go elsewhere; this sample is labeled AD, indicating they were also *a*ccepted by State but *d*eclined the offer.

The use of these two samples of respondents has several advantages. First, the AA respondents provide a sufficiently large sample of students going to a single institution to permit systematic analyses of their perceptions of this particular college in terms of their social backgrounds (gender, age, religion, parental characteristics, high school grades, "collegiate orientation," etc.). Second, the AA respondents provide a sample of students who are likely to share a reasonably common academic and social milieu. Third, the use of an AD sample, comprised of students attending a number of different colleges and universities, allows an examination of whether the findings of the AA group are limited to the particular context of a specific college (State) or whether they represent the consequences of a more general college experience (a point to be touched on in this paper but not extensively analyzed).

Students in both samples completed two questionnaires. The first questionnaire was distributed to the students in the spring of their senior year in high school after they had been offered admission by State and had made their decision as to whether or not to accept, but before they actually had arrived on campus. The second questionnaire was completed by them in the spring of their second year at college, when they were sophomores. Thus, the first questionnaire contains the adolescents' reports of their hopes, desires, and expectations about the campus situation they were to face; the second questionnaire asks about their presumably more realistic assessment of campus life after approximately two years of experience with it.

Sampling Plan

A comprehensive list of all persons who applied for admission to State beginning with the fall 1970 semester was compiled and stratified into three populations:

AA—Those students who had been *a*ccepted by State and had stated their intention to *a*ttend.

AD—Those students who had been *a*ccepted by State but *d*eclined the offer of admission.

R—Those students whose application for admission had been *r*ejected.

A systematic probability sample of 450 AAs, 300 ADs, and 450 Rs was taken from this list. (The R category was subsequently dropped when the rate of return of the mail questionnaire was considered too low to be useful in the longitudinal study planned.) We received 275 usable completed questionnaires from the AA sample (61 percent of the original mailing) and 170 from the AD sample (a response rate of 57 percent).

Each of these 445 respondents was mailed another questionnaire two years later. Respondents for whom two completed usable questionnaires were available total 156 in the AA sample and 121 in the AD sample. Thus the response rate of students from the original sampling list was 35 percent for the AA sample and 40 percent for the AD sample, and no major differences in the response rate exist between the two samples ($t = 1.06$, $p =$ n.s.). Considering the usual dropout rate in longitudinal studies, the 35 to 40 percent return in this study seems adequate for our purposes. Furthermore, the samples were found to be comparable in terms of gender, age, religion, and socioeconomic status of family. Both samples contain slightly more males than females; and both consist of a basically white, middle class Jewish clientele, though there is a significant minority of Roman Catholic students.

The Questionnaire

The primary focus of the first questionnaire is on the respondents' initial expectations of the characteristics of State as well as those of their ideal college. In addition, the questionnaire emphasizes the factors that played an important part in the respondents' choice of college, including the reasons and the sources of influence for that choice. Several questions deal with the expectations the respondent has about the opportunities for student participation (or "student power," if you will) in many university activities. Since teaching is so obviously an important part of the university experience, respondents were asked what they expected in the classroom; for example, the respondents were asked for their expectations of whether their instructors would take a personal interest in the students and, more mundane questions, such as whether they expected the instructor to take class attendance. Also included were standard background items (occupation, education, and income of parents; the nature and extent of religious activity of the student's family; family size; the number of siblings who have attended college; and the like).

The questionnaire administered two years later focused on the college actually attended and included most of the material of the earlier questionnaire along with additional questions about the respondent's perception of the major subcultural orientations (derived from the typology formulated by Clark & Trow, 1966) in the university they are attending as well as their own particular orientation. Other questions dealt with the social and sexual activities of the respondents.

For this analysis, we have concentrated exclusively on the respondents' prior expectations of State (whether or not they attended this school), the subsequent perceptions of the characteristics of the college they did attend (State or elsewhere), and their descriptions of the ideal institution of higher education.

PRELIMINARY RESULTS

The data analysis reported in this paper is only a small part of the analyses contemplated for the data set. Here, we report the results of the use of factor analysis to develop a set of scales for the description of the characteristics of the college attended and the ideal college, differences between the two respondent samples on the "college characteristic scales," the relationship between prior expectations and subsequent perceptions of college characteristics, and, finally, the preliminary results of two regression analyses using the respondent's social background characteristics and the college characteristics scales at two points in time.

The College Characteristics Scales

Separate factor analyses were carried out for each of the two respondent samples (AA and AD) as to their expectations of State (and their ideal college) while they were still high school seniors, and their perception of the attributes of the college they attended and their ideal college after two years' experience as a college student. The factor structures of these eight different analyses were sufficiently similar and the importance of comparability of variables sufficiently great, so that a single set of scales on college attributes was developed. These scales were initially defined by the responses of those in the AA sample (while they were still high school seniors) to the perceived attributes of State. Each of the scales in the set was then slightly modified to take into account the factors emerging from the additional analyses. Thus the final set of seven scales on college attributes is a reasonable compromise between the existence of initially similar, but not identical, orthogonally-based factors and the need for a completely comparable set of scales to define college attributes for the entire sample of respondents.

The resulting seven scales, which define the attributes of the colleges attended and the student's conception of the ideal college, seem to make intuitive sense on the basis of the investigators' experiences at colleges and universities as well as in terms of the relevant research literature in this area (see Feldman & Newcomb, 1969, Chs. 4, 5). The scales and their defining variables are as follows:

1. *Permissive ambience* (4 items): "Permissive attitudes towards drugs," "permissive attitudes towards sexual activities," "opportunity to do just about what you want," "strict drug regulations" (reverse scoring).
2. *Primary-group emphasis* (4 items): "Mostly small classes," "close contact with faculty," "friendly student body," "many cultural activities."
3. *Liberal arts emphasis* (4 items): "Emphasis on liberal arts," "emphasis on arts," "emphasis on science" (reverse scoring), "can meet academic pressure without strain."
4. *Specialized and useful training reputation* (5 items): "Has the special curriculum I want," "good reputation for helping to get into graduate school," "good reputation for getting a job," "lot of hard work but worth it," "meet different kinds of people."
5. *An inexpensive and convenient college* (4 items): "Close to home," "away from home" (reverse scoring), "relatively mild winter," "low cost."
6. *A high-quality institution* (4 items): "High scholastic standards," "faculty of high academic quality," "intellectual stimulation," "small city."
7. *Opportunities for student involvement* (3 items): "An opportunity to become politically active," "student voice in administration," "good athletic program."

Scores created for the respondents' responses to the items in these scales have been used as the main variables in the analyses to be reported.

Mean Differences on the College Characteristics Scales

Given the research design of the present study, there are essentially two main types of comparisions that can be made. First, one can look at the data *cross-sectionally*, comparing the perception of the particular college with the perception of an ideal college (both before the students came to college and after they have been there two years). Second, *longitudinal* comparisons can be made assessing the similarity or differences between the AA respondent's expectation of what State would be like and his/her perception of what it was like after being there for two years (for the AD student the comparison is between State and the actual college attended); and a similar longitudinal comparison can be made for conceptions of an ideal college. In both cross-sectional and longitudinal comparisons, the results can be examined separately for the AAs and the ADs, in order to assess the effects of a particular institution as opposed to the "college experience" more generally. The AAs and the ADs can also be directly compared on their expectations and perceptions of the college they attended as well as on their views of the ideal college. Finally, it is possible to compare the AA and AD samples to see whether there are any differences in the amount of change over time (i.e., from 1970 to 1972) as a result of the college experience. All of these comparisons have been completed except the last, which is currently under way.

Cross-sectional comparisons. An actual college is compared with the ideal, both before students arrived at the college and after the students had been there two years. With only one exception each for the AA and AD samples in 1970, the mean scores for the ideal college are higher than the means scores for the actual college. (See Table 8.1 for the means and standard deviations and Table 8.2 for the t values.[1]) Using a sign test, this pattern of mean differences is highly significant both separately for the AAs and ADs and when the two samples are combined. In essence, what this pattern of differences suggest is that the respondents, whether they went to State or elsewhere, are more likely to perceive their ideal college as having those attributes defined by our scales than the actual college they expected to and in fact attended. In short, and not surprisingly so, perceived reality falls short of the ideal.

We turn now to consideration of the t values for the mean differences on each of the individual college characteristics scales (see Table 8.2). With the exception of the scale "permissive ambience," not only is there supportive evidence for the pattern of reality falling short of the ideal (discerned through the sign test), but the individual differences themselves are highly significant. The only exception is quite interesting. On permissive ambience the respondents in both the AA and AD samples prior to their college experience, believe that State is even more permissive than their ideal college would be. And this particular difference between the perception of State and the ideal college is itself statistically significant. One of the possible reasons for this expectation of a highly permissive situation at State results from the reputation State received in the period 1968-70 because of the highly publicized police raid on campus to arrest some thirty students on the basis of Grand Jury indictments for drug offenses. The result of the publicity led to an exaggerated belief about the degree of the permissiveness that existed on the State campus, and quickly became part of the underground student culture.

---

[1] The size and significance of the t values are not relevant at this point in the discussion; only their sign, which indicates which mean was higher, is relevant here.

TABLE 8.1

Means and Standard Deviations on the College Characteristic Scales for Both the AA and AD Samples, 1970 and 1972

College characteristics scales	1970 AA State		1970 AA Ideal college		1970 AD State		1970 AD Ideal college		1972 AA College attended		1972 AA Ideal college		1972 AD College attended		1972 AD Ideal college	
	$\bar{X}$	SD	$\bar{X}$	SD	$\bar{X}$	SD	$\bar{X}$	SD	$\bar{X}$	SD	$\bar{X}$	SD	$\bar{X}$	SD	$\bar{X}$	SD
1. Permissive ambience	1.782	.348	1.655	.368	1.829	.287	1.625	.364	1.849	.238	1.864	.263	1.762	.297	1.813	.293
2. Primary-group emphasis	1.699	.300	1.983	.071	1.622	.362	1.978	.096	1.348	.276	1.979	.082	1.596	.301	1.972	.100
3. Liberal arts emphasis	1.244	.304	1.585	.328	1.302	.315	1.598	.309	1.188	.225	1.724	.304	1.497	.322	1.638	.279
4. Specialized and useful training reputation	1.914	.210	1.980	.067	1.790	.277	1.979	.066	1.599	.344	1.956	.108	1.739	.293	1.962	.091
5. Inexpensive and convenient	1.676	.301	1.759	.245	1.621	.306	1.683	.305	1.681	.304	1.794	.254	1.386	.314	1.694	.271
6. High-quality institution	1.831	.162	1.873	.136	1.787	.226	1.869	.140	1.597	.268	1.830	.179	1.688	.269	1.852	.157
7. Opportunity for student involvement	1.868	.233	1.909	.199	1.831	.286	1.886	.209	1.504	.332	1.890	.230	1.673	.304	1.867	.231

TABLE 8.2

Cross-Sectional Comparisons on the College Characteristics Scales for Both the AA and AD Samples, 1970 and 1972

College characteristics scales	AA				AD			
	1970		1972		1970		1972	
	State vs. ideal college		State vs. ideal college		State vs. ideal college		Present college vs. ideal	
	t^a	p	t	p	t	p	t	p
1. Permissive ambience	3.231	.002	-0.745	.458	3.863	<.001	-1.554	.124
2. Primary-group emphasis	-11.657	<.001	-27.182	<.001	-9.009	<.001	-12.191	<.001
3. Liberal arts emphasis	-10.676	<.001	-17.996	<.001	-6.796	<.001	-4.056	<.001
4. Specialized and useful training reputation	-4.304	<.001	-12.951	<.001	-6.533	<.001	-7.360	<.001
5. Inexpensive and convenient	-3.115	.003	-3.896	<.001	-1.973	.052	-8.139	<.001
6. High-quality institution	-2.892	.005	-10.274	<.001	-3.328	.002	-6.224	<.001
7. Opportunity for student involvement	-1.699	.092	-12.342	<.001	-2.012	.048	-5.510	<.001

[a]A negative sign indicates that the mean on the ideal college is greater.

TABLE 8.3

Cross-Sectional Comparisons of AA versus AD on the College Characteristics Scales, 1970 and 1972

College characteristics scales	1970				1972			
	State		Ideal college		Present college		Ideal college	
	t[a]	p	t	p	t	p	t	p
1. Permissive ambience	-1.249	.213	0.646	< .50	2.528	.013	1.428	.155
2. Primary-group emphasis	1.760	.08	0.433	> .50	-6.694	< .001	0.547	> .50
3. Liberal arts emphasis	-1.413	.16	-0.317	> .50	-8.876	< .001	2.232	.027
4. Specialized and useful training reputation	3.941	< .001	0.118	> .50	3.402	< .001	0.499	> .50
5. Inexpensive and convenient	1.378	.17	2.152	.033	7.424	< .001	2.914	.004
6. High-quality institution	1.774	.078	0.227	> .50	-2.618	.01	-1.020	.309
7. Opportunity for student involvement	1.018	.310	0.896	.372	-4.028	< .001	0.735	.463

[a] A negative sign indicates that the mean of the AD sample is greater.

The results of these cross-sectional comparisons were consistent within both the AA and the AD samples. However, when the two samples are directly compared, several interesting findings emerge. As shown in Table 8.3, there are three major differences between the AAs and ADs in terms of their expectations about State. The AAs are more likely to see State as having a primary-group emphasis, a specialized and useful training reputation, and as being a high-quality institution. However, after both samples of students have attended college for two years, the State students compared to the AD students see their university as being more permissive, more impersonal, more science-oriented, more inexpensive and convenient, of lower quality as an institution, and as having fewer opportunities for student involvement in university affairs. The only consistency across two years between the AAs and ADs is that the State students, at both points in time, were more likely to see State as having a specialized program and having a useful reputation in terms of a job or graduate school than do AD students. The only differences with respect to descriptions of the ideal college are that the AAs are more likely to point to a liberal arts emphasis as being important for an ideal college and to reaffirm their earlier belief that the ideal college should be inexpensive and convenient, which is probably a reality for them at State.

Longitudinal comparisons. Focusing first on the AA group only, the most immediately obvious finding in Table 8.4, which is consistent with all other relevant studies, is that for all statistically significant differences between expectations and perceived reality, precollege students have higher expressed expectations of what college would provide than they subsequently came to experience, according to their own reports. Thus the AAs expected State to be of somewhat higher quality and to provide more opportunity for student involvement than they subsequently reported finding there. As a prefreshman, the State student similarly overestimated the amount of primary-group emphasis (in terms of small classes and high faculty/student contact) as well as the specialized curriculum and the usefulness of State's reputation (for help in getting a job or getting into graduate school). More refined analysis based on profiles of different kinds of students may shed further light on whether this sort of expectations/actuality discrepancy is a finding for students in general or whether it holds true for certain types of students and not others.

It is interesting to examine Table 8.4 with respect to the AD students. Recall in the initial questionnaire that these students reported their expectations of State, while in the subsequent questionnaire they reported their perceptions of the institution they eventually attended. In all but one case ("liberal arts emphasis"), they expected State to have more of the characteristics than their present college is seen to have. That is, they expected State to have more of a primary-group emphasis, to have more of a specialized and useful training reputation, to be more permissive, to be more inexpensive and convenient, to be of higher quality, and to provide more opportunities for student involvement than they found in their own institutions (although the first two do not attain

TABLE 8.4

Longitudinal Comparisons (1970 versus 1972) on the College Characteristics Scales for Both the AA and AD Samples

College characteristics scales	AA				AD			
	State		Ideal college		State vs. Present college		Ideal college	
	t^a	p	t	p	t	p	t	p
1. Permissive ambience	-1.427	.157	-6.497	<.001	2.083	.041	-5.121	<.001
2. Primary-group emphasis	10.435	<.001	0.660	>.50	0.264	>.50	0.467	>.50
3. Liberal arts emphasis	1.630	.106	-4.799	<.001	-4.204	<.001	-1.143	.256
4. Specialized and useful training reputation	10.872	<.001	2.745	.007	1.297	.199	1.364	.176
5. Inexpensive and convenient	-0.117	>.50	-1.113	.268	5.250	<.001	-0.055	>.50
6. High-quality institution	9.329	<.001	2.743	.007	2.938	.005	0.957	.341
7. Opportunity for student involvement	9.682	<.001	0.819	.415	3.699	<.001	0.470	>.50

[a] A negative sign indicates that the mean of the 1972 responses is greater.

statistical significance). If it is true that incoming college students have a generally inflated and partially stereotyped view of college (and there is evidence to this effect, as discussed in Feldman & Newcomb, 1969, p. 78), then—within limits of course—practically any college actually attended by ADs (or any other students, for that matter) would score low in comparison to the initially inflated, partly stereotypic expectations of State (and presumably of many other schools).

Descriptions of the ideal college also changed over time, as shown in Table 8.4. Thus State students (AA) report permissiveness and liberal arts emphasis as somewhat *more* important for their ideal college than they did earlier; the same is true for the AD students, although the liberal arts emphasis does not attain statistical significance. Conversely, for both samples of students (although not statistically significant for the AD students), the importance of the institution being of high quality is *lower* subsequent to college attendance than prior to it. If it is correct to interpret that expectation/actuality discrepancy on this same dimension (noted earlier) as showing that incoming students in fact expected and *wanted* high institutional quality but did not get it, then the lowering of importance of this characteristic for the ideal college is especially unsettling. For the two findings taken together can be seen as revealing a growing cynicism on the students' part: since the institution was not as good as they thought it was and wanted it to be, they appear to have revised (downwards) their conception of the importance of a high-quality institution in their ideal scheme of things.

Preliminary Results of the Regression Analyses

One of the major goals of this study was to explore the relationship between expectations and perceptions of reality, focusing in particular on the nature of the college experience. One way of exploring this relationship is to regress the college sophomores' perceptions of the characteristics of their college on what these same persons' expected during their senior year in high school. We also felt it would be useful to understand, at least in part, the genesis of the expectations themselves. In order to approach both these goals, two linear regression analyses have been completed. In the first, the 1970 expectations of college and ideal attributes have been regressed on a variety of social background variables. In the second, 1972 perceptions of college and ideal attributes have been regressed on the 1970 expectations. Although the full implications of these two regression analyses have not yet been adequately explored, two things already seem clear enough to warrant comment. First, as can be seen from Table 8.5, social background factors[2] explain very little of the variance in the 1970 expectations. The traditional background variables used by sociologists are not very helpful in predicting the expectations that high school students have of the attributes for

---

[2] These background characteristics are: age, gender, religion, parent's income, father's occupation, father's education, number of siblings with college experience, and most-liked high school subjects.

TABLE 8.5

R^2s from Regression of 1970 Expectations on Social Background
Characteristics for Both the AA and AD Samples

| College characteristics scales | R^2 | | | |
| | AA | | AD | |
	State	Ideal	State	Ideal
1. Permissive ambience	.154	.122	.300	.205
2. Primary-group emphasis	.131	.083	.100	.139
3. Liberal arts emphasis	.088	.352	.087	.317
4. Specialized and useful training reputation	.154	.196	.173	.121
5. Inexpensive and convenient	.073	.302	.187	.118
6. High-quality institution	.073	.125	.187	.199
7. Opportunities for student involvement	.121	.075	.131	.076

Note: The background characteristics are: age, gender, religion, parent's income, father's occupation, father's education, number of siblings with college experience, and most-liked high school subjects.

the college they expect to attend or even of their ideal college. These expectations are apparently the result of a much more subtle set of social-psychological processes than are captured in these background variables. There is one notable exception, which leads us to our second comment. One social background variable crops up continually as a predictor of classifications—the number of siblings the respondent has who have already been to college. It is interesting that this variable occurs more frequently in analyses performed on the AD respondents than in analyses performed on the AA respondents. We have not as yet assessed the full significance of this finding, but feel it is sufficiently interesting to merit comment at this point. At this early stage of analysis, we believe that this variable has relevance to the discussion in the school-to-college literature of the presumed naiveté and lack of realistic expectations of high school seniors, a point about which we will speculate later. However, we wish to explore this variable and its interrelationships further before trying to draw more definitive conclusions.

SOME PROGRAMMATIC COMMENTS

This paper reports only a small part of an extensive longitudinal study of the transition from high school to college. The data presented represent the early stages of analysis of a data set based on longitudinal study. However, some interesting findings have already emerged, although they have not been adequately explored at this time. The overall research deals with a larger set of variables than the college characteristic scales discussed here; the analysis of these additional variables will be reported on in subsequent work. But even with respect to the seven variables that formed the mainstay of the reported analyses in this paper, much more needs to be done, and some of this work is in fact already in progress. For example, we think it is important to develop profiles of different types of students in order to explore any differences among them with respect to the impact of the transition to college. These profiles are to be based on differing "subcultural orientations," gender, commuter or residential status, and so on. Furthermore, although we found that general social background characteristics were not particularly useful in predicting expectations for college, we think it might be useful to investigate further certain of the variables, such as "siblings with college experience," and to explore the extremes of those who changed a great deal with those who changed not at all.[3] We also think it important, though we do not have the data for doing so, to analyse the roots of the prior expectations of college. Finally, we think it is important to separate the AD's by the type of college they attended to see whether there is any systematic relationship between type of college and the variables we have studied.

THE SIGNIFICANCE OF THE SCHOOL-TO-COLLEGE TRANSITION: A DISCUSSION

An interesting characteristic of researching the transition to college is that it involves the study of two different kinds of transitions, one nested within the other. For many young persons, the transition from one status (child) to another (adult) includes the transition from one social organization and surrounding community (high school) to another (college). An investigation of the interrelationships among expectations, ideals, and reality gains in analytic power when placed in the context of either of these two transitions, just as a discussion of either of these transitional passages benefits from being embedded in more general social psychological and sociological contexts. Some of the major features of such grounding, as we see it, are briefly presented in this section.

The Passage to Adulthood

The statement that adolescence is a transitional status in American society may have the ring of a cliché, but this does not mean that the transitional period it implies does not exist nor that this transitional period does not have important consequences for youths. To point out the transitional nature of adolescence is to imply that there is a status from which the adolescent is emerging (childhood) and one toward which he or she is heading (adulthood). These bracketing stages

---

[3] Although there are a few exceptions (see Fisher, 1966; Dean, 1966; Buckley, 1969, 1971b), the focus of most of the research in the area has been on the general existence of the sorts of discrepancies we have described rather than on variation in the *degree* of discrepancies among students in given samples.

appear to have clearer substantive and temporal definition than does adolescence. One is a child longer and an adult longer than one is an adolescent. However, even this is in a state of change; with better nutrition, puberty (one commonly accepted signal to mark the onset of adolescence) occurs earlier and, with the increasing complexity of our society requiring advanced education and training, adolescence is extended at the other end as well.[4] Also there is somewhat more consensus on what it means to be a child and what it means to be an adult, irrespective of the individual involved, than is the case for adolescence. We all pretty much know what a child and an adult should do; but for the adolescent, it depends on who the individual is and the type of situation in which he or she is found.

As Ruth Benedict (1938) pointed out in her classic paper, "Continuities and Discontinuities in Cultural Conditioning," a child is expected to be nonresponsive (i.e., concerned with play rather than with work, with rights rather than with obligations), submissive rather than dominant in social relationships, and to be relatively uninformed about the sexual side of human experience. The adult, on the other hand, is expected to be responsible, dominant, and to know about, as well as participate in, the human sexual experience. But how a person is to move from having the characteristics of childhood to acquiring those of adulthood is not only a problem of theoretical significance, but one of pragmatic salience in the day-to-day lives of adolescents.

It should be clear that these three-dimensions—responsibility-nonresponsibility, dominance-submission and sexuality-nonsexuality—are only a small sample of the total area of concerns in an individual's life that require clear and systematic social structural definition as one moves from childhood to adulthood. Our society (and other societies as well) does not systematically provide the necessary guidelines that would permit its members to move smoothly from childhood to adulthood without the attendant stresses and strains generally found. Although it may be argued that these stresses and strains are useful in establishing an identity, it should also be noted that the problems generated may well exceed the bounds of utility.

To a large degree, then, the problems usually associated with adolescence are due to its status as a transitory and transitional stage in the life cycle. More important, it is a stage that is viewed ambivalently by society itself. On the one hand, admiration and concern are professed for youths; on the other hand, they are generally treated as less than full citizens long past the time when this is necessary (see Ausubel, 1954; Berger, 1965, 1971; Smith 1962). An adolescent is a person who will act like a child unless treated as an adult, or so it is said.[5]

---

[4] Indeed, the span of time has become so long that Bennett Berger (1971, pp. 91–92) has been prompted to no longer speak of it as a relatively fleeting "transitional stage" but as a major and substantial "segment of life."

[5] None of the comments made to this point are intended to imply that there is an abrupt change in the social demands on youth at puberty. The change is often so gradual that we only dimly perceive the transition except in the context of specific issues that arise.

Some Problems of the Adolescent Transition

The family, the school, and the peer group are the three major social settings in which American adolescents are engaged. Put another way, adolescents are family members, students, and friends, three key roles in society. Many of the problems inherent in adolescence in contemporary American society stem from the ambiguities, uncertainties, and conflict of expectations that exist within each of these social settings and across them as well. Using a familiar example from the context of school, a number of adolescents are occasionally faced with conflicting demands from their teachers, their peers, and their parents regarding how much work they should put in, what kinds of work they should do, and the exact importance the school should take in their total life scheme.[6] In addition, adolescents often face the problem of allocating their time, concerns, and resources among these three (and other) important social contexts in which they are involved. Again, a well-known example may be cited—the one involving the adolescent who is confronted the night before an examination (for which he or she planned to study) with solicitations from friends to join them at an important party that they have planned. What should be done? How shall these conflicting demands be resolved? What are the criteria to be used in making the decision? General adult expectations lean in the direction of studying, adolescent peer culture expectations in the other direction. No systematic provisions have been made by society to facilitate solutions to these common problems.

Another set of problems during the transitional period of adolescence concerns the disruption, or at the very least, the alteration, of previous social relationships that comes with movement to adulthood. One of the clearest instances of just such an unsettling factor is attendance at a college or university that permits (or requires) the youth to live away from home. This experience clearly alters the nature of a person's social as well as residential relationships, though to varying degrees for different individuals. Also, going away to college invariably includes not only the establishing of new peer relationships, but often the breaking off or modification of previous ones. With respect to the new school setting, not only are the peer relations changed, but the nature of the required academic performance (the role of student) differs as well. In fact, it is precisely this view of entrance to college as an unsettling factor that has led to its use as a strategic entry point into the analysis of the transitional nature of adolescence in the present research.

Another major problem of adolescence, and a basic issue with which the research reported in this paper has been concerned, is the adolescent's increasing need to deal with the confrontation between expectations and reality. Although this confrontation is certainly not limited to adolescents, it is likely to be more problematic and troublesome at this point in the life cycle than in either

---

[6] For a discussion and some data on the effect of these conflicting expectations on the development of autonomy among adolescents, see Goodman (1969).

childhood or adulthood. In childhood, two factors combine to make the difference between hopes, desires, and expectations, on the one hand, and reality on the other less unsettling than it is during adolescence. First, the relative inexperience of the young child often does not permit him or her to distinguish very clearly between what he or she expects (or what he or she would like) and adult reality. The young child tends to transform the world into an image of what he or she would like it to be. Second, this distinction between perception of adult reality and adult reality itself is often of somewhat lesser importance for children. Most people, most of the time, expect and thus excuse children for confusing the two. However, for adults, knowing the distinction is often crucial. It is expected that the adult can and will separate hope from fact, desire from reality. Moreover, the broader life experiences of the adult provide ample opportunities for practice in making such decisions, so that making the distinction becomes a relatively routine matter in which most adults have become reasonably proficient. Once more, the youth finds himself facing the gulf called adolescence, located between the peaks of childhood and adulthood, with little explicit guidance as to how to move easily from one side to the other. The distinction between expectations and adult reality becomes problematic for the adolescent.

The Passage to College

The most global finding of the research reported earlier was that students' perceptions of the colleges they attended did not, generally speaking, live up to their expectations of what an ideal college would be like; moreover, these perceptions did not even match their own precollege expectations. These results are in total accord with the findings of the other research in this area of study (see references cited earlier): students entering college say they expect more of a college than it actually provides; and they tend to expect more of themselves than circumstances will allow. The predominant approach in interpreting such disparities among stated ideals, expressed expectations, and perceived reality has been to credit incoming college students for their enthusiasm and idealism, while at the same time noting how misinformed, naive, and unrealistic they are. Consider, for example, the following excerpts from George Stern's recent book (1970):

> What the data do indicate is that the new arrivals on these campuses share stereotyped expectations of college life that combine some of the most distinctive academic characteristics of the elite liberal arts colleges with the community spirit, efficiency, and social orderliness of the church-related schools. University-bound high school seniors evidently share a highly idealized image of college life representative of no actual institution at all (p. 173).
>
> The incoming freshman's expectations for the college he has just entered are neither cynical, indifferent, nor dissolute. On the contrary, he brings with him to college a naive, enthusiastic, and boundless idealism concerning its ways and purposes. Although he probably feels that he knows well enough how his school differs from others, the particular pattern of activities that makes for these

differences is not nearly so evident to him as the common stereotype of college life that he shares with other incoming freshmen (p. 176).

... the new student arrives with great expectations, reinforced by everyone save the curiously cynical upperclassmen or faculty member whom he is not likely to know anyway.... No mere college could fulfill such expectations. The student comes to realize this after he has been on campus for a short while, and the disillusion can nowhere be more acute than at the large universities where the discrepancy between student needs and institutional environment is the most extreme (p. 177).

James Stanfiel and Frederick Watts (1970) have put this more briefly, if more colloquially: "entering freshmen tend to expect the moon and usually find something more mundane" (p. 134). In this context, if blame is cast at all, it usually lands at the feet of high school counselors and at the doors of the colleges themselves; both groups are seen as wittingly or unwittingly misinforming the young recruits to college.

Although we do not exactly fault this interpretation, we do feel that caution must be exercised in accepting it as the total or main picture—for it takes at absolute face value prefreshmen's public expressions of their ideals, expectations, and perceptions. From the research to date—including that presented here—not much is known about the degree to which incoming students to college are saying the things they feel they are supposed to be saying, but are really feeling something quite different. However, there are hints in the existing research, especially with respect to intellectual commitments, that incoming students may be exaggerating their ideals and expectations in educationally desirable directions (see Feldman & Newcomb, 1969, pp. 86-88). At any rate, we think it not too cynical to point out that, at least for some students, their more private beliefs and sentiments may not fully coincide in content with the publicly expressed aspirations and perceptions.

The faulting of colleges and counselors does have an underlying assumption that is worth making explicit. Knowledge of a group's culture, norms, and social arrangements does not accidentally vary empirically among individuals (for members and nonmembers alike). Rather, this knowledge is structurally patterned, as Robert Merton (1968, Chs. 10, 11) has pointed out as part of his analysis of anticipatory socialization and reference-group behavior. The visibility of a group's internal social environments to persons not yet in the group is dependent on the structural constraints of that group as well as the social structure of the groups from which the "new" recruits come and the existing conditions of intergroup contact. Although the structured visibility of college environments is far from total, it is certainly greater than that of some other organizations. While it may be true that high school counselors' knowledge of particular college environments is sometimes less complete than is optimally desirable (see, for example, Seymour, 1968) and that colleges often glamorize themselves in public presentations (see, for example, Donato & Fox, 1970), it is also the case that colleges are not secret societies (to put the matter in its extreme form). The public can visit them. Above-ground as well as underground consumer guides to colleges do exist. Students already in college are free to report back to their younger brothers and sisters, their families, and their home communities about the setting in which they are participating. This last, in fact, may help to explain the peculiar potency of the variable of number of siblings in college in the regression (reported earlier) of precollege expectations on a variety of background variables.

The discussion of structured visibility leads us to our larger point. It is our impression that studies of the transition to college would benefit if they were embedded more systematically than they typically are in theoretical frameworks of appropriate generality and relevance. An important part of this embedding would involve comparing the high school-to-college transition with other kinds of transitions. For instance, the transition to college provides a good site for the study of anticipatory socialization and reference-group behavior, but it is only one of many such sites. Put, more generally, the move from high school to college is but one of a wide variety of "status passages" that an individual might undergo in a lifetime. And, as Glaser and Strauss (1971) point out in their "formal theory" of status passage, there are a number of important dimensions along which different kinds of passages can be compared. Passages vary, for example, in their desirability, their inevitability, their reversibility, and their repeatability. Some other dimensions of comparisons are the degree to which the passage is voluntary, the clarity of the signs of passage, the degree of control over aspects of the passage by various agents (including the person undergoing the passage), and the nature of the passage in terms of whether it is done alone, collectively, or aggregatively. We take the following contention of Glaser and Strauss seriously: "Unless a researcher is explicitly sensitive to [the] multiple properties of status passage, he can be expected to make a relatively incomplete analysis of his data" (p. 8).

The study of status passage sheds light on both the larger social structure in which a given passage occurs and on the individuals who are undergoing the passage. Not only does the nature of given status passages reflect the particular cultural and social structural conditions in which they are embedded, but any changes in the properties of these passages have consequences for the larger cultures and social structures of which they are a part. At the level of the individual, status passage usually entails modification in persons' identities—varying in degree, of course, according to the exact nature of the passage. As a student leaves high school and enters college, he leaves his formerly validated social statuses and is incorporated into new social positions. In this move, those around him define and label him according to the new positions he either does or will occupy in college. In addition to (and as part of) others' view of him, he is given opportunities to engage in behaviors that were previously either not open to him, not particularly feasible, or not easily doable. As new social identities are pressed on him, and as he is given the structural opportunities to practice and enact their behavioral implications, the student may well begin to conceive of himself as being a different person from what he once was. Changes in overall self-conceptions are intertwined with changes in a variety of more specific personality and attitudinal attributes, including expectations, aspirations and perceptions (see Feldman, 1972).

It may turn out that the "identity" construct is particularly useful in the study of the transition to college. High school students have expectations, aspirations, and perceptions in a variety of substantive areas; and many of these change as individuals enter and begin their progress through college. It is possible that many of the bits and pieces in this area of study can be parsimoniously incorporated into the more global analysis of identity and identity change. Moreover, the issue of "realism" raised earlier might benefit from being analyzed in terms of the components of identity. For example, the exalted expectations of prefreshmen regarding their social and intellectual success can be viewed in terms of claimed identities—to be compared with their actually felt identities as well as their perceptions of the social identities being imputed to them (cf. Goffman, 1959, 1963; Lofland, 1969; Lyman & Scott, 1970; Strauss, 1959; Weinstein, 1969). It seems to us that our knowledge of the transition to college might be increased by studying the conditions under which these various identity components are most or least likely to overlap and the conditions under which they are most or least likely to change in college.

The research reported in this paper has focused on the interrelationships among the expressed expectations of those about to enter college, their descriptions of the ideal college, and their reports two years later of what the colleges they actually attended were like. In the more general discussion of this last section, we have presented several interrelated theoretical contexts that seem to us useful in interpreting specific results of this particular research and others like it. Such embedding, after all, is what gives any one study its real punch.

REFERENCES

Ausubel, D. P. *Theory and problems of adolescent development.* New York: Grune & Stratton, 1954.

Bagley, C. H. College expectations and educational goals for differing collegiate groups. Paper read at the annual meeting of the American Educational Research Association, Los Angeles, February 1969.

Benedict, R. Continuities and discontinuities in cultural conditioning. *Psychiatry*, May 1938, 1(2), 161–167.

Berdie, R. F. Changes in university perceptions during the first two college years. *Journal of College Student Personnel*, March 1968, 9(2), 85–89.

Berger, B. M. Teen-agers are an American invention. *New York Times Magazine*, June 13, 1965, 12–13, 83–87.

Berger, B. M. *Looking for America: Essays on youth, suburbia, and other American obsessions.* Englewood Cliffs, N.J.: Prentice-Hall, 1971.

Buckley, H. D. The relationship of achievement and satisfaction to anticipated environmental press of transfer students in the State University of New York. Unpublished doctoral dissertation, Syracuse University, 1969.

Buckley, H. D. A comparison of freshman and transfer expectations. *Journal of College Student Personnel*, May 1971, **12**(3), 186–188. (a)

Buckley, H. D. The relationship of transfer expectations to achievement. Experimental Publication System, Issue No. 11 (April), Ms. No. 403-26. Washington, D.C.: American Psychological Association, 1971. (b)

Caple, R. B. Freshman students' expectancy of the campus climate at a community college. *Journal of College Student Personnel*, January 1971, **12**(1), 20–25.

Chapman, T. H., & Sedlacek, W. E. Differences between student expectations and perceptions of the University of Maryland. Research Report No. 5-69. College Park, Md.: Counseling Center, University of Maryland, 1969.

Clark, B. R., & Trow, M. The organizational context. In T. M. Newcomb & E. K. Wilson (Eds.), *College peer groups: Problems and prospects for research*. Chicago: Aldine, 1966.

Cramer, S. H., & Stevic, R. R. What's new in precollege guidance? A review of the 1966–67 literature. *College Board Review*, Fall 1967, No. 65, 24–29.

Cramer, S. H., & Stevic, R. R. Research in the school-to-college transition: A review of the 1967–68 literature. *College Board Review*, Winter 1968–69, No. 70, 23–29.

Cramer, S. H., & Stevic, R. R. Research on the transition from school to college: A review of the 1968–69 literature. *College Board Review*, Fall 1969, No. 73, 22–30.

Cramer, S. H., & Stevic, R. R. Research on the transition from high school to college: A review of the 1969–70 literature. *College Board Review*, Winter 1970–71, No. 78, 22–28.

Cramer, S. H., & Stevic, R. R. Research on the transition from high school to college: A review of the 1970–71 literature. *College Board Review*, Fall 1971, No. 81, 32–38.

Cramer, S. H., & Stevic, R. R. Research on the transition from high school to college: A review of the 1970–71 literature. *College Board Review*, Fall 1972, No. 85, 32–38.

Dean, G. S. High school seniors' preferences and expectations for college environment in relationship to high school scholastic achievement and intellectual ability and as a predictor of college success and satisfaction. Unpublished doctoral dissertation, University of California, Los Angeles, 1966.

Donato, D. J. & Fox, G. C. Admissions officer, faculty, and student perceptions of their college environment. *Journal of College Student Personnel*, July 1970, **11**(4), 271–275.

Feldman, K. A. Some theoretical approaches to the study of change and stability of college students. *Review of Educational Research*, February 1972, **42**(1), 1–26.

Feldman, K. A., & Newcomb, T. M. *The impact of college on students*. San Francisco: Jossey-Bass, 1969.

Fisher, M. S. Environment, expectations, and the significance of disparity between actual and expected environment at the University of Utah. Unpublished doctoral dissertation, University of California, Los Angeles, 1966.

Flanagan, J. C., & Cooley, W. W. (Eds.) Project TALENT: One-year follow-up studies. U.S. Department of Health, Education, and Welfare Cooperative Research Project No. 2333. Pittsburgh: School of Education, University of Pittsburgh, 1966.

Folger, J. K., Astin, H. S., & Bayer, A. E. *Human resources and higher education: Staff report of the Commission on Human Resources and Advanced Education*. New York: Russell Sage Foundation, 1970.

Glaser, B. G., & Strauss, A. L. *Status passage: A formal theory*. Chicago: Aldine, Atherton, 1971.

Goffman, E. *The presentation of self in everyday life*. Garden City, N.Y.: Doubleday Anchor, 1959.

Goffman, E. *Stigma: Notes on the management of spoiled identity*. Englewood Cliffs, N.J.: Prentice-Hall, 1963.

Goodman, N. Adolescent norms and behavior: Organization and conformity. *Merrill-Palmer Quarterly of Behavior and Development*, April 1969, **15**(2), 199–211.

Herr, E. L. Student needs, college expectations, and "reality" perceptions. *Journal of Educational Research*, October 1969, **65**(2), 51–56.

Lofland, J. *Deviance and identity.* Englewood Cliffs, N.J.: Prentice-Hall, 1969.

Lyman, S. M., & Scott, M. B. *A sociology of the absurd.* New York: Appleton-Century-Crofts, 1970.

McMahon, W. W., & Wagner, A. P. A study of the college investment decision: Responses, with comparisons to the characteristics of other recent microeconomic surveys. ACT Research Report No. 59. Iowa City, Iowa: American College Testing Program, 1973.

Merton, R. K. *Social theory and social structure* (Enlarged ed.) New York: Free Press, 1968.

Offer, D., Marcus, D., & Offer, J. L. A longitudinal study of normal adolescent boys. *American Journal of Psychiatry*, January 1970, **126**(7), 917–924.

Offer, D., & Offer, J. L. Growing up: A follow-up study of normal adolescents. *Seminars in Psychiatry*, February 1969, **1**(1), 46–56.

Pate, R. H., Jr. Student expectations and later expectations of a university enrollment. *Journal of College Student Personnel*, November 1970, **11**(6), 458–462.

Quay, A. T., & Dole, A. Changes in community college perceptions before and after matriculation. *Journal of College Student Personnel*, March 1972, **13**(2), 120–125.

Remaly, D. E. What happens to college freshmen: The post admissions syndrome. Paper read at the annual meeting of the American Personnel and Guidance Association, Las Vegas, April 1969.

Schoemer, J. R., & McConnell, W. A. Is there a case for the freshman women resident hall. Student Services Report No. 22. Fort Collins, Colo.: Colorado State University, 1968.

Sewell, W. H., & Hauser, R. M. Causes and consequences of higher education: Models of the status attainment process. *American Journal of Agricultural Economics*, December 1972, **51**(5), 851–861.

Sewell, W. H., & Hauser, R. M. Education, occupation, and earnings: Achievement in the early career. (Final report) Social and Rehabilitation Service Social Security Administration, Department of Health, Education, and Welfare. Madison, Wis.: Department of Sociology, University of Wisconsin, 1974.

Seymour, W. R. Student and counselor perceptions of college environments. *Journal of College Student Personnel*, March 1968, **9**(2), 79–84.

Smith, E. A. *American youth culture: Group life in teenage society.* New York: Free Press, 1962.

Sockloff, A. L., & Uhl, N. P. Changes in non-cognitive variables during the freshman year at Emory. Research Report 3 (1968–1969). Atlanta, Ga.: Office of the Dean of Faculties, Testing and Evaluation Services, University of Georgia, 1969.

Stanfiel, J. D., & Watts, F. P. Freshman expectations and perceptions of the Howard University environment. *Journal of Negro Education*, Spring 1970, **39**(2), 132–138.

Stern, G. G. *People in context: Measuring person-environment congruence in education and industry.* New York: Wiley, 1970.

Strauss, A. *Mirrors and masks: The search for identity.* Glencoe, Ill.: Free Press, 1959.

Taube, I., & Vreeland, R. The prediction of ego functioning in adolescence. *Archives of General Psychiatry*, August 1972, **27**(2), 224–229.

Trent, J. W., & Medsker, L. L. *Beyond high school: A psychological study of 10,000 high school graduates.* San Francisco: Jossey-Bass, 1968.

Walsh, W. B., & McKinnon, R. D. Impact of an experimental program on student environmental perceptions. *Journal of College Student Personnel*, September 1969, **10**(5), 310–316.

Weinstein, E. The development of interpersonal competence. In D. A. Goslin (Ed.), *Handbook of Socialization Theory and Research.* Chicago: Rand McNally, 1969.

School Experience
and Status Attainment

KARL L. ALEXANDER
Johns Hopkins University

and

BRUCE K. ECKLAND
University of North Carolina

INTRODUCTION

The structure of stratification systems and the dynamics of mobility within them have long attracted the interest of social scientists. Much of the early empirical research in this area is systemic and structural in orientation, with a major interest in issues such as the relative "openness" or "rigidity" of status systems.[1] Recently, however, there has been a significant reorientation of much stratification research from the systemic to the individual level of analysis. In particular, the frequently documented correlation between fathers' occupational attainments and those of their male offspring, often the end-point of social system inquiries, has been recognized as a phenomenon requiring explanation in its own right, raising the question of how such intergenerational status influences are transmitted. Interest in the actual process of status transmission, and of

This is a revised version of a paper presented at the NICHD Conference on Adolescence in the Life Cycle, October 1973. We are grateful to Glen H. Elder and William Owens for their thoughtful comments on an earlier version of this paper. This research was supported, in part, by the Center for the Social Organization of Schools, Johns Hopkins University.

[1] See Lipset and Bendix (1959) for a review of much of the early literature in this area.

individual attainment dynamics in general, is the unifying theme of a rapidly expanding body of research known as the status attainment literature.

The American Occupational Structure, the seminal work of Blau and Duncan (1967), set forth a conceptual-analytical strategy for the study of attainment processes that has had a profound impact on subsequent work in this area. Blau and Duncan conceptualized the attainment process in terms of multiple and complexly interrelated influences impinging on youth as they progress through the life course. For example, they believed that much of the importance of parental status characteristics for their offspring's occupational attainments is mediated through the educational system. Their analysis provided strong support for this assumption, indicating a marked family status influence on offspring's level of education, but only negligible effects on occupational outcomes when educational attainments were themselves controlled. Educational level, in turn, is identified as the major direct determinant of outcomes in the occupational marketplace. Demonstration of this progression of attainment influences is an important first step[2] in interpreting the intergenerational linkages between status positions.[3] This formulation of the attainment process has subsequently been replicated in other studies employing quite different measurement strategies and additional indicators of background status.[4]

Although Blau and Duncan were principally concerned with the matter of status transmission, their work focused attention on a much more general objective, the explanation of variations in educational and occupational attainments. This work has progressed along two closely related fronts: the boundary of Blau and Duncan's "structural" framework has been extended to include additional exogenous, or antecedent, variables, such as academic ability, family composition, race, and sex; and, additional intervening mechanisms have been introduced to further explicate the processes by which these background variables ultimately affect status outcomes.[5] We are primarily interested in "school process" extensions of the framework.

[2] An earlier study by Duncan and Hodge (1963) actually employed a conceptual model and analytical strategy quite similar to Blau and Duncan's (1967). The latter, however, seems to have had a much greater impact on subsequent work in this area.

[3] It should be mentioned, however, that although educational attainment does serve in part to mediate background influences on occupational outcomes, most of the education effect on occupational attainment is independent of social origins (Blau & Duncan, 1967; Alexander & Eckland, 1973a). The conclusion that educational certification serves more to dissociate adult attainments from the ascriptive bonds of social origins than to directly transmit either status advantage or disadvantage (Duncan, 1968; Sewell, 1971) severely strains much of the rhetoric of the anticertification literature (Berg, 1970; Miller & Reissman, 1969; Sexton, 1961).

[4] See Alexander and Eckland, 1973a, b; Haller and Portes, 1973; Sewell, Haller, and Ohlendorf, 1970; Sewell, Haller, and Portes, 1969.

[5] See Duncan, 1968, 1969; Jencks, 1972; Alexander, 1973; Alexander and Eckland, 1973a, b, c; Sewell, Haller, and Ohlendorf, 1970; Sewell, Haller, and Portes, 1969; Spaeth, 1968, 1970; Williams, 1972; Duncan, Featherman, and Duncan, 1972; Hauser, 1972; Sewell and Hauser, 1972; Elder, 1968; Featherman, 1972; Treiman and Terrell, 1973. Actual

Blau and Duncan's documentation of educational certification as an important source of subsequent attainments and as mediator of antecedent influences
is consistent with long-standing assumptions (Wolfle, 1954; Folger & Nam, 1965;
Parsons, 1959) and explains, in part, why policy and analytical considerations
focus on educational institutions in assessments of "equality of opportunity"
(Coleman, Campbell et al., 1966). Persistence through the educational system
and the attendant certification clearly represent valuable currency in the occupational marketplace. Consequently, the dynamics of educational attainment[6]
have become the topic of extensive investigation.

Within educational settings, attention has been directed toward some of the
more interpersonal and subjective mechanisms long suggested as pertinent to
educational outcomes. Goal-setting processes, interpersonal influences, and
reference-group theory have received particular attention in this respect. The
sociological and educational literatures are replete with studies of interpersonal
influence on goal-setting, of status and ability effects on goal levels, of goal
orientations and other motivational variables on attainments,[7] but rarely are all
such influences considered in conjunction. The result is often a disquieting lack
of closure. Modeling approaches to the attainment process are well suited for the
simultaneous assessment of structural, interpersonal, and subjective influences
on status outcomes, under the constraint of an explicitly formulated causal
order.

By including social structures and individual characteristics in a single analytical framework, these models are particularly useful for exploring the interface between social structure and personality development (Elder, 1973).
Furthermore, by indicating the direct and indirect mechanisms by which various
influences are transmitted, they make explicit the importance of particular
effects relative to others. Such information guards against inflated claims that so
often attend the study of incomplete models.[8]

This project will evaluate one such school process attainment model. Its
specific components (to be elaborated in the following section) include social
status, academic ability, and sex as "background" variables, and a variety of

academic achievement, as distinct from educational attainment (or years of education
obtained), may also be profitably studied within this general framework. See Hauser (1969,
1971), McDill, Meyers, and Rigsby (1967), and McDill, Rigsby, and Meyers (1969).

    [6] In this literature "educational attainment" usually refers to either years of schooling
received or degrees conferred, while "educational achievement" pertains to standardized
achievement test scores.

    [7] See Bell, 1965; Crockett, 1969; Ellis and Lane, 1969; Furstenburg, 1971; Haller and
Butterworth, 1960; Herriott, 1963; Kahl, 1961; Kandel and Lesser, 1969; McDill and
Coleman, 1965; Rehberg, Schafer, and Sinclair, 1970; Simpson, 1962; Wilson, 1959.

    [8] Jencks' evaluation (1972) of the actual attainment consequences of estimated genetic
contributions to differences in measured IQ is a good example (it is the general strategy that
is being endorsed here, not the particulars of Jencks' estimate). Gordon's rather elaborate
model (1972) of educational and occupational goal orientations, on the other hand, fails to
address the crucial issue of their consequence for tangible outcomes in the stratification
system. Thus, multivariate modeling in itself does not assure closure for the inquiry.

subjective, interpersonal, and organizational variables as intervening between these and actual status outcomes. The variables are arrayed in a causal structure presumed to reflect the actual pattern of influence among them. In evaluating the model, we will estimate the importance of each background and school variable for educational and occupational attainments, their influences on one another (under the constraint of our causal ordering), and the indirect effects of family background through school processes. The analysis is based on longitudinal data from a national sample of youth, first sampled in 1955 as high school sophomores and followed up in 1970.[9] With this overview of the research issues in mind, we will present in the next section the details of our particular model of the attainment process. This will be followed by a discussion of sex effects in the attainment model and finally by a presentation of our results, which, in this report, are restricted to working men and women.

SCHOOL EXPERIENCES IN ADULT ATTAINMENT: THE ANALYTIC MODEL

Our model follows in the tradition of those developed by Sewell and his colleagues.[10] Sewell's "social-psychological" extensions of the Blau and Duncan framework have examined the mediation of ability and family background in educational and occupational attainments through various school-related mechanisms—academic performance, the influences of "significant others," and educational and occupational goal orientations. Sewell's modeling efforts, conducted on data from 1957 Wisconsin high school seniors, are the most definitive to date regarding the role of subjective and interpersonal variables in the attainment process.

In our research program, we have "replicated" a number of earlier studies of status attainment. These replications provide independent confirmation for most of the conclusions from Blau and Duncan's structural model (Alexander & Eckland, 1973a, b) and Sewell's school process models (Alexander, 1973; Alexander & Eckland, 1973c), despite substantial differences in research design and measurement.

Figure 9.1 is a schematic representation of the causal relationships among background and school process variables in our approximation of one of the Wisconsin models (developed and evaluated by Hauser, 1972). The informative value of our comparison of EEO and Wisconsin models is enhanced by their use of data from the same cohort of youth (the Wisconsin sample consisting of 1957 Wisconsin high school seniors and the EEO of 1955 high school sophomores).

---

[9] The fifteen-year follow-up project, directed by Bruce K. Eckland, has been named "Explorations in Equality of Opportunity" (EEO).

[10] See Sewell, Haller, and Ohlendorf, 1970; Sewell, Haller, and Portes, 1969; Hauser, 1972; Sewell and Hauser, 1972.

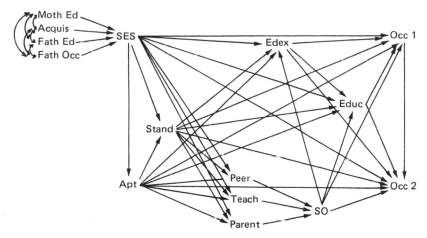

Figure 9.1   EEO "replication" of the Hauser-Sewell model of status attainment. Variable abbreviations used in Figures 9.1 and 9.2 and throughout the analysis are: SO, the composite index of significant others' influence; Moth Ed, mother's education; Acquis, household acquisition index; Fath Ed, father's education; Fath Occ, father's occupation; SES, unmeasured socioeconomic status construct; Apt, academic aptitude; Stand 1 and Stand 2, sophomore and senior class standing; Curric 1 and Curric 2, sophomore and senior curriculum enrollment; Peer, peer plans index; Teach, teacher contacts regarding college plans; Parent, parental contacts regarding college plans; Image, self-conceptions of academic competence; Edex, educational expectations; Educ, educational attainment; Occ 1 and Occ 2, early and present occupational attainments.

Despite differences in measurement and conceptual formulation,[11] the two analyses are strikingly consistent.

The highlights of this analysis introduce the substantive concerns of this report, which involve a number of extensions of the Hauser-Sewell model. Our analysis (consistent with the conclusions of Blau & Duncan, 1967; Duncan, 1968; Sewell, Haller, & Portes, 1969; Sewell, Haller, & Ohlendorf, 1970; and Sewell & Hauser, 1972) identified educational attainment as, by far, the major determinant of occupational outcomes. Indeed, of all variables in the analysis, only high school class standing had a notable, but still minor, direct effect on occupational attainments. Thus, the importance of family background, ability, and school processes for occupational sorting is almost entirely mediated through educational certification.

Our research and that of Sewell and Hauser (1972) identify a wide array of direct influences on educational attainment itself, with no single variable being

[11] Our version was actually not a "true" replication of Hauser's model. It excludes occupational aspirations and includes occupational status as an attainment outcome. Moreover, the measurement strategies employed in the two analyses often differed markedly. For a more thorough discussion of these matters, see the original research reports (Alexander & Eckland, 1973c; Hauser, 1972; Sewell, Haller, & Portes, 1969).

of overriding importance. In our models, socioeconomic status, academic ability, class rank, educational expectations, and a composite index of significant others' influence all have moderate direct effects on educational levels. The direct effects of ability and SES are reduced considerably when the school variables are included in the analysis, indicating that school processes are an important mediating link between the family background of youths and their level of educational attainment.

In this analysis the influence of significant others is the most important direct determinant of educational attainments, followed by family status background and senior class standing. Peers and parents represent exceedingly important sources of this interpersonal influence, followed at a distance by school personnel. The influence of all three types of significant others is responsive to variations in status background and demonstrated academic performance, while performance is primarily determined by measured ability. Neither the EEO nor the Wisconsin analysis suggested any substantial direct effects of family background on academic performance.

This brief overview suggests the value of identifying key mechanisms that link status background to adult status. The relationship between background factors, such as academic ability and SES, and eventual adult attainments is maintained, in large measure, by a variety of more proximate determinants of these adult outcomes. Information regarding these processes is crucial for understanding the full complexity of attainment dynamics and, regarding our particular substantive interests, the functioning of educational institutions.

The objective of this paper is to evaluate the school process model presented schematically in Figure 9.2. Except for the composite index of "Significant Others" (which was deleted for reasons to be noted shortly), all variables from the Hauser-Sewell replication were retained in this version. Its additions include sophomore- and senior-year measures of class rank and curriculum enrollment and an index of academic self-conceptions. Curriculum tracking has often been identified as one of the more consequential "sorting and selecting" mechanisms of school organization (Parsons, 1959; Folger & Nam, 1965), but its importance has yet to be evaluated within this conceptual framework. These measures of tracking and performance permit a rather detailed portrayal of within-school attainment dynamics. The responsiveness of both streaming and rank to "functionally relevant" (i.e., ability and motivation) and "functionally irrelevant" (i.e., SES) influences, the degree to which terminal outcomes are anchored by earlier ones, and the extent to which the linkage between early and later outcomes is mediated by intervening mechanisms may all be assessed with such data. The index of academic self-conceptions, a subjective construct often thought to be critically important in the attainment process (Gordon, 1972), will supplement our measure of goal orientation.

The arrangement of variables in Figure 9.2 is determined largely by either their actual time of measurement or, if measured retrospectively, their temporal referent. Nevertheless, there is some arbitrariness in the ordering of contemporaneously measured variables that are likely to be mutually influencing, either

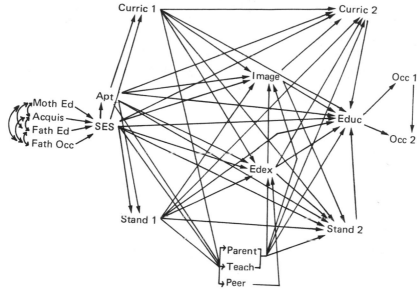

Figure 9.2 The EEO school process model of status attainment. [All antecedent variables in the model except Peer and the four status background items, should also have arrows leading into both early and present occupational attainments.]

simultaneously or over time. While such reciprocal effects can be estimated under certain circumstances (see, for example, Hauser, 1972; Duncan, Haller, & Portes, 1968), the recursive model employed here reflects both the temporal constraints imposed by variable measurements and reasonable assumptions regarding direction of causation derived from other studies of these processes (Sewell, Haller, & Ohlendorf, 1970; Sewell, Haller, & Portes, 1969; Sewell & Hauser, 1972).

Some of the patterns of influence diagrammed in Figure 9.2 perhaps merit brief elaboration. While the parental and teacher-counselor contact items are allowed to directly influence all subsequent outcomes in the model, the peer plans index has been constrained to directly affect only "own" plans.[12] The peer index actually measures interests and plans rather than influence, and does not necessarily imply persuasive intent. Parental and teacher contacts regarding college plans, on the other hand, more clearly suggest efforts at interpersonal influence, and, because of this, they are permitted to directly affect all later outcomes. These differences in the interpersonal influence variables prompted our deletion of the composite "Significant Others' Influence" index from this analysis. It is anticipated, nevertheless, that much of the importance of all interpersonal variables, adult and peer, will be mediated through "own" plans. Also, the "significant others" variables were themselves contemporaneously

[12] Allowing peer plans to directly influence all subsequent outcomes in the model would result in only one additional "significant" effect. The peer plans–educational attainment coefficient for males, at .131, would exceed the .100 level. These "sex-controlled" full models have not been included in this report.

measured and are assumed not to directly affect one another. Thus, their covariances are treated as functions of their mutal dependence on antecedent and unmeasured influences.

Academic self-concept has been measured retrospectively with data from the 1970 follow-up survey.[13] Although the items in the index refer to the overall high school experience, we have assumed that cumulative and terminal experiences would weigh most heavily in such recollections. Hence, the scale has been placed subsequent to all variables measured in 1955 when the respondents were sophomores but prior to senior rank and curriculum enrollment. Sewell and his associates have speculated that such a construct might mediate some of the ability-performance linkage (Sewell, Haller, & Portes, 1969), but they lacked the data necessary to test this assumption. Substantial importance is often implied for such subjective variables without actually assessing their importance for tangible attainment outcomes (Gordon, 1972; Crockett, 1966). The evidence to date, however, suggests only modest effects for most subjective-motivational variables (Elder, 1968; Featherman, 1972; Crockett, 1969). As noted earlier, multivariate models such as these are particularly useful for avoiding exaggerated claims of consequence.

Just as was the case with out indicators of interpersonal influence, the relationship between contemporary measures of class rank and curriculum enrollment is attributed to their mutual dependence on antecedent variables. Thus, only academic ability and status background will be entered into the regression equations for these variables at the sophomore year. Sophomore rank and curriculum enrollment are, however, permitted to directly affect both of their senior-year counterparts. While these "lag" effects should be the largest in each senior-year equation, the extent to which sophomore influences on senior outcomes are mediated by intervening mechanisms and the causal efficacy of these mechanisms independent of sophomore-year anchoring will be of particular interest.

Finally, principally for analytical convenience, academic ability is treated as dependent on status background in our models. As Hauser (1972) notes, this conceptualization inflates the importance of social origins for ability to the extent that both are mutually dependent on parental genetic characteristics. Since the ability-SES correlations and regression coefficients are almost identical throughout the analysis, the results and their implications, aside from those

---

[13] Our reliance on retrospective data for the self-concept index is, of course, problematic. Unfortunately, none of the data from the original 1955 survey were suitable for this purpose. Although such a scale has been constructed from these data (Meyer, 1970), selective nonresponse by college-goers precluded its adoption here. Although it might be feared that retrospective data would inflate the relationship between self-conceptions and attainment outcomes, the correlations actually obtained were all of moderate magnitude (ranging between .22 and .29 for educational and early and current occupational attainments). If the measurement of self-conceptions does exaggerate their importance, then the conclusion to be presented of their only modest importance would actually overstate the case somewhat.

involving the ability-SES linkage itself, are essentially unaffected by our conceptualization.

To this point we have outlined the dimensions of our school process model and the information to be culled from its consideration. We have not yet touched on one major substantive concern of this project, that of sex differences in attainment dynamics. This topic has been set aside for separate consideration, and we turn now to a discussion of how it will be examined within this modeling framework.

SEX EFFECTS IN THE ATTAINMENT MODEL

The topic of differences in the attainment dynamics of men and women is sorely neglected in the attainment process literature. Almost all of the studies alluded to thus far, including Hauser's analysis (1972) and our "replication" of that model (Alexander & Eckland, 1973c), have been restricted to samples of males. Indeed, an inspection of the multivariate modeling literature might easily suggest that "status attainments" are often treated as synonymous with male attainments. Our analysis of sex differences will examine the pertinence of sex for school process dynamics and the adequacy of this rather narrowly circumscribed framework in accounting for sex differences in attainment outcomes. Census data and numerous tabular and correlational studies of variables such as school retention and educational plans (Flanagan & Cooley, 1966; Wolfle, 1954; Folger & Nam, 1965) have long suggested the importance of sex for status outcomes, yet this issue has received scant attention in the attainment modeling literature.

The little information that is available does indeed suggest sex-specificity in the importance of background influences, identifying academic ability as more consequential for the attainments of males and status background for females (Hauser, 1971; Sewell & Shah, 1967, 1968). Contrary to what might have been anticipated, however, these results have not stimulated further consideration of such differences. With the exception of our own recent study (Alexander, 1973), sex effects have yet to be considered in any of the more complex attainment models in the literature.

In relation to educational outcomes, we evaluated the model shown in Figure 9.2 for selected main and interaction effects of sex for the entire EEO sample. The analysis produced a marked educational liability for women that was largely independent of the numerous school process variables. Furthermore, we found considerably greater status ascription in the attainment outcomes of women, whereas male educational attainments were, as in Sewell's studies, more closely tied to ability.

Recently, however, Treiman and Terrell (1973) have obtained somewhat different results. Comparing the attainment outcomes of employed men and women in variations of the Blau and Duncan "basic model," they found male and female attainment dynamics to be quite similar, with the most marked differences occuring for income levels. Their finding of minor sex differences regarding educational attainments differs from the findings of the few other studies, including our own, that have considered this issue, but none of these other inquiries are restricted to samples of *working women*. In view of these contradictory findings, and the relative neglect of female attainment dynamics in general, a replication of our other analysis, but restricted to currently employed women, should be quite informative and is what we plan to do in this report. While it may be the case that women who, for whatever reasons, pursue labor-force careers are not subject to the same educational attainment disabilities affecting the total female population, it is not entirely clear why this should be anticipated. It is suspected, rather, that Treiman and Terrell's findings may result from the omission of certain key variables from their analysis, most notably academic ability.

We will begin by evaluating the model presented in Figure 9.2, but include sex as an additional exogenous, or background, variable. First, the effects of sex, ability, and SES alone on each of the school process and attainment outcomes will be assessed, following which all patterns of influence portrayed in the model will be estimated. Next, an explicit test of significance for the sex main effects in the above analyses and for sex interactions with ability and status background will be presented. Finally, the substantive implications of these interactions will be evaluated by examining the status background and ability effects on each of the school process and attainment outcomes separately for males and females. As in our other analysis, it is anticipated that social origins will be more consequential for the attainment outcomes of women, while ability influences will be more pronounced for men (Sewell & Shah, 1967; Alexander, 1973). This analysis, then, is essentially a replication of our earlier work, but with the female sample restricted to currently employed women. Contrary to Treiman and Terrell (1973), it is expected that the sex effects in this analysis will generally be similar to those obtained for the total EEO female sample. Of course, restricting the analysis to "working" women considerably reduces the size of our usable female sample. The number of women with complete information on all variables in this attainment model is 486, as compared with 854 in our other study. Such attrition is to be anticipated, and at a later date we intend to explicitly explore the processes affecting female labor-force participation. It might be noted that the total EEO female sample numbers 1130. The reduction of this figure to 854 in our other analysis reflects attrition due to missing data on any variable in the model.

More than 95 percent of the 947 males in the EEO follow-up sample did provide usable data on current occupation. Those few who did not were omitted from our other inquiry to retain comparability with this analysis. Consequently, the male models in the two studies correspond exactly, while differences between the total sample and female models result from the omission of unemployed women from this analysis.[14]

---

[14] It is somewhat unfortunate that we were not able to apply more rigorous criteria for identifying career-oriented women. We have merely selected out those women who reported

Further discussion of the data set is presented in the Appendix to this paper. The Appendix also includes a detailed description of our measures and how we generated an unmeasured SES construct while retaining the disaggregated effects of the SES indicators, plus a brief discussion of our method of analysis, which employs both recursive path models and a dummy variable technique for assessing the significance of sex main and interaction effects.

RESULTS

We will begin by considering the standardized effects of ability, SES, and sex alone for each of the school process variables and status outcomes in the attainment model. These are presented in Table 9.1. Comparing the relative importance of background variables would be considerably more arduous in the full model, in which these effects are decomposed into indirect and residual direct influences. In order to restrict the discussion to effects of some substantive importance, coefficients of less than .100 will be considered trivial. With our relatively large sample, considerably smaller coefficients would be statistically significant at conventional levels.

It is apparent from the data in Table 9.1 that the effects of background variables are far from uniform throughout the model. Academic ability is identified as the dominant influence for class standing and self-concept. Sex has a secondary effect on each of these outcomes. And SES is of negligible importance in all three instances (although the status coefficient for sophomore rank falls just below the .100 level). Thus, academic performance and self-evaluations thereof are principally responsive to academic ability, and we find little evidence of the often presumed status bias in grading. Furthermore, women tend to score somewhat higher on each of these outcomes, even independent of ability and status background.[15] Presumably this reflects some unmeasured sex-related motivational influence.

Although SES is relatively unimportant for these dependent variables, it has substantial effect on almost all others in the model. It is the principal determinant of the three types of "significant others' influence" and of educational expectations. Furthermore, though these differences are somewhat less marked, SES is also more important than ability for both sophomore- and senior-year curriculum enrollment and early and present occupational attainments. Clearly, then, social origins are quite influential, both for actual attainments and for many of the school process mechanisms. Consistent with much of the adolescent-society literature (Coleman, 1961), high-status youth disproportionately express college-going intentions regardless of academic ability, and perhaps of scholarly interest as well. Similarly, academically pertinent interpersonal experiences, and even curriculum tracking decisions, are more

---

both an early and current occupation. This procedure would pick up temporary workers and exclude career-oriented women who were unemployed at the time of the follow-up survey.

[15] Females are coded "1" and males "0" in this analysis. Hence, a negative coefficient indicates a negative consequence of being female.

TABLE 9.1

Standardized Regression Coefficients for the "Background Effects" Model (Combined-Sex Sample, $N = 1,205$)

	Curric 1	Stand 1	Peer	Teach	Parent	Edex	Image	Curric 2	Stand 2	Educ	Occ 1	Occ 2
Apt	.232	.440	.126	.017	.122	.124	.358	.313	.477	.324	.259	.265
SES	.330	.099	.386	.192	.312	.413	.023	.319	.082	.323	.302	.322
Sex	−.088	.142	.006	−.024	.095	−.007	.204	−.044	.240	−.127	.146	−.055
R^2	.217	.258	.196	.040	.154	.219	.183	.264	.328	.287	.235	.230
R^2 (uncon)[a]	.221	.260	.199	.046	.161	.219	.188	.267	.328	.289	.240	.236

[a]The proportions of explained variance obtained with unconstrained (or, observed) interitem correlations are presented in the last row of the table. The difference between constrained and unconstrained R^2s is the loss of explanatory power due to the use of the canonical index construction strategy.

responsive to the influence of social origins than of ability. Being related to status background in this fashion, such school processes may constitute important mechanisms of status transmission. This possibility will be explored more thoroughly in the full attainment model.

As was suggested in our introduction, educational attainment is important both as a status outcome itself and as mediator of antecedent influences. Our analysis identifies SES and academic ability as being equally important determinants of such attainment, with respective coefficients of .324 and .323. Most other multivariate inquiries, however, have reached a somewhat different conclusion, granting measured ability a modest advantage in influencing educational outcomes (Duncan, 1968; Sewell, Haller, & Portes, 1969; Sewell, Haller, & Ohlendorf, 1970).

While the reliability of our aptitude measure may account for this discrepancy, a more substantive explanation appears to apply. All of the inquiries just mentioned were based on male samples, whereas our analysis includes both sexes. It will be demonstrated later that sex interactions with ability and SES are confounded in this analysis, resulting in some important distortions (it will be recalled that the multiple regression strategy assumes linear, additive influences). For males, ability is indeed somewhat more important than SES as a determinant of educational attainment, but just the reverse is the case for women. The conclusion of their equal importance in this analysis, then, results from the confounding together of these sex-specific differences in the relative importance of ability and status background. A similar confounding of effects occurs for the two occupational attainment outcomes in Table 9.1. Hence, to ignore sex effects, or to study them without considering important interactions, may result in a partial and/or misleading portrayal of attainment dynamics.

The remaining sex effects in Table 9.1 also merit brief mention. Even with ability and status controlled, women tend to suffer a modest educational disability. At the same time, however, they are relatively advantaged in terms of early occupational attainments (the negative sex coefficient for present occupational status is statistically significant, but falls below our .100 cutoff for the attribution of substantive importance). In more substantive terms, this last result reflects a tendency for males to disproportionately report an "unskilled or semiskilled" first job (35 percent of males versus 18 percent of the women in the total sample—not shown in tables), while women are overrepresented in the "office, clerical, and sales" category (50 percent and 12 percent for females and males, respectively).

Although our relatively crude occupational classification generally functions in the attainment model as do more refined scales (Alexander & Eckland, 1973a), this early attainment advantage for women may still reflect either lack of sufficient detail in the coding scheme or some peculiarity of the measurement of "first occupation" (see Blau & Duncan, 1967, for a discussion of the adequacy of a similarly worded item in their analysis). Nevertheless, a modest early occupation advantage is indicated for women, and its "robustness" has yet to be evaluated with more refined measurements.

Finally, a brief comparison of these results with our other sex effect inquiry is in order (Alexander, 1973). The educational disability for women in Table 9.1 is quite similar to that obtained for the entire EEO female sample, as are the other sex effects in the analysis. Thus, restricting the study to currently employed women does not produce the sex similarity in attainment dynamics suggested by Treiman and Terrell (1973).

The full attainment model is evaluated in Tables 9.2 and 9.3. These analyses trace the patterns of relationship among school process and attainment variables themselves and will allow us to assess their role in mediating the background influences just discussed. Table 9.2 includes all effects implied in the schematic presentation of the model in Figure 9.2; "trivial" effects, those falling below .100, are deleted in Table 9.3. Our discussion will focus on this second set of coefficients.

Comparison of the coefficients of determination in Tables 9.1 and 9.3 indicates that the additional complexities of the full model do far more than mediate the various background influences already identified. In every comparison except those for sophomore rank and curriculum enrollment (for which the three background variables remain the only regressors), the full model's explanatory power is substantially greater. It accounts for at least 40 percent of the variance for six dependent variables (the largest R^2 being .579, for senior class standing), while the largest coefficient of determination in the background effect analysis was only .328 (also for senior class standing). Indeed, the proportions of explained variance in the full model fall below 20 percent in only one instance, the teacher influence item. These differences in explanatory power indicate that school processes contribute uniquely to the explanation of subsequent outcomes, as well as possibly serve to mediate background influences. We will be sensitive to their importance in both these respects in discussing the patterns of influence reflected in this relatively powerful model.

The direct influences on occupational attainment in Table 9.3 are consistent with the Wisconsin analyses in identifying educational attainment both as the major determinant of occupational outcomes and as an important mediator of antecedent influences. Only educational attainment and early occupational status directly affect current occupation, and only SES, sex, and educational level have notable direct influences on early occupational sorting. It is interesting that the indirect effects of SES, sex, and educational attainment through the early-present occupation linkage exhaust almost all of the importance of early attainments for later ones. These indirect effects are .037, .063, and .168, respectively, whereas the "career continuity" linkage is only .283. Hence, knowledge of early occupational levels contributes little unique explanatory power to the current occupation equation.

These patterns of influence in the full model indicate, once again, that practically all of the background and school process consequences for

TABLE 9.2

Standardized Regression Coefficients for the Full Status Attainment Model (Combined-Sex Sample, $N = 1,205$)

	SES	Apt	Curric 1	Stand 1	Peer	Teach	Parent	Edex	Image	Curric 2	Stand 2	Educ	Occ 1	Occ 2
Moth Ed	.216													
Acquis	.427													
Fath Ed	.333													
Fath Occ	.291													
SES		.320	.330	.099	.303	.112	.207	.169	-.025	.090	.017	.137	.097	.055
Apt			.232	.440	.014	-.097	-.042	-.029	.222	.132	.186	.109	.008	.003
Sex			-.088	.142	.005	-.028	.088	-.028	.163	-.032	.137	-.158	.181	-.046
Curric 1					.210	.198	.280	.180	.012	.420	.031	.090	.033	.013
Stand 1					.143	.155	.226	.117	.288	.124	.499	.090	.067	.024
Peer								.290	***	***	***	***	***	***
Teach								-.001	-.019	-.019	-.025	-.017	.011	-.026
Parent								.192	.014	.062	-.009	.008	.040	.070
Edex									.037	.150	.021	.177	-.012	-.005
Image										.008	.175	.009	.039	-.010
Curric 2												.200	.038	.045
Stand 2												.140	.049	.026
Educ													.497	.469
Occ 1														.257
R^2	1.00	.102	.217	.258	.253	.095	.268	.442	.251	.503	.582	.450	.479	.588
R^2 (uncon)		.107	.221	.260	.256	.102	.274	.444	.259	.505	.582	.452	.485	.592

***Peer effects not computed in the "full" model.

TABLE 9.3

Standardized Regression Coefficients for the Full Attainment Model, with "Trivial" Effects Deleted
(Combined-Sex Sample, $N = 1,205$)

	SES	Apt	Curric 1	Stand 1	Peer	Teach	Parent	Edex	Image	Curric 2	Stand 2	Educ	Occ 1	Occ 2
Moth Ed[a]	.216													
Acquis	.427													
Fath Ed	.333													
Fath Occ	.291													
SES		.320	.330	.099	.305	.111	.202	.164	.162	.150	.133	.144	.132	
Sex				.142					.225		.200	-.160	.224	
Apt			.228	.440		-.097						.129		
Curric 1					.212	.202	.261	.180		.452				
Stand 1					.149	.149	.227	.100	.298	.129	.505			
Peer								.289						
Parent								.189						
Edex										.197		.203		
Image											.177			
Curric 2												.249		
Stand 2												.192		
Educ													.592	.547
Occ 1														.283
R^2	1.00	.103	.209	.258	.252	.094	.259	.441	.249	.494	.579	.442	.457	.573
R^2 (uncon)		.107	.213	.260	.256	.101	.266	.444	.249	.494	.579	.444	.463	.573

[a]Teach is omitted from column of independent variables because none of its coefficients in the full model exceeded .100.

occupational attainment are mediated through the intervening mechanism of educational certification, which will now be considered as an outcome variable itself.

Educational attainment is found to be influenced by a sizable number of antecedent factors, none of which is clearly predominant. Senior-year curriculum enrollment has the largest direct effect at .249, attesting to the importance of such streaming (Parsons, 1959). All other effects retained in Table 9.3 range between .13 and .20 (rounded to two significant digits). The two school process variables of consequence in addition to curriculum enrollment are senior class rank and educational expectations, both of whose direct effects exceed those of the background variables in the model. Moreover, the direct influences of ability and SES, though still large enough to warrant retention in Table 9.3, are considerably reduced from their magnitude in Table 9.1. Thus, much of the importance of these background variables for educational attainment is indeed mediated through the model, with goal orientations, class rank, and curriculum enrollment being identified as the important proximate mechanisms of that mediation.

In contrast to SES and ability effects, the sex coefficient for educational attainment in Table 9.3 is actually somewhat larger than its counterpart in Table 9.1, at $-.160$ and $-.127$, respectively. This increment offsets modest salutary sex effects on educational retention that are mediated through female class standing and self-concept advantages. Hence, even when the influences of a multiplicity of school variables are controlled, women still suffer a direct educational liability. Unlike SES and ability influences, then, the importance of sex for educational attainment is almost entirely direct, and not mediated by these intervening mechanisms.

Thus, the extensions of the basic structural framework examined here do not appreciably enhance our understanding of the dynamics of sex inequalities in educational attainment. Although this framework has proven quite useful for the study of male attainments, it apparently must be extended yet further for the explanation of the sex differences. At this point, the only definitive conclusion that we can put forth is that those educationally pertinent factors found to mediate much of the ability and SES consequences for educational outcomes are not similarly important for sex differences. Presumably, then, the explanation for such inequalities must lie outside the realm of the "purely" academic.

Although sex and social origins are certainly not as important for educational attainment as is suggested by some of the more vitriolic anticertification literature, it is clear that universal achievement standards are far from the sole determinants of success in the stratification process. These sex inequalities and the importance of status background for occupational sorting attest to this. At the same time, it should be recognized that the combined effects of ability and performance considerably outweigh any other direct influences on status outcomes in the model and that, on balance, *educational certification serves more to dissociate adult attainments from social origins than to perpetuate either status advantage or disadvantage* (Alexander & Eckland, 1973a; Duncan, 1968; Sewell, 1971). *That is, most of the importance of educational certification for occupational attainments is independent of the influence of social origins.*

The omission of some direct school process effects on educational attainment in Table 9.3 does not necessarily imply their complete inconsequence. Most have at least modest *indirect* effects. Sophomore class standing and academic self-conceptions, for example, both affect senior class rank, and sophomore curriculum enrollment, parental influences, and peer plans all influence educational expectations. Indeed, the only variable that does not affect educational attainment either directly or indirectly, or any other subsequent outcome in the model for that matter, is teacher influence. This is consistent with the Wisconsin analyses, which identified teachers as the least consequential of the three categories of significant others (Hauser, 1972; Sewell & Hauser, 1972).

We may now consider, somewhat more concisely, the patterns of influence on school processes, moving "backwards" through the model. As anticipated, the sophomore counterparts of senior rank and curriculum enrollment are their major determinants. There are, however, a number of additional direct influences on the two senior-year outcomes that suggest both "late blossoming" of academic talent and some mediation of the sophomore-year influences. Aptitude, sex, and educational expectations directly affect senior rank, while aptitude and expectations are consequential for senior tracking.[16]

The self-concept effect on class rank perhaps deserves special note since it does mediate a portion of the ability-performance relationship, as had been speculated by Sewell and his colleagues (Sewell, Haller, & Portes, 1969). Its importance in the model, though, is far less than is often implied for such constructs (Gordon, 1972); goal orientations are clearly more consequential.[17] Even in concert, however, these variables are less important for the explanation of actual attainment outcomes than are the more "objective" influences of status background, academic ability, and so forth.

Influences on self-conceptions and expectations are themselves of interest. Self-conceptions of academic competence are affected only by ability, class standing, and sex, with the last being the least important of the three. These self-evaluations, then, are principally responsive to what might be considered "educationally relevant" influences.

---

[16] Although the direct ability effect on senior rank in the full model might be a consequence of error in the self-reported measure of sophomore rank, at least one other study with multiple measures of class standing has reported a similar residual effect (Williams, 1972).

[17] The possibility should be considered that the sizable expectation effect on attainments may actually combine influence in both directions. Tangible feedback on the likelihood of admission to college should be expected to have considerable impact on educational expectations. Such "contamination" would likely be less problematic in our sophomore sample than in samples of seniors. This matter is discussed more fully elsewhere (Alexander & Eckland 1973a, c).

Educational expectations, on the other hand, are most strongly affected by the interpersonal influences of parents and peers. SES, sophomore rank, and curriculum enrollment are also identified as being of some consequence in the goal-setting process. The modest direct social origins influence on educational expectations in Table 9.3 is somewhat less than half its magnitude in Table 9.1, which omitted school process variables. Thus, much, but not all, of the status background effect on educational expectations is indeed mediated by interpersonal (Furstenberg, 1971; Kandel & Lesser, 1969; Simpson, 1962; Duncan, Haller, & Portes, 1968) and other school process mechanisms.

It is interesting that the subjective variable most responsive to the performance-relevant influences of ability and class standing, self-conceptions, is by far the less consequential for attainment outcomes. It appears that the educational system provides little tangible reward for high self-evaluations of academic competence, failing to exploit a potentially valuable motivational mechanism. Educational expectations, on the other hand, are both more important for later attainments and more closely tied to social origins, thereby constituting a not inconsequential subjective linkage in the status transmission chain.

The remaining influences in the extended model can be dealt with briefly. All three "significant others" variables are somewhat affected by status background, sophomore rank, and sophomore enrollment. In each instance, ability effects are almost entirely mediated through class rank and tracking. The modest negative ability coefficient for teacher influences may indicate some minor reaction against youth who fail to translate academic aptitude into performance; but this effect is of marginal importance and should not be overinterpreted.[18] Teacher responsiveness to the status background of youth is quite modest, though significant (no such effects were obtained by Sewell and his associates with their somewhat different indicator of interpersonal influence, 1969), while the somewhat stronger status effects on both peer and parental influences are as would be anticipated. In evaluating the last of these effects, though, it should be noted that curriculum enrollment and class rank are more important direct determinants of parental influence than is status background, suggesting that considerations beyond merely those of status transmission are involved in such interpersonal influence processes.

The major determinant of class rank is measured ability, but modest secondary influences are also obtained for sex and SES. This status effect on class standing was not obtained in either Hauser's analysis (1972) or our replication of his model (Alexander & Eckland, 1973c); however, both of these analyses were restricted to male samples. As will be demonstrated shortly, the confounding of sex interactions with main effects in Table 9.3 accounts for the present

---

[18] The aptitude influence on teacher contacts was essentially zero in the background effect model (Table 9.1). The negative direct effect here offsets modest positive ability influences mediated through rank and curriculum enrollment.

"discrepancy," just as was the case with educational attainment. It will be shown that status effects on class standing are somewhat more pronounced for women than for men. In fact, the coefficient for males alone does indeed fall below the .10 level, and thus is consistent with the Wisconsin analyses.

Finally, both academic ability and status background affect sophomore curriculum enrollment, with the influence of status background somewhat larger. Comparing the rank and tracking variables, it appears that early streaming decisions are considerably more subject to influences of social origin than is the evaluation of academic performance. This might be considered the organizational counterpart of status influences on educational expectations. The importance of status background for curriculum sorting, particularly in relation to academic ability, represents a significant departure from universal achievement standards in the functioning of our educational institutions. Nevertheless, the moderate coefficients of determination in Table 9.3 indicate that, even in conjunction, status background and ability are hardly adequate to account for these school process outcomes (Hauser, 1971). On the other hand, both curriculum enrollment and rank in class do play roles in mediating the influence that such background variables have on subsequent outcomes.

Sex Interactions

Sex differences in the importance of ability and status background will be evaluated by recomputing the analysis presented in Table 9.1, but this time separately for each sex. Before presenting these models, however, it will be useful to explicitly test for the significance of the sex interactions that will underlie them. This has been accomplished with the dummy variable regression strategy described in the appendix to this chapter. The results of this analysis, which also tests the significance of the sex main effects already discussed in Tables 9.1, 9.2, and 9.3, are presented in Table 9.4.

The entries in Table 9.4 indicate the amount of variance explained by different combinations of predictor variables. For example, the combined explanatory power of academic ability and status background for each of the school process and attainment variables in Figure 9.2 is presented in the first row of Table 9.4. The second row indicates the joint explanatory power of ability, SES, and sex; hence, the difference between entries for rows 1 and 2 is the increment in explained variance attributable solely to sex. The significance of this increment is evaluated with the appropriate F test (Lane, 1968), the results of which are reported in the lower portion of the table.

Sex interactions are added to the prediction equations in the third row as multiplicative terms involving the product of sex with ability and status indicators; consequently the difference between entries for rows 2 and 3 is the explained variance attributable to such interactions alone. The analysis is repeated in rows 4 through 6, but this time in addition to sex main effects and interactions all predictor variables implied in the full model are included in the equations. This is a somewhat conservative strategy for assessing the significance

TABLE 9.4

Sex Main Effects and Interactions with Status Background and Ability for School Process and Status Outcomes in the EEO Model (Combined-Sex Sample, $N = 1,205$)

Independent variables	Dependent variable explained variance											
	Curric 1	Stand 1	Peer	Teach	Parent	Edex	Image	Curric 2	Stand 2	Educ	Occ 1	Occ 2
(1) Apt, SES	.213	.240	.199	.046	.152	.219	.147	.264	.271	.273	.218	.233
(2) Apt, SES, sex	.221	.260	.199	.046	.161	.219	.188	.267	.328	.289	.240	.236
(3) Apt, SES, sex, sex interactions	.226	.261	.202	.049	.170	.230	.190	.272	.337	.301	.248	.241
(4) Full model[a]	.213	.240	.256	.101	.267	.444	.234	.504	.565	.431	.458	.590
(5) Full model, sex	.221	.260	.256	.102	.274	.444	.259	.505	.582	.452	.485	.592
(6) Full model, sex, sex interactions	.226	.261	.258	.103	.280	.449	.261	.506	.588	.461	.486	.594
					F test							
(2) versus (1)	***	***	n.s.	n.s.	***	n.s.	***	*	***	***	***	*
(3) versus (2)	*	n.s.	n.s.	n.s.	**	***	n.s.	*	***	***	**	*
(5) versus (4)	***	***	n.s.	n.s.	***	n.s.	***	n.s.	***	***	***	*
(6) versus (5)	*	n.s.	n.s.	n.s.	**	**	n.s.	n.s.	***	***	n.s.	n.s.

Note: Only sex interactions with ability and status background are included in the model.

[a]Includes all main effects implied in Figure 9.2.

$*p < .05.$
$**p < .01.$
$***p < .001.$

of such effects, since the modest covariance of sex with ability and SES is included in the "sex-free" equations.

The analysis indicates wide-ranging sex effects in the school process model. Consistent with the analysis already discussed, nine of the twelve possible sex main effects are significant at conventional levels. Similarly, eight of the twelve tests for interaction are also significant.

Statistical significance does not necessarily imply substantive importance though, and the proportions of explained variance associated with these significant effects vary from modest to negligible. The largest sex main effect, that for senior class standing, accounts for almost 6 percent additional variance, while the largest of the sex interactions, involving educational attainment as the dependent variable, involves an increment in explained variance of just over 1 percent. Thus, the latter effects, though statistically significant, are modest at best.

Not reflected in these data is their close correspondence with the results obtained for the total EEO female sample (Alexander, 1973). While the specific proportions of variance explained in the two analyses differ somewhat, practically all the effects found to be statistically significant in our other inquiry are also found here. The selective, sizable sample attrition as a consequence of limiting this analysis to currently employed women, then, does not alter our conclusions regarding the importance of sex influences in the attainment process.

These conclusions differ markedly from those put forth by Treiman and Terrell (1973). That their inquiry did not directly evaluate sex main effects, failed to test for the significance of interactions, and had no measure of academic ability avialable[19] may account for much of this disagreement. Whatever the reasons, though, our data clearly suggest the relevance of sex for various attainment outcomes, even when restricting the analysis to samples of currently employed men and women. The substantive importance of these sex main effects has already been considered in the total sample model. We will turn now to the interactions just documented.

Table 9.5 presents the effects of academic aptitude and SES on each outcome in the attainment model separately by sex. Based on earlier inquiries (Sewell & Shah, 1967; Hauser, 1971; Alexander, 1973),[20] it was anticipated that ability influences would be more consequential for the attainment outcomes of males,

---

[19] Treiman and Terrell are not to be faulted for failing to include ability in their analysis, since it was not measured in the data set they employed (Blau & Duncan, 1967). In omitting ability, though, the ability-status covariance would be attributed entirely to status background. As we have seen, status and ability differ in importance for men and women. Hence, ignoring either might result in the conclusion of essentially similar importance for the other.

[20] In Hauser's analysis (1971) ability was more consequential for the goal orientations of men than of women, but social origins were still more important than ability for both sexes. In Sewell and Shah's (1967) and our (1973) analyses, the relative importance of these variables actually differed by sex.

TABLE 9.5

Standardized and Unstandardized Ability and SES Regression Coefficients for School Process and Status Outcomes in the EEO Model, by Sex

| | Males (N = 719) | | | | | | Females (N = 486) | | | | | |
| | SES | | Apt | | | | SES | | Apt | | | |
	Stand	Unstand	Stand	Unstand	R^2	R^2 (uncon)[a]	Stand	Unstand	Stand	Unstand	R^2	R^2 (uncon)[a]
Curric 1	.298	.092	.269	.034	.221	.223	.378	.128	.182	.022	.210	.219
Stand 1	.072	.038	.462	.100	.244	.245	.136	.075	.426	.086	.229	.234
Peer	.358	.346	.156	.063	.194	.199	.424	.474	.085	.034	.205	.206
Teach	.178	.067	.041	.006	.039	.048	.210	.089	-.017	-.003	.042	.048
Parent	.296	.121	.162	.028	.150	.167	.358	.154	.065	.010	.144	.150
Edex	.373	.192	.213	.046	.244	.246	.454	.278	.010	.002	.209	.209
Image	.036	.018	.380	.077	.156	.162	.008	.005	.345	.072	.121	.131
Curric 2	.292	.088	.358	.045	.291	.294	.354	.120	.251	.031	.232	.237
Stand 2	.052	.043	.547	.187	.323	.325	.127	.110	.420	.131	.219	.223
Educ	.302	.302	.374	.155	.315	.319	.356	.354	.249	.089	.233	.244
Occ 1	.274	.269	.310	.127	.234	.242	.353	.330	.186	.063	.192	.198
Occ 2	.285	.267	.314	.122	.247	.255	.368	.368	.197	.071	.210	.215

[a] R^2s for unconstrained interitem correlations are presented in this column.

while status ascription would be more pronounced for women. Since some item variances differ considerably for the two sexes, both standardized and unstandardized regression coefficients are reported in Table 9.5. The import of both sets of coefficients is the same, however, and we will restrict our discussion to the somewhat more readily interpretable standardized effects.[21]

Although there are no formal statistical standards to guide these comparisons, the consistency of sex differences in Table 9.5 is indeed impressive. Academic ability is less important for every attainment outcome except one for women, with self-conceptions being the lone exception. For seven of these comparisons, the coefficients for males and females differ by .100 or more. For example, ability is essentially irrelevant to the educational expectations of women, but its effect is well above the minimal level for men, at .213. Similarly, the female ability coefficients for both senior rank and curriculum enrollment and the three attainment outcomes are all less than the corresponding effects for males.

Sex variations in status effects are also in line with our expectations, but are less pronounced relative to ability effects. In every comparison except for academic self-conceptions, female outcomes are more strongly status-ascribed. The coefficients generally differ by between .06 and .09.

The interactions noted in discussing the extended model merit particular mention here. Ability is somewhat more consequential than are social origins for the educational and occupational attainments of men, while just the reverse is the case for women. The combined-sex analysis confounded these differences, resulting in the "discrepant" conclusion that status effects on educational attainment exceeded those of ability. Actually, our data are quite consistent with those of other inquiries in identifying ability as somewhat more important than social origins for men.

Similar sex interactions affect the class rank results. The male SES coefficients for both sophomore and senior class rank fall below our minimal level for the imputation of substantive importance, while the corresponding female paths both exceed this standard. Although these differences are not dramatic, their confounding in the full model accounts for the "significant" status-rank effect obtained. Thus, the data for our male sample are also consistent with those presented by Sewell and his colleagues (1969, 1970, 1972) in failing to identify marked status biases in the evaluation of academic performance. Female rank, however, is somewhat more strongly affected by such status considerations.

Although it would be informative to examine sex differences in attainment dynamics further by evaluating the full model separately for men and women, this would entail a rather extended discussion and will not be pursued in this already lengthy report. The data that have been presented are sufficient to suggest the relevance of sex for status attainments. Sex main effects and interactions with status background and ability are evident for numerous school

---

[21] The models computed from unconstrained interitem correlations (i.e., the original data before generation of the SES construct) are similar in import. These are not reported here.

process and attainment variables. Of particular importance, perhaps, is the direct educational disability suffered by women even with all other influences in the model *simultaneously* controlled. The explanation for this sex liability must lie outside the school process framework studied, since it was not accounted for by any of the mediating mechanisms in the model. These complexities in attainment dynamics would be masked in single-sex inquiries. Our analysis suggests, further, that even the study of direct sex effects would provide a somewhat deceptive portrayal of attainment influences if important interactions were slighted.

INTERPRETATION

Longitudinal data on a national sample of youth, first sampled in 1955 as high school sophomores and followed up in 1970, were employed in the evaluation of a rather elaborate model of the status attainment process. The analysis provides insight into both the dynamics of status attainment and the functioning of our educational institutions.

As has frequently been documented, academic ability, status background, and sex were found to have far-reaching and varied consequences for school process and attainment outcomes. Simple generalizations regarding the influence of these "background variables" are clearly inappropriate, however, since both their relative and absolute importance vary markedly across dependent variables.

That the "sorting and selecting" mechanisms of our stratification system depart significantly from the meritocratic "ideal"[22] is indicated by the considerable importance of status background for educational and occupational outcomes and the lower educational attainments of women, even with the influences of academic ability and social origins controlled. Moreover, our analysis of sex interactions with other background variables suggests a not inconsequential compounding of the liabilities of status ascription: the educational attainments of women, already lower on the average than those of equally competent males, are themselves more responsive to the influence of social origins than of ability, while just the reverse applies to men. Thus, we find evidence of substantial sex and status ascription, with the latter being more pronounced for women. At the same time, however, academic ability is identified as a major influence on both educational attainment, exceeding status background in importance for men, and occupational outcomes. In its broad outlines, then, the process of status attainment combines both considerable status ascription and selection for academic competence.

The responsiveness of school processes to these background influences is quite varied. While academic ability is the major determinant of outcomes

---

[22] Some potentially serious implications of "meritocracy" are only recently beginning to receive the consideration they require (Eckland, 1967; Herrnstein, 1973; Wrong, 1969). As our understanding of these matters develops, the meaning of the concept, and perhaps its appeal, may undergo considerable change.

involving the evaluation of academic performance (either by others through grading or by oneself in self-conceptions of competence), social origins are clearly important in other instances. The three categories of "significant others," educational expectations, and curriculum tracking are all more responsive to the influence of status background than of ability.

Although documentation of these gross effects is itself informative, many subtle questions regarding their meaning as indications of status influence remain open. Some of these questions were addressed in the full attainment model, but the definitive resolution of others awaits further research. A few examples will suggest the current gaps in our understanding of these matters.

The status background linkage with peer plans presumably reflects, in large measure, the importance of status homophyly for peer-group formation and networks of association (Duncan, Haller, & Portes, 1968; Rhodes, Reiss, & Duncan, 1965) and its effect on parental contact likely implies status-related differences in the value of educational attainment, but the appropriate interpretation of other status effects is somewhat less clear. Do the dependency of educational expectations on social origins and the subsequent effect of such expectations on actual attainments reflect class-related differences in scholarly values and their importance as motivating mechanisms or merely the recognition by high-status youth that their economic advantage practically assures them a college education?

Similarly, an explanation for the relation between status background and curriculum enrollment is problematic. Is this relationship maintained through the efforts of high-status parents and their offspring in pursuit of a college education, or by educational gatekeepers (administrators, counselors, and teachers, in particular), whose judgments regarding the "suitability" of their charges for college might be influenced by considerations of status origin.[23] Finally, with regard to sex effects, what are the more proximate mechanisms that account for the class rank and self-concept advantages enjoyed by women in comparison with men of similar ability, or, for that matter, for the disadvantage of women in terms of enrollment in college preparatory curricula?

Despite our inability to answer all such questions definitively, the analysis identifies some important mechanisms for the transmission of these background effects. Consistent with numerous other inquiries, educational attainment represents the major determinant of occupational outcomes, mediating substantial background influences and contributing uniquely to the explanation of subsequent attainments. The role of educational certification in the stratification process is indeed far-reaching, with almost all the effects of antecedent variables in our model being mediated through it. This crucial importance accounts, in large measure, for the considerable interest in the dynamics of educational attainment itself, which occupied much of our attention in the analysis.

[23] Our analysis of the teacher contact variable has not addressed this particular issue, and the variable itself is not suited to do so. Data pertaining directly to interpersonal influences on the initial streaming decision, which commonly occurs earlier in the school career than when our respondents were sampled, would be required to consider this question.

The school process model evaluated here contributes substantially to our understanding of these dynamics. Of the three background variables studied, only the direct effects of sex are not appreciably affected by the additional complexities of the full model. By contrast, more than half the ability and SES consequences for educational attainment are transmitted via various intervening mechanisms. Educational expectations, senior rank, and senior curriculum all directly affect actual educational attainments, and these, in turn, are themselves responsive to interpersonal and subjective variables in the model.

A brief review of some of these intermediate processes might be useful at this point. Academic self-conceptions are principally affected by ability and academic performance, and have a modest impact on senior rank. Educational expectations are influenced directly by status background and interpersonal variables, and, in turn, have notable effects on both senior curriculum and educational attainment. The linkages between corresponding sophomore- and senior-year measures of class rank and curriculum enrollment, though substantial, are far from determinant, suggesting considerable opportunity for the "late blossoming" of academic talent. Furthermore, the independent effects on these senior-year outcomes indicate some freedom from the constraints of early anchoring.

Some "negative" conclusions regarding the efficacy of school process influences deserve particular note. Teacher influences were identified as the least consequential of the variables examined, suggesting the need to consider strategies by which the interpersonal influences of adult "significant others" in educational settings might be better exploited. Similarly, it may come as some surprise that self-conceptions of academic competence are not more consequential. In view of their almost total dependence on ability and performance (among the measured variables in the model), educators committed to universal achievement standards might profitably explore mechanisms by which such self-conceptions can be more effectively channeled into educational payoffs. Educational expectations, the more important of the two subjective influences examined, are also more closely tied to status background.

Finally, somewhat different "routes" of influence are indicated for the various background variables. Curriculum sorting, the interpersonal influences of parents and peers, and educational expectations are the principal linkages between status background and attainment outcomes, while class standing, self-conceptions of competence, and curriculum enrollment emerge as major vehicles for the influences of ability. In order to minimize status advantages, we would need to make the status "transmitters" either more responsive to the influence of ability or less consequential for subsequent attainments. Obviously, strategies for achieving either of these ends would imply far-reaching changes for both our educational system and society at large. Compared to these insights on the mediation of ability and status effects, the school process model leaves largely unexplained the mechanisms by which sex differences in educational attainment are maintained. While sex bears on a number of school process outcomes (rank, curriculum enrollment, and self-conceptions in particular), its direct importance for actual educational attainment is not modified appreciably by the inclusion of these intervening variables in the model. Thus, it appears that further elucidation of these sex differences will require extending the bounds of the school process framework.

The numerous sex and SES main effects uncovered (and the sex interactions to be noted shortly), imply considerable discrepancy between the "ideal" of universal achievement standards for educational and occupational attainment and the reality of attainment dynamics. However, we have identified some important school determinants of attainment outcomes that are presumably more malleable than the influence of social origins and sex (Sewell, Haller, & Ohlendorf, 1970). Although the actual effects of these variables are far from dramatic, their potential value for redressing inequities deserves close scrutiny. Our understanding of attainment dynamics and educational institutions would benefit from further study of their determinants; both subjective and inter-personal variables were not adequately explained in our model (about 25 percent of the variance).

Finally, the implications of our analysis of sex interactions with ability and SES merit reiteration. As anticipated, almost all school process and attainment outcomes were somewhat more status-ascribed for women and more responsive to academic ability for men. Had the results of our "main effects" model been accepted uncritically, these differences and their important implications would have remained undetected. The moral, of course, is that suspected deviations from linear-additivity must be pursued if the complexities of complex phenomena are to be adequately understood.

Our analysis, then, has examined some of the interrelationships among school-related administrative, interpersonal, and subjective variables and their roles in the attainment process. These interrelationships, and the dynamic processes that they imply, stand in sharp contrast to the simple status transmission model underlying most pre-"status attainment" inquiries. While status transmission is indeed an important element in the attainment process, the mechanisms of that transmission are themselves exceedingly complicated; moreover, many important influences on attainment outcomes are entirely independent of social origins. An appreciation of these complexities is absolutely essential whatever the basis of one's interest in these matters, be it analytical, policy-oriented, or political.

Our model as a whole was rather powerful, explaining 45 to 60 percent of the variance in both senior-year variables (curriculum and class standing) and each of the three outcome variables (educational attainment, first job, and present occupational status). Its consistency with earlier inquiries in this tradition reinforces our conclusion that we have indeed documented some of the complex processes of status attainment. Yet the analysis also suggests fruitful areas for further research. In particular, the mechanisms by which the "nonfunctional" sex and SES consequences for status attainments are mediated deserve further attention. This might require moving outside the confines of the school to consider phenomena such as sex-role socialization, noneducational networks of association, and institutional discriminatory practices. Similarly, the link between early and present occupational attainments remains almost entirely unspecified, and variables affecting career mobility and continuity require consideration.

Finally, the importance of "school quality" variables has not been considered at all in this inquiry. While school differences in educational "hardware" and student body composition do not appear to have dramatic effects on educational outcomes (Hauser, 1969; Hauser, 1971), they certainly merit inclusion in a comprehensive model of attainment dynamics (Alexander & Eckland, 1973b; Coleman et al., 1966).

It is apparent from this brief consideration of "open" issues that the informative value of this analytic framework is far from exhausted. The multivariate modeling strategies employed here constitute a coherent and informative framework for the study of attainment dynamics. The relatively simple analytical model originally put forth by Blau and Duncan (1967) has been progressively elaborated to the point where we are now beginning to appreciate some of the more intricate complexities of the process of stratification. Every extension of the analysis suggests new areas of inquiry, and in so doing promotes both continuity and cumulativeness in this research domain.

APPENDIX

Sample

The data were derived from a survey of some 40,000 public high school sophomores and seniors conducted by the Educational Testing Service in 1955. The nationally representative sample included all seniors in 516 schools and all sophomores in 97 of the 516 schools. The original survey consisted of two major sections: a twenty-item test of academic aptitude, measuring both verbal and mathematical ability, and a questionnaire survey eliciting self-reported information on such items as family background status, occupational and educational goals, and peer, parental, and teacher influences on college plans. The 1955 data have already been employed in a number of inquiries (Meyer, 1970; Michael, 1961; Rogoff, 1962; Stice & Ekstrom, 1964).

The 1970 follow-up survey was restricted primarily to the national sophomore sample. Schools constituted the basic sampling units. These were stratified by region and size, and to some extent by parental education, group test scores, and school dropout and college-going rates. The final sample consisted of 42 schools with 4,151 sophomores from all regions. More detailed descriptions of the EEO schools (Eckland & MacGillivray, 1972) and sampling procedures (Alexander & Eckland, 1973b) are available elsewhere. Usable data were obtained for 2,077 of the 4,151 sophomores in the final sample, 1,130 females and 947 males. The 50 percent nonresponse consists of 32 percent "true" nonrespondents, 16 percent lost cases (for whom current addresses could not be located), and 2 percent known deceased. The major sample selection biases involve an underrepresentation of urban and large schools (partially an intended consequence of the sample stratification), and, not surprisingly, an underrepresentation of low-aptitude students. These sample biases, of course, temper the generalizability of our results.[24] Similarly, the sample, consisting as it does of high school sophomores, excludes that not inconsequential segment of youth who terminated their education earlier (Folger & Nam, 1965).

Variable Measurement

In order to minimize sample attrition due to missing data on different items, procedures were employed for estimating missing data whenever it appeared empirically and logically sound to do so. A comparison of means, standard deviations, interitem correlations, and parallel path analyses with and without missing data estimates revealed no notable estimation-biasing effects. These procedures are reported elsewhere (Alexander & Eckland, 1973b).

Family background status. The unavailability of any of the "conventional" occupational status classificatory schemes,[25] in conjunction with recent critiques of the use of single status indicators and indices as universally applicable to all substantive problems (Hodge, 1970; Haug & Sussman, 1971), prompted us to explore the influence of several status background variables on attainment

---

[24] If the primary objective of this study were to produce a set of descriptive statistics on college-going rates, dropout rates, and the like, then these sample biases might present a more serious problem. We are not, however, interested in the marginals per se, but in the relationships among variables. It is such relationships that tell us something about the causal network involved in the attainment process. Thus, the critical question is: Would the correlations among variables differ substantially from those we obtained had everyone in the original sample (or, ideally, the universe) been included in the study? What evidence we have suggests that these differences would not be great. There were eleven "status attainment" variables in the 1955 data for which information was available from the EEO respondents, the total EEO sample, and the original Educational Testing Service sample, the last data set including schools not in the EEO follow-up survey. Separate intercorrelation matrices for these eleven items were generated, by sex, for each of these three samples. The average difference in the magnitude of these coefficients for all possible comparisons ($N = 330$) was only .023, although for a few comparisons the difference was as large as .08. In general, the coefficients tended to be slightly higher in both the Respondent and Full EEO samples than in the original ETS sample, indicating that the major source of bias, to the extent that it exists here, involves sampling error in the selection of follow-up schools and not low response rates.

[25] An attempt to estimate Socio-Economic Index (SEI) scores from a ninety-category coding of father's occupation developed by ETS was unsuccessful. The major difficulty involved the too liberal use of residual categories in the original 1955 coding. Son's present occupation SEI scores (Reiss, Duncan, & Hatt, 1961) were coded from the 1970 schedule; however, no such information was obtained on "first occupation." The six-category scale finally employed (described in test) was the only scheme available that would provide comparable measures for all three occupational status variables, i.e., father's occupation and son's present and first jobs.

dynamics. Four such variables are employed in this analysis and, except for some missing data estimates, all were obtained from the 1970 schedule:

A. Mother's education—Nine precoded response categories were provided.
   1. None, or some grade school.
   2. Finished grade school.
   3. Some high school.
   4. High school graduate.
   5. Some college.
   6. Bachelor's degree.
   7. Some graduate work.
   8. Master's degree.
   9. Ph.D. or professional degree.

B. Father's occupational status—An item pertaining to father's occupational status "while you were in high school" contained ten precoded response categories. These were reduced to a heirarchical set of six occupational prestige-status categories (see Alexander & Eckland, 1973b, for details).
   1. Unskilled and semiskilled workers.
   2. Skilled workers, blue-collar foremen, craftsmen, and service workers.
   3. Salesmen, clerical workers, and technical workers.
   4. Small and large business managers and owners.
   5. Professionals, typically not requiring advanced degrees.
   6. Professionals, typically requiring advanced degrees.

C. Father's education—Same categories as provided for mother's education.

D. Acquisition index—A factor-weighted index of possessions in the respondent's high school household was constructed, using Maxwell's weighting scheme (1971). The initial set of twenty-two household commodity items in the questionnaire was reduced to thirteen for the final scale by eliminating items with modest factor loadings. The final scale, with a reliability coefficient of .83, consists of items ranging from the possession of a "globe of the world" to "more that one bathroom."

An unmeasured SES construct will be generated through a canonical correlation analysis (Hauser, 1972) to mediate the joint effects of these four status background items. For models in which the effects to be constrained by the construct are the only exogenous variables, the procedure is rather straightforward. The canonical analysis is performed on the two sets of variables created by dividing the model into variables whose effects are to be mediated through the construct and all other variables in the analysis. The canonical procedure generates unmeasured variates as linear functions of their respective sets of variables such that the correlation between variates is at a maximum, under the constraint of orthogonality between pairs of variates. Thus, in contrast to the factor analysis model, which selects linear functions of items that maximize variance within domains, the canonical model maximizes covariance between domains (Cooley & Lohnes, 1971, p. 169).

The model for a canonical analysis with three indicators in each set or domain and one significant canonical correlation is presented schematically in Figure 9.3. As is suggested in this schematic diagram, the model posits a causal structure in which the unmeasured construct is an exact function of its "cause" indicators, and variables in one set only affect those in the other through the mediating mechanism of the intervening construct(s).

Since the bs are standardized regression coefficients, the application of the basic theorem of path analysis ($r'_{xy} = \Sigma b_{yx_i} \cdot r_{xx_i}$ for $i = 1$ to n) readily provides estimates of the simple zero-order correlations between canonical variates and items in their respective sets. Next, the second canonical variate is absorbed into the set of dependent variables by multiplying through the canonical correlation with each $r_{c_2 y_i}$. The remaining first variate is the "SES construct." These various manipulations reduce the original model to the set of estimated zero-order correlation coefficients presented in Figure 9.4.

Finally, the r_{xy} between-set constrained correlations are computed as the products of the appropriate correlations with the SES construct (i.e., $r_{x_i y_i} = r_{x_i s} r_{y_i s}$). Interitem correlations among variables within sets are unaffected by the index construction procedure. This matrix of observed and constrained correlations is then employed as the basic data in the multiple regression analysis.

In models such as ours, in which the constrained effects between sets of variables will be affected by their mutual relationship to other exogenous or causally antecedent variables, the index construction procedure is somewhat more complex than the one we described (Hauser, 1972, pp. 174–176). Although the estimation procedure remains conceptually similar, this mutual dependence (or covariance in the case with exogenous variables) must be taken into account. This is accomplished by partialing the preliminary zero-order correlation matrix on those variables whose effects must be controlled (sex, in our case) and using this matrix of partial correlations as the basic data for the canonical analysis. Of course, the coefficients then generated in the canonical analysis will be partials (or, in the case of the regression weights, "double

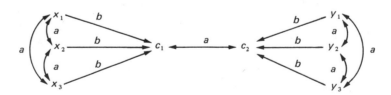

where c_1 and c_2 are canonical variates;
    xs are items whose effects are to be mediated;
    ys are dependent variables in the model;
    as are simple correlation coefficients;
    bs are standardized partial regression coefficients

Figure 9.3

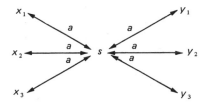

where *as* are simple zero-order correlation
coefficients;
s is the status construct

Figure 9.4

partials") that must then be transformed back into constrained zero-order correlations. The technical aspects of this procedure are discussed in considerable detail elsewhere (Hauser, 1972), as is canonical correlation analysis itself (Cooley & Lohnes, 1971; Anderson, 1958).

As mentioned before, the canonical analysis generates sets of orthogonal variates. Given the possibility of significant higher-order canonical correlations, indicating linear covariance between sets of variables not subsumed under the first correlation, some standard is needed to determine when this strategy entails too great a loss of information. Statistically significant higher-order canonical correlations are often of negligible importance, and correlations of .30 or less are frequently disregarded (Cooley & Lohnes, 1971). All the second canonical correlations derived in our analysis fall below this level. The difference in coefficients of determination computed from "constrained" and "observed" correlations is the explanatory power lost in neglecting between-set covariance not subsumed under the first canonical correlation. Both measures of explained variance are reported in our tables.

It is important to note that this index construction strategy posits a model in which the measured indicators are causally prior. The factor analysis model, on the other hand, conceptualizes empirical indicators as reflections or consequences of some underlying "causal" factor. Although factor analysis is commonly employed in the construction of indices for variables such as social status, its use often appears to be determined more by considerations of convenience than of conceptual adequacy. It strains the common usage of the concept to conceive of SES as somehow "causing" such varied phenomena as educational level, income, occupational status, consumption habits, life styles, and so forth. The canonical model, on the other hand, assumes that the effects of these factors combine in some fashion to affect other variables of interest.

Academic aptitude. Aptitude was measured with a twenty-item test administered by ETS during the 1955 survey. Stice and Ekstrom (1964) describe the test as follows:

The test, administered under untimed conditions, was constructed to give approximately equal weight to vocabulary and to arithmetic reasoning. It was designed for maximum discrimination between the sixth and eighth deciles of an unselected twelfth-grade population. Consequently, it was somewhat difficult for the tenth-grade population of the present study (p. 10).

It is unfortunate that we do not have good validity or reliability data for this relatively short test of academic aptitude. Our earlier inquiries do suggest, however, that it operates within the context of these models very much as it "should," taking as our standard of comparison the results of similar substantive analyses (Alexander & Eckland, 1973a, b). Nevertheless, we must be sensitive to the fact that the likelihood of differential (and uncorrected) unreliability in our various measures is high, precluding undue "concreteness" in interpreting parameter estimates and in comparing the relative importance of variables (Kelley, 1973).

Peer college plans. An index of peer college orientations was constructed by summing responses to two pertinent items from the 1955 schedule.

a. What are the college plans of the friend you like most?

Available responses were:
1. Definitely planning to go to college, or is already in college.
2. Thinking about college, and will probably go.
3. Thinking about college, but will probably decide not to go.
4. Not planning to go to college.

b. Of the people your own age with whom you spend most of your free time, how many of them plan to go to college, or are already going to college?

The response categories for the second item were:
1. All of them.
2. Most of them.
3. Only a few.
4. None.

Sophomore and senior class standing. The sophomore class standing measure was included in the 1955 schedule as a quartile self-ranking: "How good, on the average, have your high school grades been?" Response categories were: "in the top quarter of your class"; "in the second quarter of your class"; "in the third quarter"; "in the lowest quarter."

In the distribution of responses, the two middle categories were overrepresented, whereas considerably fewer than the "expected" 25 percent of the sample placed themselves in the highest and lowest quartiles (with 18 percent in the first and 7 percent in the last). Similar biases were obtained for the total 1955 samples of sophomore (Stice & Ekstrom, 1964, p. 23) and senior males (Rogoff, 1962, pp. 20–21). This "homogenization" of the distribution will likely attenuate somewhat the explanatory power of the sophomore rank item.

Data on senior- or terminal-year rank were obtained in a 1959 follow-up survey of high school principals and a 1969–70 survey of schools. Information on actual class standing was obtained in 1969 and on quintile placement in 1959. Because of the considerably higher response rate in 1959, the quintile measure is employed in the analysis. The 1969 information, which correlated .93 with the quintile data, was used (rescaled into quintiles) when 1959 data were not available.

Sophomore- and senior-year curriculum enrollment. Sophomore- and senior-year curriculum enrollment items were included in the 1955 and 1970 schedules, respectively. Both items were dichotomized into "college preparatory" and "other" categories. In both instances the "other" categories included business, vocational, general, and "other" curricula.

Adult influences. Two indicators of the influence of adult "significant others" were obtained from the 1955 schedule. The first item pertained to school personnel, and asked: "To what extent have you discussed going to college with the teachers or guidance counselors (advisors) in your school?" The other comparably worded item pertained to parents. The response categories for both items were "not at all"; "some"; "quite a lot."

The wording of these adult-influence items is somewhat different from that employed by Sewell and his colleagues (1969, 1970), which more directly tapped the encouragement of college plans.

Academic self-concept. A factor-weighted scale involving self-descriptions of academic performance and problems was constructed with Maxwell's weighting scheme (1971). The nine-item scale has an estimated reliability of .90. The items, from the 1970 schedule, involve self-evaluations of high school performance and problems.

1. I usually did a bit more than the teacher required.
2. I considered myself to be a fast reader.
3. My grades reflected my ability fairly accurately.
4. In class, I could seldom keep my mind on what the teachers were saying.
5. Slow reading held me back in my schoolwork.
6. I wasn't able to concentrate on what I read.
7. The tasks often seemed insurmountable in school.
8. I kept up to date in my assignments by doing my work every day.
9. I had trouble remembering what I read.

Four response categories, ranging from "strongly agree" to "strongly disagree," were available for each item. Missing data were estimated by assigning the individual's average item score to unanswered items if as least half of the index items had been completed.

Educational expectations. Plans after high school were measured in 1955 with an item that asked: "What do you think you *will* do when you finish high school? (Suppose that you do not go into the military service.)"

The response categories available were:

1. Go to college.
2. Work for a year or two and then go to college.

3. Get a part-time job and go to college.
4. Get a full-time job and go to college at night.
5. Go to trade school, or take some special training.
6. Get a job.
7. Become an apprentice.
8. Other.

These eight categories were reduced to a set of three. Category 1 was designated "college-goers"; categories 2 through 4 were collapsed into a "possible college" group; and categories 5 through 8 were designated "non-college-goers."

Educational attainment. Educational attainment was measured with the same set of categories employed for the parental education items. With the sample consisting of high school sophomores, the lowest level of attainment feasible was "some high school" (50 of the 947 males in the follow-up sample), while the upper bound was the "Ph.D. or professional degree" category (64 cases).

Occupational attainments. Early and present occupational statuses were measured with the hierarchically ranked categories described for the father's occupation item. Early occupational attainments were obtained from an item requesting "the first job engaged in when you finished school or college."

Sex. Sex data were obtained during the original 1955 survey.

Analysis

Path analysis is our principal analytic technique. In path analysis a model is expressed as a set of linear, additive regression equations, each of which includes a residual error effect that completely determines the dependent variable of interest. The coefficient of determination (dependent variable explained variance) will be presented in the analysis in lieu of this residual effect.

In recursive models such as ours, the path coefficient, the basic statistic of path analysis, is equivalent to a standardized regression coefficient. It assesses the direct, unmediated influence of a given independent variable on a dependent variable, with the effects of other variables entered into the regression equation partialed out. Indirect effects implied in the model can be readily computed according to the "tracing" rules of path analysis. The techniques and assumptions of this analytic strategy are discussed in detail in a number of sources (Duncan, 1966; Heise, 1969; Land, 1969).

The convention of employing diagrammatic models in path analysis to summarize the flow of hypothesized causal effects compels the researcher to make these causal assumptions explicit. The double-headed curved arrows linking exogenous, or predetermined, variables in such schematic presentations indicates an empirical relationship in which no assumptions regarding causal priority in that relationship are being made. The statistic associated with that linkage is the simple zero-order correlation. All other effects in the model involve the decomposition of the correlation between two variables into direct and indirect effects, constrained by the pattern of causal influences implied in the model.

The dummy variable technique for assessing the significance of sex main and interaction effects (or, more specifically, the significance of the increment in dependent variable explained variance attributable to such influences) is formally equivalent to an analysis of covariance (Fennessey, 1968). Interactions are entered into the regression equations as multiplicative terms involving the product of sex with each other variable involved in the interactions. A detailed example of this strategy is presented by Lane (1968). A more general discussion of the use of dummy variables in multiple regression analysis is provided by Suits (1957).

REFERENCES

Alexander, K. L. Sex effects in the status attainment model. Paper presented at the Annual Meetings of the American Sociological Association, New York, 1973.

Alexander, K. L., & Eckland, B. K. Basic attainment processes: A replication and extensions. Mimeo. Johns Hopkins University, Baltimore, 1973. (a)

Alexander, K. L., & Eckland B. K. Effects of education on the social mobility of high school sophomores fifteen years later (1955-1970). Chapel Hill, N.C.: Final Report to the National Institute of Education, 1973. (b)

Alexander, K. L., & Eckland, B. K. The Hauser-Sewell model of status attainment: A "quasi-replication." Mimeo, Johns Hopkins University, Baltimore, 1973. (c)

Anderson, T. W. An introduction to multivariate analysis. New York: Wiley, 1958.

Bell, R. L. "Lower class Negro mothers' aspirations for their children." Social Forces, May 1965, 43(4), 493-500.

Berg, I. Education and jobs: The great training robbery. New York: Praeger, 1970.

Blau, P. M., & Duncan, O. D. The American occupational structure. New York: Wiley, 1967.

Coleman, J. S. The adolescent society. New York: Free Press, 1961.

Coleman, J. S., Campbell, E. Q., Hobson, C. J., McPortland, J., Mood, A. M., Weinfeld, F. D., & York, R. L. Equality of educational opportunity. Washington, D.C.: U.S. Government Printing Office, 1966.

Cooley, W. W., & Lohnes, P. R. Multivariate data analysis. New York: Wiley, 1971.

Crockett, H. J. Psychological origins of mobility. In N. J. Smelser & S. M. Lipset (Eds.), Social structure and mobility in economic development. Chicago: Aldine, 1966.

Crockett, H. J. Social class, education, and motive to achieve in differential occupational mobility. In B. C. Rosen, H. J. Crockett, & C. Z. Nunn (Eds.), Achievement in American society. Cambridge, Mass.: Schenkman, 1969.

Duncan, O. D. Path analysis: Sociological examples. American Journal of Sociology, July 1966, 72, 1-16.

Duncan, O. D. Ability and achievement. Eugenics Quarterly, March 1968, 15, 1-11.

Duncan, O. D. Inheritance of poverty or inheritance of race? In D. P. Moynihan (Ed.), On understanding poverty. New York: Basic Books, 1969.

Duncan, O. D., Featherman, D. L., & Duncan, B. Socioeconomic background and achievement. New York: Seminar Press, 1972.

Duncan, O. D., Haller, A. O., & Portes, A. Peer influences on aspirations: A reinterpretation. American Journal of Sociology, September 1968, 74, 119-137.

Duncan, O. D., & Hodge, W. Education and occupational mobility: A regression analysis. American Journal of Sociology, May 1963, 68(6), 629-644.

Eckland, B. K. Genetics and sociology: A reconsideration. *American Sociological Review*, April 1967, 32(2), 173–194.

Eckland, B. K., & MacGillivray, L. School profiles: Working paper No. 1. Institute for Research in Social Science, Chapel Hill, N.C., 1972.

Elder, G. H. Achievement motivation and intelligence in occupational mobility: A longitudinal analysis. *Sociometry*, December 1968, 31(4), 327–354.

Elder, G. H. Linking social structure and personality. Paper presented at the Annual Meetings of the American Sociological Association, New York, 1973.

Ellis, R., & Lane, W. Structural supports for upward mobility. In B. C. Rosen, et al. (Eds.), *Achievement in American society*. Cambridge, Mass.: Schenkman, 1969.

Featherman, D. L. Achievement orientations and socioeconomic career attainments. *American Sociological Review*, April 1972, 37, 131–143.

Fennessey, J. The general linear model: A new perspective on some familiar topics. *American Journal of Sociology*, July 1968, 74(2), 1–27.

Flanagan, J. C., & Cooley, W. W. Project talent one-year follow-up studies: Cooperative research project #2333. School of Education, University of Pittsburgh, Pittsburgh, 1966.

Folger, J. K., & Nam, C. B. A study of education and the social structure: Cooperative research project #2065. Florida State University, Tallahassee, Fla., 1965.

Furstenberg, F. F. The transmission of mobility orientation in the family. *Social Forces*, June 1971, 49(4), 595–603.

Gordon, C. Looking ahead: Self-conceptions, race, and family as determinants of adolescent orientation to achievement. Washington, D.C.: American Sociological Association, Arnold M. and Caroline Rose Monograph Series, 1972.

Haller, A. O., & Butterworth, C. E. Peer influences on levels of occupational and educational aspirations. *Social Forces*, May 1960, 38(4), 289–295.

Haller, A., & Portes, O. Status attainment processes. *Sociology of Education*, Winter 1973, 46, 51–91.

Haug, M. R., & Sussman, M. B. The indiscriminate state of social class measurement. *Social Forces*, June 1971, 49(4), 549–563.

Hauser, R. M. Schools and the stratification process. *American Journal of Sociology*, May 1969, 74(6), 537–611.

Hauser, R. M. Socioeconomic background and educational performance. Washington, D.C.: American Sociological Association, Arnold M. and Caroline Rose Monograph Series, 1971.

Hauser, R. M. Disaggregating a social-psychological model of educational attainment. *Social Science Research*, June 1972, 1, 159–188.

Heise, D. R. Problems in path analysis and causal inference. In E. F. Borgatta (Ed.), *Sociological methodology*, San Francisco: Jossey-Bass, 1969.

Herriott, R. E. Some determinants of educational aspiration. *Harvard Educational Review*, Spring 1963, 33(2), 157–177.

Herrnstein, R. J. *I.Q. in the meritocracy*. Boston: Little, Brown, 1973.

Hodge, R. W. Social integration, psychological well-being, and their SES correlates. In E. O. Laumann (Ed.), *Social stratification: Research and theory for the 1970's.* Indianapolis: Bobbs-Merrill, 1970.

Jencks, C. *Inequality: A reassessment of the effect of family and schooling in America.* New York: Basic Books, 1972.

Kahl, J. A. Common man boys. In A. H. Halsey, J. Floud, & C. A. Anderson (Eds.), *Education, economy, and society: A reader in the sociology of education.* New York: Free Press, 1961.

Kandel, D., & Lesser, G. S. Educational plans of adolescents. *American Sociological Review*, April 1969, 34(2), 213–223.

Kelley, J. Causal chain models for the socioeconomic career. *American Sociological Review*, August 1973, 38(4), 481–493.

Land, K. C. Principles of path analysis. In E. F. Borgatta (Ed.), *Sociological methodology*, San Francisco: Jossey-Bass, 1969.

Lane, A. Occupational mobility in six cities. *American Sociological Review*, October 1968, **33**(5), 740-749.

Lipset, S. M., & Bendix, R. *Social mobility in industrial society*. Berkeley: University of California Press, 1959.

McDill, E. L., & Coleman, J. Family and peer influences in college plans of high school students. *Sociology of Education*, Winter 1965, **38**(1), 112-126.

McDill, E. L., Meyers, E. D., Jr., & Rigsby, L. C. Institutional effects on the academic behavior of high school students. *Sociology of Education*, Summer 1967, **40**(3), 181-199.

McDill, E. L., Rigsby, L. C., & Meyers, E. D., Jr. Educational climates of high schools: Their effects and sources. *American Journal of Sociology*, May 1969, **74**(6), 567-586.

Maxwell, A. E. Estimating true scores and their reliabilities in the case of composite psychological tests. *British Journal of Mathematical and Statistical Psychology*, 1971, **24**, 195-204.

Meyer, J. H. High school effects on college intentions. *American Journal of Sociology*, July 1970, **76**(1), 59-70.

Michael, J. A. High school climate and plans for entering college. *Public Opinion Quarterly*, Winter 1961, **25**(4), 585-595.

Miller, S. M., & Reissman, F. The credentials trap. In S. M. Miller & F. Reissman (Eds.), *Social class and social policy*. New York: Basic Books, 1969.

Parsons, T. P. The school class as a social system. *Harvard Educational Review*, Winter 1959, **29**(4), 297-318.

Rehberg, R. A., Schafer, W. E., & Sinclair, J. Toward a temporal sequence of adolescent achievement variables. *American Sociological Review*, February 1970, **35**(1), 34-48.

Reiss, A. J., Jr., Duncan, O. D., & Hatt, P. K. *Occupations and social status.* New York: Free Press of Glencoe, 1961.

Rhodes, A. L., Reiss, A. J., & Duncan, O. D. Occupational segregation in a metropolitan school system. *American Journal of Sociology*, May 1965, **70**(6), 682-694.

Rogoff, N. *Social structure and college recruitment.* New York: Bureau of Applied Social Research, Columbia University, 1962.

Sewell, W. H. Inequality of opportunity for higher education. *American Sociological Review*, October 1971, **36**, 793-809.

Sewell, W. H., Haller, A. O., & Ohlendorf, G. W. The educational and early occupational attainment process: Replication and revision. *American Sociological Review*, December 1970, **35**(6), 1014-1027.

Sewell, W. H., Haller, A. O., & Portes, A. The educational and early occupational attainment process. *American Sociological Review*, February, 1969, **34**(1), 82-91.

Sewell, W. H., & Hauser, R. M. Causes and consequences of higher education: Models of the status attainment process. *American Journal of Agricultural Economics*, December 1972, **54**(5), 851-861.

Sewell, W. H., & Shah, V. P. Socioeconomic status, intelligence, and the attainment of higher education. *Sociology of Education*, Winter 1967, **40**(1), 1-23.

Sewell, W. H., & Shah, V. P. Parents' education and children's educational aspirations and achievements. *American Sociological Review*, April 1968, **33**(2), 191-209.

Sexton, P. C. Education and income: Inequalities of opportunity in our public schools. New York: Viking Press, 1961.

Simpson, R. L. Parental influence, anticipatory socialization, and social mobility. *American Sociological Review*, August 1962, **27**, 517-522.

Spaeth, J. L. Occupational prestige expectations among male college graduates. *American Journal of Sociology*, March 1968, **73**(5), 548-558.

Spaeth, J. L. Occupational attainment among male college graduates. *American Journal of Sociology*, January 1970, Part 2. 632–644.

Stice, G., & Ekstrom, R. B. High school attrition. Princeton, N.J.: Educational Testing Service, 1964.

Suits, D. B. The use of dummy variables in regression equations. *Journal of the American Statistical Association*, December 1957, **25**, 585–595.

Treiman, D. J., & Terrell, K. Sex differences in the process of status attainment: A comparison of working men and women. Paper presented at the Annual Meetings of the American Sociological Association, New York, 1973.

Williams, T. H. Educational aspirations: Longitudinal evidence on their development in Canadian youth. *Sociology of Education*, Spring 1972, **45**, 107–133.

Wilson, A. B. Residential segregation of social classes and aspirations of high school boys. *American Sociological Review*, December 1959, **24**(6), 836–845.

Wolfle, D. *America's resources of specialized talent*. New York: Harper and Brothers, 1954.

Wrong, D. H. Social inequality without stratification. In C. S. Heller (Ed.), *Structured social inequality*. Toronto, Ont.: Macmillan, 1969.

10

Social Influences
on Marital Choice

ROBERT A. LEWIS
Pennsylvania State University

INTRODUCTION

Marriage as a "Fulfillment"
of Adolescent Development

Although a driver's license and the right to vote have increasingly become symbols of adulthood in contemporary America, marriage continues to be regarded by many as the badge of adult status. This appears to be the case, since marriage not only occurs most frequently during the latter phases of adolescent physical and intellectual maturation,[1] but marriage also signals the major shift in socialization. That is, late adolescents turn from being the object of socialization within the parental family to assuming the incipient role

---

[1] In 1970 the median age in the United States at first marriage was 23.2 years for males, which was somewhat higher than the "legal age" of 21 set by many states, and 20.8 years for females, which was slightly lower (Davis, 1972, p. 243). One of the difficulties, however, in delimiting and thus conceptualizing adolescence is the arbitrary nature of the alleged beginning and ending of this stage of development.

of socializer through the acceptance of responsibility vis-à-vis a marital partner and possible children.

Thus, since the decision to marry or to not marry is one of the major decisions customarily considered in late adolescence,[2] the topic of marital choice is most appropriate for a conference such as this, which has focused on "adolescence as a developmental process."[3]

Two Related Questions

This paper is concerned with positional socialization, the process whereby adolescents are readied and motivated to assume adult statuses through positions such as husband and wife (Winch, 1962). As Hill and Aldous (1969) have pointed out, happily, the focus on later socialization avoids "the thorny issues of the development of core personality involved in identification and the process of transmitting deeply rooted response sets from generation to generation" (p. 886). Thus, this paper deals with the components of "successful" socialization into adult roles, that is, adolescents' knowledge of marital roles, their ability to play marital roles, and their motivation to assume them, which Brim (1964) has suggested are necessary for the successful performance of roles.

The primary focus of this paper, however, is on the *social influences* that affect the processes of premarital dyadic formation and marital choice. As such, our task could encompass two related questions that most adolescents ask themselves: (1) "*Whom* shall I marry?" and (2) "*When* shall I marry?" As one may note, these questions are inexorably related, since often the "when" greatly determines the "whom" and vice versa. These causal sequences are reasonable, nevertheless, if one accepts the premises that: (1) a marriageable person in an open (free choice) marital system *could* marry any number of similar persons; and (2) final choices of marital partners are frequently predicted on chance events that help one define the present as the "right time" to be married and therefore one's current partner as *the* one to marry (Reiss, 1960; Bolton, 1961; Blood, 1962). Or, as some cynics have suggested, the sole condition for many marriages is having someone . . . anyone . . . make an offer of marriage. Nevertheless, in spite of the relatedness of these two research questions, time and space constraints limit our attention to the *persons* from whom mates are

---

[2] Broderick (1966) has reported that 75 percent of some 17-year-old boys and 94 percent of some 17-year-old girls fully intended to be married someday.

[3] The decision to marry, however, is not only of interest to social scientists who have developmental concerns for the effective functioning of young persons in our society; marital choice has become a focal point for some biologists as well. In fact, a number of scientists have called for a rapprochement between geneticists and social scientists who are concerned about the possible evolutionary effects of differential fertility rates on gene changes within our population (Eckland, 1968; Garrison, Anderson, & Reed, 1968). Although demographers always have been interested in the proportion of those within a population who marry and in the variance in age at marriage, since these variables are critical in relation to fertility, these writers are additionally concerned about the genetic quality of life for those who are yet to be born.

chosen, while leaving residual the equally interesting question of the timing of marriage.[4]

Two Levels of Analyses

Scientific studies of marital choice appear to have been conducted nearly exclusively on one or another of two levels. By and large, the study of assortative mating by geneticists and sociologists has been conducted at the macroscopic level through large-scale analyses of social structural variables, that is, demographic characteristics of mates and nonmates. In decided contrast, social psychologists within their human laboratories have focused primarily on the dyad (the pair) and thus have usually ignored the dyad's social context. Attempts to bridge the hiatus between sociocultural norms and intradyadic mate selection behavior have been few and far between.

SOCIOCULTURAL ANALYSES: THE MACROSCOPIC LEVEL

The Principle of Homogamy

Personal freedom to choose one's own mate in our society has been grossly overrated in the face of overwhelming data that the number of eligible persons who are "appropriate" as mates is severely restricted. This restraint is due to extensive, homogamous cultural norms with predictable parameters that substantially reduce the probability of free choice. If there is any social phenomenon in the United States that has reached the rate necessary to receive the label of systematic, modal behavior, it is the practice of homogamy (the tendency of similar persons to marry). As a colleague of mine has remarked: "No matter which operational definition or sample has been chosen, no matter what measurements, research designs or statistics have been utilized, homogamy is continually confirmed."[5]

A few studies have suggested the possibility of future decreases in the practice of homogamy (Thomas, 1951; Dinitz, Banks, & Pasamanick, 1960; Leslie & Richardson, 1956) and marriage mobility (Rubin, 1968) or "marrying up" especially among lower class women (Elder, 1969). Nevertheless, the bulk of evidence demonstrates that most Americans continue to choose their marriage partners from eligibles who are similar to themselves in a number of social

[4] For research on social influences and the timing of marriage, see Auken (1965); Moss (1965); Perrucci (1968); Bartz and Nye (1970); Elder (1972); Aldous and Hill (1969); de Lissovoy (1973).

[5] Homogamy, however, is *not* the predominant or only pattern in *all* societies. For example, some African states encourage marriage between different social groups, presumably for the purposes of minimizing conflicts between social groups and thus strengthening national bonds (Goody, 1971).

characteristics,[6] while in some societies homogamy has been shown to operate even for eye color, hair color, and physical stature (Beckman, 1962).

Some Implications of Homogamy

Although some geneticists have been engrossed with various biological implications of homogamy, social implications of this phenomena have rarely been examined or anticipated. In spite of the crucial place that homogamy occupies in the continuity/discontinuity of the family and other social institutions, few social scientists have explored the possible effects of mate selection practices such as homogamy on social structures.

Generally speaking, in the absence of differential fertility, homogamy should not change the gene frequencies in a population. However, there is evidence in one analysis of 1960 census data (Kiser, 1968) that assortative mating (homogamy) for education has enhanced differential fertility. Parenthetically, Hirsch (1967) has suggested that

> universally compulsory education, improved methods of ability assessment and career counseling and prolongation of the years of schooling further into the reproductive period of life can only increase the degree of positive assortative mating in our population. From a geneticist's point of view our attempt to create the great society might prove to be the greatest selective breeding experiment ever undertaken (p. 128).

Thus, continued homogamy in education might become one of the major mechanisms in the continued evolution of mankind. As Eckland (1968) has reported:

> Long-term mate selection (homogamy) for educability or intelligence increases the proportion of relevant homozygous genotypes which over successive generations tends to produce a biotic model of class structure in which a child's educability and, therefore, future social status are genetically determined (p. 223).

An Area for Research and Theory Building

Despite the massive evidence for homogamy, there have been few comprehensive or systematic explanations of *how* homogamy works. In other words, it is not fully known why like persons are attracted to each other. Though homogamy has been shown to operate even among spiders and various insects (Lutz, 1905), it is obviously much more than a biological phenomenon.

Some suggestions and "theories" have been advanced to explain why persons seek mates who are similar to themselves. For instance, Katz and Hill (1958) in their norm-interaction theory suggest that the probability of marriage covaries

---

[6] For example, Dinitz et al. (1960), on the basis of marriage licenses secured for 2,706 couples in Columbus, Ohio, for 1933, 1939, 1949, and 1957–58, argued that, in spite of the passage of time, most marriages were still characterized by relative class homogamy.

Homogamy, however, is less evident for relationships that are initiated at college rather than in one's home town (Leslie & Richardson, 1956); and, age homogany has been shown to decrease with remarriage and increasing ages for partners.

with the probability of interaction, which itself is determined by time and distance costs (propinquity), which is due to homogeneous residential patterns. Others have suggested that similar values are the mechanisms that mediate between homogamous norms and marital choices (Coombs, 1961, 1962; Selfors, Leik, & King, 1962; Hudson & Henze, 1969). According to Coombs (1961), dyadic interaction between similar persons is rewarding, and perpetuated, because they share similar values and a "universe of discourse" that fosters communication and a "minimum of tension and ego threat."

Surprisingly, however, no current theory has implied that homogamous norms are internalized early in life as the result of effective socialization by parents and others. Thus, a more fruitful explanation may lie in answers to the research questions: By whom, when, how, and how effectively are homogamous norms *mediated* to adolescents prior to their choosing a mate? It is no chance event that children and adolescents choose those similar to themselves as friends and later as spouses, since parents admit to consciously choosing schools and neighborhoods for their children, as well as directly or indirectly manipulating their children's courtship (Sussman, 1953). Thus, future study of social influences on marital choice might well be defined for research purposes as the study of social norms *mediated through interaction with parents, siblings, and peers.* [7]

SOCIOPSYCHOLOGICAL ANALYSES: THE MICROSCOPIC LEVEL

Experimental social psychologists at the microscopic level of analysis have been more systematic in their study of interpersonal attraction and dyadic formation than have been those at the macroscopic level. They have also been more oriented toward the building and testing of conceptual paradigms. For instance, Heider's balance theory (1958), Festinger's cognitive dissonance theory (1957), Winch's theory (1958) of complementary needs, Byrne's reward theory (1971), and the exchange theory (Thibaut & Kelley, 1959; and many others) have done much to stimulate a flow of propositions, empirical findings, and hence accretive theory.

Generally speaking, however, social psychologists have ignored the linkages between social structural variables and dyadic formation or marital choice in

[7] Other studies of marital choice have identified additional social correlates that deserve mention here: age at marriage (Auken, 1965; Moss, 1965; Bartz & Nye, 1970; Elder, 1972); income (Cutright, 1970); education (Perrucci, 1968); class and kinship systems (Rosen & Bell, 1966; Firth, Hubert, & Forge, 1970); the proportion of in-group members in a given population (Thomas, 1951); the incest taboo (Parsons, 1954); residential propinquity and the sex ratio (Clarke, 1952; Kerckhoff, 1956; Katz & Hill, 1958; Catton & Smircich, 1964); marital status (Bowerman, 1956); wars, business cycles, political crises, epidemics, natural catastrophes, and other socioeconomic factors (Jacobsohn & Matheny, 1962). Yet, these social influences appear to operate more as proscriptions than prescriptions, i.e., norms against one's marrying from within certain groups. These social influences thus are more passive and limiting than active and selecting.

their quest of intradyadic phenomena. Some of these studies have compared the degree of similarity/dissimilarity in the social backgrounds of couples who vary according to differing levels of attraction or involvement. However, these researchers have tended to conceptualize social similarities as characteristics or traits of individuals rather than as environmental factors.

In addition, the primary concern of these experimentally oriented researchers has been directed toward early pair attraction and interaction rather than toward later dyadic phenomena such as the crystallization of pair commitment and couples' decisions to marry. In fact, over 80 percent of these studies have involved strangers who had never met prior to the experiment. And yet, in spite of the fact that many past experiments did not involve well-established pairs or follow couples longitudinally, there has been a recent, increasing effort to study interpersonal attraction in terms of long-time relationships (Huston, 1974).

THE MEDIATING AGENTS:
"SIGNIFICANT OTHERS"

Reflecting Behavior

Heterosexual dyads do not form in a social vacuum. Yet, one neglected area in the American literature on mate selection and dyadic formation has been the interface between the socialization processes and the formation of the premarital dyad. For instance, while much attention has been directed to the societal and personal characteristics of potential mates and to their own dyadic interaction, few theoretical or empirical efforts have focused on the importance of "significant others" on the formation and maintenance of heterosexual dyads.

Nevertheless, Waller and Hill (1951) once described the roles of significant others in mate selection in terms of a "looking-glass reflection of unity provided by a friendly public." In other words, friends and relatives may react toward a courting couple as to a social unit; for example, they may invite them to social events as a pair, think of them together, and arrange for them to be together. If couples accept these favorable reactions to their pair relationship, they may increasingly perceive themselves to be a dyad and to adopt the roles prescribed by dyadic norms. Dyadic interaction thus rises in part out of positive social rewards and interaction with significant others.

Only a few researchers, however, have drawn attention to parents and peers as vital, mediating agents between sociocultural norms, such as homogamy, and heterosexual dyadic formation (Bates, 1942; Kirkpatrick, 1945; Sussman, 1953; Coombs, 1962; Ryder, Kafka, & Olson, 1971). This is strange, since a number of analysts have long focused attention on this research need (Burgess & Wallin, 1944; Burgess & Locke, 1945; Hollingshead, 1950; Leslie & Richardson, 1956).

Coombs (1962) has evidence that suggests that, since parents are usually the primary socializing agents for their children, they still exert indirect reinforcements in family value transmission to ensure that the marital partners of their children will be homogamous. Earlier, Bates (1942) gathered extensive interview data from unmarried college students to the effect that their parents directly or indirectly had influenced their courtship choices. For instance, 79 percent of the males and 97 percent of the females admitted that their mothers had sought in one way or another to influence their choice of opposite-sex companions. The percentages were somewhat lower in reports of fathers' influence; furthermore, parents played more positive roles in the courtships of their daughters than their sons.

Similarly, Ryder et al. (1971) have explicated the roles played by friends in dyadic formation as: (1) introducing and initiating meetings between the two persons; (2) providing further opportunities and occasions for their early interaction; (3) offering protective situations, mediation services, and benevolent attitudes toward their developing relationship; and (4) acting toward the two as to a pair.

Labeling Behavior

Positive reflection and situational structuring, however, are relatively passive processes, compared to the process of labeling. Although labeling theory has been developed particularly for the study of social deviance (Lemert, 1951, 1967; Kitsuse, 1962; Becker, 1963; Erickson, 1962, 1966), it may also help to explain the formation of "normal" social groups such as marriages. For example, contemporary labeling theorists (cf. Schur, 1969), following the earlier thought of Durkheim, suggest that social groups create deviance in their promotion of social cohesion by providing labels for residual rule violators. Thus, susceptible violators accept deviant labels for themselves, internalize the evaluations, and act out deviant roles in conformity to the labels. Therefore, not only does labeling establish and maintain boundaries between social groups, but it also initiates and reinforces social behavior *within* social groups.

Needed: A Labeling Focus for Dyadic Formation

The findings of a recent study (Lewis, 1973c)[8] suggest that a labeling focus in the study of marital choice might be beneficial in so far as it would enlist a societal context and the processes of socialization. Scheff (1966) has offered a set of hypotheses as an initial labeling theory for the study of social deviance. Adapted for the investigation of mate selection behavior, these propositions might be restated in the following manner:

1. Values, models, and symbols of marital dyadic unity are learned throughout childhood and preadolescence (Broderick & Rowe, 1968; Hill

[8] It is interesting that higher intercorrelations were found between dyadic formation assessed for 316 premarital pairs and the reflecting/labeling behavior of their family members, as compared to their friends. These data suggest that significant others within one's family may be more instrumental than one's friends in effecting pair formation. At least, these data demand a closer investigation of the impact that various significant others have on dyadic formation and marital choice.

& Aldous, 1969), particularly in the family of orientation (Mayer, 1967).

2. These values and symbols are reaffirmed in social interaction and increasingly anticipated throughout preadolescence and adolescence (Broderick, 1966; Broderick & Rowe, 1968).

3. Loosely joined and low-committed premarital pairs form for indeterminant periods of time as the result of rewarding interaction and pair achievements in the perception of similarity, rapport, self-disclosure, accurate role-taking, and need satisfaction (Lewis, 1972, 1973a). See Figure 10.1.

4. Pairs reacted to and labeled as "viable dyads" by significant others are rewarded for their symbiotic interaction and punished for their separatist behavior (Bates, 1942; Sussman, 1953; Ryder et al., 1971).

5. Particularly in times of individual disorientation, pair members are more susceptible to the cues given by the reactions of significant others (Erickson, 1966, p. 88; Ryder et al., 1971) and at those times are more accepting of dyadic labels and norms (Bolton, 1961).

6. Internalization of dyadic labels and norms enables pairs to play reciprocal roles in conformity to these labels and norms, that is, to act and react as comprehensive dyads with increasing interaction and commitment (Waller & Hill, 1951).

In sum, labeling theory suggests that significant others play key roles in initiating, perpetuating, and crystallizing premarital dyadic commitments. Included in these roles are the critical evaluations of a pair by friends and relatives, their labeling the two as a viable or nonviable pair, and their reflecting and reacting toward the two actors in terms of their proffered labels. On the other hand, chief roles played by the incipient dyad include their acceptance or rejection of the given labels that may reinforce conceptualizations of themselves as a viable or nonviable pair. The general assumption is that when dyadic labeling is withheld by significant others, pair relationships are transitory and few develop into comprehensive dyads. But, when dyadic labeling is offered by significant others and is accepted and internalized by the partners, the resulting dyad is launched into a more permanent trajectory, e.g., a marital career.

The interrelated concepts and hypotheses necessary for a labeling emphasis on dyadic formation and marital choice (Figure 10.2) are as follows:

Hypothesis 1: The amount and effectiveness of anticipatory socialization into marital-dyadic values positively influences the degree of initial attraction between pair members of the opposite sex.

Hypothesis 2: The amount and effectiveness of anticipatory socialization into marital-dyadic values positively influences the amount of rewards given by significant others for symbiotic behavior.

Hypothesis 3: The amount and effectiveness of anticipatory socialization into marital-dyadic values positively influences the amount of punishments given by significant others for separatist behaviors.

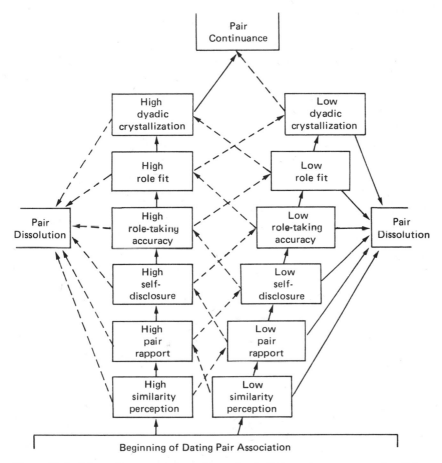

Figure 10.1   Schematic presentation of postulated dating pair processes and anticipations of those developments generally needed for the achievement of premarital dyadic formation. *Solid lines* suggest relationships that correspond to hypotheses of the family developmental framework. *Dotted lines* suggest alternatives that do not. (From "A Developmental Framework for the Analysis of Premarital Dyadic Formation" by R. A. Lewis, *Family Process,* 1972, **40**, 40. Copyright 1972 by The Waverly Press. Reprinted by permission.)

Hypothesis 4: The amount of visibility of dyadic exclusiveness positively influences the amount of dyadic labeling of heterosexual pair relationships by significant others.

Hypothesis 5: The amount of rewards for symbiotic behavior positively influences the amount of pair members' susceptibility to dyadic labels.

Hypothesis 6: The amount of punishments for separatist behavior positively influences the amount of pair members' susceptibility to dyadic labels.

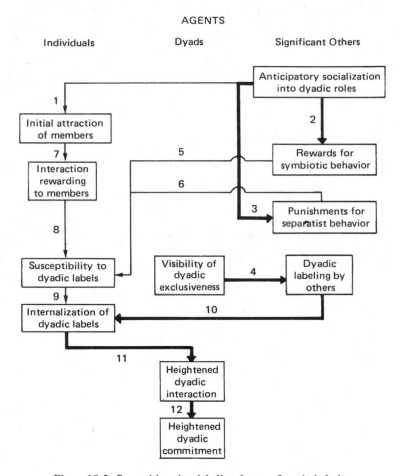

Figure 10.2 Propositions in a labeling theory of marital choice.

Hypothesis 7: The amount of initial attraction between pair members positively influences the amount of rewards that accrue to pair members' early interaction.

Hypothesis 8: The amount of rewards within pair members' early interaction positively influences members' susceptibility to dyadic labels.

Hypothesis 9: The amount of members' susceptibility to dyadic labels positively influences their internalization of dyadic labels.

Hypothesis 10: The amount of dyadic labeling by significant others positively influences the amount of members' internalization of dyadic labels.

Hypothesis 11: The amount of pair members' internalization of dyadic labels positively influences the amount of the pair's dyadic interaction.

Hypothesis 12: The amount of a pair's dyadic interaction positively influences the amount of the pair's dyadic commitment.

Some Values of a Labeling Emphasis

A labeling emphasis on marital choice proffers several benefits. Primarily, it offers bridging concepts, as "significant others," "definition of the situation," "socialization," "role-taking," "interaction," "reaction," and "labeling," which span the macrocosm, the social system, and the microcosm, the developing dyad.

Likewise, this focus roots dyadic processes within the complex web of social interrelationships of which it is in reality a part. As such, a critical variable is the social audience, the significant others, who both act and react to a pair as reflectors and labelers. As Erickson (1962) has suggested in another context, friends and relatives may act as a "community screen," thus functioning as filters that select, reinforce, and sustain certain heterosexual pairs in preference to others. Thus, one value of this emphasis would be its potential contribution to predicting which heterosexual pairs may survive or be extinguished over time from a direct knowledge of significant others' reactions to the pair.

Another value of a labeling emphasis on mate selection is its central focus on *process*. It is a dynamic, rather than a static, approach and as such necessitates sequential (longitudinal) analyses. Dyadic formation can be better understood, therefore, in light of the constant changes that occur for couples as a result of their interaction with significant others, as well as between themselves. In the words of Bolton (1961): "Mate selection must be studied not only in terms of the variables brought into the interaction situation but also as *a process* in which a relationship is built up, a process in which the transactions between individuals *in certain societal contexts* are determinants of turning points and commitments out of which marriage emerges" (p. 235.) Therefore, these propositions need to be tested empirically.

NEEDED RESEARCH AND THEORY

In this relatively forsaken area of positional socialization, a number of other research topics cry out for study:

1. According to Hill and Aldous (1969), the large body of research on maternal separation and maternal deprivation has not been extended to positional socialization in general or sex-role learning in particular, due to its heavy concentration on cognitive and personality variables for young children. Likewise, there is much current research on the effects of father-absence on sex-role learning. But these studies too have not specified the direct relation between this deficit of a family position and adolescents' later acceptance and/or adequate playing of marital roles in adulthood. Longitudinal studies through the late adolescent years are desperately needed to understand the antecedents and consequences in this substantive area.

2. It may not seem possible, but even less is known about the roles that siblings play in positional socialization (Irish, 1964). For instance, there is

practically no empirical work on adolescents' assumption of marital positions, choice, and playing of marital roles, as a result of having no sibs, having no older cross-sex sib, or other family conditions related to birth order. At this time, such neglect perpetuates a blind spot in the eye of scientific inquiry (cf. Toman, 1971).

3. Furthermore, at this time it is not certain whether parents or peers are more effective role models for adolescent positional socialization or under what conditions parents and others may be more effective agents of socialization. There is much evidence that parents are effective socializers in the transmission of certain adult attitudes, values, and roles (Lewis, 1971, 1973b). This effectiveness suggests for some areas more continuity than discontinuity between generations (Bowerman & Kinch, 1959; Bath & Lewis, 1962). However, there are others who intimate the prevalence of little generational continuity in values (Hobart, 1958; Solomon, 1961; Brim & Wheeler, 1966). Further clarification of these issues would do much to identify those strategies and supports that human service systems may provide to assist those adolescents who have received deficient socialization into marital and other adult positions.

However, in conclusion, what appears to be most needed at this time is a set of "interlocking theories between the social and biological sciences with regard to mate selection" (Eckland, 1968, p. 233), a multivariate, interaction model that specifies the interaction between heredity and environment, genes and cultural forces, in the area that has been neglected by scientists on both sides.

But, prior to erecting a grand theory of marital choice, it is incumbent on social scientists to systematically draw together a well-articulated theory from all present empirical evidence by means of interdefined and interrelated concepts. Gone is the day (hopefully) when sociologists and psychologists had the excuse, in the name of discipline formation and protection, to ignore each other's contributions to knowledge!

REFERENCES

Aldous, J., & Hill, R. Breaking the poverty cycle: Strategic points for intervention. *Social Work*, 1969, **14**, 3–12.

Auken, K. Time of marriage, mate selection and task accomplishment in newly formed Copenhagen families. *Acta Sociologica*, 1965, **8**, 128–141.

Bartz, K. & Nye, F. I. Early marriage: A propositional formulation. *Journal of Marriage and the Family*, 1970, **32**(2), 258–268.

Bates, A. Parental roles in courtship. *Social Forces*, 1942, **20**, 483–486.

Bath, J., & Lewis, E. Attitudes of young female adults toward some areas of parent-adolescent conflict. *Journal of Genetic Psychology*, 1962, **100**, 241–253.

Becker, H. *Outsiders: Studies in the sociology of deviance.* Glencoe, Ill.: Free Press, 1963.

Beckman, L. Assortative mating in man. *Eugenics Review*, 1962, **2**, 63–67.

Blood, R. *Marriage.* New York: Free Press, 1962.

Bolton, C. Mate selection as the development of a relationship. *Marriage and Family Living*, 1961, **23**, 234–240.

Bowerman, E. Age relationships at marriage, by marital status and age at marriage. *Marriage and Family Living*, 1956, **18**, 231-233.

Bowerman, E. & Kinch, J. Changes in family and peer orientation of children between the fourth and tenth grades. *Social Forces*, 1959, 37, 206-211.

Brim, O. Socialization through the life cycle. *Social Science Research Council Items*, 1964, 18, 1-5.

Brim, O., & Wheeler, S. *Socialization after childhood: Two essays*. New York: Wiley, 1966.

Broderick, C. Social heterosexual development among urban Negroes and whites. *Journal of Marriage and the Family*, 1966, 27, 200-203.

Broderick, C., & Rowe, G. A scale of preadolescent heterosexual development. *Journal of Marriage and the Family*, 1968, **30**(1), 97-101.

Burgess, E., & Locke, H. The Family. New York: American Book, 1945.

Burgess, E., & Wallin, P. Homogamy in personal characteristics. *Journal of Abnormal and Social Psychology*, 1944, **29**, 475-481.

Byrne, D. *The attraction paradigm*. New York: Academic Press, 1971.

Catton, W., & Smircich, R. A comparison of mathematical models for the effects of residential propinquity on mate selection. *American Sociological Review*, 1964, **29**, 522-529.

Clarke, A. An examination of the operation of residential propinquity as a factor in mate selection. *American Sociological Review*, 1952, **17**, 17-22.

Coombs, R. A value theory of mate selection. *Family Life Coordinator*, 1961, **10**, 51-56.

Coombs, R. Reinforcement of values in the parental home as a factor in mate selection. *Marriage and Family Living*, 1962, **24**, 155-157.

Cutright, P. Income and family events: Getting married. *Journal of Marriage and the Family*, 1970, **32**(4), 628-637.

Davis, K. The American family in relation to demographic change. In C. Westoff, and R. Parke (Eds.), *Demographic and social aspects of population growth*. Vol. 1. Washington, D.C.: U.S. Government Printing Office, 1971.

de Lissovoy, V. High school marriages: A longitudinal study. *Journal of Marriage and the Family*, 1973, **35**(2), 245-255.

Dinitz, S., Banks, F., & Pasamanick, B. Mate selection and social class: Changes during the past quarter century. *Marriage and Family Living*, 1960, **22**, 348-351.

Eckland, B. Theories of mate selection. *Eugenics Quarterly*, 1968, **15**(2), 71-84.

Elder, G. Appearance and education in marriage mobility. *American Sociological Review*, 1969, **34**(4), 519-533.

Elder, G. Role orientations, marital age and life patterns in adulthood. *Merrill Palmer Quarterly*, 1972, **1**, 1962-1966.

Erickson, K. Notes on the sociology of deviance. *Social Problems*, 1962, 9, 307-314.

Erickson, K. *Wayward Puritans*. New York: Wiley, 1964.

Festinger, L. *A theory of cognitive dissonance*. Stanford, Calif.: Stanford University Press, 1957.

Firth, R., Hubert, J., & Forge, A. *Families and their relatives: Kinship in a middle-class sector of London—An anthropological study*. New York: Humanities Press, 1970.

Garrison, R., Anderson, V., & Reed, S. Assortative Marriage. *Eugenics Quarterly*, 1968, **15**(2), 113-127.

Goody, J. Class and marriage in Africa and Eurasia. *American Journal of Sociology*, 1971, **76**(4), 585-603.

Heider, F. *The psychology of interpersonal relations*. New York: Wiley, 1958.

Hill, R., & Aldous, J. Socialization for marriage and parenthood. In D. Goslin (Ed.), *Handbook of socialization theory and research*. Chicago: Rand McNally, 1969.

Hirsch, J. Behavior-genetic, or "experimental," analysis: The challenge of science versus the lure of technology. *American Psychology*, 1967, **22**, 118-130.

Hobart, C. Emancipation from parents and courtship in adolescence. *Pacific Sociological Review*, 1958, **6**, 25-29.

Hollingshead, A. Cultural factors in the selection of marriage mates. *American Sociological Review*, 1950, **15**, 619-627.

Hudson, J., & Henze, L. Campus values in mate selection: A replication. *Marriage and Family Living*, 1969, **24**, 722-775.

Huston, T. *Foundations of interpersonal attraction*. New York: Academic Press, 1974.

Irish, D. Sibling interaction: A neglected aspect in family life research. *Social Forces*, 1964, **42**, 279-288.

Jacobsohn, P., & Matheny, A. Mate selection in open marriage systems. *International Journal of Comparative Sociology*, 1962, **3**, 98-123.

Katz, A., & Hill, R. Residential propinquity and marital selection: A review of theory, method and fact. *Marriage and Family Living*, 1958, **20**, 27-35.

Kerckhoff, A. Notes and comment on the meaning of residential propinquity as a factor in mate selection. *Social Forces*, 1956, **34**, 297-313.

Kirkpatrick, C., & Caplow, T. Courtship in a group of Minnesota students. *American Journal of Sociology*, 1945, **51**, 114-125.

Kiser, C. Assortative mating by educational attainment in relation to fertility. *Eugenics Quarterly*, 1968, **15**(2), 98-112.

Kitsuse, J. Societal reaction to deviant behavior: Problems of theory and method. *Social Problems*, 1962, **9**, 247-256.

Lemert, E. *Social pathology*. New York: McGraw-Hill, 1951.

Lemert, E. *Human deviance, social problems, and social control*. Englewood Cliffs, N.J.: Prentice-Hall, 1967.

Leslie, G., & Richardson, A. Family versus campus influences in relation to mate selection. *Social Problems*, 1956, **3**, 117-121.

Lewis, R. Socialization into national violence: Familial correlates of hawkish attitudes toward war. *Journal of Marriage and the Family*, 1971, **33**(4), 699-708.

Lewis, R. A developmental framework for the analysis of premarital dyadic formation. *Family Process*, 1972, **11**(1), 17-48.

Lewis, R. A longitudinal test of a developmental framework for premarital dyadic formation. *Journal of Marriage and the Family*, 1973, **35**(1), 16-25. (a)

Lewis, R. Parents and peers: Socialization agents in the coital behavior of young adults. *Journal of Sex Research*, 1973, **3**(2), 156-170. (b)

Lewis, R. Social reaction and the formation of dyads: An interactionist approach to mate selection. *Sociometry*, 1973, **34**(3), 409-418. (c)

Lutz, F. Assortative mating in man. *Science*, 1905, **22**, 249-250.

Mayer, J. People's imagery of other's families. *Family Process*, 1967, **6**, 27-36.

Moss, J. Teenage marriage: Crossnational trends and sociological factors in the decision of when to marry. *Acta Sociologica*, 1965, **8**, 98-117.

Parsons, T. The incest taboo in relation to social structure and the socialization of the child. *British Journal of Sociology*, 1954, **5**, 101-117.

Perrucci, C. Mobility, marriage and child-spacing among college graduates. *Journal of Marriage and the Family*, 1968, **30**(2), 273-282.

Reiss, I. Toward a sociology of the heterosexual love relationship. *Marriage and Family Living*, 1960, **22**, 139-145.

Rosen, L., & Bell, R. Mate selection in the upper class. *Sociological Quarterly*, 1966, **7**(2), 157-166.

Rubin, Z. Do American women marry up? *American Sociological Review*, 1968, **5**, 750-760.

Ryder, R., Kafka, J., & Olson, D. Separating and joining influences in courtship and early marriage. *American Journal of Orthopsychiatry*, 1971, **41**, 450-464.

Scheff, T. *Being mentally ill.* Chicago: Aldine, 1966.

Schur, E. M. Reactions to deviance: A critical assessment. *American Journal of Sociology*, 1969, 75, 309–322.

Selfors, S., Leik, R., & King, E. Values in mate selection: Education versus religion. *Marriage and Family Living*, 1962, **24(4)**, 399–401.

Solomon, D. Adolescents' decisions: A comparison of influence from parents with that from other sources. *Marriage and Family Living*, 1961, **23(4)**, 393–395.

Sussman, M. Parental participation in mate selection and its effects upon family continuity. *Social Forces*, 1953, **32**, 76–81.

Thibaut, J., & Kelley, H. *The social psychology of groups.* New York: Wiley, 1959.

Thomas, J. The factor of religion in the selection of marriage mates. *American Sociological Review*, 1951, **16**, 487–491.

Toman, W. The duplication theorem of social relationships as tested in the general population. *Psychological Review*, 1971, 78, 380–390.

Waller, W., & Hill, R. *The family: A dynamic interpretation.* New York: Dryden Press, 1951.

Winch, P. *Mate selection.* New York: Harper, 1958.

Winch, P. *Identification and its familial determinants.* Indianapolis, Bobbs-Merrill, 1962.

11

Adolescence and Socialization for Motherhood

JESSIE BERNARD
Pennsylvania State University

This paper consists of four parts. The first presents a descriptive statement of current changes in adolescence and motherhood and a critique of the manner in which girls have been socialized for motherhood in the past. The second part, using the concepts of tipping points and turning points, attempts to pinpoint the time when certain changes relevant to the present context have occurred or will occur, namely, the time when the institutional structures of our society dealing with basic aspects of marriage and motherhood have tilted or will tilt, restructuring the three fundamental roles of women—worker, wife, mother. Part three deals with the critical turning point in the lives of adolescents that occurs with sexual initiation. The fourth part tries to assess the impact of feminism on adolescents today.

Appreciation is due Dr. William Spillane, discussant of this paper, who called my attention to Kantner and Zelnik's studies of the sexual experience of unmarried women in the United States.

THREE KEY CONCEPTS: ADOLESCENCE, MOTHERHOOD, SOCIALIZATION

The psychosocial nature of *adolescence* as a luxury of affluent societies has been discussed by Diana Baumrind (selection 7 in this volume) and needs little further elaboration. I would like only to sketch some of the aspects most relevant for the adolescent girl today. These young women, say 13 to 19 years of age, were born from 1954 to 1960, just at the crest of the so-called feminine mystique. They were under 10 when Betty Friedan (1963) analyzed that mystique for us and initiated the recrudescence of feminism. They are among the first adolescent generations to: vote for a president; see abortion as a political issue; confront a drug culture; know that there were communes or "pads" to which they could escape from home if they wanted to; be exposed to the environmental, or ecological, movement; learn of zero population growth; see their elder sisters deciding where to live on the basis of the quality of the air as well as the quality of the schools.

During the lifetime of these adolescents, new life styles have emerged among their mothers as well as among their peers. Their mothers have less elaborately coiffed hair, more subdued lip makeup, if any at all. Their mothers' clothes are more casual and comfortable; they wear slacks instead of skirts a good deal of the time; stiletto heels are uncommon, and entertaining is less formal. If their mothers are in the 35 to 44 or the 45 to 54 age brackets, over half (52 and 54 percent, respectively) were in the labor force in 1972. (President's 1973 Manpower Report, Tables 1, 2.) So, far from encouraging the coquettish arts, many of these mothers are disappointed when they find their daughters still reluctant to take the initiative in asking boys to dance with them at high school parties. They are more feminist than their daughters. They cry as well as laugh when their 5-year-old daughters say they want babies of their own to play with.

These adolescents are the first generation to find their textbooks challenged for the sexism of their contents, their school boards challenged for the disparity in funds expended on boys' and girls' atheletic programs, their schools challenged for not permitting girls to take shop courses.

They are among the first adolescents to be exposed to the new feminist movement of the late sixties and early seventies and to hear about respectable women who deliberately bear children outside of marriage because they want motherhood but not marriage (Brandwein, 1973; Klein, 1973a). They are the first young women to see the ideal to which young women used to look forward—marriage to an affluent husband who could provide them a life of leisure—in the process of devaluation to the status of a luxury that should be taxed (Preston, 1972). They are among the young women who have, since 1948, been showing less and less interest in marriage.

They are the first adolescents to arrive on the scene at a time when there is a rebellion in process against motherhood as we institutionalize it in our society, when a spate of books appears shouting that *Mother's Day is Over*! (Radl, 1973), the first generation to hear of *The Baby Trap* (Peck, 1972), to read of happily married mothers who "really feel like screaming" (McBride, 1973, p. xi). These books are not, be it noted, written only by radical feminists, but also by conventional women as well. Women have protested motherhood in the past, to be sure. But then it was excessive motherhood—fifth, sixth, seventh babies they could not prevent (Sanger, 1928). Now, it is mothers of one or two, even no, children who are protesting. Mothers who love children, but not motherhood as it is institutionalized in our society today. And they are protesting in public! In the past, such protests were secret, woman-to-woman, so that on the surface the illusion of the happy, self-fulfilled mother could be maintained. Now the protest is open, unashamed, without guilt. Earlier adolescents did not hear such protests.

They are the first adolescents to arrive on the scene when the protests of the mothers are supplemented by strong antinatalism in the media as part of the environmental movement, when young women expect kudos not sanctions when they say they do not want to have babies, when a National Organization for Nonparenthood has arisen to help women make motherhood truly voluntary (Bernard, 1974, Ch. 3) and the choice to remain "child-free" an acceptable option.

A great deal of the research on which our knowledge of adolescence rests does not fit this new generation. Certainly the classic Erikson developmental schema does not fit.

Motherhood, as it is currently institutionalized, is, historically speaking, new and unique and, like adolescence itself, a product of affluence (Bernard, 1974, Ch. 1). Until recently, and in most parts of the world still, able-bodied adult women have been too valuable as workers to be spared for the full-time care of small children. Communes today are learning the same lesson; some will accept no children because their care is too costly in terms of labor-hours. Only those that are relatively affluent or subsidized can afford them. Our own society has been able to spare women for the full-time, exclusive care of children for only a relatively brief period of time. This allocation of adult time is good for neither mother nor children, psychologically nor economically. Questions about it are now being raised.[1]

Quite aside from any economic argument is the current antinatalist argument that women should be encouraged to enter the labor force in order to discourage them from having the third or fourth child. Or, for that matter, the second. Or first, for there is even a nascent movement to encourage childlessness. Its message is being heard. Although the proportion of young women who say they want no children is still small—3.9 percent as of June 1972—it had tripled in the three previous years, and may conceivably rise higher (Bureau of the Census, 1972). Also in 1972, in a sample of adolescent girls, 7 percent replied "false" to the statement "someday I will probably want to get married and have children" (Sorensen, 1973, p. 502). Although it is probably safe to say that at least nine

---

[1] The supporting data for the discussion of motherhood are presented in Bernard (1974).

out of ten girls who are adolescents today are going to be mothers, it is probably also safe to say that they are not going to have many babies.

The role of mother is no longer being defined as monopolizing a woman's whole life or, even when her children are in school, her exclusive attention. The mother of school-age (but not preschool) children who is not in the labor force is today becoming the exception rather than the rule. This point will be elaborated in greater detail later.

When we speak of the socialization of adolescents for motherhood, we have to ask: "Socialization for what stage of motherhood?" For motherhood is by no means a unitary or homogeneous phenomenon. At least four stages can be delineated: (1) early motherhood—the children are preschoolers and the mother is approximately 25 to 34 years of age; (2) middle motherhood—the children are of school age and the mother is in the 35 to 44 or 45 to 54 age bracket; (3) late motherhood—the children are 18 years of age or older and the mother is 55 or over; and (4) for some long-lived women, when mother-child roles are reversed. The present discussion deals primarily with middle motherhood.

So far as socialization is concerned, it would be carrying coals to Newcastle to review for this group the way we have bent the female twig for motherhood. As long ago as 1916, Leta Hollingworth was pointing out the many techniques used to impress on girls the importance of bearing children. Judith Blake Davis reminded us again in 1972. And the many studies of sex stereotyping from the primer on up have documented how insistently, almost coercively, and pervasively we have socialized girls to believe that the primary lifetime role for them was that of mother (New Jersey NOW, 1972). Only recently has the coercive nature of this socialization come under challenge. Only now is there a concerted effort on the part of at least some to counteract this pressure and make motherhood genuinely voluntary.

Not only has the socialization for motherhood been all-pervasive, it has also been counterproductive, structured in such a way as to produce precisely the characteristics in girls that were dysfunctional for motherhood. Girls were socialized for dependency rather than for the strengths required for the role of mother (Newton, 1955). In Erikson's schema (1968), the young woman at marriage moved from one dependency to another, from "the care received from the parental family in order to commit herself to the love of a stranger and to the care to be given to his and her offspring" (Erikson, 1968, p. 205). Erikson conceded that she might have a brief moratorium between the two dependencies. But for the most part, "such women . . . assumed that, after college, they need not make a life of their own but could live their lives through boyfriends and, later, husbands. They agreed with the young women who said: 'I had always been taken in by the myth that all you have to do is find a man and you'll be happy.' If they were 'to find a man,' they must not be too self-assertive" (Carden, 1973, p. 18). And this is how it looked to the young women:

> "I had always been told that men wouldn't like me because I was too aggressive. I thought I had gotten over that. I had, to a large extent, but . . . in my senior year,

when lots of women were getting married, I worried about not being married and about there being no position in this society for a single woman. Until I left [college] I accepted the myth that women are submissive, not speaking at SDS meetings, sitting in the dorms waiting to be asked out" (Carden, 1973, p. 26).

Surely this was not the caliber required for effective motherhood.

Not only has the model for socializing girls for motherhood been counter-productive so far as dependency is concerned, but it has also become increasingly inadequate for socializing young women for motherhood in the world they live in today, that is, in a world where, as documented later, the norms of virginity, which in the past protected against irresponsible motherhood, are in process of dissolution. They are not being adequately socialized for responsible as well as voluntary motherhood.[2]

In the past, a major component of the socialization for motherhood consisted of the maintenance of virginity as a first line of defense against involuntary or irresponsible motherhood. It is an absolutely certain way to avoid motherhood. (There is a folk saying that the best contraceptive is ten feet of space.) In a society that makes so little provision for infants borne outside of marriage, responsibility includes involving the father as well as the mother in a serious commitment if motherhood is undertaken. In our society, therefore, among teen-agers, if not among mature women, responsibility still precludes premarital motherhood. If virginity is not to serve as the first line of defense against irresponsible motherhood, there must be other defenses, including the desire to prevent conception in the first place.

Such second-line defenses are far from normative today. Some of the salient findings of a survey among adolescents aged 13 to 19 in 1972 are presented in Table 11.1. Although 70 percent of the initiated adolescents worry about becoming pregnant, fewer than half (44 percent) are inhibited by fears of becoming pregnant, and an almost equal proportion (45 percent) consider contraception (except the pill) too much trouble. Fewer than a third (31 percent) use the pill. Understandably, in view of such irresponsibility, almost a fourth (23 percent) have had a pregnancy. Among all the initiated adolescents, 14 percent feel the availability of abortion relieves them of worry about pregnancy and if they become pregnant, 18 percent would seek an abortion; almost a third would marry the father. It is true that the older teen-agers show more responsibility than the younger ones, and the young women with current sexual experience show more responsibility than the others; still even they seem less than prudent in their behavior. Responsible use of contraception has not yet achieved for society even the limited success of virginity as a defense against

---

[2] This harsh judgment should be tempered by recognition that young people are increasingly viewing parenthood with concern for the environment. Thus, overall, half (49 percent) of all the young women surveyed in 1972 (Sorensen, 1973, Table 296) agreed that it was immoral to have an unwanted child in our overpopulated world, especially since abortion is so available. More of the older women (54 percent) than of the younger women (43 percent) agreed. There is also recognition of the dysgenic effects of drug use (see vignette 8).

TABLE 11.1

Behavior and Attitudes of Adolescent Nonvirgins as Related to Sexual Responsibility, by Age and Experience

Attitude or behavior	All	By age		By experience	
		Ages 13–15	Ages 16–19	With current intercourse experience	With no current intercourse experience
Sometimes worry about becoming pregnant (451, 452)	70%	61%	72%	71%	68%
Used contraception first time (385)	19			29	3
Used contraception most recent time (507)				40 (13–15, 23%; 16–19, 46%)	
Do not know where to secure contraceptive information (301)	16	32	9	62	
Precaution taken in past month (481)				63	
Never trusted to luck in past month (503)					
Would have abortion if became pregnant (457, 458)	18	2	23	23	3
Would get married if became pregnant (458)[a]	31	10	39	31	30
Have used pills (386)	31				
Fear has prevented intercourse (476)	44			38	58
Contraception (except pill) too much trouble (308)	45	35	49		
Neither used contraception last time (507)	40	45	38		
Have never thought about getting pregnant in last month (505)				82	
Don't worry because abortion so available (330)	14	21	11		
Have been pregnant (479, 480)	23	11	28	28	7

Note: Figures in parentheses refer to tables.
[a] In 27 percent of the cases the young man said he would marry the young woman; in 46 percent of the cases he might marry her (Table 472).
Source: Sorensen, 1973.

irresponsible motherhood. How to socialize adolescents for the prevention of irresponsible motherhood in a world where virginity can no longer hold the line against it is still an unsolved problem.[3]

In brief, socialization for a new kind of adolescent in a new kind of world for a new kind of motherhood calls for a thoughtful new look.

TIPPING POINTS AND TURNING POINTS

Daniel Patrick Moynihan (1973) has interpreted the eruptions of the 1960s in terms of what might well be called a societal "quake" theory. The eruptions were brought about by demographic forces. In that decade, the children born during the era of the feminine mystique "rushed" our society. We were quite unprepared for their assault on our institutions. Our 15-year-old adolescent girl—taken here to represent her generation—was a bit too young to participate in those eruptions, but not too young to be exposed to their reverberations.

To say that our society is in the throes of rapid change is banal. But to say that we can now pinpoint the exact moment when a whole institutional structure, like a geological one, tilts is not banal. And that is what we can now do for at least some components of the institutional structures dealing with marriage and motherhood. If we had a Richter scale for societal, as well as for earth, quakes, the present societal quake would surely register 8. We cannot pinpoint all of these tiltings with precision, but within a year or two in either direction, we can zero in on the time when such institutional tilts have taken place, or are about to take place. This very moment may be such a time.

The concept of the *tipping point* comes from the study of urban communities, where it refers to the process by which one land-use succeeds another. It has been applied especially to the racial composition of an area. Traditionally, a neighborhood, primarily white, attracts a few black families; their number increases. For a while it remains biracial. But as the number of black families increases, the white families become uneasy. One by one they sell their homes to black families until, at the tipping point, there is a kind of panic selling and the whole neighborhood tilts to become all black.

The concept of the tipping point as applied here is not identical to this ecological use. It merely denotes the fact that there comes a time when what was formerly typical or modal now becomes "deviant"—in a statistical and non-pejorative sense—or nonmodal, and vice versa. As Ruth Hartley (1970) notes, when a pattern becomes modal, it tends to become normative, even coercive if not panicky as in ecological tipping.

[3] Not until 1973, after two years of controversy, did the Board of Education in one of the most affluent and educated counties in the country finally approve of the study of contraception for high school seniors. Even so, it will require parental approval. And a Local Advisory Committee will decide when each school is ready to offer such study (*Washington Post*, September 12, 1973). Parental disapproval remained strong.

In the present context, the societal tipping point is defined as the point in time when the 50 percent level is reached. When half of the members of a society do or accept or believe something, the chances are that it will tend to become normative.

At this point I strongly resist the temptation to soar off in a theory of anomie and anomia. It would take some such form as this, that the societal tipping point—the moment when a 50-50 balance has been reached—is a time of true normlessness in the sense that two different norms cancel one another out. Rather than leading to a different normative pattern that then becomes coercive, it is conceivable that the worst possible situation—the absence of any definitive norm—results. The adolescent does not know which norm to follow; the woman in middle motherhood does not know whether or not to enter the labor force. Anomia results. Fascinating as I find this approach, I relinquish it here.

In addition to the concept of tipping points, I have found it useful to use the concept of *turning points*. Without investing too much time in fine distinctions, I will say only that turning points are here distinguished from tipping points in that they refer to changes in the direction of a curve rather than, as in the case of tipping points, simply a level in a continuing trend in a given direction. A turning point is countertrend, a tipping point is trend-conforming and trend-confirming.

It is, admittedly, not always easy to distinguish between a tipping point and a turning point. A curve may turn when its tipping point is reached; any curve may hit an asymptote at the tipping point. Birth, marriage, and divorce rates commonly show turning points; they may also show tipping points. The proportion of mothers of school-age (but not preschool) children in the labor force appears to be approaching a ceiling. The upward trend in labor-force participation by women in middle motherhood since 1948 may be interpreted simply as the fancy of one cohort or generation of women, as the feminine mystique was for the generation of the 1950s. There are always pitfalls in projecting statistical trends and always numerous ways to interpret them.

The question arises also: Can we prevent a tilt if we wish to do so? Or reverse it? Did we turn the tide against the heroin "epidemic"? Did or can Nixon reverse the trend toward centralized government? Did we turn the trend toward violence in the cities, as John Spiegel (1973) thinks we did? For him, the Chicago convention and the Kent State shooting "represent the cutoff [turning] point of the old era and the entering point for the new era which we are entering or already have entered." Is the so-called equilibrium theory correct in the sense that there is a kind of homeostatic mechanism at work that tends to maintain a system and prevent tilts, that puts corrective processes to work when or if it is disturbed so it returns to its original balance? Will sex roles return to pre-"quake" definitions? I believe not.

Societal Turning Points

Two turning points relevant for our discussion here have to do with the birth rate since 1957 and the first-marriage rate since the late forties. Both will now begin to have important implications for the 15-year-old adolescent girl as she approaches marriage or motherhood.

The young woman who is 15 years old today was born in 1958, the turning point that marked the end of the era of the feminine mystique. The birth rate, which had crested the year before she was born, now resumed its long-time secular trend downward. She belongs, therefore, to the first female cohort since World War II not caught in the Parke-Glick marriage squeeze (1967), there were more boys born in 1956-1957 than girls born in 1958. For young women born during the 1950s with its rising birth rate, the marriage squeeze was on them; there were not enough young men born in the year or two before they were born to become their husbands twenty years later. For the present generation of adolescent girls, by 1977, when they are 20, there will be more young men a year or two older than they. Young women will not therefore be so vulnerable to panic about "getting their man" when there are enough young men of the right age for them to go around. Indeed, the very concept of getting one's man is, I believe, becoming anachronistic for this generation of adolescents.

In the current marriage squeeze until 1977, still reflecting the rising birth rate of the 1950s, young women have been waiting for the young men, with a consequent slight rise in age at marriage. One might expect a return to the lower age at marriage when the squeeze reverses itself to fall on the men rather than on the women. But there is reason, I believe, to anticipate a somewhat different pattern.

In the past, when a young women—"wired for marriage" by the socialization she had undergone—went to a young man in the marriageable years, she proposed, in effect, if not in words, something like this: Please father the two or three children I need for my self-fulfillment; support me while I bear them; support them until they are about 18 and me for the rest of my life. In return I will promise to take care of your personal needs as long as you live or until you can afford to relieve me and hire others to do so. That was the image of life that formed her mentality, her sexuality, her emotionality. She was set in that course or, in the literal sense, career, from the moment of birth.

That proposal looked quite reasonable in view of the way roles were structured in the past. It took into account the enormous disadvantage women labored under in the work force; it anchored them safely within the bonds of marriage. It was about the best they could hope for. They got what they were socialized to want, although, in some cases, at enormous cost.

Our 15-year-old adolescent is not likely to view marriage in this light. She is not so likely to think of herself as forever "taken care of" by the man she marries. Her proposal may now take a form such as this: Give me a baby or two for self-fulfillment and help me also in my career or job by sharing with me the costs of motherhood, including any time out from career or job required. In return I will share with you the provider role for the family and help you also in your job or career. The young man—who needs marriage more than she does (Bernard, 1972, Ch. 2)—will feel less reluctant about the financial obligations when they are to be shared. And since the young woman is not necessarily

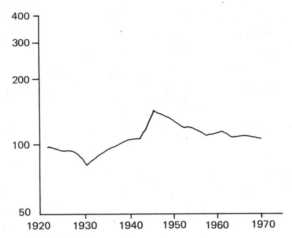

Figure 11.1   First-marriage rates per 1,000 single women:
United States, three-year averages, 1921 to 1971. (Source:
Glick & Norton, 1973, p. 302.)

asking for lifelong support nor, for that matter, in a growing though still small number, even for children, she is less likely to consider marriage the *ultima thule* of her life. There are, further, extramarriage life styles available as the rapid increase in female-headed households shows (Bernard, 1968). Marriage itself will seem less important to her.

Will marriage have the same urgency for these young women as it had for young women in the past? Will they feel pressured to "get their man" while the getting is good, in the prime years of the late teens and early twenties? If there are agreeable alternatives to marriage, will that make a difference?

We are beginning to get data to help firm up our knowledge and help answer such questions. These data come from the analyses of the marriage rate by Paul C. Glick and Arthur J. Norton (1973). They report a strange but interesting downward trend in the first-marriage rate since a turning point in the late 1940s, as shown in Figure 11.1.

I had been watching the overall marriage rate with a great deal of interest for several years. After a steady rise during the early 1960s, it began to waffle, leveling off in 1969, and beginning to show declines from time to time. For the first seven months of 1971, for example, both the rate and number of marriages were lower than in 1970, "indicating a possible reversal of the long upward trend" (National Center for Health Statistics, 1971, p. 1). The 1970 census showed a smaller proportion of young women ages 18 to 24 married than the 1960 census showed. Something, it was clear, was happening, but exactly what it was did not become apparent until the work of Glick and Norton (1973) clarified it. They found that a downturn in the *first*-marriage rate compensated for the rising *re*marriage rate, suggesting a lessening of enthusiam for marriage among the young women.

If the downward trend in the first-marriage rate was due to delayed marriage resulting from the marriage squeeze or from such historical war-generated influences as pressures among young men to continue a college education or to ensure draft deferment, it had not been compensated for by 1970 (Glick & Norton, 1973, p. 306). This led Glick and Norton to ask whether "a decline in eventual marriage [was] developing" (Glick & Norton, 1973, p. 305). They are cautious in their reply. It is "too early to assert with confidence that there is an impending upsurge in lifetime singleness" or, stated more relevantly for our purposes, an impending decline in marriage for oncoming teen-agers.

So much, then, for two societal turning points—the decline in the first-marriage rate since the late forties and the decline in the birth rate since 1957—which, twenty years later, have major implications for today's adolescent female. They affect the marital matrix in which motherhood as she will know it will be embedded. Both are related to equally relevant tipping points, one having to do with the redefinition of the role of mother now in process and one with the norm of virginity.

Societal Tipping Points

Figure 11.2 presents a tipping point which I consider of major significance for our concerns here. It deals with the proportion of mothers with school-age (but not preschool) children who were in the labor force 1948-72. In 1972, for the first time, the proportion of these mothers who were in the labor force reached a tipping point. To be sure the tilt was not great. (It would have been greater if it had included mothers who were in the labor force for as much as a week.) Nor was it rapid. By 1990, when our teen-agers are in their early thirties, the

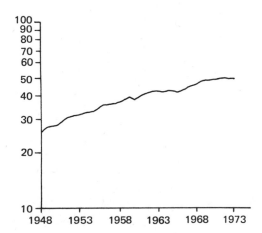

Figure 11.2 Proportion of mothers with school-age (but not preschool) children in the labor force, 1948 to 1972. (Source: *Manpower Report of the President*, 1973, Table B-4, p. 168.)

proportion of women in the age brackets 35–44 and 45–54—who are most likely to be mothers of school-age (but not preschool) children—is projected to be only 55 and 58 percent, respectively (President's 1973 Manpower Report, Table E2, p. 220). Nevertheless, these data suggest that the role of mother into which adolescent girls today are to be socialized is in the process of being redefined to involve labor-force participation as well as child rearing. When we face the adolescent girl, we see a young woman who is likely to be simultaneously a mother and a labor-force participant for a good many years of her life. We can no longer socialize her for motherhood without socializing her also for a serious worker role as well. We have long been thinking of this in connection with women in the late—or, as sometimes it is called, the "empty-nest"—stage of motherhood, when their children are over 18. And the labor-force participation of women in the 45 to 54 age bracket is, indeed, already fairly high—54.0 percent in 1970. But we must now begin to think of labor-force participation among mothers with school-age children still in the home as well.

A considerable amount of "motherwork" now includes a job, as Ruth Hartley (1959–60) was already finding in her interviews with working mothers some time ago. As noted earlier, adolescent girls can no longer assume that they will be taken care of for the rest of their lives once they become mothers. Nor can we any longer encourage a casual attitude toward the work history of these young women. The socialization of adolescents for motherhood as it is now coming to be institutionalized calls not only for the acquisition of marketable vocational skills, but also, seriously, for their maintenance.

A second great tipping point has to do with female virginity. Researchers have been watching with a kind of near-voyeurism the changing mores with respect to premarital sexual relations, especially among women. This is understandable, for premarital virginity was one of the bedrocks of traditional marriage. Because of the centrality of female virginity, it became one of the major strains in research on marriage and the family as soon as this field was opened up for study. Kinsey and his associates (1953, Table 37, p. 337) startled an incredulous world with their finding that about half of all the women in his sample—49 percent—had engaged in premarital intercourse. The bald fact was softened when the details were examined. The proportion varied from only 4 percent if the woman married at age 14 to as much as 56 percent if she married at age 28. Also mollifying the impact was the further finding that for the most part, the premarital relations were with the future husband.

Our concern here is not with marital status at first intercourse but with age, for the most recent survey finds the concept of premarital intercourse of only marginal interest. Sorensen (1973, p. 341) tells us, in fact, that the concept of "premarital sex" is becoming "increasingly outmoded, because young people are not scheduling marriage on their life agenda simply to gratify their sexual needs or in order to legalize their sexual relationships." Marital status at sexual initiation is thus becoming increasingly irrelevant. The discussion here deals only with teen-age, not with premarital, intercourse. (Actually only 2 percent of the

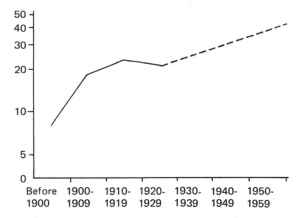

Figure 11.3 Proportion of young women who had sexual intercourse by age 20, by decade of birth. (Sources: For the first four decades, Kinsey et al., 1953, Table 83, p. 339; for the 1950s, Kantner & Zelnik, 1972, p. 9, and Sorensen, 1973, Table 404, p. 441. The Kantner-Zelnik sample yielded the figure of 46 percent for 1971, the Sorensen sample, 45 percent for 1972.)

respondents in the Sorensen sample were married, so, in effect, the data deal almost entirely with premarital sexual relations; the Kantner-Zelnik data (1972, 1973) deal only with never-married young women.) The tipping point for teen-age young women is shown in Figure 11.3. In 1971, in a sample of 4,240 young women, 46 percent had had coitus by the age of 19; in the Sorensen sample of 181 young women, 45 percent had had sexual intercourse by that age. For young women born in the 1950s, the tipping point, 50 percent, will probably be reached around 1976 or 1977.

It will be recalled that during the 1960s there was considerable controversy with respect to trends in premarital coitus. Some argued that there had been no increase since the 1920s when the great revolution had occurred; there was only more talk about it since then. But others, observing the current scene, could hardly accept this conclusion. They could not prove it, but they *felt* or intuited that premarital intercourse had increased (Packard, 1968, pp. 124–126).

The research finally corroborated their hunch. There had been a second wave of change. In 1938, L. M. Terman had predicted that if the trends that he had traced continued, no girl born after 1940 would enter marriage a virgin. He was wrong. The sharp rise of the 1920s abated in the thirties. If they married in their early twenties, half of the young women born in 1950 would still be virgins at the time of their marriage. But this figure would not necessarily hold for young women born later.

The reason for the controversy was, precisely, that we were approaching a tipping point in the 1960s. The young people themselves were talking a great deal about the pros and cons of intercourse outside of marriage, the nature of sexual relations, of marriage, of virginity, and a host of other interpersonal relationships. The talk apparently had its effect.

Another tipping point that may be just ahead of us—or just behind us—has to do with the nature of marriage the 15-year-old adolescent girl will face, as revealed in several measures of divorce trends. Figure 11.4 presents three such measures. All show tipping points in the 1970s. The period divorce rate for married women 14 to 44 years of age, which was 28.0 percent in 1971 (Glick & Norton, 1973b, p. 67), may "tip" in the last year or two of the decade; the precentage of all marriages entered into during the last thirty-five years that have ended in divorce—40.9 percent in 1970 (Glick, 1973, p. 69)—may reach a "tip" some time next year; and the percentage of all marriages that end in divorce seven years later—43.2 percent in 1970 (Glick, 1973, p. 73)—may have "tipped" in 1972. It is not inconceivable that in the lives of today's teenagers the stable lifelong marriage may become deviant. For women fifteen years older than today's teen-agers—born from 1935 to 1944—Glick and Norton (1973, p. 308) project that about 29 percent will end their first marriages in divorce. The projected tipping point on this measure would come for the generation born 1970-75.

There is, of course, no reason to believe that the current upward trend in divorce will continue forever. The tipping points may prove to be turning points, for we know that divorce rates do fluctuate over time. The rates may level off and even decline. Still, in reply to their own question, "Is the upward trend in divorce 'phasing out'?" Glick and Norton (1973, p. 311) reply that although "a leveling off or decline in the divorce rate must come sometime, . . . such a change is still awaited."

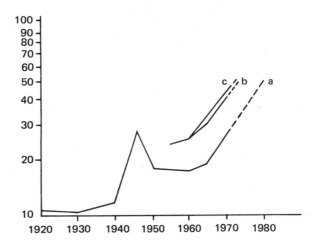

Figure 11.4 Trends in three measures of divorce, 1920–
1971. (Source: Glick, 1973, pp. 67, 69, 73.)

What we may be witnessing is the approximate form that current experiments in life style will be taking—either the two-step form of marriage that Margaret Mead has predicted or, at least, some form of experimental or limited or temporary marriage, dissolved when it fails and followed by a more stable and permanent relationship.

The relevance for motherhood and the adolescent girl can be inferred. She will have to be socialized for a form of motherhood that does not have the supports it has had in the past, weak as such supports proved to be all too often. The more fluid kinds of relationships will have to provide for any children that result. Although men are increasingly asking for and accepting a greater share in the rearing of children, for at least the immediate future it will remain easier for men than for women to renege on parental responsibilities. Although more and more women are rejecting custody of children in divorce, still the preconceptions of judges continue to influence them in granting custody to mothers. The general loosening up of sexual relations and the lag in contraceptive practice by young women also increases the probability of mother-supported children. Berger, Hackett, and Millar (1972) in their study of the anarchist communes in the West noted that young women, knowing that Aid to Dependent Children support was available, were more willing than young women in the past to engage in transitory sexual relations that might end in pregnancy.

Related Tipping Points

Related to changes in adolescent practices, there has also been a change with respect to standards, an increase in what Ira Reiss (1967) calls the permissive standard. In 1964, I noted that "there was a time when those arguing for premarital virginity could be assured of a comfortable margin of support in the group [NCFR]. This is no longer always true. Especially the younger members no longer accept this code. A more permissive position is emerging" (Bernard, 1964). Somewhere along the line a tipping point had been reached. The work of Ira Reiss (1967), though dealing primarily with college-age students rather than with teenagers, has shown the rise of this more permissive standard, although the precise date of the tipping point cannot be pinpointed.

One tipping point of interest to our 15-year-old adolescent girl has to do with the man she marries. Among white male high school graduates, 20 to 24 years of age, the tipping point for college entrance came in 1968. Since then, at least half of all white male high school graduates have been going on to college. In 1972, it was 53.3 percent (Bureau of the Census, 1973). This means that at least among white 15-year-old adolescent girls the chances are better than even that when or if they marry, their husbands will have had some college education. I do not underestimate the importance of this fact. Several years ago a survey of young people by the Daniel Yankelovich (1969) polling service showed us that the great divide was between college and noncollege youth rather than between the generations. I have noted elsewhere that dealing with any system primarily of the college-educated is different from dealing with one with a less educated personnel. Marriage, we know, is different among the college educated, as is motherhood also.

Related to this tipping point is another one relevant for our teen-ager. In 1972, for the first time the proportion of male freshmen entering college who hold to the ideology that woman's place is in the home fell below 50 percent (American Council on Education, 1972). The tilt here is in the direction of a more feminist position. The chances are good that by 1976, when the 1972 entering freshmen graduate, a larger proportion will be tilted toward a feminist position. A study by Bernice Lott (1973, p. 577) shows that the mean score on a liberation scale of college men is almost as high (18.49) as that of women (20.26).

Yet another related tipping point relevant to the adolescent girl that cannot be located with precision but can be documented in the research literature has to do with the image of the career woman. After a period of denigration, the career woman's image has been rehabilitated. She is no longer viewed as a deviant eccentric, a misfit, a victim of inauspicious family trauma (Helsen, 1972). Indeed, Zella Lurie (1972) now warns us against putting sanctions on the college woman who is not career-oriented.

There are doubtless other tipping points at this very moment that we have no time series to document. But whether there are or not, we know of enough of them to conclude that the years we are now living through, the early 1970s, are witnessing a tilt in the institutional structure of our society of truly spectacular magnitude. It will surely have profound influence on the motherhood today's teen-ager will engage in.

Before moving to developmental turning points in the lives of the young women themselves, I offer a brief aside on the significance for adolescent girls today of the societal turning and tipping points reviewed above. I believe they will have the effect of giving young women more control over the contigencies that have dominated their lives in the past, as Glen Elder (1974) has so cogently noted:

> A life style dependent on marriage and the husband's career are features of a woman's contingent life. Depending on the man she marries, a young woman's occupational plans and preparations may be invalidated, modified, or receive the support needed for eventual fulfillment. Lacking control over this event, on which everything seems to hinge, most young women have been understandably reluctant "to take their future careers seriously" during the premarital years, or even until after the childbearing and rearing phases of marriage.[4]

It seems to me that, although for most young women these contingencies still persist, the general tiltings in the institutional structures of our society dealing with work, marriage, and motherhood will give more and more young women increasing control over the contingencies that affect their lives. Deci-

---

[4] Present citation from manuscript.

sions about marriage and motherhood will be more contingent on their own preferences; and the men they marry will increasingly expect this to be the case. I do not foresee arrogant rejection of husbands' preferences. The young women I know expect to respect them. The vignettes presented later flesh out these comments.

DEVELOPMENTAL TURNING POINTS

Although opposed to the concept of development that implies an orderly sequence of changes, the concept of the psychological turning point is old in the folk mind. The best known turning point in the Christian world is the case of Saul on the road to Damascus. The psychology of conversion has confirmed the reality of that kind of experience. The member of Alcoholics Anonymous who recounts his story further confirms the reality of such individual turning points. Most of us have heard people tell of events or experiences that changed them completely from one course to another. *Ms.* magazine (O'Reilly, 1972) has been reporting the "click" phenomenon among women; it refers to the critical moment when a woman's consciousness is suddenly raised by some remark or incident to the chauvinism in the world about her. In a way such "clicks" constitute turning points. A new definition of reality creates a new reality for her. Her world "tilts" in a new direction.

Parents report their uneasiness as they observe their children teetering between two worlds, fearful that something may happen to "tilt" their lives in the—to them—wrong direction. The son's downfall dates from the moment he met John; the daughter's, from the day she met Mary, or John, as the case may be.

In a study of mother-daughter relations, women college students were asked to write autobiographies. The young women with middle class backgrounds wrote vaguely and nondramatically of their personal histories. The upwardly mobile young women with working-class backgrounds, who showed the psychological malaise that characterizes those we used to call marginal, were different. They frequently noted critical experiences that changed the course of their lives, such as the change resulting from having an ethnic boyfriend, or from a college course. The experiences changed their reality and, they thought, their whole lives (Millman, 1973). In a way, the Freudian approach is a form of the crisis concept. One traumatic experience at the age of 4 or earlier, one glimpse of the primal scene, could lead to the psychiatrist's couch years later.

This approach does not lend itself easily to the hard-nosed research techniques so favored today. The crises that can be subjected to agentic-style research have to be expectable ones, the garden variety. Adolescence does offer examples of this kind. Sexual initiation, at whatever age, is such an expectable "crisis," this time in quotation marks, that lends itself to the turning-point approach.

An enormous literature documents the sexual initiation of boys. It has been said that almost every first novel is such a document. But although the loss of virginity has been a far more serious turning point for women than for men—loss of virginity in Western cultures has led almost universally to lowered status, if not disgrace—few novels deal with it except if it results in pregnancy. If, or when, it does, it too becomes a major theme. The seduced child, the raped girl, the seducing young woman are—perhaps morbidly—fascinating figures.

It is interesting to note that in all the schemata for developmental stages in women, based as they are almost exclusively on childbearing, so little attention has been paid to the importance of sexual initiation. There has been an overwhelming preoccupation with virginity and the importance of preserving it until marriage, and the girl's whole life seemed to be centered on protecting it as did also an all-pervasive insititutional structure designed for that purpose. Chaperones, restrictions, a thousand little rules of etiquette were devised to keep the girl's virginity intact. In our society it would not have been absurd to label the stage in a young woman's development between, say, 16 and 20, as the "stage of virginity protection." Be that as it may, the adolescent now entering the scene has had less exposure to the concept of marriage on which the cult of virginity rested. Virginity of women at marriage is important to only 23 percent of young men 16 to 19 years of age (Sorensen, 1973, Table 103).

Sexual initiation does, in fact, constitute a turning point in the development of adolescent girls.

> Once she has had her first sexual intercourse, a girl often feels different about herself—not deprived or bereft of her virginity, but different *within* herself. She seldom feels raped or violated by the experience, although she may feel her first sex partner was insensitive. She does feel more mature and experienced—but in a mildly defensive sense. She sometimes feels the need to rationalize what she has done and to feel more sympathetic with girls who have also had their first sexual experience. This reaction is not diminished even when she continues to have intercourse with the same boy or other boys. She is, as one girl told us, "now on the other side of the fence," or, as another girl put it, "You're like trying to justify it in your mind . . . so you change your views really drastically." Many girls characterize their first intercourse as a "learning experience"; girls, far more frequently than boys, report reactions of guilt, sorrow, and disappointment (Sorensen, 1973, p. 190).

Sexual initiation changes an adolescent's relationship not only with herself and her peers, but also with her mother. The one and, in many cases, only ground for superior status or claim for authority of a mother vis-à-vis her daughter is sexual experience. She has been initiated; the daughter, according to the mores so far, has not. But sexual experience is a great equalizer. Once the daughter has been initiated, once she, too, shares the adult secret, a major support for the mother's authority is gone. Even "sex education" short of actual experience may add a trump card to the daughter's hand.

Sexual initiation changes the perception of self among teen-agers. "They view their bodies differently. They react to their sexual partners, to their families, and

to society in a different way because they perceive themselves differently"
(Sorensen, 1973, p. 203).

In view of the significance of this turning point, it is of interest to learn that
the age at which it occurs among young women as of 1971–72 is just over 20
years. Among the teenagers who have had intercourse, the modal age at first
intercourse is 15, the median between 15 and 16.[5]

A comparison between girls 13 to 15 years of age and girls 16 to 19 years of
age suggests that there may be a movement toward even earlier age at first intercourse since it was 16 among the older girls but only 15 among the younger ones
(Sorensen, 1973, Table 405).

The crisis nature of pregnancy among teen-agers, especially among unmarried
young women, needs no elaboration for this audience. Inside or outside of marriage, early pregnancy—the earlier the first child is borne the larger the total
number of babies borne will be—is not only "demographically disastrous," but
also almost determinative of a restricted life history for the mother thereafter.
This fact is of interest to educators and social workers who try to head off the
dysfunctional results of such early pregnancies, as well as to demographers and
policy makers. The recommendations of the President's Commission on Population Growth and the American Future (1972, p. 168) on the subject were that:
"(1) States eliminate existing legal inhibitions and restrictions on access to contraceptive information, procedures, and supplies; and (2) States develop statutes
affirming the desirability that all persons have ready and practicable access to
contraceptive information, procedures, and supplies." But, as we saw earlier, socialization of girls—let alone boys—for the use of such information, procedures,
and supplies even when available is quite another matter. A matter that we are
not now expert in dealing with. In Kantner and Zelnik's sample (1973), among
white young women, 10 percent of the sexually experienced had had a pregnancy, and among black young women, more than 40 percent had (p. 31). In the
Sorensen sample, more than a fourth (28 percent) of the nonvirgin teenagers 16
to 19 years old had experienced a pregnancy (Sorensen, 1973, Table 479, p.
450).

The age at sexual initiation is related to the age at menarche, which has been
declining for over a century and seems now to have leveled off at the age of 12.
The significance for motherhood of a growing spread between age of menarche
and age of marriage cannot be ignored in our thinking about socialization for
motherhood in adolescence.

[5] The data on age at first sexual intercourse are not entirely comparable for Kantner and
Zelnik (1972) and Sorensen (1973). The first include more black respondents, and the
second, more younger subjects. The Kantner-Zelnik data show that "the likelihood that a
young never-married woman 15–19 years of age has experienced coitus rises from 14
percent at age 15, to 21 percent at age 16, to 27 percent at age 17, to 37 percent at age 18,
and to 46 percent by age 19" (Kantner & Zelnik, 1972, p. 9). The corresponding figures in
the Sorensen sample of young women 12 to 19 years of age were: 25 percent by age 15; 34
percent by age 16; 37 percent by age 17; and 45 percent by age 19 (Sorensen, 1973, table
405, p. 441).

FEMINISM, MOTHERHOOD, AND
TODAY'S ADOLESCENT

As Diana Baumrind notes, adolescence takes on the character of the society that creates it. The adolescent girl today lives in an ambience in which feminism is exerting an impressive influence. For this reason the way feminism is dealing with motherhood is a legitimate factor to glance at when considering the socializing of adolescents for motherhood.

The feminist movement, as has now been made clear, is not a disciplined phalanx with a sacred revealed text. It has had to hassle a number of issues.[6] One of the most difficult was that of lesbianism. For a while it looked as though that issue would split the movement. An accommodation has now been reached. The movement became secure enough to accommodate both lesbians and non-lesbians without insisting that either obliterate or dominate the other. Feminists can accept choices in the matter of relations between the sexes provided only that they be purely voluntary, not coerced.

Now an issue emerges on the horizon—as yet a cloud no larger than the size of a man's fist—dealing not with relations between the sexes but with motherhood. Some of the most talented early feminists were vehemently antinatalist. Not only were they hostile to the maternal role, but they also actively propagated the idea of mechanical gestation to minimize women's role as mothers. More recently women with a strongly promotherhood point of view have become articulate and active, extolling the joys of motherhood and breast-feeding (which they may sometimes engage in until the child is 3 years old). Among some, this cult of motherhood is merely a personal preference; but among others, it is an almost knee-jerk reaction against the rampant antinatalism evoked by the environmental movement. Any kind of pressure on women—antinatalist as well as pronatalist—is rejected.

There are political as well as individual implications for teen-agers of the motherhood issue. For although there is no official feminist "line" on motherhood, the antinatalist feminists—like other antinatalists—have criticized the movement's support of child-care centers, provisions for maternity leave with pay, and other services for mothers as assuming that motherhood was to be taken for granted for all women. Efforts to help women integrate their roles as mothers and as labor-force participants are therefore viewed by them as misguided because they see motherhood as an inevitable choice, not an established fact, for women.

If the emphasis on choice, which is a fundamental belief of feminists, is achieved—as I believe it will be—there will be no difficulty. Neither a promotherhood nor an antimotherhood position will be taken. The emphasis

---

[6] Only issues relevant to motherhood are commented on here. The most serious issue in the early years was between political and strictly feminist emphases, the so-called politicos, wished to subordinate strictly female issues to general socialist ones; the feminists wished to emphasize the strictly female issues. That struggle is not pertinent in the present context.

will be on voluntary motherhood, with no hard feelings for those who disagree with one's own preference. The opinions will run something like: OK, have your babies, but don't put us down if we don't. Or, conversely, OK, don't have any babies, but don't put us down if we do. The issue of motherhood will certainly be resolved, as the issue of lesbianism was.

Until recently, high school girls showed an apathetic reaction to feminism. Poorly informed, they tended "to see 'women's libbers' as 'a bunch of man-haters and bra-burners.'" They found the "implied rejection of men . . . very threatening." And, at their age, they had not yet experienced "the full impact of conflicting values" rampant in our society today, nor could they "anticipate what their lives [would] be like after graduation" (Carden, 1973, p. 30). Since 1970, however, high school groups have increasingly asked for speakers on the subject of feminism. It may be that the hostile antinatalism that characterized some of the early leaders has now been dissipated, rendering the movement more congenial to the young women, especially as some of the feminist groups see "children's liberation" as a way to make them better mothers: "A group from New Haven commented: 'although most of us are rejecting the Freudian notion that the only fulfillment of a woman's life is her children, many of us see children as a beautiful and important part of our lives. We want to be able to provide settings which will allow our children to grow and develop happily'" (Carden, 1973, p. 192). Feminism is seen by these mothers as a guide for rearing their children.

Age does make a difference. In 1972, although only a third of the 13 to 15-year-olds (32 percent) believed that the women's liberation movement was good for women, almost half (47 percent) of the 16 to 19-year-olds did, the nonvirgins (51 percent) more than the virgins (37 percent) (Sorensen, 1973, Table 268).

Actually, whether or not there is an official rapprochement between feminists and high school girls, there are many high school girls who follow the lines delineated by the feminists. In 1970, for example, a survey of YWCA teen-age leaders found that by that time a tipping point had been passed. About 60 percent of the respondents favored child-care facilities outside of the home, believed that men should help with household chores, and that a man's identity should not be given priority at the wife's expense (Carden, 1973, p. 159). As leaders, they are, by definition, ahead of the young women they deal with. But if they are, in fact, harbingers, young women are being socialized for a style of motherhood consonant with the times.

Young women rarely ask the old marriage-versus-career question any longer. More and more they ask instead: What *else* am I going to do besides being a mother? They take the "else" for granted. Taped interviews (Thompson, 1972) with eight high school seniors, 16 and 17 years of age, show that neither marriage nor motherhood is the *sine qua non* of a fulfilled life. Only three were unequivocally for motherhood; one would adopt children; two did not plan to have children; and two were equivocal. Certainly early marriage was not their preference. The mid or late twenties were favored among the seven who planned to marry; the one who planned to adopt children wanted to wait until she was close to 40. Late twenties and early thirties were the preferred ages for child-bearing. All took some sort of profession for granted (four in science, two in the arts, one in law, one in medicine). The contingencies Elder (1974) has noted are recognized: these young women expect to have husbands who will share their career interests and will assume their share of household and parental functions. They do not want to marry men who would not accept such responsibilities. They wish to take care of their children in the early years (although some are unrealistic about how much time they could take out of their professional careers for this), but they do not wish to become the martyred, self-sacrificing mothers of tradition. To put flesh on these bare bones, vignettes of these young women follow.

EIGHT VIGNETTES OF CONTEMPORARY ADOLESCENTS

I. "[Motherhood] just seems the logical step for me after I've done everything I'd want to do. . . . Once I get married, I think I'll just kind-of give up on the career and do what I can to keep up with it. . . . I really enjoy biology and there's no way that anybody's going to keep me from doing what I want. . . . [Before marriage] I would like at least to have accomplished a little something. . . . I would like to know I'd done something . . . and that somebody would develop what I started out with. . . ." Her preferred time to marry was mid-twenties; to have children, late twenties and early thirties.

II. "[My future will] possibly include motherhood" despite "[my] anti-feelings due to conditions in society." But recently, "I've been thinking maybe I would [have children] . . . . The father will have to take more of a part in the family, will have to be a parent. . . . Hopefully I can pursue both marriage and whatever career I may choose. . . . The mother image isn't the total parental image. . . . so she doesn't become the great martyr who gives up everything for her children. . . . I wouldn't start a family until I knew I could function independently on my own. And once I was a mother I wouldn't give up my whole life. . . . I have images, after I get out of college, of spending a few years *not* settling down—doing something where . . . you had lots of time to travel. . . . She hopes for "a very liberated lifestyle, not the kind of thing that one day I'll say to myself, 'I'm in a rut.' Hopefully I'll always be free to make more choices in my life. . . . For a while I thought motherhood was dying. But I think it'll change so that it'll not be the all-inclusive facet of being a woman. But I don't think it will die out. It will continue, but it won't be a woman's reason for existing. That'll change." She wants one or two children in her late twenties. She recognizes she will be influenced by her husband but hopes that will not change her plans.

III. "When I get married, I'm not going to do all the dishes and cook all the food. My husband will help out. . . . The woman who sits around the house all day and mends the clothes and washes the dishes and all that stuff is . . . very boring. Mothers should get out and do things. . . . I'm going to go into architecture, and I'm going to work for a while before I even plan on getting married. . . . When the children are small, I could be a draftsman . . . at home. If I went into architecture and the guy I married was going into teaching—well, a lot of times an architect will make more than a teacher. So I might say, 'Look, I can go into architecture and you can stay home with the kids, because I'll be making more money.' . . . He'd probably be upset because the man is supposed to bring home the money; it might be a problem. It would depend on financial need. . . . My mother feels I should go to college and the first week I'm out of college I should marry some guy and have six kids. . . . I'd like to work for a while first. Maybe I'd . . . get good at it, get a decent salary. Then maybe I'd think about getting married. Just so I'd accomplish something. Not just to be a woman so you can have babies and perpetuate life. I would naturally not marry some guy who had completely different views from mine." She does not want more than two children.

IV. "As of now, my plans do not include motherhood. Partly because I want to 'save the world' and I plan to be very involved in that, and partly because of my own convictions that this world cannot support an expanded population. I don't see any way I can successfully deal with raising children and with my own career. In the future I may see how this could happen but I don't see it right now. . . . The changes up to now have already affected me. In the future I think it will be easier for me to do what I want to do and not face so much of 'Oh, you haven't had any children yet? Oh, that's sad.' I think people will realize that not to have children is also a sound choice. What I do won't necessarily be what most people do. . . . I assume I will get married eventually, maybe in ten years. . . . I imagine I will spend most of my life working. I can't see myself getting out of my career . . . just to raise children. I can't see that it's that important in our society. It would be unfair to marry someone who wanted to have children. . . . but also it wouldn't be fair to me to make me give up my career to have his children. I don't believe I could ever marry a man with whom I could not have this understanding. I just hope [motherhood] becomes more of a choice for women rather than foregone conclusion. Then our society will become liberal enough so that any woman who decides to have children—that's fine. And any woman who decides not to have children—that's equally fine, equally good—can be seen to be equally logical and reasonable. I think both choices are equally legitimate."

V. "[Motherhood, yes, but] I see a real dilemma, since I want to get a law degree and have a career, and I don't know if I'll have time to raise a family. I love children and I want to get married, but it might be difficult if I were a lawyer, to be a good mother, which is something to think about. . . . You have to combine [marriage and career]. I just don't see how you could be happy just being a housewife. . . . I wouldn't mind getting married when I was in my third year of law school. But I think I'd want to have a life of my own . . . and just be free, in a sense, and independent because I feel like for the rest of my life I won't be, so why not try to prolong it as long as possible. . . . If I'm a good mother, and a loving mother, I don't know that maybe those hours in the day when I went to work would really matter. I doubt we'll ever get to the stage where men are at home with the children as much as women are. I chose law because of the state of the world. I just felt I wanted to do something. I didn't want to just sit home and watch what was happening or read about it in the newspaper. I wanted to be involved and I wanted to help."

VI. "I want to have a career as a doctor, and I don't think I will have time for marriage because I don't want it. It's just that I was in a family that was very unhappy, and I've seen motherhood with my own mother. It didn't work for her and I don't trust myself that it would work for me. I'm pretty sure I won't change my mind. . . . I would like to be a medical officer on a ship. I want an exciting and dangerous life. I'm an adventurer. That's my problem."

VII. "I've been thinking that because of the population explosion I would want only two children of my own but maybe adopt some. . . . I notice [changes] in young people, just talking about them. Girls complain about their fathers' male chauvinism toward their mothers, and even boys do. One boy I was talking to at school was complaining about how his father dominated his mother. And if boys take this attitude, then I don't think they'll dominate their wives. . . . If a woman has a career and she's as well educated as a man, she shouldn't be tied down with all the housework duties. And the man shouldn't come home from work and put his feet up and rest for the rest of the evening. The woman has worked all day long, too. . . . I feel that the man should take more part in raising the children. I would force more of the responsibility for the children on my husband. I definitely would not drop my career to raise a family. While taking time out from my career to raise children, I could be taking courses to back it up and help keep in touch with it without actually working or maybe I could do part-time work. . . . I don't want to be stationary in a suburb. . . . I'd like to get into my career first and then [around 27 or 28] get married. . . . If you just get married after you get out of college, chances are you won't get back into your career. You start having kids and you're tied down with them. . . . If my husband doesn't like my career, that's his problem. I'm not going to have my interests changed by my husband. But I imagine if he disapproved of my career then I wouldn't have married him in the first place."

VIII. "If I fall in love with someone who has been into drugs, where the genes have even a possibility of having been 'messed up' I don't want to run the risk of having children who would have to live with not being whole. I would be more willing to adopt children anyway. There are plenty of children. . . . For a woman not to have a career while she is married is almost foolish, because she's giving her life away to her children. If I got married at all, I would expect to share the housework and the financial support. . . . I would like to see the mother image changed from the mother who stays at home all the time with the children to the mother who teaches the children, gives herself to her children, and has a life of her own also. And it's very possible because of day care and because of the changing ideas of many men. . . . I could probably work at home [in art, her career choice] and have my children with me a good deal of the time. But it would be a good experience for the children to spend some of their time in a day care center. . . . I don't really foresee getting married until I'm close to 40. Maybe I would want the emotional security, although right now I don't feel that I need that much. . . . I might adopt an older child rather than a baby. . . . I would try to show my husband that I derive as much pleasure from my career as he does from his." She wants no children of her own, she will adopt.

REFERENCES

American Council on Education, Staff of the Office of Research. *The American freshman: National norms for fall 1972.* Washington, D.C.: Author, 1972.

Berger, B. M., Hackett, B. H., & Millar, R. M. Child rearing in communes. In L. K. Howe (Ed.), *The future of the family.* New York: Simon & Schuster, 1972.

Bernard, J. Developmental tasks of the NCFR–1963–1988. *Journal of Marriage and the Family*, 1964, **26**, 29–38.

Bernard, J. Present demographic trends and structural outcomes in family life today. In J. A. Peterson (Ed.), *Marriage and family counseling, perspective and prospect.* New York: Association Press, 1968.

Bernard, J. *The future of marriage.* New York: World, 1972. (Paper ed., New York: Bantam, 1973.)

Bernard, J. *The future of motherhood.* New York: Dial Press, 1974. (Paper ed., Baltimore: Penguin, 1975.)

Brandwein, R. A. The single parent family revisited. Paper presented at the meetings of the Society for the Study of Social Problems, New York, Fall 1973.

Bureau of the Census. *Birth expectations and fertility: June 1972.* Series P-20, No. 240, September 1972.

Bureau of the Census. *Characteristics of American youth: 1972.* Series P-23, No. 94, March 1973.

Carden, M. L. *The new feminist movement.* New York: Russell Sage Foundation, 1973.

Davis, J. B. *Coercive pronatalism and American population policy.* Berkeley, Calif.: International Population and Urban Research, September 1972.

Elder, Glen H., Jr. *Depression Generation.* Chicago: University of Chicago Press, 1974.

Erikson, E. *Identity, youth and crisis.* New York: Norton, 1968.

Friedan, B. *The feminine mystique.* New York: Norton, 1963.

Glick, P. C. Dissolution of marriage by divorce and its demographic consequences. Liege, Belgium: International Population Conference, 1973.

Glick, P. C., & Norton, A. J. Perspectives on the recent upturn in divorce and remarriage. *Demography*, 1973, **10**, 301–314.

Hartley, R. Some implications of current changes in sex role patterns. *Merrill-Palmer Quarterly of Behavior and Development*, 1959–60, **6**, 153–164.

Hartley, R. American core culture: Changes and continuities. In G. H. Seward & R. C. Williamson (Eds.), *Sex roles in changing society.* New York: Random House, 1970.

Helsen, R. The changing image of the career woman. *Journal of Social Issues*, 1972, 28, 33–46.

Hollingworth, L. S. Social devices for impelling women to bear and rear children. *American Journal of Sociology*, 1916, 22, 19–29.

Kantner, J. F., & Zelnik, M. Sexual experience of young unmarried women in the United States. *Family Planning Perspectives*, 1972, 4, 9–18.

Kantner, J. F., & Zelnik, M. Contraception and pregnancy: Experience of young unmarried women in the United States. *Family Planning Perspectives*, 1973, 5, 21–35.

Kinsey, A. C., and Associates. *Sexual behavior in the human female.* Philadelphia: Saunders, 1953.

Klein, C. *The single parent experience.* New York: Walker, 1973. (a)

Klein, C. Socialization of the child in voluntary, single parent home. Paper presented at the meetings of the Society for the Study of Social Problems, Fall 1973. (b)

Lott, B. Who wants the children? *American Psychologist*, 1973, 28, 573–582.

Lurie, Z. Women college graduates. Presidential address to the New England Psychological Society, November 1972.

McBride, A. B. *The growth and development of mothers.* New York: Harper & Row, 1973.

Manpower Report of the President, transmitted to the Congress, March, 1973. Washington: U.S. Government Printing Office, 1973.

Millman, M. Autobiography and social mobility: Life accounts of working-class daughters. Paper presented at the meetings of the Society for the Study of Social Problems, New York, Fall 1973.

Moynihan, D. P. Peace—Some thoughts on the 1960s and 1970s. *The Public Interest*, 1973, No. 32, 3–12.

National Center for Health Statistics. Births, marriages, divorces, and deaths for July 1971. *Monthly vital statistics report.* September 1971, 20, 1.

New Jersey NOW Task Force. *Dick and Jane as victims.* Princeton: Authors, 1972.

Newton, N. *Maternal emotions.* New York: Hoeber, 1955.

O'Reilly, J. The housewife's moment of truth. *Ms.*, Spring 1972, 54–55, 57–59.

Packard, V. *The sexual wilderness: The contemporary upheaval in male-female relationships.* New York: McKay, 1968.

Parke, Robert, Jr. and Glick, Paul. Prospective changes in marriage and the family. *Journal of Marriage and the Family*, 1967, 29, 249–256.

Peck, E. *The baby trap.* New York: Pinnacle, 1972.

President's Commission on Population Growth and the American Future. *Population and the American future.* New York: Signet, 1972.

Preston, S. H. Female employment policy and fertility. Research paper for the Report of the President's Commission on Population Growth and the American Future. Reproduced, 1972.

Radl, S. *Mother's Day is over.* New York: Charterhouse. 1973.

Reiss, I. L. *The social context of premarital sexual permissiveness.* New York: Holt, Rinehart and Winston, 1967.

Sanger, M. *Motherhood in bondage.* New York: Brentano, 1928.

Sorensen, R. C. *Adolescent sexuality in contemporary America, personal values and sexual behavior ages 13-19.* New York: World, 1973.

Spiegel, J. Quoted in R. J. Donovan, U.S. said solving violence problem. *Washington Post*, September 3, 1973.

Terman, L. M. *Psychological factors in marital happiness.* New York: McGraw-Hill, 1938.

Thompson, E. Taped interviews, unpublished, 1972.

Washington Post, September 12, 1973.

Yankelovich, D. *Generations apart: A study of the generation gap.* New York: Columbia Broadcasting System, 1969.

Adolescence in Social-Historical Context

Youth and Social Movements

RICHARD G. BRAUNGART
Syracuse University

All societies experience stability and change, and this is one of the most puzzling paradoxes in social and political theory. The persistence of social structure in society establishes order without which chaos would result. A desire for change may come about when established institutions fail to meet or to represent the legitimate needs of groups in society. Then again, because societies never achieve permanent integration and continue to develop over time, they may generate the sources of their own conflict and change. The generational cycle is one of the constant sources of social strain in history. Young people always have been impatient with the traditional order, and in recent years youth has emerged as a formidable agent of social and political change (Ortega y Gasset, 1958; Feuer, 1969).

Most members of society in the course of their life cycles experience frustration and the desire for change. However, it is only when a significant

This is a revised version of the paper presented to the conference. The author would like to thank Margaret M. Braungart, Glen H. Elder, Jr., and David L. Westby for numerous helpful comments, many of which were incorporated into this paper.

number of people become aware of their common circumstances and feel something can be done to alleviate their dissatisfaction that a social movement may appear. The discrepancy between the individual needs or aspirations of young people and the existing social and political conditions lies at the root of youth movements (Heberle, 1951; Killian, 1966; Sherif & Sherif, 1969; Bakke & Bakke, 1971; Demerath, Marwell, & Aiken, 1971; Liebert, 1971).

YOUTH

Youth is defined as a biosocial age stratum in society, following childhood and adolescence and preceding adulthood. This stage in the life cycle is considered to begin somewhere between the ages of 14 and 18 and to continue until approximately 22 to 25 years of age, or when youth enter the labor market on a full-time basis (Flacks, 1971; Keniston, 1971; Moynihan, 1973). Empirical evidence is mounting that suggests that specific biosocial changes occur during each stage of the life cycle, such that certain needs and developments are considered more important at one stage than at another (Ausubel & Sullivan, 1972). The stage of the life cycle defined as youth is considered crucial for the development of: (1) formal, critical thinking and future orientation (Piaget, 1967); (2) the evaluation of moral principles and values in society (Kohlberg, 1964; Piaget, 1965); and (3) the conscious search for self-identity (Erikson, 1968). Beginning in adolescence and continuing through the stage of youth, young people gradually expand their intellectual horizons and attempt to define their relationship to society. It is during this period that youth search for a sense of fidelity—a congruence in ideals, beliefs, and actions—within themselves, their parents, peers, and in society at large.

Awareness and concern with the sociopolitical world increase during youth, but the extent of this concern is determined largely through political socialization (Hyman, 1959; Block, Haan, & Smith, 1968; Ausubel & Sullivan, 1972). Political socialization begins in early childhood and is described as a general cognitive, affective, and motivational predisposition toward politics. By the middle and upper elementary school grades, children acquire political knowledge and facts; during adolescence and youth, their ability to conceptualize on a higher symbolic or ideological level increases rapidly; and in the adult years, greater emphasis is placed on the formal aspects of politics such as issues, candidates, and programs (Greenstein, 1968; Dawson & Prewitt, 1969; Sigel, 1970). It is during the socialization period, somewhere between adolescence and early adulthood, that youth are drawn into radical social movements. While the intensity of political behavior appears to result in part from their heightened psychosocial energy, the ideological direction youth follow generally remains consistent with what they have learned in the home (Braungart, 1969).

In recent history, the presence of large numbers of young people throughout the world appears to be related to social and political change. Demographic growth during the 1960s, both in the significant numbers of youth and the increased proportion of students attending colleges and universities across the country, provides some indication about the origin and nature of youth movements. While the average total population increase in the United States from 1960 to 1968 for all age groups was 12 percent, the age group 18-24 experienced a 43 percent increase—the largest increment for all age cohorts during that time period. This rapid increase stands in sharp contrast to the population growth from 1950 to 1960. Whereas the overall growth rate during the 1950s was 19 percent, the growth rate for youth between the ages of 18 and 24 was − 1 percent (Douglas, 1970). These figures provide a clue to the numerical impact this age group had on society over the last two decades. The recent surge in the youth population, however, is not expected to continue indefinitely. Although Moynihan (1973) reported the 14- to 24-year-old age cohort grew by 52 percent during the 1960s, he predicts only an 11 percent increase in the 1970s, and an 8 percent decline in the adolescent-youth population during the 1980s.

The earlier predictions that the World War II "baby boom" would have an unprecedented impact on American society were borne out. The sudden appearance of large numbers of young people in this country during the 1960s had a direct effect on higher education. For example, the number of youth per 100 persons 18 to 21 years of age enrolled in institutions of higher education in 1946 was 22 percent (2,078,095). By 1967, this figure had reached 47 percent (6,348,000)—in other words, the percentage of the youth population attending college had doubled in two decades. When one considers the absolute number of youth attending colleges and universities during the period 1946-67, the figure tripled (Douglas, 1970).

What occurred in the United States during the 1960s was that suddenly a new class of youth appeared on the college scene, isolated from the rest of society. Statements to the effect "you can't trust anyone over 30," "we are alone and separate from them," were heard, and this new generation developed its own culture with its unique life style, music, dress, argot, and political rhetoric (Denisoff & Peterson, 1972). The proliferation of youth placed a strain on society, especially on colleges and universities. During this period of rapid demographic change, institutions of higher education became increasingly more involved with the growth and development of the economy, since they were responsible for providing the critical resources—intellectual manpower, and scientific, technological knowledge—necessary to sustain the postindustrial society. As the creators and allocators of many of these resources, universities themselves became centers of power and politics. And this new political role was destined to be played out on their campuses. While the great majority of students appeared relatively uncommitted to radical campus politics, a "critical mass" of students did emerge who were recruited into protest activity. Although the percentage of activist youth has remained relatively small over the years (under 2 to 5 percent), their absolute numbers increase steadily with the growing number of students attending college.

SOCIAL MOVEMENTS

Although the youth movement appeared to many as a new "phenomenon" of the 1960s, social movements are as old as history (Geschwender, 1968; McLaughlin, 1969; Davies, 1971; Rush & Denisoff, 1971). They represent ways dissatisfied groups bring about change in society and may be defined as those "socially shared activities and beliefs directed toward the demand for change in some aspect of the social order" (Gusfield, 1970, p. 2). Social movements appear to be reactions against major trends that threaten the sense of identity, self-esteem, and stability of groups in society. Out of the main drifts in contemporary history have developed countervailing forces that challenge their legitimacy. Recently, a growing dissatisfaction among ethnic minorities, college youth, and women over the traditional forms of segregation, war, bureaucracy, and sex-role stereotyping has led to a desire and effort for collective change. Traditional images in these areas are being replaced by a sense of personal self-development and efficacy that appear to transcend one's color, age, or sex. Among the many youth movements that have appeared in recent history are: the Civil Rights Movement, Peace Movement, Pacifist Movement, Amnesty Movement, New Right, New Left, Feminist Movement, Counterculture, Jesus Freaks, Gay Liberation Movement, Communalism, Free Love Movement, and the Ecology Movement.

The involvement of youth in social movements reflects a worldwide phenomenon (Albornoz, 1967; Lipset, 1967; Shimbori, 1968; Emmerson, 1968; Lipset & Altbach, 1969; Flacks, 1970a; De Conde, 1971; Bakke & Bakke, 1971; Allerbeck, 1971; Liebman, Walker, & Glazer, 1972). Although the issues over which youth protest vary from country to country, certain similarities partially explain the appearance of student movements on college and university campuses. First, increasing numbers of youth are attending institutions of higher learning today—although the figures are considerably higher in industrial and postindustrial societies than in modernizing nations. Second, universities share the characteristics of being "cities of youth" and centers of critical thinking and discussion over numerous domestic, national, and international issues—racism, military and economic repression, citizenship, war, poverty, pollution, and so on. Youth attending universities participate in these debates, and many share similar feelings over the eradication of these problems. Third, colleges and universities furnish an international medium for the rapid dissemination of "new" ideas and the spread of cultural and ideological values. These structural conditions the world over provide the opportunity for a "critical mass" of youth to emerge who actively participate in social and political behavior (Weinberg & Walker, 1969; Tygart & Holt, 1972; Meyer & Rubinson, 1972).

The appearance of youth movements in recent history, however, cannot be explained solely in terms of large numbers of isolated college youth in close proximity to one another—even though the historical slope of political attitudes among youth has been moving slowly toward the left (Lipset & Ladd, 1971).

Although these structural features have increased steadily over the years, youth movements occur sporadically and usually develop in direct response to specific changes and transformations that have taken place in society. The obvious question arises: Why do youth movements appear at one particular time in history rather than another—why in the 1930s and 1960s and not in the 1950s and early 1970s? The complexity of social and historical events lies at the root of this question. No single factor can account for the sudden appearance of youth movements. Rather, the unique mix or blend of demographic factors in combination with historical, social, and cultural conditions provides some understanding into the origin of youth's behavior. If this line of thinking is correct, the youth movement in the 1960s developed as a result of a particular kind of interaction between generational, historical, social, and cultural forces in society.

Historical Factors and Youth Movements

Historical moods and fashions shift over time, and these interact with social, political, and cultural movements. The changing political *Zeitgeist* or shifts in the climate of politics and public opinion between the status quo and liberal reform have gone through a series of ebbs and flows in this country since the turn of the century. The temporal location of youth in relation to decisive political events appears to be associated with the rise and fall of youth movements (see Table 12.1). The period 1900–29 was characterized by economic conservatism and cultural liberalism. That is, laissez-faire capalism, imbued with the social Darwinist ethic, suddenly thrust the country into the status of an international industrial giant. At the same time, a romantic, indulgent youth culture challenged Victorian social and sexual mores, and created for their generation the "Roaring Twenties." This historic period was followed by the Great Depression, and from 1930 to 1940, the political pendulum swung to the left with increased governmental growth and control. It was during this "liberal" historic period that many college youth signed the Oxford Pledge and pressed for international peace through noninvolvement with the impinging land war in Europe. Reports of rallies and demonstrations suggest that as many as 185,000 youth took an active part in these protests (Lipset, 1972). With the onset of World War II, the pendulum swung once again to the right, and during the period 1941-59, patriotism, global reconstruction, the Cold War, McCarthyism, and returning GIs blanketed college campuses. In the middle 1950s, anxiety over communism and alleged international subversion permeated American society. During these Eisenhower years, youth were quiescent and generally disinterested in politics, thereby earning the title the "silent generation."

The historical pendulum reversed itself once again during the 1960s, and this decade witnessed a perceptible shift toward the side of young people. With the inauguration of John F. Kennedy—who symbolized the romantic, apocalyptic vision for a fresh and idealistic generation of black and white youth—new legal and political fronts were created on civil rights and poverty. It was during this period that student movements emerged on both the political left and right, with

TABLE 12.1

Temporal Location, Decisive Political Events, and Youth Movements

Temporal location	Decisive political events	Youth movements
1900–1929	Economic growth and cultural liberalism Industrialization, U.S. develops favorable balance of trade and becomes world industrial power World War I Isolationism Prohibition Women's Suffrage "Roaring Twenties"	Youth culture challenges Victorian social and sexual mores
1930–1940	The Great Depression Poverty Election of FDR–"New Deal" Government economic programs Growth of national socialism in Germany	Youth join antiwar movement Sign Oxford Pledge Campus strikes
1941–1949	World War II Truman administration Atomic bomb Returning GIs Global reconstruction, U.N.	Little youth movement activity
1950–1959	The Cold War–Eisenhower Years Growth of "military-industrial complex" Dulles foreign policy Recession McCarthyism 1954 Supreme Court desegregation decision House Un-American Activities Committee	"The silent generation"
1960–1968	Kennedy-Johnson Years "New Frontier" Civil rights demonstrations Peace Corps, poverty programs Vietnam escalation Assassinations of Kennedy brothers and Martin Luther King "Great Society" programs Ghetto riots and campus disruption	New Left New Right Civil rights and Black Power Protest demonstrations, strikes, violence
1969–1973	Nixon-Agnew Years Emphasis on "law and order" Vietnam war ends, fighting in Southeast Asia continues Inflation, job squeeze Growth of multinational corporations Watergate	Women's rights Ecology movement

such groups as Students for a Democratic Society (SDS), Young Americans for Freedom (YAF), Student Nonviolent Coordinating Committee (SNCC), and Congress of Racial Equality (CORE) organizing and springing up on campuses across the country (Braungart, 1969). The most significant and vehemently contested issues during the early years of this decade were civil rights, university reform, and the war in Southeast Asia. By 1970, this priority had reversed itself, and the Vietnam—Cambodia war became the overriding national issue, closely followed by university reform and civil rights (Braungart & Braungart, 1972a). During the mid-1960s, a youth movement emerged that challenged the very foundation of American society. Nurtured on college campuses, youth groups divided by a process of ideological mitosis and became increasingly revolutionary, militant, and nihilistic as the decade drew to a close.

With the election of a "law-and-order" president in 1968, a new conservative mood began to grow throughout the country. The Nixon-Agnew strategy favored a combination of confrontation-centrist politics, and appeared fairly successful until the exposure of the Watergate affair, which revealed that the White House was administered by an overzealous, clandestine right-wing staff. Today campuses are relatively calm, but this appears to be an uneasy calm. It is as though the present campus quiet were seated in the eye of the storm around which historical events continue to swirl and rage. Numerous social problems still plague American society, and civil rights, women's rights, and ecology remain high on the list. Since the precedent for radical student movements has been established, only time and the development of future events will determine whether the scenario of student activism repeats itself.

What this view of history suggests is that consistent as well as opposing historical forces have been operating since the turn of the century, and these factors in combination with other conditions have influenced the form and substance of student movements in the United States. Youth attending college during the 1960s were born in the 1940s. What made this generation different from previous age cohorts was that these youth were the products of social and historical forces that developed during the 1950s and extended into the early 1960s. Youth born in the 1940s were the first generation to grow up under the specter of nuclear annihilation and mass indifference ushered in by the atomic age. These youth had never experienced the direct, personal dislocations and fears of the Depression and World War II years, but instead witnessed the presence of a victorious and affluent United States playing the role of a dominant superpower—with all of its negative connotations and implications. These factors in combination with the scare tactics of the McCarthy era in the 1950s and the events of the early 1960s—the struggle by blacks to achieve legal and social equality, the violent assassinations of civil rights workers and a young president—helped produce a generation of college youth, a large proportion of whom were cynical, strongly antiwar, and politically liberal. Youth attending college in the early 1970s were different from those of the previous decade in that they did not experience the direct thrust of many of the historic events that took place in the late 1940s and the 1950s. They did experience, however, the dramatic events of the 1960s, in addition to the excesses of radicalism exhibited by youth groups during that period. This may have persuaded them to tone down their own political style, although the form of youth's politics continues to move toward the left.

Social Structural Factors and Youth Movements

History is not the only force in society related to youth movements. There have also been perceptible shifts in social and economic institutions in this country over the last half century, which in turn have influenced the relationships and concerns of youth with society. Economic trends have revolved around the decline in the manufacturing sector and the growth of social services, especially in the areas of government, trade, finance, and utilities. In fact, the service sector now accounts for over half of national employment. The composition of the labor force also has changed, with white-collar employees now outnumbering blue-collar workers (Miles, 1971). The net result of this change is that youth have been forced out of the labor market. During the 1960s, the number of males 16 to 19 years of age increased by 44 percent, yet the number of employed males the same age grew by only 11 percent. As the unemployment rate for youth went up, so did signs of dislocation, alienation, and lack of connection with society (Moynihan, 1973).

Structural shifts are taking place throughout society that appear to have a direct bearing on student movements—some trends are noted as follows. Regionalism in the form of local institutional and cultural segmentation is breaking down. The family-based enterprise and the middle-sized business are being taken over by national or multinational corporations. At the same time, the mobility of individuals appears to be on the increase. Bell (1973) argues the United States is moving toward a mass or postindustrial society. He perceives postindustrial society principally in terms of a communal society wherein public mechanisms rather than markets become the allocators of goods and services, public choice rather than individual demand becomes the arbiter of services, and a communal society translates the claims of its members into claims of the community. Postindustrial society is divided into three sectors: (1) the social structure, which encompasses the economy, technology, and occupational and educational systems; (2) the culture, involving the sphere of expression, symbolism, and meaning; and (3) the polity, which regulates the distribution of power and adjudicates conflicting claims and demands of individuals and groups.

The growth of postindustrial society is generating additional needs for its members, along with a new type of labor force recruited primarily from institutions of higher learning. These changes in society have created a stratum of professional, technical, and intellectual elite who are actively promoting cultural values and demands. Whether this new labor force becomes more militant or remains in the traditional guild form will be decided over the next few decades (Miles, 1971; Bell, 1973). In the meantime, knowledge continues to be a major source of innovation and economic growth, placing the university in the strategic position as one of the dominant institutions in society. As generators of cognitive developments and technical manpower, universities have become centers of structural and cultural change.

A century ago, an elite of some 50,000 youth were enrolled in 563 institutions of higher learning. Today, over 6,500,000 youth attend 2300 colleges and universities across the country (Peterson, 1966, 1968b). What has occurred in the interim period has been an unprecedented transition from class-based institutions of higher learning to mass institutions, the latter of which recruit students from all class and status sectors of society. As Gusfield (1963) noted, before the Civil War, education was considered a luxury and was reserved primarily for the upper class gentry. However, since the turn of the century and with the industrialization and rapid growth of the American economy, college and university enrollment has increased substantially. Curricula have also undergone changes, with professional and occupational programs replacing the purely classical orientation. This trend has continued to the present time, and particularly since the early 1960s, American universities have moved into an era of mass education. In many respects, these modern multiversities are no longer the intellectual sanctuaries of a bygone era, but have become proving grounds for youth in their confrontation with themselves and with society as well.

Youth movements during the 1960s reflected the power of a new adversary class reacting against a scientific, technologically based society. Students (primarily recruited from the liberal arts and humanities) reacted against the deteriorating conditions created by postindustrial society: especially, congested and polluted cities, poverty, mass education, wholesale discrimination, bureaucratic hardness, and alienation. Although interest in the social sciences and humanities has increased, there has been a decline in intellectual motivation and orientation among students. Youth attending college are less interested in competition, the achievement motive, and traditional Protestant ethic values toward money and work. This leads into a discussion of the cultural changes that have taken place during recent American history and their impact on the youth movement.

Cultural Factors and Youth Movements

Another index of a changing society can be seen in the shifts in values and attitudes over time. Prevailing cultural moods appeared to be associated with the growth or demise of political youth movements. For example, college students in the mid-1920s were reported to be most concerned with values centering around personal ideals, vocations, fraternity life styles, cheating on examinations, coeducation, moral choices in life, and religiosity (Katz & Allport, 1931). These youth were not noted to be particularly interested in politics, and youthful political activity was relatively nonexistent during this time (Draper, 1967). In the 1930s, however, political interest heightened among youth, and the moral political consideration of war became a paramount issue that triggered numerous strikes on campuses across the country. In the mid-1930s, students were reported to be concerned with academic freedom, university reform, the labor movement, as well as student rights and privileges (Draper, 1967). During the 1940s and through the 1950s, however, youth appeared less interested in politics and more concerned with personal goals, with the result that their political activity subsided.

An inverse relationship appeared to exist between youth's religious values and political activity over the last twenty years (Hastings & Hoge, 1970). Among college students from 1948 to 1967, there was a reported decline in traditional religious beliefs and behavior, a greater questioning of religious precepts especially among younger age groups, and a general liberalizing of personal values. Conversely, during this same period there was a noticeable increase in the politicization of youth that paralleled the growth of the student movement. Hastings and Hoge (1970) suggested that the history of American student political activism—which showed considerable activity during the middle 1930s and 1960s, with almost no activity in the early 1950s—is represented by a curve exactly the inverse of the curve for traditional religious commitment.

Matza (1961), Clark and Trow (1960), Peterson (1968b), and Block, Haan, and Smith (1968) have developed typologies concerning American collegiate subcultures. Each provides a profile or paradigm of the cultural styles exhibited by college youth over the last two decades. In the 1950s, Matza studied the "spirit of rebelliousness" among nonconforming college youth and classified them into three groupings: delinquents, radicals, and bohemians. Clark and Trow (1960) identified and described four major types of student subcultures in the late 1950s and early 1960s: collegiate, vocational, academic, and nonconformist. The incidence of college youth falling into each of these categories was reported by Bolton and Kammeyer (1967) in a 1964 survey of 13,000 freshmen entering twenty-three colleges and universities. These authors report that 51 percent of the youth surveyed indicated their major interests in college centered around an active social life and carrying on the college tradition—the collegiate type. Vocational goals were given priority by 27 percent, while the pursuit of ideas (the academic type) was listed by 19 percent. Three percent of the freshmen surveyed were classified as nonconformists.

The Matza (1961) and Clark and Trow (1960) typologies stand in contrast to subcultural typologies developed by Peterson (1968b) and Block, Haan, and Smith (1968), whose typologies reflected the more politicized student subcultures of the middle and late 1960s. Peterson's paradigm (1968b) consisted of eight student types distinguished by their overriding value commitments. He arranged his subcultural groups along a continuum ranging from acceptance through neutral to the rejection of American institutions: professionalist (most accepting), vocationalist, collegiate, ritualist, academic, intellectual, left activist, and hippie (most rejecting). Another useful and comprehensive political paradigm of American college youth was constructed by Block, Haan, and Smith (1968). These authors differentiated six student subcultural types: politically apathetic youth, alienated youth, individualist youth, activist youth, constructivist youth, and antisocial youth. In comparison to Clark and Trow's model, all the categories in the Block, Haan, and Smith typology could be classified as nonconformist, with the exception of politically apathetic youth who represent the academic, collegiate, and vocational types.

What these four typologies indicate is a shift in student cultural and political styles from the late 1950s to the 1960s. Whereas political themes were not considered by Matza or Clark and Trow, they became the overriding theme or core for the schemes developed by Peterson and Block, Haan, and Smith. The student subcultural paradigm developed by Block, Haan, and Smith appears especially applicable to the range of youth politics that was characteristic of the late 1960s. For example, the political styles of SDS, SNCC, and CORE were representative of activist youth, while the style of YAF strongly resembled individualist youth. The more pragmatic and less ideological youth political groups, such as Young Democrats and Young Republicans, most nearly represented the political style of constructivist youth.

National surveys of college youth in the late 1960s and early 1970s undertaken by the American Council on Education (1966, 1967, 1968, 1969, 1970, 1971, 1972) and Yankelovich (1972) indicated an association between the changing values of youth and the growth of campus-based activism. With regard to cultural values, the following trends among college youth were cited. In the late 1960s and early 1970s, fewer young people than usual were interested in marriage and raising a family (71 percent in 1969, 65 percent in 1972); they were less prone to join fraternities or sororities (31 percent in 1967, 14 percent in 1971); less satisfied with attending college (65 percent in 1970, 57 percent in 1971); less concerned with being administratively responsible (29 percent in 1966, 20 percent in 1971); less pressed to develop a philosophy of life (83 percent in 1967, 68 percent in 1971); not particularly interested in checking out books from the library (54 percent in 1967, 43 percent in 1971); not particularly interested in the traditional cultural pursuits such as visiting art galleries (71 percent in 1967, 66 percent in 1971) and playing a musical instrument (51 percent in 1966, 38 percent in 1971) (American Council on Education, 1966, 1967, 1969, 1970, 1971, 1972).

Along with the changing cultural values during the late 1960s and early 1970s, these national surveys reported an increased interest in politics among college youth. More students appeared concerned with: consumer protection (72 percent in 1969, 76 percent in 1972); government legalization of marijuana (19 percent in 1968, 47 percent in 1972); the elimination of poverty (78 percent in 1969, 80 percent in 1970); equality for women (81 percent in 1970, 91 percent in 1972); participation in a demonstration (5 percent in 1967, 10 percent in 1972); taking part in university decisions (68 percent in 1969, 76 percent in 1971); and in community action (26 percent in 1971, 29 percent in 1972) (American Council on Education, 1967, 1968, 1969, 1970, 1971, 1972). A general dissatisfaction with American society was reported, accompanied by support for protest movements such as the New Left and Black Power movements.

Although ostensibly interested in politics, these youth did not care to identify with either of the two major political parties, but instead chose to classify themselves as "Independents." Ladd, Hadley, and King (1971) compared the number of political Independents under 30 years of age over the last four elections and discovered that in the 1948 presidential election, 27 percent of the young people under 30 classified themselves as Independents. In 1968, this percentage rose to 40 percent, the highest of all age groups identifying with the Independent political classification. Forty-seven percent of the college youth surveyed in 1969 by Yankelovich (1972) identified with the Democratic party, while 25 percent considered themselves Republicans, and 28 percent did not identify with either of the two major political parties. Two years later in 1971, a similar survey revealed 36 percent of college youth identified with the Democratic party, 21 percent classified themselves as Republicans, and a sizable plurality 43 percent did not choose to identify with either major political party. These data suggest that the direction of political identification among youth has shifted toward the independent position. The term Independent, of course, tells us little about the direction of political preference. During the last decade, a greater number of college youth moved toward the political left or liberal orientation. For example, in 1961, Middleton and Putney (1963) elicited the political views of youth attending sixteen colleges and universities and reported: 2 percent claimed they were socialist, 11 percent highly liberal, 47 percent moderately liberal, 30 percent moderately conservative, 3 percent highly conservative, and 7 percent were uncodable. The American Council on Education (1969) reported the political preference for entering freshmen in 1969 reflected the following ideological range: 3 percent identified with the far left, 30 percent liberal, 44 percent middle of the road, 21 percent conservative, and 2 percent far right.

After 1970, there appeared to be a shift away from the mood of the 1960s, with considerably less political radicalism. While certain values continued to liberalize in the 1970s, others became more conservative. The continued liberal trend could be seen in those youth who: agree that marriage is obsolete (24 percent in 1969, 34 percent in 1971); easily accept the authority of a "boss" in a work situation (56 percent in 1968, 36 percent in 1971), or the authority of the police (59 percent in 1968, 45 percent in 1971); consider religion very important (38 percent in 1969, 31 percent in 1971); believe hard work always pays off (69 percent in 1968, 39 percent in 1971), or that competition encourages excellence (72 percent in 1969, 62 percent in 1971); welcome less emphasis on money (65 percent in 1968, 76 percent in 1971); favor sexual freedom (43 percent in 1969, 56 percent in 1971); believe extramarital sex is morally wrong (77 percent in 1969, 57 percent in 1971); consider patriotism very important (35 percent in 1969, 27 percent in 1971); believe in living a clean, moral life (45 percent in 1969, 34 percent in 1971); welcome more emphasis on law and order (60 percent in 1968, 50 percent in 1971); and perceive education as very important (80 percent in 1969, 74 percent in 1971). During this same period other values appeared to be headed back in the direction of tradition, such as youth who: believe big business is in need of fundamental reform (45 percent in 1970, 40 percent in 1971); consider it immoral for capable people to collect welfare (31 percent in 1969, 34 percent in 1971); place emphasis on working hard (41 percent in 1968, 44 percent in 1971); take affluence for granted (45 percent in 1968, 39 percent in 1971); are career-minded (55 percent in 1968, 61 percent in 1971); exhibit self-doubts about making money (40 percent in 1969, 50 percent in 1971); are concerned with job security (33 percent in 1970, 46 percent in 1971); and view privacy as very important (61 percent in 1969, 64 percent in 1971). Although no comparative data from previous surveys are available, the majority of youth (56 percent in 1971) rejected violence as an acceptable tactic to achieve one's ends (Yankelovich, 1972).

By 1971 and 1972, political orientations among college youth continued to shift away from the radical politics typical of the late 1960s. When compared with the 1969 data, the American Council on Education (1972) reported a lessening of political radicalization and polarization among college youth, as the percentage distribution for student political orientation in 1972 indicated: 2 percent far left, 33 percent liberal, 48 percent middle of the road, 16 percent conservative, and 1 percent far right. In addition, while two-thirds of the students in 1970 thought radicalism would continue to grow, a year later in 1971, the majority of youth believed radicalism would level off or decline. By 1971, students were reported to be less critical of major American institutions, the two-party system, business, universities, unions, and the Supreme Court. Nine out of ten students expected to register and vote in the 1972 presidential election, and three out of four believed social change could best be brought about by working within the system (Yankelovich, 1972).

Yankelovich (1972) argued that an "unlinking" of cultural and political values among youth occurred in the early 1970s. That is, the continued liberalizing of cultural (or countercultural) values concerning marriage, work, sex, and drugs represented a distinct departure from the more conventional and middle-of-the-road political orientations that reappeared among college youth. However, this separation of cultural from political values did not take place among students who identified with the far left. For these youth, the values of the counterculture and radical politics continued to correlate very highly. However, the vast majority of college youth—the 90 to 95 percent who did not identify with the revolutionary left—moved in their search for certain cultural changes while steering clear of the more radical forms of politics. Yankelovich (1972) concluded that these shifts in values among contemporary youth reflected a new "naturalism" revolving around three major themes: emphasis on the community rather than the individual, anti-intellectualism and nonrationalism, and the search for sacredness in nature.

The 1960s appears to have witnessed a profound demographic change in American society that was unlike the 1950s and is different from the 1970s. Youth emerged as an independent source of change and interacted with historical, social, and cultural forces to produce unique forms of political behavior.

YOUTH AND SOCIAL MOVEMENTS

A number of propositions have been employed to describe the relationships between youth and social movements. These relationships were derived from empirical research and appeared relatively consistent throughout the 1960s. While each proposition offers a partial understanding into the possible roots of youth movements, they individually lack the ability to differentiate and synthesize a wide range of historical, social, cultural, and psychological forces into a coherent and meaningful theoretical explanation. There is one theory in sociology that appears to have the analytic capacity to explain the complex origins of youth movements—and that is the generational unit theory (Mannheim, 1944, 1952). Mannheim has developed a theory that is capable of identifying and tracking a large number of variables over time. While it has never been formally tested, one index of the popularity of this theory can be seen in the number of discussions it has generated (Feuer, 1969; Bengtson, 1970; Westby & Braungart, 1970; Brunswick, 1970; Lambert, 1970, 1971, 1972; Braungart, 1971c; Simmons, 1971; Flacks, 1971; Goertzel, 1972; Riley, Johnson, & Foner, 1972; Lipset, 1972; Bengston & Black, 1973; Braungart, 1974). The remaining portion of this paper will present a series of propositions that describe the relationship between youth and social movements over the last decade. This will be followed by an attempt to identify and analyze the formal and emerging properties of Mannheim's generational unit theory.

Propositions

The youth movement was made up of a minority of students in relation to the total university student population (Peterson, 1966, 1968a; Peterson & Bilorusky, 1971; Block, Haan, & Smith, 1968; Braungart & Braungart, 1972a). Estimates of hard-core membership in all radical groups comprising the youth movement rarely exceeded 5 percent of the total student body in this country at any one time throughout the last decade. In fact, the largest national left-wing group, SDS, has never reported more than 10,000 dues-paying members. The right-wing YAF claimed 20,000 collegiate members on 200 campuses. Nevertheless, on occasions, such as the incidents that occurred at Berkeley, Columbia, and San Francisco State, radical youth were successful in mobilizing strong and widespread support among moderate students and faculty for student grievances, especially after police and National Guard were brought on campus. Evidence also suggested that while the youth movement was growing at a relatively moderate albeit consistent rate, it sparked a general campus malaise and cynicism among a much wider spectrum of college youth. Support for protest activity peaked in 1970, with 57 percent of the nation's colleges and universities experiencing a "significant impact" on campus operations as the result of Cambodia, Kent State, and Jackson State.

Members of the youth movement were recruited from the most selective and prestigious colleges and universities across the country—the highest incidence of protest occurred at private universities, private liberal arts colleges, and large public universities (Skolnick, 1969; Bayer & Astin, 1969; Scott & El-Assal, 1969; Dunlap, 1970; Flacks, 1970b; Hodgkinson, 1970; Shotland, 1970; Gergen, 1970; Foster & Long, 1970; Scurrah, 1972; Bayer, 1972; Braungart & Braungart, 1972a; Riesman & Stadtman, 1973). The liberal traditions of schools like Reed, Swarthmore, Bennington, Antioch, and Oberlin contributed to the selective recruitment and styles of activism that took place on their campuses. Although the majority of students on these campuses were liberal and active, their total numbers remained minuscule when compared to the over 6,500,000 young people attending colleges and universities during that time. A variety of research sources suggested that large state universities were more likely to produce politicized student bodies and demonstrations than small universities and colleges. These multiversities, as they have been characterized, possessed both the size and heterogeneity to support nonconformist subcultures that were more likely to ignore conventional academic pursuits. Larger institutions were also under enormous competitive, organization, and economic pressures that inhibited communication at all levels, exacerbated student-faculty rapport, and increased student alienation. While selective colleges and large universities were predictably centers of student unrest, this phenomenon spread throughout the country to most institutions of higher learning and filtered down to many high schools as well.

Youth who majored in the social sciences, humanities, and in the theoretically oriented fields of science were more politicized and active than those in the practical, applied, and experimental fields (Heist, 1966; Gamson, Goodman, & Gurin, 1967; Flacks, 1967; Auger, Barton, & Maurice, 1969; Braungart, 1969; Fenton & Gleason, 1969; Dunlap, 1970; Lipset, 1972; Braungart & Braungart, 1972b). Youth majoring in the social sciences were more likely to become knowledgeable about social problems and society's ills. Sociology, anthropology, history, and philosophy courses instilled in youth a sensitivity and a heightened consciousness toward personal, social, and political problems. It is not unreasonable to expect youth experiencing such disparities to search for a more perfect society. Likewise, artistic and creatively inclined youth who were strongly opposed to a technologically ordered society were more likely to manifest frustrations and be drawn into critically motivated movements. Later in the 1960s, physics and chemistry majors were becoming politicized by the threat of impending annihilation through unleashed military power or the destruction and pollution of the environment.

Leftist activist youth within American universities aspired to service and creative-expressive occupations (Gamson, Goodman, & Gurin, 1967; Flacks,

1967; Whittaker & Watts, 1969; Geller & Howard, 1969; Baird, 1970; Cowdry, Keniston & Cabin, 1970; Demerath, Marwell, & Aiken, 1971; Fendrich, Simons, & Tarleau, 1972). This stands in sharp contrast to the more success-oriented, economically motivated and rewarded professions of business, medicine, law, government, or natural science. Most research on left-wing students suggested these youth planned on becoming teachers, social scientists, entering creative-expressive occupations, and becoming actively involved in community development and change. Follow-up studies a number of years later proved this to be the case.

In terms of scholastic aptitude and interest, activist youth appeared somewhat more intellectually oriented than nonactive college students (Gamson, Goodman, & Gurin, 1967; Keniston, 1968; Geller & Howard, 1969; Braungart, 1969; Flacks, 1967, 1970b; Watts, Lynch, & Whittaker, 1969; Miller & Everson, 1970; Kerpelman, 1972). Typically, left- and right-wing youth were reported high on measures of intelligence and grade-point average. This is a consistent finding in most research, especially in the early years of the youth movement. These youth tended to rank themselves in the upper half of their classes, even though some studies reported no actual difference in intellectual achievement between protesting versus nonprotesting youth. Activists did not see grades as important, nor were they as vocationally oriented as the nonactivists.

Extracurricular activities of activist youth showed them to be more involved in community-related activities, social services, and political organizations and less involved in athletics (Haan, Smith, & Block, 1968; Geller & Howard, 1969; Cowdry, Keniston, & Cabin, 1970; Demerath, Marwell, & Aiken, 1971; Kerpelman, 1972; Fendrich, Simons, & Tarleau, 1972). In general, leftist youth reached out for extra-academic experiences while attending college. They not only joined numerous campus organizations, especially those appealing to their political persuasion, but were more likely to become involved in wider community activities such as tutorial projects, voter registration drives, and social action projects. Leftist youth were more prone than the average college students to exhibit nonconformist countercultural behavior such as experimenting with drugs and sex, but unlike the hippie subculture, this seldom resulted in their complete withdrawal from society.

Demographic background characteristics, such as age, year in college, and sex, indicated left-wing activists did not differ significantly from the general undergraduate student population (Lyonns, 1965; Auger, Barton, & Maurice, 1969; Braungart, 1969; Whittaker & Watts, 1969; Geller & Howard, 1969; Clarke & Egan, 1969; Smith, Haan, & Block, 1970; Kerpelman, 1972; Braungart & Braungart, 1972b). Free Speech Movement activists at Berkeley were more often than not in their late teens, drawn predominantly from the freshman and sophomore classes, and slightly overrepresented with females, as compared to the general campus population. Conversely, data from SDS and other left-wing protest groups on various eastern colleges and universities revealed activists to be in their early twenties, upperclassmen, graduate students, and highly represented with females. Because of regional differences and specific university profiles, there appeared to be few background characteristics differentiating student activists from nonactivists. The one demographic feature that remained consistent suggested that leftist activists were slightly more equalitarian in the sex composition of their membership than were other campus-based political groups.

Activist youth within American universities were recruited originally from relatively well-to-do backgrounds with high-status parents as compared to the general student population. Later in the 1960s, the movement spread to include all segments in the college student population (Westby & Braungart, 1966; Flacks, 1967; Keniston, 1968, 1971; Paulus, 1968; Block, Haan, & Smith, 1968; Braungart, 1969; Clarke & Egan, 1969; Dunlap, 1970; Hodgkinson, 1970; Lewis, 1971; Braungart & Braungart, 1972b). A number of studies conducted in the early and mid-1960s described activist youth as coming from middle and upper middle class backgrounds. These were the sons and daughters of privileged, high-income families where both parents often had four or more years of college and frequently were employed in occupations for which advanced education was a necessary prerequisite. Within more homogeneous college and university populations, such as those at Harvard, Yale, Columbia, and Stanford, where the modal income was predictably high, parents' income, education, and occupation failed to discriminate protesters from nonprotesters. As the decade of the 1960s drew to a close and the youth movement (especially the antiwar wing of the movement) became more hotly debated and diffused throughout society, family-status background was less able to differentiate activists from nonactivists. Participants in campus-based activist groups typically came from urban and suburban environments rather than small towns. They were more likely to be recruited from the East and West Coasts, and they were seldom the first in their families to attend college. In fact, many activists came from families in which parents had been attending college for several generations.

Activist youth typically came from homes in which parents were politically liberal and exhibited a high interest in politics (Westby & Braungart, 1966; Haan, Smith, & Block, 1968; Thomas, 1968; Keniston, 1968, 1971; Flacks, 1967, 1970b; Watts, Lynch, & Whittaker, 1969; Braungart & Braungart, 1972b). The majority of these youth were from politically "liberal" homes with a small proportion from left-wing or radical backgrounds and even fewer who had converted or rebelled from politically conservative parents. The bulk of empirical evidence supported the thesis that youth, *qua* activists, were not rebelling against their parents' political views but were the products of privileged environments, liberal antiauthoritarian socialization experiences, and thus were acting out what they were taught in the home. While data revealed that college may have been a liberalizing experience during late adolescence and early adulthood, empirical evidence likewise suggested that many youth brought their parents' liberal political attitudes and values with them to college, especially strongly held opinions toward foreign policy, civil rights, freedom of speech, and social welfare programs. And further, when parents themselves were actively involved in politics, the probability of their progeny becoming involved was predictably high.

Liberal Protestant and Jewish family backgrounds were overrepresented among left-wing youth when compared with conservative Protestant and Catholic backgrounds, with a greater proportion of activist youth exhibiting nonreligious and secular attitudes than the campus population in general (Solomon & Fishman, 1964; Gamson, Goodman, & Gurin, 1967; Flacks, 1967, 1970a; Braungart, 1969; Auger, Barton, & Maurice, 1969; Watts, Lynch, & Whittaker, 1969; Smith, Haan, & Block, 1970). Liberal Protestant denominations, such as Quaker, Unitarian, and Episcopalian, produced a disproportionately large number of youth who participated in leftist political behavior when compared with the more conservative Protestant sects. While few left-wing youth came from Catholic homes, the number of students who reported coming from Jewish families was disproportionately high, higher in some instances than the combined religious affiliation of all other denominations. The general trend in research indicated left-wing youth tended to be low on conventional religiosity—they were less likely to attend worship services and more readily defined themselves as agnostic or atheist. This stands in contrast to right-wing youth who were recruited from Protestant and Catholic homes with more traditional religious beliefs.

The political liberalism and religious secularism exhibited by activist youth were expressions of moral principles and underlying clusters of values learned in the home (Kohlberg, 1964, 1970; Flacks, 1967, 1970b; Keniston, 1968, 1971; Haan, Smith, & Block, 1968; Thomas, 1968; Watts, Lynch, & Whittaker, 1969). Research suggested that radical youth followed the intellectual, expressive, romantic, humanitarian, and idealistic values of their parents. Parents fostered autonomy, self-expression, and strongly encouraged socially responsible attitudes in their offspring. Researchers reported that many student activists were highly principled youth acting out a "postconventional" level of morality. Such findings suggested that these youth defined right and wrong in terms of universalistic criteria, as opposed to the "preconventional" and "conventional" levels of morality that were based on egocentric precepts and institutionally sanctioned norms. This is not to say that preconventional and conventional moral youth were not found among left-wing groups. In one study at least, a minority of preconventional and conventional radical youth were identified. And although no direct causal relationship has been developed, preconventional youth may have been largely responsible for campus violence and disruption that took place in the 1960s.

Activists more often came from homes in which democratic and equalitarian child-rearing practices were employed; there was little evidence to support the notion that radical youth were reared by overpermissive or overindulgent families (Flacks, 1967, 1970b; Keniston, 1968, 1971; Thomas, 1968; Haan, Smith, & Block, 1968; Braungart, 1969, 1971a). Although evidence exists suggesting left-wing youth came from permissive families, permissiveness per se has never been demonstrated to be an independent cause of student activism. It was reported that leftist parents were slightly more egalitarian than apolitical or conservative parents in allowing their offspring to express themselves and to openly experiment with life. However, parental dedication to humanitarian causes, democratic family values, and political socialization appeared to have a greater impact in explaining political activism among youth.

There was little evidence to support the proposition that parental role identification of sons toward their mothers was related to left-wing youth politics (Keniston, 1968, 1971; Thomas, 1968; Braungart, 1971b; Fengler & Wood, 1973). Although one study suggested left-wing males identified with their mothers, other research reported that student activists were consistent in their attitudes toward both parents. That is, the plurality of youth surveyed did not identify more with one parent vis-à-vis the other. Of those few who did identify with one parent over the other, both sexes appeared to identify more with mothers than with fathers, albeit this maternal relationship was found to be slightly greater for females than for males. And finally, evidence also suggested that left-wing male youth identified less often with their mothers when compared with other apolitical and politically active youth groups.

Although personality profiles of activists pictured them as alienated, these youth were not noted to be maladjusted psychologically (Winborn & Jansen, 1967; Astin, 1968; Whittaker & Watts, 1969, 1971; Miller & Everson, 1970; Loken, 1970; Bakke & Bakke, 1971; Demerath, Marwell, & Aiken, 1971; Kerpelman, 1972). Researchers reported left-wing youth scored high on verbal aptitude and low on math; they were more sensitive to aesthetic expression, had well-developed social consciences, perceived themselves as altruistic and humanitarian, exhibited idealized views, manifested high empathy, held less rigid and authoritarian views, were open to new ideas, and were impulsive, critical, and restless. Other research suggested both left- and right-wing youth were highly ego-involved in politics, were less needful of emotional support and nurturance, valued leadership, were socially ascendant, assertive, and sociable. Still other studies argued left-wing militant radicals were more paranoid than most students, perceived themselves as less efficacious than nonmilitants, and expressed greater feelings of alienation and estrangement.

As the 1960s drew to a close, the goals and objectives but not the tactics of the youth movement spread to a much larger segment of the youth population (Yankelovich, 1969; Hadden, 1969; President's Commission on Campus Unrest, 1970; Gergen, 1970; Peterson & Bilorusky, 1971; Braungart & Braungart, 1972b). This trend was demonstrated by the increasing number of youth who turned out for demonstrations and mass meetings at both the college and high school levels. While the majority of these youth did not define themselves as radicals or militants, they nevertheless felt the need to demonstrate when the "right" cause or issue presented itself. The majority of youth on college campuses remained privatists and success-oriented; however, there developed a growing number of young people who were dissatisfied with society and the "system." Empirical evidence revealed that many of the same characteristics that described activist youth existed in their sympathetic but nondemonstrative peers. Now, let us turn to the generational unit theory, which pulls some of this material together.

Generational Unit Theory

A generation, according to Mannheim (1952, p. 289), appears structurally similar to a social class, wherein individuals hold similar locations in the economic and power structure. He opens his argument on generations and social movements by emphasizing the importance of biological age, since this factor provides a vital base in social and historical change. Biological location partially determines the range of experience, and by being "location-bound," one is limited to certain modes of thought and behavior. In the words of Mannheim (1952), belonging to the same age group and background has this in common:

> Both endow the individuals sharing in them with a common location in the social and historical process, and thereby limit them to a specific range of potential experience, predisposing them for a certain characteristic mode of thought and experience, and a characteristic type of historically relevant action (p. 291).

Like Feuer (1969), Ortega y Gasset (1958), Davis (1940), and Eisenstadt (1956), Mannheim (1952) argues that generations have played an important role in the creation of new social and historical forms. He maintains that while the phenomenon of generations is ultimately rooted in the biological rhythm of birth and death, the determining sociological fact of a generation hinges on the "common location" (*Lagerung*) of its members:

> "Generation" represents nothing more than a particular kind of identity of location, embracing related "age groups" embedded in a historical-social process (p. 292).

Feuer (1969, p. 25) suggests that biological generations are not necessarily sociological generations until the shared historical experiences produce similar perceptions and understandings of reality. Lambert (1970) likewise argues that the sociological problem of generations begins where the biological problem leaves off.

Generational unit, on the other hand, represents a much stronger bond than actual generations:

> Youth experiencing the same concrete historical problems may be said to be part of the same actual generation; while those groups within the same actual generation which work up the material of their common experience in different specific ways, constitute separate generational units (Mannheim, 1952, p. 304).

Generational units share a similar location and common destiny in history. Within a generation there can exist any number of protagonistic or antagonistic generational units competing with one another. The units themselves respond to similar social and cultural forces and impose a parallelism of response on their members—that is, pressure to conform to partisan points of view. From the eighteenth century on, Mannheim (1952, p. 304) argues, there emerged two rivaling political mentalities—the romantic-conservative and the rationalist-liberal. Although both schools belonged to the same historical generation, their membership responded to social and cultural stimuli in divergent ways and thus constituted different generational units. Mannheim (1952, p. 310) is explicit, however, in pointing out that not every generation produces the same number and kind of social configurations. The existence of any unit is partially determined by the unique interplay or blend of social, cultural, and historical forces. These, in turn, are selectively filtered and amplified through shared collective impulses and values.

Since each generation need not develop its own unique bond or consciousness, the rhythm of successive generations based on biological and sociological factors need not evolve in parallel form. Whether a particular "generational style" or *entelechy* develops every year, every thirty years, or every hundred years depends on the "trigger action" of the combined historical, social, cultural, and psychological forces (Mannheim, 1952, p. 310). The quantity and quality of influences within a particular historical period are important since natural data, according to Mannheim—and he considers the concept of biological rhythm natural data—remain constant in history, and as such possess little explanatory power. The understanding of generational phenomena results when we view these natural data as having been influenced by the dynamic factors that "seize upon" the different characteristics and potentialities inherent in the natural datum. That is, according to Mannheim (1952, p. 305), natural data receive their shape and form from the emerging social, cultural, and historical processes. And while the natural data of age, class, and status provide the range of ingredients that constitute the substance of society, the special features and transformations that occur within certain historical periods give these natural factors their unique character and form.

Mannheim suggests, however, that history is too one-sided and monistic to explain adequately the totality of social and cultural change. Certain entelechies, which reflect social and intellectual trends, provide the underlying currents that evolve into basic attitudes and behavior within generations. Youth movements are heavily influenced or molded by these intellectual trends, and the particular style of the period itself—whether it is liberal or conservative, static or dynamic—is expressed in the dominant force or *Zeitgeist* ("spirit of the age"). However, this relationship is not asymmetrical; while history or the *Zeitgeist* influences generational entelechies, generational units influence the structure of society and course of history. By selecting and amplifying certain entelechies and not others, generational units create both the genesis and the dynamics for new social and historical order.

Although members must be born in the same historical period to constitute a generation, they must also experience the interplay of social and cultural forces to become a part of the same generational unit. While age similarity and historical themes influence generations and generational units, another factor in

Mannheim's theory involves the actual participation in a common social and cultural "nexus." Implied in this "nexus" is the "participation in a common destiny" on the part of group members themselves (Mannheim, 1952, p. 303). Membership in a particular social-historical community is a crucial ingredient for generational location and solidarity. Mannheim (1952, p. 303) suggests that a generational unit exists only when a "concrete bond" is created among its members as a result of their exposure to similar social and intellectual forces in the process of "dynamic destabilization." Youth must be drawn into the "vortex of social change" to become members of the same actual generation, and at this point Mannheim distinguishes between the "actual" versus "potential" generational units. Isolated youth, that is, peasant or rural youth, who have the potential for experiencing generational solidarity, rarely become involved in generational movements. Membership implies participation in the social and intellectual currents of the day—which typically occur in urban centers experiencing rapid change (Mannheim, 1952, p. 303).

Social and cultural change have the effect of accelerating the "stratification of experience" (*Erlebnisschichtung*) of each successive generation (Mannheim, 1952, p. 309). During periods of rapid social and historical change, attitudes take on new meaning and quickly becomes differentiated from traditional patterns of experience. As these newly emerging patterns of experience consolidate, they form fresh impulses and cores for generational configuration that result in unique generational styles. The importance of the acceleration of social change for the realization of potentialities inherent in generations is absent in slowly changing communities. Static or slowly changing societies: (1) display no such generational units sharply set off from preceding generations; (2) articulate no unique collective entelechy; and (3) since the tempo of change is gradual, new generations evolve out of old generations without visible cleavage—there remains a strong homogeneity between generations (Mannheim, 1952, pp. 309-310). Periods characterized by war, natural catastrophe, and total political mobilization rarely develop generational differentiation due to the homogenization of values resulting from fear and/or national solidarity. However, during times of relative security and protracted institutional growth, the quicker the tempo of social and cultural change (due to science, technology, nationalism, overpopulation), the higher the probability that successive generations will develop their own entelechies.

Generational units likewise participate in the transmission of culture. Each successive generation experiences a "fresh contact" with traditional values and principles, and this "fresh contact" introduces new psychosocial units to the cultural and historical process. Inherent in this "fresh contact" is a radical revitalization process, which forces youth to make novel interpretations and adjustments to the cultural heritage. The transmission of cultural data usually occurs through formal teaching, and these conscious forms often become the older stratum of consciousness. Around age 17 or so, youth begin to reflect on problematical issues and begin to live "in the present." As they struggle to clarify the issues of the day, they are more prone to transform the upper-most stratum of consciousness into serious reflection, while the deeper stratum (habits) remains untouched. Youth appear to be "up to date" and close to the "present" problems by virtue of their "fresh contact" and in the fact that they are "dramatically aware of a process of destabilization and take sides on it" (Mannheim, 1952, p. 301). But their consciousness appears more substantive than formal, and although contemporary and timely, some-what superficial.

Perhaps the most critical factor in Mannheim's generational unit formula involves the psychological structuring of consciousness or what he terms the "stratification of experience." Merely being born during the same period in history does not guarantee similarity of consciousness with a generational unit. The sharing in the same "inner-dialectic" provides the critical experience—with its perceptions, gestalt, and linguistic expressions that structure and modify environmental and sensory data—"partly simplifying and abbreviating it, partly elaborating and filling it out" (Mannheim, 1952, p. 306). The perceptions of generational units are formed in a particular way, and the structure and con-tent of these psychological configurations depend on the collective values and goals to which their members subscribe. The importance of these formative and interpretive principles is that they provide the link between spatially separated individuals who may never have come into contact with one an-other. Whereas the common location in the generational cycle is of potential importance, the generational unit emerges when similarly located contempo-raries share ideas and values and participate in a common destiny.

Although no one has directly measured the generational unit theory, there exists considerable bivariate empirical support for this argument. As referred to previously, Eisenstadt (1956, 1963), Ortega y Gasset (1958), Erikson (1963, 1968), Feuer (1969), Dawson and Prewitt (1969), Keniston (1971), Ausubel and Sullivan (1972), and Moynihan (1973) discussed biological fac-tors inherent in the generational cycle that affect student political behavior. All suggested that the period of youth, with its search for fidelity, identity, meaning, and strong peer-group identification, has important political impli-cations.

Holzner (1962), Mills (1963), Lipset (1967, 1972), Emmerson (1968), Alt-bach (1968), Laqueur (1969), Lipset and Altbach (1969), and Miles (1971) discussed the historical significance of youth movements, both in advanced and developing countries. They maintained that different historical configurations have influenced the form and substance of student movements around the world (see also Bakke & Bakke, 1971; Liebman, 1971; Bell, 1973).

Perhaps more than any single area of research there exist numerous empirical studies describing the social and demographic characteristics of youth move-ments. Important among these have been the works by Lyonns (1965), Somers (1965), Heist (1966), Gamson, Goodman, and Gurin (1967), Flacks (1967, 1971), Block, Haan, and Smith (1968), Bayer and Astin (1969), and Scott and

El-Assal (1969), and numerous case studies (Altbach, 1968; Foster & Long, 1970; Riesman & Stadtman, 1973).[1]

Katz and Allport (1931), Laing (1967), Draper (1967), Roszak (1969), American Council on Education (1972), Slater (1970), and Reich (1970) investigated the influence of traditional and emerging cultural forces and how these have affected the counterculture and youth politics.[2]

Finally, Gamson, Goodman, and Gurin (1967), Flacks (1967, 1971), Keniston (1968, 1971), Haan, Smith, and Block (1968), Block, Haan, and Smith (1968), Whittaker and Watts (1969) studied the psychological and ideological characteristics of activist youth.[3]

What has not been undertaken to date has been a multivariate, sequential treatment of these bivariate relationships that explain the political characteristics of generational units. In order to formalize the general theory originally outlined by Mannheim, the following features and relationships are presented as suggestive: *generational unit* is defined as the dependent variable (X_1); the *psychological structuring of consciousness* (X_2), is the intervening variable, which is both influenced by, and monitors, select *historical* (X_3), *social* (X_4), *cultural* (X_5), and *biological* (X_6) factors, and independent variables. See Figure 12.1. The generational unit model predicts that cohort membership alone will not determine generational behavior in a direct sense, but chronological age acting indirectly through exposure to select historical, social, and cultural factors in combination with a new psychological consciousness and common destiny will explain generational units. Mannheim also argues that generational units are able to act as influences on the historical, social, and cultural processes over time. There appears to be a feedback effect in operation, whereby the political behavior of the generational units themselves can partially determine the course of social and historical change.[4]

Discussion

The generational unit theory assumes the progression of society toward higher and more sophisticated forms of social and political organization. What is

[1] See also Watts, Lynch, and Whittaker (1969), Kahn and Bowers (1970), Hodgkinson (1970), Peterson and Bilorusky (1971), and Mankoff and Flacks (1971).

[2] See also Hastings and Hoge (1970), Denisoff and Levine (1970), Revel (1971), Keniston (1971), Berger (1971), Yankelovich (1972), and Gottlieb (1973).

[3] See also Geller and Howard (1969), Baird (1970), Miller and Everson (1970), Smith, Haan, and Block (1970), Demerath, Marwell, and Aiken (1971), Liebert (1971), Meyer (1971, 1973), and Kerpelman (1972).

[4] Mannheim's generational unit theory appears sequential and includes a revitalization process as the behavior and influence of youth movements affect historical, social, and cultural processes, rendering the model one of "alternating asymmetry." And while the generational unit theory appears amenable to comparative controls, longitudinal research designs, cohort analysis, or panel design, the complexity introduced by the feedback process indicates that greater methodological and statistical sophistication will be required to measure this theory.

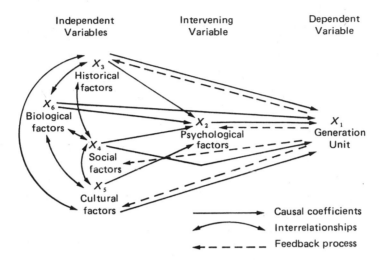

Figure 12.1 Multivariate model based on Mannheim's theory of generational units.

significant about Mannheim's theory is that he does not attribute youth movements to any single cause but to youth's reactions to the major issues and contradictions that exist in society at a particular period in time. Youth groups take sides and mobilize over issues like their parents before them, but unlike their parents and due to the "fresh contact," they are more attuned to the current issues that confront their generation. When the contradictions appear historically "new" (women's rights, minority rights, ecology) and when they cut across old conflicts of interest, there is a greater probability that society will experience youth movements.

The generational unit theory has the capacity to examine generational units both in terms of *intergenerational* and *intragenerational* behavior. In this respect, the theory can differentiate and evaluate political behavior both between and within generations. For example, Zeitlin (1966) observed differential responses to the Cuban revolution by workers in Cuba in 1962, which he attributed to their different historical experiences of being part of a particular political generation. It was the members of the "Castro generation," the age cohort 28–35, who were most likely to have favorable attitudes toward the revolution— probably due to the "common frame of reference" developed during the anti-Batista struggle. The lowest support for the revolution was given by the 21- to 27-year-old age group (the youngest age group surveyed), which Zeitlin attributed to the fact that these workers were too young to remember working conditions in prerevolutionary Cuba.

The theory also has the flexibility to explain differential political behavior within the same generation. The reason why individuals born into a particular generation display divergent political orientations appears to be in part that groups or units within the same generation may be further differentiated by social structural factors. When Zeitlin (1966) looked at "within" generational differences in attitudes toward the Cuban revolution, he found that the structural factor of prerevolutionary employment status had a significant impact on attitudes toward the revolution for each of the generations studied. Workers who were unemployed or underemployed prior to the revolution tended to be strongly procommunist and more supportive of the revolution than workers who were regularly employed before the revolution.

Mannheim's generational unit theory appears particularly applicable in accounting for the radically divergent student political styles exhibited by youth in the United States during the 1960s. Opposing political orientations among members of the same age cohort were illustrated by one study (Westby & Braungart, 1970) in 1966 of the left-wing SDS and right-wing YAF, both of whom rejected status quo politics and in its place constructed utopias that transcended the present and were oriented toward the future. SDS youth supported the goals of "participatory democracy," military disengagement, humanitarianism, and an idyllic communal order; the members of YAF favored the dominance of the free enterprise system, nationalism, militarism, and rugged individualism.

These activist youth were asked to write "the history of the United States from the present to the year 2000," and the essays were classified according to their major organizing themes (Westby & Braungart, 1970). Five utopian-dystopian conceptions of the future were identified: progressive utopia (steady improvement), revolutionary utopia (overthrow of existing structure), conversionist utopia (downward drift followed by "rapid awakening"), linear decline dystopia (steady decline), and eschatological dystopia (sudden cataclysm). SDS tended to be more dystopian (49 percent) than utopian (27 percent), with: 34 percent of these youth reporting a linear decline in the future of the United States, 15 percent expecting the eschatological end of history, 13 percent a progressive drift upward, 10 percent revolution, and 4 percent conversion to radical goals. YAF youth, on the other hand, favored utopian themes (52 percent) in their essays as opposed to dystopian conceptions (33 percent), with: 36 percent foreseeing a drift toward state control followed by a sudden "conversion" to conservative principles, 29 percent linear decline, 15 percent progressive themes, 4 percent eschatological doom, and 1 percent revolution. These conceptions of the future were not determined solely by opposing political styles but appear to be partially the result of divergent social background experiences. When comparing the status characteristics of SDS versus YAF members, it was reported that: members of the left-wing group tended to come from upper middle class (55 percent), "low" ethnic status (63 percent), and Jewish or nonreligious (62 percent) backgrounds; while members of the right-wing group were often from lower middle class and working-class (72 percent), "high" ethnic status (69 percent), and predominantly Protestant or Catholic (84 percent) backgrounds (Braungart, 1969, 1971c). It appears that youth groups or units "within" the same generation who exhibit different structural locations experience or interpret the sociopolitical world differently. In modern American society, two types of status strains may be related to the origin of radical youth groups in this study: (1) a high social class position in conjunction with low social status positions; and (2) low social class in conjunction with high social status positions. SDS members, because of high achieved status albeit low ascribed status favor the reorganization of society, while the YAF, who experience low achieved status and high ascribed status, likewise repudiate contemporary society. In the first instance, when mobility and achievement in occupation and education are not matched by comparable religious and ethnic position, one might expect a rejection of the status quo in place of more universalistic, equalitarian standards. In the second instance, when groups experience social rewards on the basis of membership in established American status groupings but lack comparable class security and insulation, one might expect a rejection of the status quo in favor of a return to traditional principles and values. This hypothesis may partially explain the radical departure from conventional politics exhibited by SDS and YAF groups in the 1960s (Braungart, 1971c).

The generational unit theory is not concerned with social statics, but with emerging forces and creative syntheses that continually give rise to new patterns of social organization over time. Unlike the functionalist theory of generational conflict (Eisenstadt, 1956, 1963; Bettelheim, 1963; Parsons, 1963), the generational unit theory suggests that youth are not rebelling against society but instead are creating new forms of consciousness that are in part the result of generational and social structural forces. What makes the generational unit theory different from the homeostatic or functionalist theory is that youth movements in the former represent *destabilizing* forces within history. The newer units represent the vanguard or "cutting edge" of specific entelechy that interact and compete for the definition and control of reality.

Since youth movements are not constant throughout history but occur at different times and places, their explanation cannot be attributed solely to generic social and historical forces. Although history, culture, social structure, and psychological factors all add to the drama of human behavior, these factors alone cannot explain the unique "system of coordinates" or the "space between evolving events" that precipitate youth movements.[5] Although these forces are necessary, they do not appear to be sufficient to explain the sporadic or unique

---

[5] Both Biderman (1969) and Moynihan (1973) allude to the importance of measuring the "uniquely crucial regularities and interconnections" of forces in society. Biderman (1969, p. 72) is concerned with abandoning the artificial compartmentalizations "that have grown up to fit the abstract theoretical formulations of the several social science disciplines," and argues we must provide practical empirical measures of those key aspects in the social process that permit one to study social change over time. Moynihan (1973, p. 9) suggests that the youth population explosion of the 1960s interacted in a "synergistic" way with interdependent social and historical forces to produce a much greater consequence than would have taken place had any of these forces occurred in isolation or at different periods.

conditions that produce change at certain periods in time. Mannheim (1940) called the unique blends of social and psychological factors *principia media*—the underlying principles or interactions that represent "transmission belts" of human behavior.[6] Mannheim defines principia media as the

> temporary groups of general factors so closely intertwined that they operate as a single causal factor, . . . universal forces in a concrete setting as they become integrated out of the various factors at work in a given place at a given time—a particular combination of circumstances which may never be repeated (pp. 178-182).

Mannheim (1940, p. 183) argues that epochs are not dominated by a single principium medium but by a whole series of them that are intertwined in a multidimensional way. Reality consists of the mutual relationships between economic, political, and ideological spheres and of the concrete principia media operating among them. In Mannheim's view (1940, p. 184), a large number of mutually related principia media form a structure or social psychological pattern, and interdependent change in a number of principia media constitutes structural change.

The task of sociologists is to understand the principia media of each new period—not just to identify them in form, but to "study them in their mutual relationships" as well. Mannheim (1940, p. 185) offers several suggestions concerning how to study principia media. First, the sociologist is to distinguish various "factors" and "tendencies" and to "translate the chaos of facts into a correct description of the complicated interplay of forces." Only after this is accomplished can the sociologist begin the quantitative assessment of how complex structures can be analyzed or broken down into "simpler elements" for study. However, Mannheim (1940, p. 187) warns of the danger in "placing principia media side by side as equally significant factors without the attempt to relate them to one another." It is possible that the historical and social psychological forces at work in society are of unequal weight and that there is such a thing as a hierarchy of mediating principles,

> particularly when the multidimensional structure is being described as a whole. As against a method which assigns equal weight to all factors and principles and which is, at the very best, merely cumulative, there can be no doubt that those methods which give an axis to the structure in the sense that they seek to establish either "independent variables" or a "hierarchy of causal factors," are on the right track. But such a "hierarchy" can be constructed only empirically (Mannheim, 1940, p. 187).

[6] Mannheim (1940, p. 177) derives his conception of principia media from John Stuart Mill, and implicit in this concept is the question of causation. If one accepts the causal reasoning of Mill and Mannheim, then there are a number of methodological and statistical techniques that may be employed to test the generational unit theory. Several causal techniques in sociology that appear applicable are: (1) causal analysis (Blalock, 1969, 1971; Braungart, 1973); (2) path analysis (Duncan, 1966; Land, 1969; Finney, 1972); (3) parameter estimation (Anderson, 1973); and (4) multiple indicators or block variables (Sullivan, 1971). However, the existence of interactions and interrelationships—critical in measuring the generational unit theory—will require statistical sophistication in handling causal techniques (see Duncan, 1966; Althauser, 1971; Hannan, 1971).

Mannheim's discussion of the generational unit theory and principia media have important implications for the study of youth movements. The generational unit theory provides a model specifying formal properties that interact in a certain way, whereas principia media reflect the unique substantive interconnections among and between components of the theory over time. Only when we are able to understand the structural and emerging properties of historical, social, cultural, and psychological forces will we be in a better position to measure and predict the multidimensional relationship between youth and social movements.

REFERENCES

Albornoz, O. *Estudiantes norteamericanos: Perfiles politicos.* Caracas, Venezuela: Instituto Societas, 1967.

Allerbeck, K. R. Soziale bedingungen für Studentischen radikalismus. Inaugural-dissertation zur erlangung des Doktorgrades der Philosophischen fakultät der Universität zu Köln, 1971.

Altbach, P. G. *Student politics and higher education in the United States: A select bibliography.* St. Louis, Mo., and Cambridge, Mass.: United Ministries of Higher Education and Center for International Affairs, Harvard University, 1968.

Althauser, R. P. Multicollinearity and nonadditive regression models. In H. M. Blalock (Ed.), *Causal models in the social sciences.* Chicago: Aldine, Atherton, 1971.

American Council on Education. National norms for entering college freshmen—Fall 1966. *ACE Research Reports*, 1966, 2(1).

American Council on Education. National norms for entering college freshmen—Fall 1967. *ACE Research Reports*, 1967, 2(7).

American Council on Education. National norms for entering college freshmen—Fall 1968. *ACE Research Reports*, 1968, 3(1).

American Council on Education. National norms for entering college freshmen—Fall 1969. *ACE Research Reports*, 1969, 4(7).

American Council on Education. National norms for entering college freshmen—Fall 1970. *ACE Research Reports*, 1970, 5(6).

American Council on Education. The American freshman: National norms for Fall 1971. *ACE Research Reports*, 1971, 6(6).

American Council on Education. The American freshman: National norms for Fall 1972. *ACE Research Reports*, 1972, 7(5).

Anderson, J. G. Causal models and social indicators: Toward the development of social system models. *American Sociological Review*, 1973, 38(3), 285–301.

Astin, A. W. Personal and environmental determinants of student activism. *Measurement and Evaluation in Guidance*, 1968, 1(3), 149–162.

Astin, A. W., & Bayer, A. E. Antecedents and consequents of disruptive campus protests. *Measurement and Evaluation in Guidance*, 1971, 4(1), 18–30.

Auger, C., Barton, A., & Maurice, R. The nature of the student movement and radical proposals for change at Columbia University. *The Human Factor*, 1969, 9(1), 18–40.

Ausubel, D. P., & Sullivan, E. V. *Theory and problem of child development.* New York: Grune & Stratton, 1972.

Baird, L. L. Who protests: A study of student activists. In J. Foster & D. Long (Eds.), *Protest! Student activism in America.* New York: Morrow, 1970.

Bakke, E. W., & Bakke, M. S. *Campus challenge.* Hamden, Conn.: Archon Books, 1971.

Bayer, A. E. Institutional correlates of faculty support of campus unrest. *Sociology of Education*, 1972, 45(1), 76–94.

Bayer, A. E., & Astin, A. W. Violence and disruption on the U.S. campus, 1968–1969. *Educational Record*, Fall 1969, 337–350.

Bell, D. *The coming of post-industrial society.* New York: Basic Books, 1973.

Bengston, V. L. The generation gap: A review and typology of social-psychological perspectives. *Youth and Society*, 1970, 2(1), 7–32.

Bengston, V. L., & Black, K. D. Intergenerational relations and continuities in socialization. In P. Baltes & W. Schaie (Eds.), *Life-span developmental psychology: Personality and socialization.* New York: Academic Press, 1973.

Berger, B. M. *Looking for America.* Englewood Cliffs, N.J.: Prentice-Hall, 1971.

Bettelheim, B. The problem of generations. In E. Erikson (Ed.), *Youth: Change and challenge.* New York: Basic Books, 1963.

Biderman, A. D. Social indicators and goals. In R. A. Bauer (Ed.), *Social indicators.* Cambridge, Mass.: MIT Press, 1969.

Blalock, H. M. *Theory construction.* Englewood Cliffs, N.J.: Prentice-Hall, 1969.

Blalock, H. M. (Ed.) *Causal models in the social sciences.* Chicago: Aldine, Atherton, 1971.

Block, J., Haan, N., & Smith, M. B. Activism and apathy in contemporary adolescents. In J. F. Adams (Ed.), *Understanding adolescence.* Boston: Allyn and Bacon, 1968.

Bolton, C. D., & Kammeyer, K. C. *The university student.* New Haven, Conn.: College and University Press, 1967.

Braungart, R. G. Family status, socialization and student politics: A multivariate analysis. Unpublished doctoral dissertation, Pennsylvania State University, 1969.

Braungart, R. G. Family status, socialization and student politics: a multivariate analysis. *American Journal of Sociology*, 1971, 77(1), 108–130. (a)

Braungart, R. G. Parental identification and student politics. *Sociology of Education*, 1971, 44(4), 463–473. (b)

Braungart, R. G. SDS and YAF: A comparison of two student radical groups in the mid-1960's. *Youth and Society*, 1971, 2(4), 441–457. (c)

Braungart, R. G. Path analysis and causal analysis: Variations on a multivariate technique of measuring student politics. Paper presented to the annual meetings of the Society for the Study of Social Problems, New York, August 1973.

Braungart, R. G. The sociology of generations and student politics: A comparison of the functionalist and generational unit models. *Journal of Social Issues*, 1974, 30(2), 31–54.

Braungart, R. G., & Braungart, M. M. Administration, faculty, and student reactions to campus unrest. *Journal of College Student Personnel*, 1972, 13(2), 112–119. (a)

Braungart, R. G., & Braungart, M. M. Social and political correlates of protest attitudes and behavior among college youth: A case study. Paper presented to the annual meetings of the Southern Sociological Society, New Orleans, April 1972. (b)

Brunswick, A. F. What generation gap? *Social Problems*, 1970, 17(3), 358–371.

Clark, B. R., & Trow, M. Determinants of college student subculture. Unpublished manuscript, Center for the Study of Higher Education, University of California, Berkeley, 1960.

Clarke, J. W., & Egan, J. Social and political dimensions of campus protest activity. Unpublished manuscript, Center for Policy Analysis, Institute for Social Research, Florida State University, 1969.

Cowdry, R., Keniston, K., & Cabin, S. The war and military obligation: Private attitudes and public actions. *Journal of Personality*, 1970, 38(4), 525–549.

Davies, J. C. (Ed.) *When men revolt and why.* New York: Free Press, 1971.

Davis, K. The sociology of parent-youth conflict. *American Sociological Review*, 1940, 5(4), 523–535.

Dawson, R., & Prewitt, K. *Political socialization.* Boston: Little, Brown, 1969.

De Conde, A. (Ed.) *Student activism.* New York: Scribner's, 1971.

Demerath, N. J., Marwell, G., & Aiken, M. T. *Dynamics of idealism.* San Francisco: Jossey-Bass, 1971.

Denisoff, R. S., & Levine, M. H. Generations and counter-culture. *Youth and Society*, 1970, **2**(1), 33–58.

Denisoff, R. S., & Peterson, R. A. *The sounds of social change.* Chicago: Rand McNally, 1972.

Douglas, J. D. *Youth in turmoil.* Washington, D.C.: U.S. Government Printing Office, 1970.

Draper, H. The student movement of the thirties: A political history. In R. J. Simon (Ed.), *As we saw the thirties.* Urbana, Ill.: University of Illinois Press, 1967.

Duncan, O. D. Path analysis: Sociological examples. *American Journal of Sociology*, 1966, **72**(1), 1–16.

Dunlap, R. Radical and conservative student activists: A comparison of family backgrounds. *Pacific Sociological Review*, 1970, **13**(3), 171–181.

Eisenstadt, S. N. *From generation to generation.* Glencoe, Ill.: Free Press, 1956.

Eisenstadt, S. N. Archetypal patterns of youth. In E. H. Erikson (Ed.), *Youth: Change and challenge*, New York: Basic Books, 1963.

Emmerson, D. K. (Ed.) *Students and politics in developing nations.* New York: Praeger, 1968.

Erikson, E. H. Youth: Fidelity and diversity. In E. H. Erikson (Ed.), *Youth: Change and challenge.* New York: Basic Books, 1963.

Erikson, E. H. *Identity: Youth and crisis.* New York: Norton, 1968.

Fendrich, J. M., Simons, R., & Tarleau, A. Activists ten years later: A study of life styles and politics. Paper presented to the annual meetings of the American Sociological Association, New Orleans, August 1972.

Fengler, A. P., & Wood V. Continuity between the generations: Differential influence of mothers and fathers. *Youth and Society*, 1973, **4**(3), 359–372.

Fenton, J. H., & Gleason, G. Student power at the University of Massachusetts: A case study. Amherst, Mass.: Bureau of Government Research, University of Massachusetts, 1969.

Feuer, L. S. *The conflict of generations.* New York: Basic Books, 1969.

Finney, J. M. Indirect effects in path analysis. *Sociological Methods and Research*, 1972, **1**(2), 175–186.

Flacks, R. The liberated generation: Explorations of the roots of student protest. *Journal of Social Issues*, 1967, **23**(3), 52–75.

Flacks, R. Social and cultural meanings of student revolt: Some informal comparative observations. *Social Problems*, 1970, **17**(3), 340–357. (a)

Flacks, R. Who protests: The social bases of the student movement. In J. Foster & D. Long (Eds.), *Protest! Student activism in America.* New York: Morrow, 1970. (b)

Flacks, R. *Youth and social change.* Chicago: Markham, 1971.

Foster, J., & Long, D. (Eds.) *Protest! Student activism in America.* New York: Morrow, 1970.

Gamson, Z. F., Goodman, J., & Gurin, G. Radicals, moderates and bystanders during a university protest. Paper presented to the annual meetings of the American Sociological Association, San Francisco, August 1967.

Geller, J. D., & Howard, G. Student activism and the war in Vietnam. Unpublished manuscript, Department of Psychiatry, Yale University School of Medicine, 1969.

Gergen, K. J. Social background, education, attitudes and previous experience with activism. Personal communication to the President's Commission on Campus Unrest, Washington, D.C., August 1970.

Geschwender, J. A. Explorations in the theory of social movements and revolutions. *Social Forces*, 1968, **47**(2), 127–135.

Goertzel, T. Generation conflict and social change. *Youth and Society*, 1972, **3**(3), 327–352.

Gottlieb, D. Youth and the meaning of work. University Park, Pa.: College of Human Development, Pennsylvania State University, 1973.

Greenstein, F. I. *Children and politics.* New Haven, Conn.: Yale University Press, 1968.

Gusfield, J. R. Intellectual character and American universities. *Journal of General Education*, January 1963, **14**, 230–247.

Gusfield, J. R. (Ed.) *Protest, reform and revolt.* New York: Wiley, 1970.

Haan, N., Smith, M. B., & Block, J. Moral reasoning of young adults: Political-social behavior, family background and personality correlates. *Journal of Personality and Social Psychology*, 1968, **10**(3), 183–201.

Hadden, J. K. The private generation. *Psychology Today*, 1969, 3(5), 32–35, 68–69.

Hannan, M. T. Problems of aggregation. In H. M. Blalock (Ed.), *Causal models in the social sciences.* Chicago: Aldine, Atherton, 1971.

Hastings, P. K., & Hoge, D. R. Religious change among college students over two decades. *Social Forces*, 1970, 49(1), 16–28.

Heberle, R. *Social movements.* New York: Appleton-Century-Crofts, 1951.

Heist, P. Intellect and commitment: The faces of discontent. Unpublished manuscript, Center for the Study of Higher Education, University of California, Berkeley, 1966.

Hodgkinson, H. Student protest—An institutional and national profile. *The Record*, 1970, **71**(4), 337–355.

Holzner, B. Institutional change, social stratification, and the direction of youth movements. *Journal of Educational Sociology*, 1962, **36**(2), 49–56.

Hyman, H. H. *Political socialization.* New York: Free Press, 1959.

Kahn, R. M., & Bowers, W. J. The social context of the rank-and-file student activist: A test of four hypotheses. *Sociology of Education*, 1970, 43(1), 39–47.

Katz, D., & Allport, F. H. *Students' attitudes.* Syracuse, N.Y.: Craftsman Press, 1931.

Keniston, K. *Young radicals.* New York: Harcourt, Brace & World, 1968.

Keniston, K. *Youth and dissent.* New York: Harcourt Brace Jovanovich, 1971.

Kerpelman, L. C. *Activists and nonactivists: A psychological study of American college students.* New York: Behavioral Publications, 1972.

Killian, L. M. Social movements. In R. L. Faris (Ed.), *Handbook of Modern Sociology.* Chicago: Rand McNally, 1966.

Kohlberg, L. Development of moral character and moral ideology. In M. L. Hoffman & L. W. Hoffman (Eds.), *Review of child development research.* Vol. 1. New York: Russell Sage Foundation, 1964.

Kohlberg, L. Moral development and the education of adolescents. In E. D. Evans (Ed.), *Adolescent Readings in Behavior and Development.* Hinsdale, Ill.: Dryden, 1970.

Ladd, E. C., Hadley, C., & King, L. A new political realignment? *The Public Interest*, Spring 1971, **32**, 46–63.

Laing, R. D. *The politics of experience.* New York: Ballantine Books, 1967.

Lambert, T. A. Karl Mannheim and the sociology of generations. Paper presented to the annual meetings of the Eastern Sociological Society, New York, April 1970.

Lambert, T. A. Generational factors in political-cultural consciousness. Paper presented at the annual meetings of the American Political Science Association, Chicago, September 1971.

Lambert, T. A. Generations and change: Toward a theory of generations as a force in historical process. *Youth and Society*, 1972, 4(1), 21–45.

Land, K. C. Principles of path analysis. In E. F. Borgatta (Ed.), *Sociological methodology, 1969.* San Francisco: Jossey-Bass, 1969.

Laqueur, W. Student revolts. *Commentary*, 1969, 47, 33–41.

Lewis, R. A. Socialization into national violence: Familial correlates of hawkish attitudes toward war. *Journal of Marriage and the Family*, November 1971, **33**, 699–708.

Liebert, R. *Radical and militant youth.* New York: Praeger, 1971.

Liebman, A. Students and politics in the 1950's and 1960's. Paper presented to the annual meetings of the American Sociological Association, Denver, September 1971.

Liebman, A., Walker, K. N., & Glazer, M. *Latin American university students: A six-nation study.* Cambridge, Mass.: Harvard University Press, 1972.

Lipset, S. M. (Ed.) *Student politics.* New York: Basic Books, 1967.

Lipset, S. M. *Rebellion in the university.* Boston: Little, Brown, 1972.

Lipset, S. M., & Altbach, P. G. (Eds.) *Students in revolt.* Boston: Houghton Mifflin, 1969.

Lipset, S. M., & Ladd, E. C. College generations—From the 1930's to the 1960's. *The Public Interest*, 1971, **25**, 99–113.

Loken, J. O. A multivariate analysis of student activism at the University of Alberta. Unpublished doctoral dissertation, University of Alberta, 1970.

Lyonns, G. The police car demonstration: A survey of participants. In S. M. Lipset & S. S. Wolin (Eds.), *The Berkeley student revolt.* Garden City, N.Y.: Doubleday, 1965.

Mannheim, K. *Man and society in an age of reconstruction.* New York: Harcourt, Brace & World, 1940.

Mannheim, K. The problem of youth in modern society. In K. Mannheim, *Diagnosis of our time.* New York: Oxford University Press, 1944.

Mannheim, K. The problem of generations. In K. Mannheim, *Essays on the sociology of knowledge.* London: Routledge and Kegan Paul, 1952.

Mankoff, M., & Flacks, R. The changing social base of the American student movement. *The Annals*, May 1971, **395**, 54–67.

Matza, D. Subterranean traditions of youth. *The Annals*, November 1961, **338**, 102–108.

McLaughlin, B. (Ed.) *Studies in social movements.* New York: Free Press, 1969.

Meyer, J. M., & Rubinson, R. Structural determinants of student political activity: A comparative interpretation. *Sociology of Education*, 1972, **45**(1), 23–46.

Meyer, M. W. Harvard students in the midst of crisis. *Sociology of Education*, 1971, **44**(3), 245–269.

Meyer, M. W. Harvard students in the midst of crisis: A note on the sources of leftism. *Sociology of Education*, 1973, **46**(2), 203–218.

Middleton, R., & Putney, S. Student rebellion against parental political beliefs. *Social Forces*, May 1963, **41**, 377–383.

Miles, M. W. *The radical probe: The logic of student rebellion.* New York: Atheneum, 1971.

Miller, R. E., & Everson, D. H. Personality and ideology: The case of student power. Paper presented to the annual meetings of the Midwest Political Science Association, Southern Illinois University, April–May 1970.

Mills, C. W. The new left. In I. L. Horowitz (Ed.), *Power, politics and people.* New York: Ballantine Books, 1963.

Moynihan, D. Peace—Some thoughts on the 1960's and 1970's. *The Public Interest*, Summer 1973, **32**, 3–12.

Ortega y Gasset, J. *Man and crisis.* New York: Norton, 1958.

Parsons, T. Youth in the context of American society. In E. H. Erikson (Ed.), *Youth: Change and challenge.* New York: Basic Books, 1963.

Paulus, G. A multivariate analysis study of student activist leaders, student government leaders and nonactivists. Unpublished doctoral dissertation, Michigan State University, 1968.

Peterson, R. E. *The scope of organized student protest in 1964-1965.* Princeton, N.J.: Educational Testing Service, 1966.

Peterson, R. E. *The scope of organized student protest in 1967-1968.* Princeton, N.J.: Educational Testing Service, 1968. (a)

Peterson, R. E. The student left in American higher education. *Daedalus*, 1968, 97(1), 293–317. (b)

Peterson, R. E., & Bilorusky, J. A. *May 1970: The campus aftermath of Cambodia and Kent State.* Berkeley, Calif.: Carnegie Commission on Higher Education, 1971.

Piaget, J. *The moral judgment of the child.* New York: Free Press, 1965.

Piaget, J. *Six psychological studies.* New York: Random House, 1967.

President's Commission on Campus Unrest. The report of the President's Commission on Campus Unrest. Washington, D.C.: U.S. Government Printing Office, 1970.

Reich, C. A. *The greening of America.* New York: Random House, 1970.

Revel, J. F. *Without Marx or Jesus: The new American revolution has begun.* Garden City, N.Y.: Doubleday, 1971.

Riesman, D., & Stadtman, V. A. (Eds.) *Academic transformation.* New York: McGraw-Hill, 1973.

Riley, M. W., Johnson, M., & Foner, A. (Eds.) *Aging and society: A sociology of age stratification.* Vol. 3. New York: Russell Sage Foundation, 1972.

Roszak, T. *The making of a counter culture.* Garden City, N.Y.: Doubleday, 1969.

Rush, G. B., & Denisoff, R. S. (Eds.) *Social and political movements.* New York: Appleton-Century-Crofts, 1971.

Scott, J. W., & El-Assal, M. Multiversity, university size, university quality and student protest: An empirical study. *American Sociological Review,* 1969, **34**(5), 202–209.

Scurrah, M. J. Some organizational structural determinants of student protest in U.S. universities and colleges. Unpublished doctoral dissertation, Cornell University, 1972.

Sherif, M., & Sherif, C. *Social psychology.* New York: Harper & Row, 1969.

Shimbori, M. The sociology of a student movement: A Japanese case study. *Daedalus,* 1968, **97**(1), 204–228.

Shotland, R. L. The communication patterns and the structure of social relationships at a large university. Unpublished manuscript, Graduate Center, City University of New York, 1970.

Sigel, R. S. (Ed.) *Learning about politics.* New York: Random House, 1970.

Simmons, L. R. The real generation gap: A speculation on the meaning and implications of the generation gap. *Youth and Society,* 1971, **3**(1), 119–135.

Skolnick, J. H. *The politics of protest.* New York: Simon and Schuster, 1969.

Slater, P. *The pursuit of loneliness: American culture at the breaking point.* Boston: Beacon Press, 1970.

Smith, M. B., Haan, N., & Block, J. Social-psychological aspects of student activism. *Youth and Society,* 1970, **1**(3), 261–288.

Solomon, F., & Fishman, J. R. Youth and peace: A psycho-social study of student peace demonstrators in Washington, D.C. *Journal of Social Issues,* 1964, **20**(4), 54–73.

Somers, R. The mainsprings of rebellion: A survey of Berkeley students in November 1964. In S. M. Lipset and S. S. Wolin (Eds.), *The Berkeley student revolt.* Garden City, N.Y.: Doubleday, 1965.

Sullivan, J. L. Multiple indicators and complex causal models. In H. M. Blalock (Ed.), *Causal models in the social sciences.* Chicago: Aldine, Atherton, 1971.

Thomas, L. E. Family congruence on political orientations of politically active parents and their college-age children. Unpublished doctoral dissertation, University of Chicago, 1968.

Tygart, C. E., & Holt, N. Examining the Weinberg and Walker typology of student activists. *American Journal of Sociology,* 1972, **77**(5), 957–966.

Watts, W. A., Lynch, S., & Whittaker, D. Alienation and activism in today's college-age youth: Socialization patterns and current family relationships. *Journal of Counseling Psychology,* 1969, **16**(1), 1–7.

Weinberg, I., & Walker, K. Student politics and political systems: Toward a typology. *American Journal of Sociology,* 1969, **75**(1), 77–96.

Westby, D. L., & Braungart, R. G. Class and politics in the family backgrounds of student political activists. *American Sociological Review,* 1966, **31**(5), 690–692.

Westby, D. L., & Braungart, R. G. Activists and the history of the future. In J. Foster & D. Long (Eds.), *Protest! Student activism in America.* New York: Morrow, 1970.

Whittaker, D., & Watts, W. A. Personality characteristics of a nonconformist youth subculture: A study of the Berkeley non-student. *Journal of Social Issues,* 1969, **25**(2), 65–89.

Whittaker, D., & Watts, W. A. Personality characteristics associated with activism and disaffiliation in today's college-age youth. *Journal of Counseling Psychology,* 1971, **18**(3), 200–206.

Winborn, B. B., & Jansen, D. G. Personality characteristics of campus social-political action leaders. *Journal of Counseling Psychology*, 1967, **14**(6), 509-513.

Yankelovich, D. *Generations apart*. New York: Columbia Broadcasting System, 1969.

Yankelovich, D. *The changing values on campus*. New York: Washington Square Press, 1972.

Zeitlin, M. Political generations in the Cuban working class. *American Journal of Sociology*, 1966, **71**(5), 493-508.

Research Themes and Priorities

SIGMUND E. DRAGASTIN
*National Institute of Child Health
and Human Development*

As a scientist administrator with an interest in adolescence research, I bring a point of view to this volume somewhat different from those of the previous twelve contributors, all of whom are social scientists deeply immersed in actually doing research. To ask, "What are the research themes and priorities in adolescence research?" gets one immediately into the question of values, the sociology of knowledge, and the way scientific disciplines and federal funding agencies function. Before saying anything at all about research themes and priorities, I want first to say something about these problems. Second, I will sketch an alternate conference or book of readings that might have been put together if there were no limits of time and space. And finally, I will discuss certain research themes and priorities that emerged in the conference.

VALUES AND SCIENTIFIC RESEARCH

There can be little doubt that the current interest in adolescence stems from the fact that young people in society are creating problems: for their parents, for various social institutions, and for themselves. At one extreme, commentators will tell you that the problems young people are experiencing are merely a symptom of a sick society. At the other extreme, they will tell you, in somewhat modified terms, that the problem is sick adolescents. Social scientists, who are better informed than certain journalistic commentators, are willing to admit that both society and individual development are implicated in these problems. And that is the point of view taken by this volume.

But the question of where the problem lies is partly a question of values. Beyond life, health, and "adaptive" functioning, what is the meaning of human development in any philosophical sense? Ask a self-aware Catholic, Protestant, Jew, Marxist, Hindu, Buddhist, or Sufi and you get a different answer from each. What are the relative weights given to various fundamental dimensions of human behavior: active-passive, instrumental-affective, personal-social, hedonic-responsible, or any other set of dichotomies or dilemnas? Because these are value questions, the social scientist, as social scientist, has nothing at all to say about the relative merits of these values. He may survey them in populations, delineate their origins or consequences, and say how they function or fail to function in certain circumstances. But as a social scientist, he cannot tell us which ones are humanly superior. Yet, presumably, each social scientist has values of his own, and they may very well influence the way he structures his research. Social scientists, in the wake of protest from blacks and other minorities, are probably more aware of these value orientations than they have ever been before. But the problem remains. Mythology still gets into social science conceptualization, design, and conclusions by way of the investigator's own value system. In the area of adolescence research, it seems especially important that investigators be aware of their own cosmology and value systems and that they make those systems explicit, at least for themselves.

The second reason it is difficult to assign research priorities in the area of adolescence concerns the subculture and social structure of investigators themselves. Sitting as I do in an interdisciplinary research funding institute, I have ample opportunity to listen to investigators from a variety of disciplines commenting on the priorities in adolescence research. From one point of view, it is remarkable that pediatricians, psychiatrists, anthropologists, sociologists, and psychologists of many persuasions can actually come to some consensus about what the problems are. But just as frequently, investigators turn out to be lobbyists for their own point of view. This is not entirely a matter of self-interest. Investigators, like everyone else, have their own subcultures: colleagues, students, professional organizations, journals, and department chairmen. In the interest of specialization, investigators interact with, and are rewarded by, highly specialized publics. As a consequence, like other ethnic groups, they tend to have a rather specialized view of the world. The sociologist's solution to a pressing problem may strike a psychologist as excessively utopian, while the sociologist may think of the psychologist's solution as trivial. And the psychiatrist or clinical psychologist may think of either's research as exceedingly esoteric. But since all research is valuable and the professional scientist is often (and rightly) committed to the advancement of knowledge as an end in itself, investigators continue to do what they do well, and they are not particularly interested in research priorities.

Compounding the problem of scientific subcultures is the way research often comes to be funded in the federal establishment. Congress allocates public research dollars in response to felt public concern. Cancer, population, and drug use are a few examples that come readily to mind from different fields. Once a mandate is given, administrators and investigators interact to set research priorities. At this point, the values of society and the relative prestige of various disciplines compound these problems of academic subcultures. For example, because biochemistry is perceived as more "scientific" than some of the softer social sciences, drug use may be attacked more at the level of a biochemical antiagent than at the sociological level of values or the psychological level of socialization. And problems of poor performance may be seen and studied in terms of poor nutrition rather than in terms of inadequate social stimulation or even different cultural values. These perceptions may be further confounded by the policy-minded administrator who knows that certain kinds of research findings can be readily implemented and others are more difficult or impossible.

THE CONFERENCE: ACTUAL AND ALTERNATE

Having delineated some of the problems of research priorities that flow from investigators' values and subcultures, and from funding practices, let me go on to delineate, in greater detail, research themes as seen by the organizers of this conference. I will do so by outlining the conference as it was designed and as it might have been designed were there no limits of time (at the conference) and of space (in this volume).

The model of the conference combines a developmental and a sociological point of view. First, we looked at some of the major personal developments taking place in adolescence: physical growth, cognitive development, competence, self-image, and ideology. Second, we looked at the way that social patterns and social structures facilitate or impede transitions to adult roles: college success, status attainment, marriage, and motherhood. Last, we wanted an overview of how young people react when all is not going well in these processes.

Within the broad framework of development and social structure, certain topics were chosen and others were not. This was partly a function of whether or not good research was being done on a particular topic and whether a particular investigator was available to write a paper and come to the conference.

Another constraining factor was, to some extent, the research mandate of the National Institute of Child Health and Human Development, which is oriented more to the study of individual development than to the study of social structural factors. Within these constraints, the topics were chosen. But without such constraints, an alternate conference could have been designed.

Earlier drafts of conference topics contained a considerable number of additional topics complementing the papers in this volume. John Clausen's paper on the social meaning of differential physical and sexual maturation could have been followed by a paper on cross-cultural variations in physical types and their social meanings cross-culturally. David Elkind's authoritative review of recent research on cognitive development in adolescence might have been followed by a similar paper on cognitive development, but one written from a strong social-psychological perspective. At the conference, in fact, Guy E. Swanson raised a number of interesting questions from that point of view. The relationship between language and thought as they bear on identity was included as a topic in the original program, and the growing literature on minority subcultures could have provided a chapter in its own right on the relationships between language, thought, and identity.

In the area of affect development, additional papers might have reviewed the contribution of cognitive and physical, as well as social, influences as they bear on affect development. Morris Rosenberg, in his paper "The Dissonant Context and the Adolescent Self-Concept," highlights the importance of social context in the developmental process and the development of self-image in particular. He could equally well have talked about self-image development, committed versus idealized self-image, ego extensions, the relationship between self-image and academic achievement, the importance of significant others in self-image development, self-values, the stability of the self-concept over time, the relationship between physical change in appearance and self-image, and the influence of minority group status or sex on self-image.

Joseph Adelson's paper on the development of ideology in adolescence would have been nicely complemented by a presentation concerning the attainment of political competence, preferences, and roles, as well as a paper on the development and acquisition of values. (I happen to think that "values," like moral judgment, is a prescientific term but one that is here to stay.) Finally, in the ideal conference, a paper would have been presented on self-other relationships as a developmental process, what Chad Gordon (1971) calls the acceptance/achievement and intimacy/autonomy dilemmas.

Moreover, outside a strictly developmental perspective, other papers might have been presented on the demography of adolescence, selected social characteristics of adolescence in the United States, and an epidemiological survey of adolescents' health problems.

In the first part of the conference, the organizers intended to emphasize the interplay between organism and environment and the mediating linkages between the two. In the second part of the conference, the emphasis was on the relationship between adult roles and the social structural factors that facilitate or impede transition into those roles.

Papers presented were by Norman Goodman and Kenneth Feldman on the transition to college, by Karl Alexander and Bruce Eckland on status attainment, by Robert Lewis on marital choice, and by Jessie Bernard on motherhood.

An alternate conference program would have included papers on the transition from grade school to high school, on high school social and academic achievement, and on the transition to graduate school and graduate career choice; papers on job opportunities and choices for non-college-bound students; papers on social interventions in the status attainment process: the effectiveness of job training or work experience, or the effect of time spent in the military; papers delineating the effects of job market conditions for both college and noncollege students. Each of these topics might have been presented for males and females.

The social influences on marriage might have been presented not only from the point of view of marital choice, but also from the point of view of timing, stability, and alternate forms of marriage. And the whole area of childbearing and child rearing might have been explored in papers on the effects of childhood and adolescent socialization in forming concepts and values regarding childbearing and child rearing; the time of childbearing and desired size of family; the effects of children on marriage.

Finally, the ideal conference would have included a number of papers on youth in social movements. While Braungart's paper concerns student protests focused on educational structures, other papers might have focused on how noncollege youth handle their frustrations; on black protests; on sexism in the Women's Liberation movement; on other aspects of the counterculture movement: religious conversion, communes, the antiwar and peace movements, and on the trend to esoteric religion and mysticism.

There was no social engineer at the conference, but had there been one, he or she might have drawn up a provisional list of issues to be addressed in designing institutions that would facilitate the transition of youth into adulthood; and social patterns that bear on socialization. The report of the Panel on Youth of the President's Science Advisory Committee (1973) believes the following factors should be addressed: rigid versus flexible time schedules, the regularity or irregularity of daily time scheduling; continuity within an institution versus mobility between institutions, and closely allied, total versus partial institutions; age segregation within youth, segregation from adults, and segregation from the world of work and work activity. Should institutions respond to adolescents at the level of their psychological and physiological development or at the level of their chronological age? Should teaching be geared to developmental stages, or is learning more dependent on reward structures that, within certain limits, can be introduced at any time? Should adolescents be encouraged to focus their attention inward to their own identity problems, or outward toward idealistic absorption in causes? Should an adolescent be encouraged to concentrate on what he does well ("spiked learning"), or should he concentrate on a broad menu of prescribed activities ("broad front learning")? Are there certain ages at which certain activities are particularly well learned? What are the legal rights and obligations of young people? How much should society mold the young versus provide opportunities for choice? How wide the choices? What is the appropriate time for economic independence, and what are the appropriate means? What should be the cognitive–noncognitive ratio in the content of formal education?

RESEARCH THEMES AND PRIORITIES

Although the conference could have been expanded in the way I have described, or in a number of other ways, there were some questions that emerged in a fairly focused way and they would probably have emerged even in a larger conference.

There was a great deal of discussion in the first part of the conference on what it means to be responsibly independent. Whether one's concern is language development, cognitive development, or personality and social development, whether one is considering physical characteristics, organismic change, or social structure, whether one is considering any of these factors by sex, age, or social class, a primary concern is how to get at the shift from being a child to being responsibly independent.

Guy E. Swanson expressed the opinion that much of the work on cognitive development, whether in moral judgment, formal thought, or conceptual orientation, was a specialized expression of this larger question. And Robert Hogan felt that the concept of "life style" was probably the optimum unit for capturing the flavor of an individual's personality or the unique impression that he makes.

Swanson thought that much of the work on cognitive development had left out important elements that might be important for adolescents: open-mindedness, the ability to devise or apply practical tests, the extent to which people are in touch with their own feelings and put that self-awareness to work in their own interest; the extent to which people are playful, steadfast, judicious, and wise. Swanson suggested that the main difference in cognitive maturity in adolescents and adults may relate to levels of social participation: the picture one has for himself of what he is authorized to do and empowered to do and responsible for doing in particular situations.

Robert Hogan, responding to Diana Baumrind's presentation, had some interesting observations to make concerning responsibility. Drawing from his own work on moral development, as well as from Durkheim, he sketched a stage typology in which "responsibility" might be loyalty to the rules, to one's social group, or to oneself. In these stages, one acts out of fear of parental disapproval, peer disapproval, or in favor of self-approval. But another dimension in his model has to do with the degree to which a person regards the rules and established procedures as having instrumental value. This he calls the "ethics of social responsibility." The alternative he calls "higher law morality," where the ethic of personal conscience is a kind of intuitive morality. Hogan made his remarks to show the congruence between his empirically derived typology and Baumrind's typology, also empirically derived.

It was in much of this discussion by Swanson and Hogan and in the interchange around Baumrind's and Adelson's papers that I was reminded that what psychologists today call moral development would, historically, often have been called human development. It was this kind of discussion that highlighted the difficulty of talking about "responsible independence" without also considering ideology and value systems. What it means to be responsibly independent is very much like what it means to be a man or a woman.

At an earlier NICHD conference, Abraham Edel (1969) pointed out that historically the moral has been conceived according to four different models: the goal-seeking, the juridical, the self-developmental, and the hairetic. If one substitutes the term "responsibly independent" for "moral" in Edel's typology, his remarks seem very apropos to the kind of discussion that developed in the conference.

The goal-seeking model says men have certain fixed goals that they pursue by following certain rules of right and wrong. However, as a result of psychoanalytical, anthropological, and sociohistorical studies relating to morality, no neat picture of human goals as the focal point of morality remains. The juridical model of morality has its base in a system of laws or rules enjoined by men. But psychoanalytical studies of conscience and anthropological studies of variations in patterns have led to a breakdown of the juridical model. The self-developmental model of morality thinks in terms of the self and its qualities and development. But such a model ultimately depends on whether there is a stability in the self and its characteristics. The fourth model, called hairetic, from the Greek term for choice, is the prevalent model today, focusing on the whole of ethical decision and moral judgment in terms of choice. Everything else—goals, laws, stable qualities of the self—is relegated to the background as things that furnish material that generate problems for choice. Individuals, including adolescents, are being thrust more and more into situations in which they must make choices, and very much of the first part of this conference dealt with this central theme: the contemporary adolescent emerging into the role of anguished decision making with near total responsibility and little guidance.

How an investigator conceptualizes his research and what he thinks of as important will be influenced by the model he accepts of human development. If he accepts a goal-seeking model, he will be interested in how adolescents become "virtuous" men; if a juridical model, how they become good citizens; if a self-development model, how they become strong, autonomous egos; if a hairetic model, how they develop the capacity for choice. These, or other models, determine in subtle ways what one considers important about cognitive development, self-image, competence, or ideology.

What it means to adolescents in their own ideology to be responsibly independent probably also influences the types of protest they make to current social structures. The political activists can be seen as a group of young people demanding responsibility not only for themselves but from social institutions. Other young people seem to be returning to a relatively simple goal-seeking model of salvation in theistic or atheistic religious movements. Still others make a relatively easy transition to acceptance of middle class norms and values, while still others set off on quests of self-development and personal growth.

Just as responsible independence emerged as the theme in the first part of the conference, the effects of various types of social segregation emerged as the theme in the second part. If it is true that adolescents in other societies and in earlier periods of this society experienced less difficulty in these transitions, and if it is true that adolescence as a special period in the life course is a culturally and historically defined phenomenon, then one can ask what effect contemporary social structuring, especially various types of segregation, might have on adolescents' transitions to adulthood.

What is the effect of age segregation within an age cohort and across age cohorts? What are the effects of sex segregation, of segregation of youth from the world of work, of class segregation, or segregation by IQ? What are the effects of segregation by race or ethnic group? What are the effects of any of these kinds of segregation within schools and out of schools? What are the effects on educational attainment, occupational choice, status achievement, marital choice, age at marriage, type of marriage, fertility decisions, and, in general, role definitions in the world of work and in the home? What could cross-cultural studies teach us about these matters?

The conference organizers had, in fact, thought about commissioning specific papers on many of these themes but finally decided that a focus on various roles was a more economical way to proceed.

When it comes to listing actual research priorities that were mentioned in the conference interchange, one is hard pressed to produce anything more than a fairly uninteresting catalogue. For reasons previously mentioned in this paper, investigators are interested in that in which they are interested. But among the special priorities mentioned by one or more participants are the following. Research is needed on the very nature of the meaning of "adolescence" and scientific ways of talking about the period. Biological age, chronological age, and psychosocial functioning are not always synchronized. We need to develop better indicators of physical, psychological, and social growth in order to have some idea about what the baselines are during the different periods of adolescent development. In brief, we have yet to develop a common language in which to talk about adolescent development. We need a nomenclature to define adolescence as a process rather than as a period.

The problem is complicated on the social-psychological side by the fact that the roles adolescents must play as they are growing up are subject to differing definitions by different cultures and by different subcultures within a society.

These definitions also change over time. Not only is the term "adolescence" a social definition, but what society perceives as an adolescent problem is also socially defined.

Within the context of these problems of definitions, we need certain kinds of studies: (1) studies of normal adolescents to find out what the norms are, both for girls and for boys, and to arrive at baseline data, insofar as possible, for physical growth and sexual development, as well as for cognitive and personality development; (2) longitudinal studies so that adolescence can be better perceived as a process rather than as a period; and (3) cross-sectional studies of adolescents in different physical, social, and geographic settings to assess the impact of the interactions between organismic development and environment.

A number of participants noted that little research has been conducted concerning the way in which children can be transformed from concrete thinkers to persons able to form their own values. During the adolescent period, the individual's cognitive behavior becomes formalized. The child develops an ability to think hypothetically during this period just as his thinking becomes less spontaneous and the growth of his intelligence, as measured by IQ, appears to reach a plateau. We need to discover the nature of the abstract thinking that adolescents must learn in order to cope with adulthood. Within this context, there was some criticism of schools that emphasize specific behaviors or skills rather than broad intellectual growth, that is, learning and cognitive development including social, emotional, and philosophical development.

Studies of the nature of the changing self-concept, self-esteem, and sexual identity need to be undertaken. A number of investigators stressed the necessity to study the developmental process of personality and behavior over time. They noted that studies merely indicating correlations between T_1 and T_2 were not sufficient. Specifically, there is a need to know more about asynchronizations in personality and environment. These asynchronizations include those that are intraorganismic and those that are the result of asynchronizations with the environment, for example, the 16-year-old who is married and has two children; the 30-year-old graduate student who has never held a job. Some participants particularly emphasized the need for studies of the relationship between social change and generational succession, taking into account the role of the environment on adolescent development. To undertake such study successfully, it would be necessary to disentangle cohort, period or event, and life course effects in human development. Two research strategies were recommended to isolate the differential effects of historical events and social change: (1) the longitudinal study of the single birth cohort for intracohort comparisons; and (2) the comparison of two birth cohorts. A combination of these two strategies might be uniquely valuable and more quickly completed.

Studies of the ideologies that affect adolescent behavior and the factors that influence ideology were suggested. We should find out how these factors differ by culture and over time.

A number of participants suggested short-term, strategic, longitudinal studies across transition points such as entry into junior high school, high school, college, marriage, and so forth.

There was broad concensus about the need for studies of parental behavior relative to adolescence and how parental behavior and parental behavior in interaction with social structure affect self-esteem, moral and political values, social competence, achievement, and the affective life of the adolescent.

In the area of adolescent socialization, life history studies of the successful adolescent who succeeds in an unsuccessful environment would be fruitful. Both preadolescent socialization and effective intervention programs should be looked at via the life history technique.

Studies of the subcultures adolescents form and the institutions adolescents create should also be undertaken.

More studies of biological processes in the normal adolescent would reemphasize the tremendous biological variation within the bounds of "normal" and perhaps lessen concern about the "abnormal," which, in fact, is often just somewhat different from the median or mean.

A number of points were made by participants concerning general assumptions about research and adolescence. In particular, there was a plea to approach studies of adolescent development with an open mind instead of preconceived ideas and to approach the positive side of the picture instead of placing too great an emphasis on studying the negative side. It was also pointed out that there are huge differences between 12-, 16-, and 18-year-olds and that it is not appropriate to merely classify all of them as adolescents.

If a summary statement could be made, it would probably stress the need to know more about the following factors: parental behavior in relation to adolescent behavior and parental behavior in relation to social structure; early socialization as it affects the adolescent experience; the nature of the changing self-concept as this relates to adolescent self-esteem and sexual identity; social change as it affects adolescent behavior, including analysis across generations; the successful adolescent who succeeds in an unsuccessful environment; ways of developing healthy adolescent intelligence as previously discussed; good measures of competence, achievement, and so on; and adolescent subcultures and the institutions adolescents create in relation to their own problems and developmental tasks.

It is not easy, and perhaps not even wise, to talk about research priorities across several broad disciplines based on a single conference. I have tried, mainly, to show the general direction of the conference and to reflect the context within which the previous twelve papers were written.

What was most encouraging about putting the conference together was to experience the sensitive interest and wealth of talent conference participants are bringing to the underdeveloped but developing area of research in the psychology and sociology of adolescents.

REFERENCES

Edel, A. Scientific research and moral judgment. *The acquisition and development of values: Report of a conference.* Bethesda, Md.: National Institute of Child Health and Human Development, 1969.

Gordon, C. Social characteristics of early adolescence. *Daedalus*, 1971, **100**(4), 931–960.

President's Science Advisory Committee (Office of Science and Technology, Executive Office of the President). *Youth: Transition to adulthood.* Washington, D.C.: Superintendent of Documents, 1973.

Conference
Participants

Joseph Adelson
Psychology Clinic
University of Michigan
Ann Arbor, Michigan

Karl L. Alexander
Department of Sociology
Johns Hopkins University
Baltimore, Maryland

Diana Baumrind
Institute of Human Development
University of California
Berkeley, California

Jessie Bernard
Research Scholar Honoris Causa
Pennsylvania State University
University Park, Pennsylvania

Richard G. Braungart
Department of Sociology
Syracuse University
Syracuse, New York

John A. Clausen
Institute of Human Development
University of California
Berkeley, California

Robert Crain
Department of Sociology
Johns Hopkins University
Baltimore, Maryland

Robert W. Deisher
Department of Pediatrics
University of Washington
Seattle, Washington

Sigmund E. Dragastin
Growth and Development Branch
National Institute of Child Health
  and Human Development
Bethesda, Maryland

Dorothy H. Eichorn
Institute of Human Development
University of California
Berkeley, California

Glen H. Elder, Jr.
Department of Sociology
University of North Carolina
Chapel Hill, North Carolina

David Elkind
Department of Psychology
University of Rochester
Rochester, New York

Kenneth A. Feldman
Department of Sociology
State University of New York
Stony Brook, New York

Norman Goodman
Department of Sociology
State University of New York
Stony Brook, New York

Chad Gordon
Department of Sociology
Rice University
Houston, Texas

Robert Hogan
Department of Psychology
Johns Hopkins University
Baltimore, Maryland

Sheila M. Hollies
Program Analysis Section
National Institute of Child Health
  and Human Development
Bethesda, Maryland

Hester Lewis
Judge Baker Guidance Center
Boston, Massachusetts

Robert A. Lewis
College of Human Development
Pennsylvania State University
University Park, Pennsylvania

Norman Livson
Department of Psychology
California State University
Hayward, California

William A. Owens
Department of Psychology
University of Georgia
Athens, Georgia

Merrill S. Read
Growth and Development Branch
National Institute of Child Health
  and Human Development
Bethesda, Maryland

Morris Rosenberg
Department of Sociology
State University of New York
Buffalo, New York

Patsy Sampson
Growth and Development Branch
National Institute of Child Health
  and Human Development
Bethesda, Maryland

Philip Sapir
The Grant Foundation, Inc.
New York, New York

William Spillane
Center for Population Research
National Institute of Child Health
  and Human Development
Bethesda, Maryland

Guy E. Swanson
Institute of Human Development
University of California
Berkeley, California

David S. Westby
Department of Sociology
Pennsylvania State University
University Park, Pennsylvania

Name Index

Numbers in italics refer to the pages on which the complete references are cited.

Subject Index